Svetlana Chmakova's Nightschool

The Weirn Books

VOLUME TWO

Yen Press

CONTENTS

Chapter 7

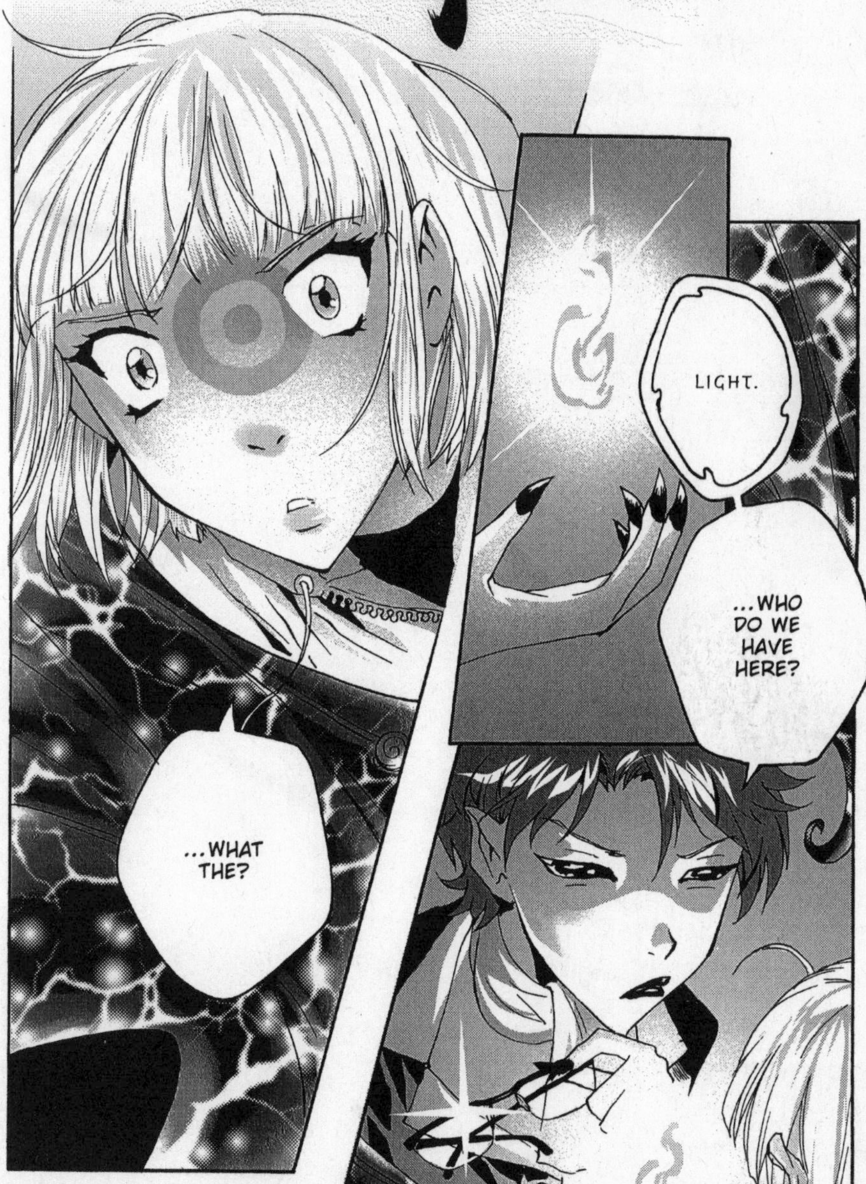

...WHAT THE?
LIGHT.
...WHO DO WE HAVE HERE?

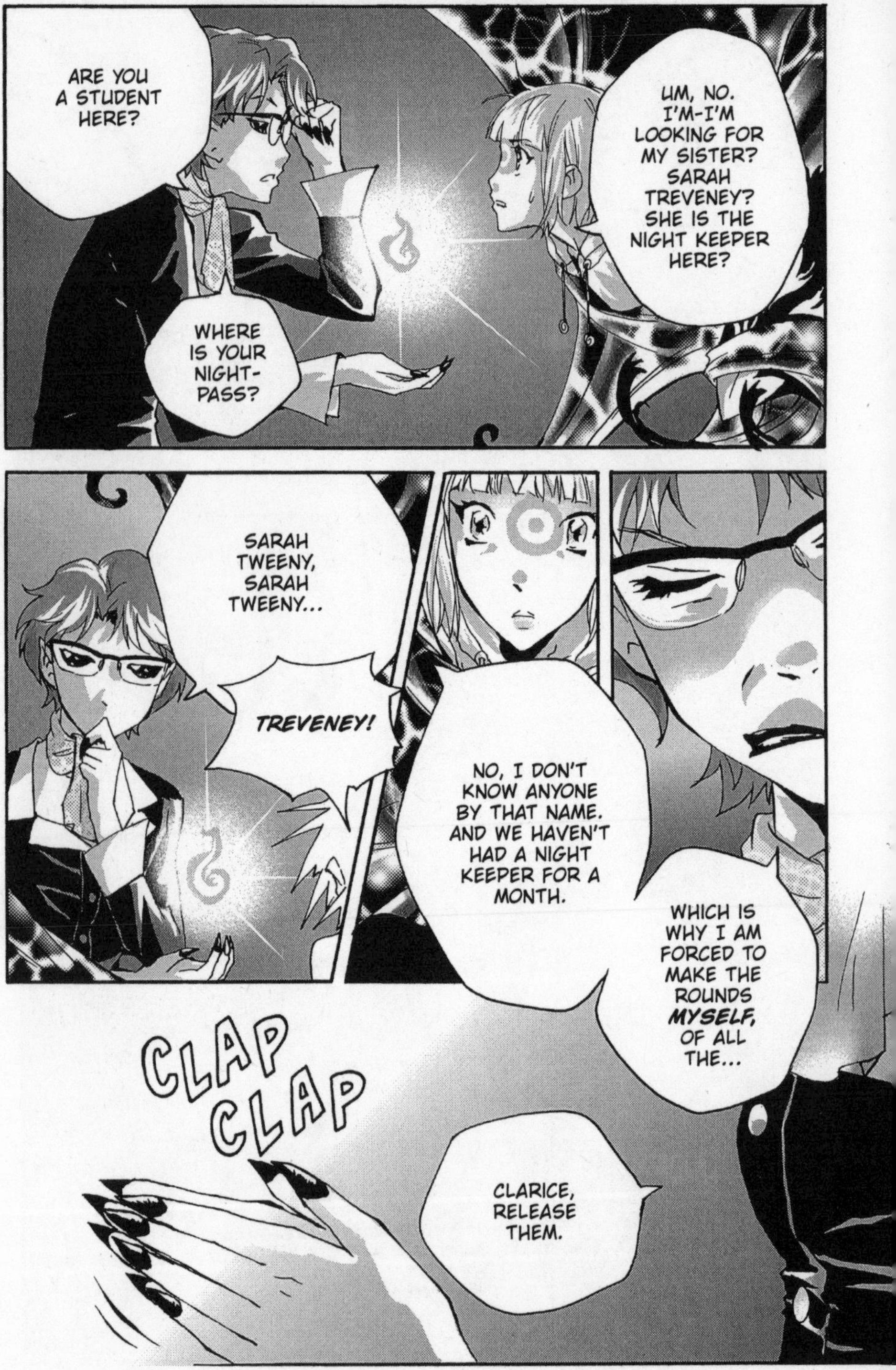
ARE YOU A STUDENT HERE?
UM, NO. I'M-I'M LOOKING FOR MY SISTER? SARAH TREVENEY? SHE IS THE NIGHT KEEPER HERE?
WHERE IS YOUR NIGHT-PASS?
SARAH TWEENY, SARAH TWEENY...
TREVENEY!
NO, I DON'T KNOW ANYONE BY THAT NAME. AND WE HAVEN'T HAD A NIGHT KEEPER FOR A MONTH.
WHICH IS WHY I AM FORCED TO MAKE THE ROUNDS MYSELF, OF ALL THE...
CLAP CLAP
CLARICE, RELEASE THEM.

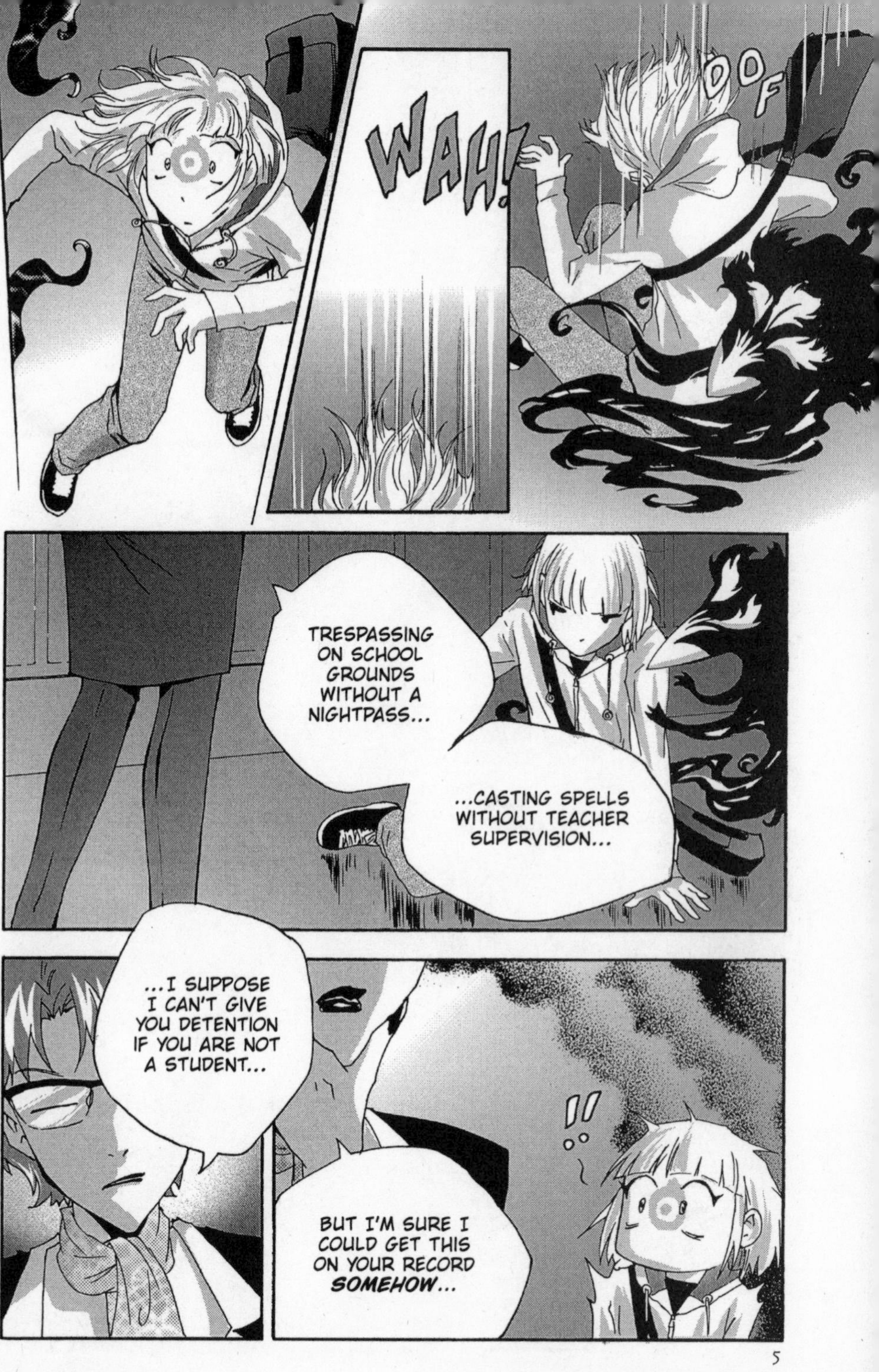
WAH!
OOF
TRESPASSING ON SCHOOL GROUNDS WITHOUT A NIGHTPASS...
...CASTING SPELLS WITHOUT TEACHER SUPERVISION...
...I SUPPOSE I CAN'T GIVE YOU DETENTION IF YOU ARE NOT A STUDENT...
!!
BUT I'M SURE I COULD GET THIS ON YOUR RECORD ***SOMEHOW***...

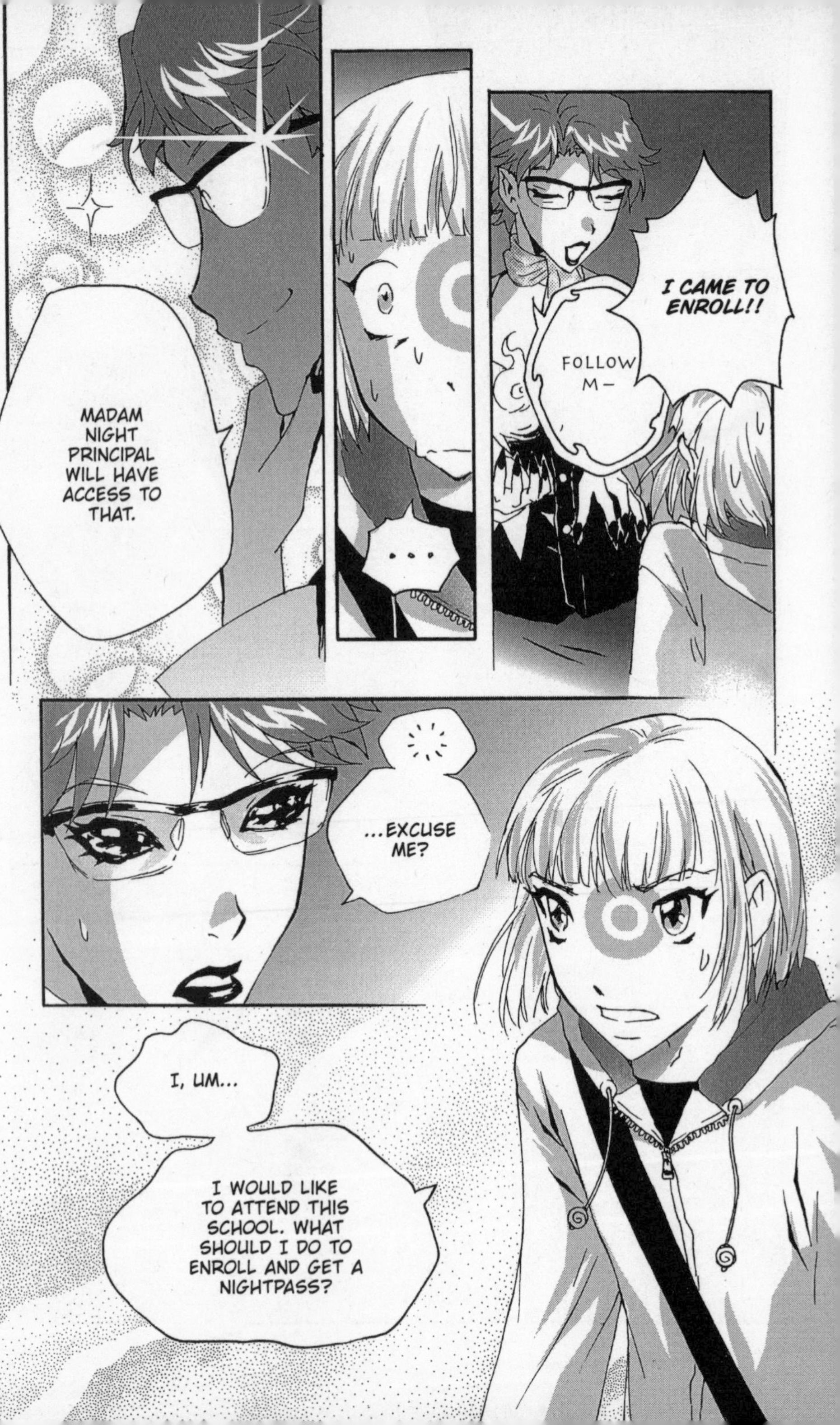
MADAM NIGHT PRINCIPAL WILL HAVE ACCESS TO THAT.
...
FOLLOW M—
I CAME TO ENROLL!!
...EXCUSE ME?
I, UM...
I WOULD LIKE TO ATTEND THIS SCHOOL. WHAT SHOULD I DO TO ENROLL AND GET A NIGHTPASS?

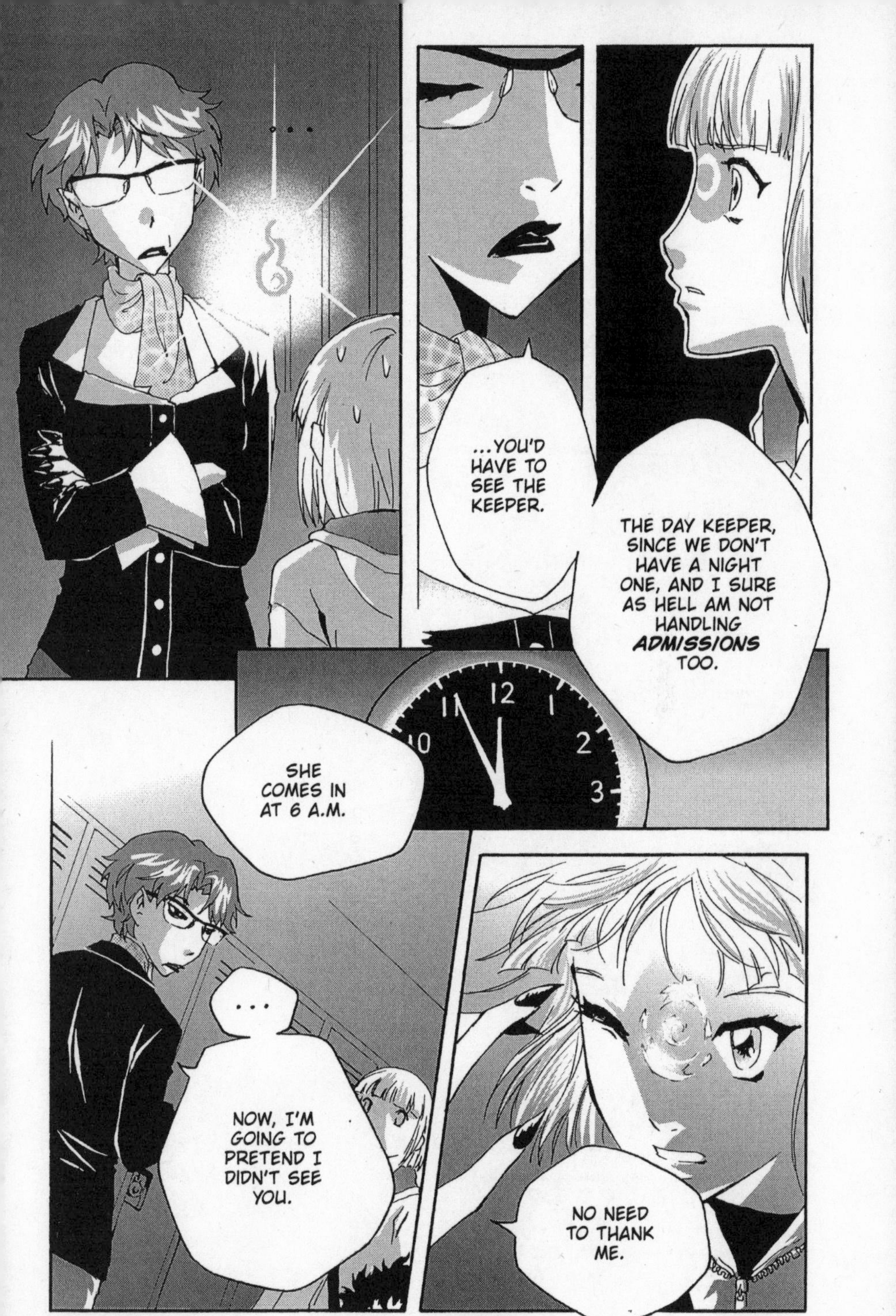
. . .
...YOU'D HAVE TO SEE THE KEEPER.
THE DAY KEEPER, SINCE WE DON'T HAVE A NIGHT ONE, AND I SURE AS HELL AM NOT HANDLING ***ADMISSIONS*** TOO.
SHE COMES IN AT 6 A.M.
. . .
NOW, I'M GOING TO PRETEND I DIDN'T SEE YOU.
NO NEED TO THANK ME.

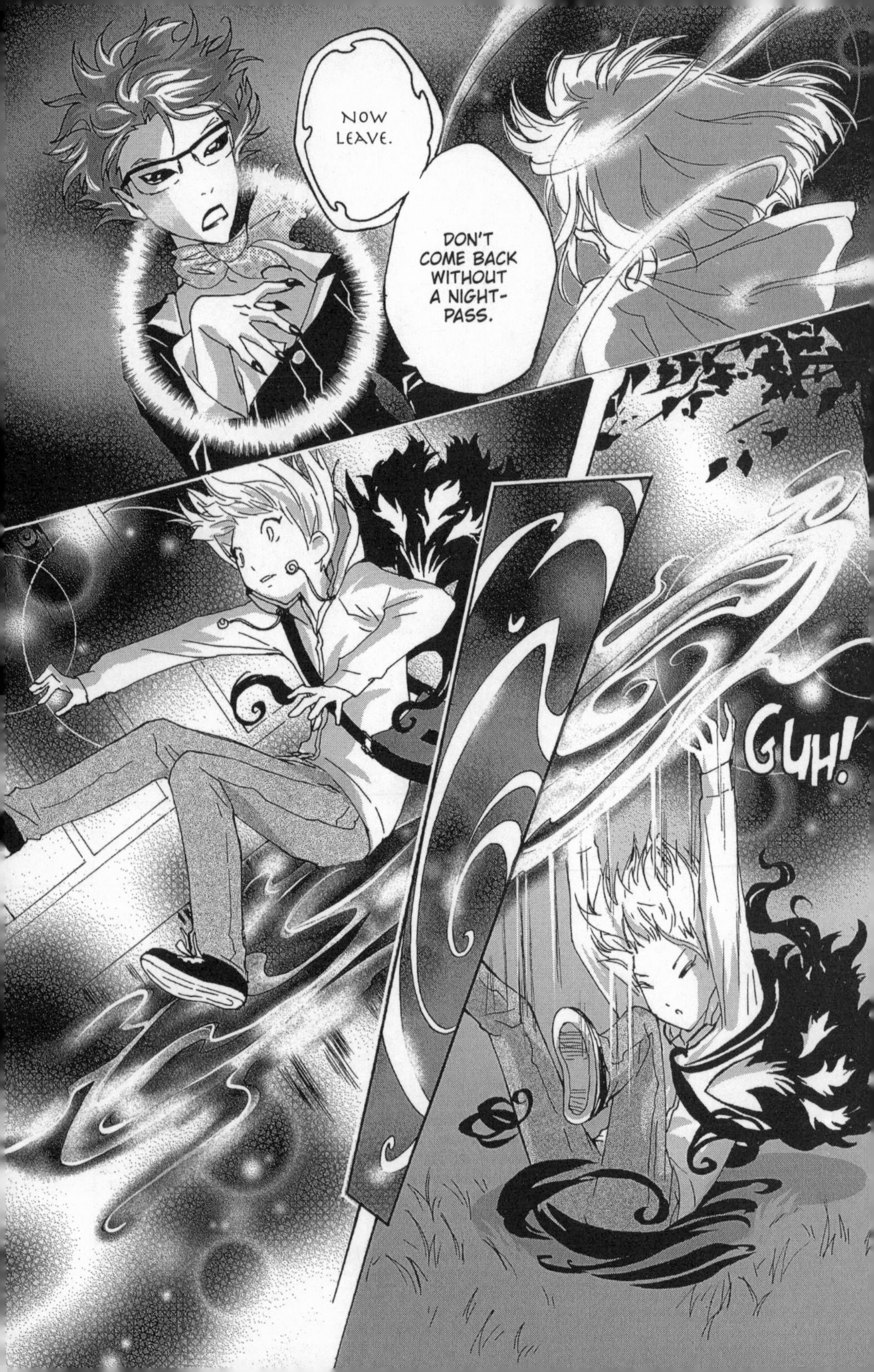
NOW LEAVE.
DON'T COME BACK WITHOUT A NIGHT-PASS.
GUH!

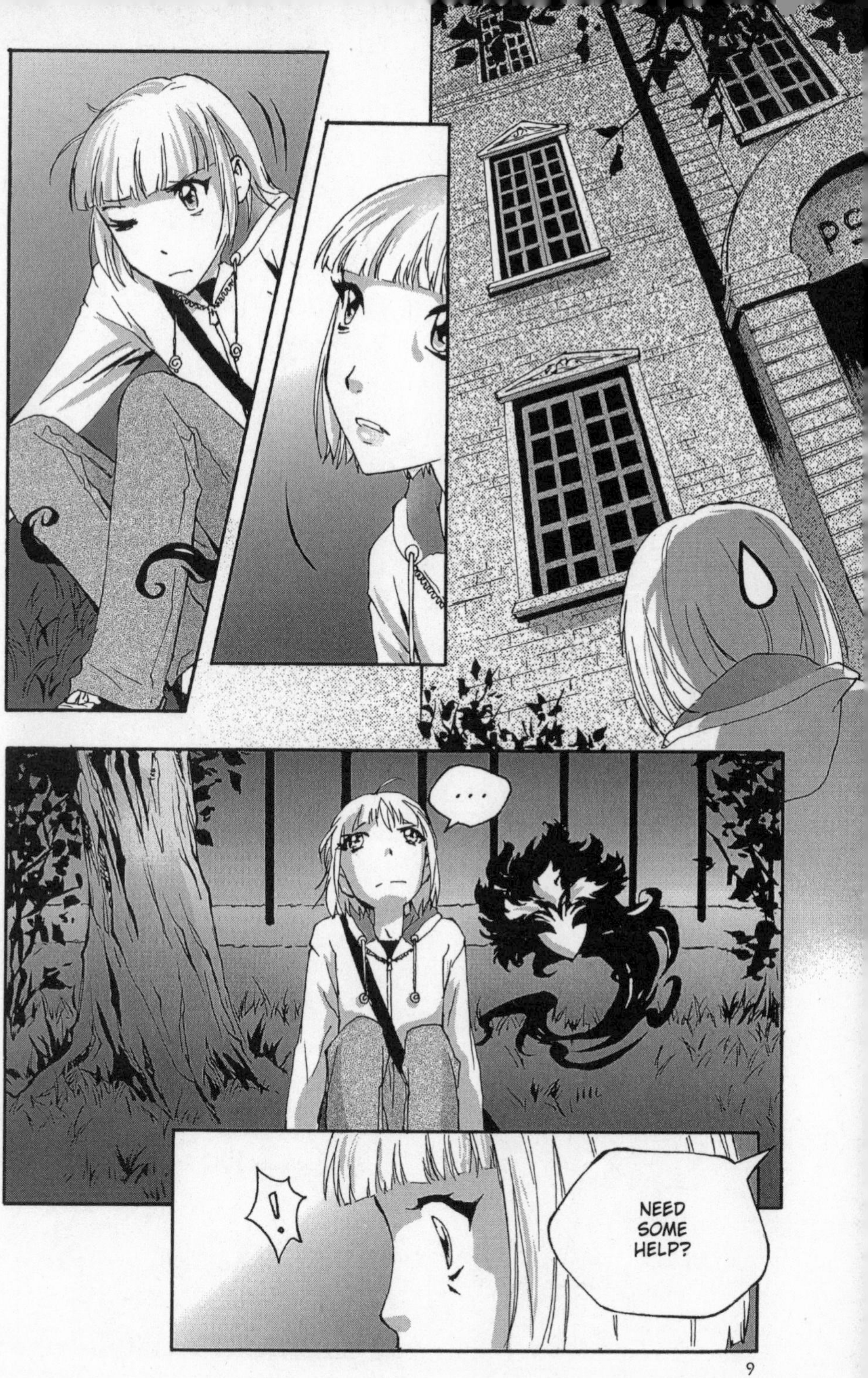
...
!
NEED SOME HELP?

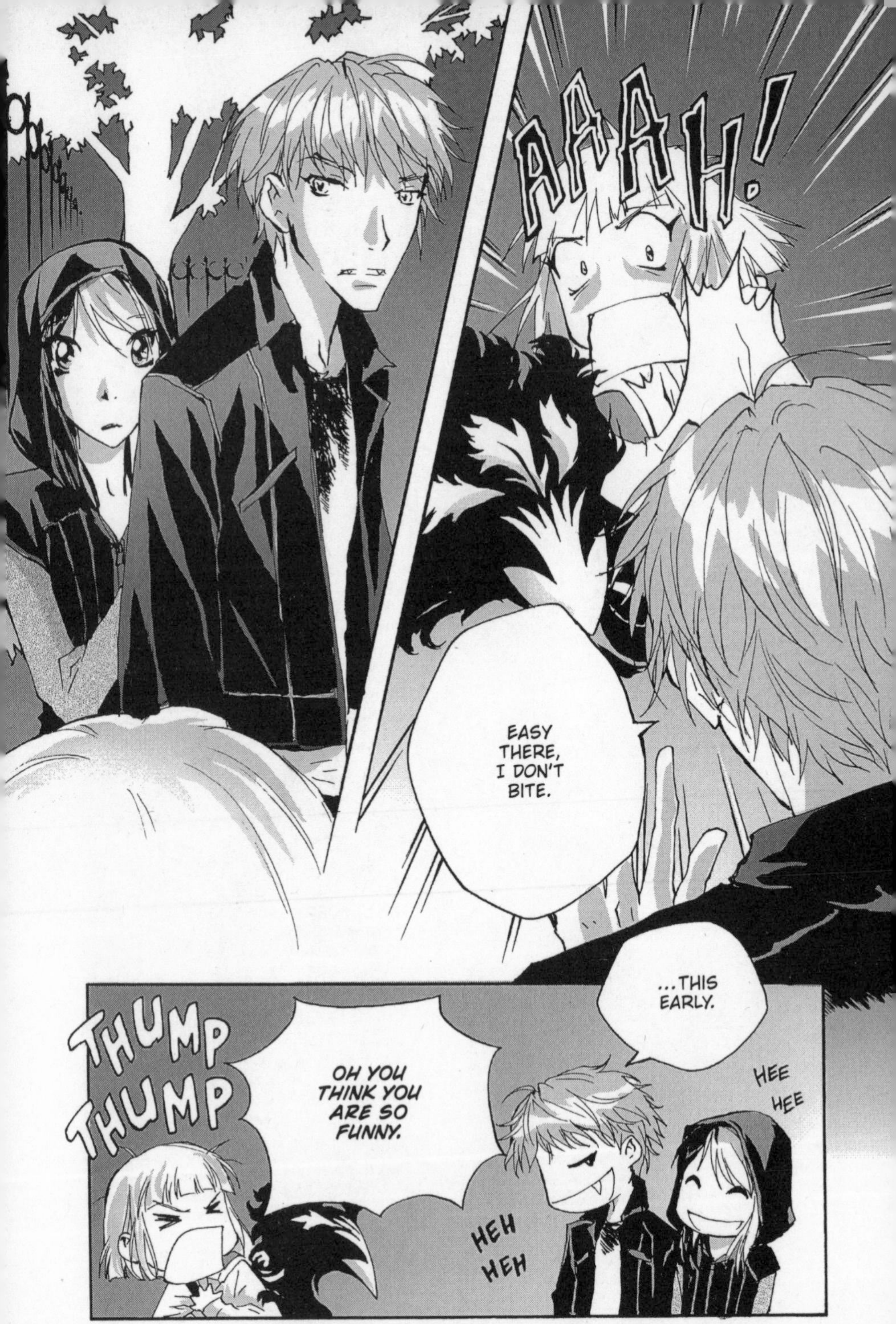
AAAH!
EASY THERE, I DON'T BITE.
...THIS EARLY.
THUMP THUMP
OH YOU THINK YOU ARE SO FUNNY.
HEE HEE
HEH HEH

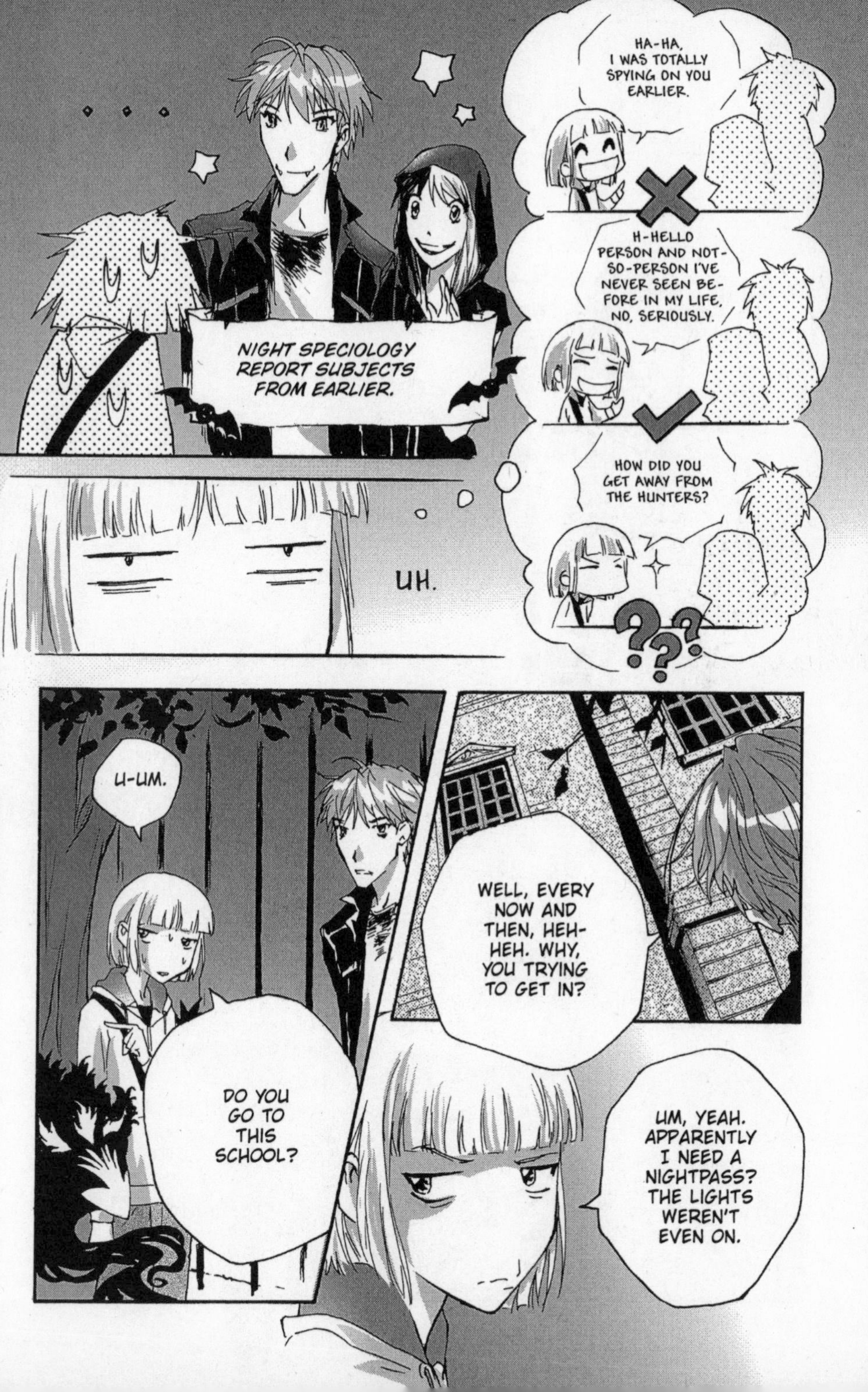
NIGHT SPECIOLOGY REPORT SUBJECTS FROM EARLIER.
UH.
HA-HA, I WAS TOTALLY SPYING ON YOU EARLIER.
H-HELLO PERSON AND NOT-SO-PERSON I'VE NEVER SEEN BE-FORE IN MY LIFE, NO, SERIOUSLY.
HOW DID YOU GET AWAY FROM THE HUNTERS?
U-UM.
DO YOU GO TO THIS SCHOOL?
WELL, EVERY NOW AND THEN, HEH-HEH. WHY, YOU TRYING TO GET IN?
UM, YEAH. APPARENTLY I NEED A NIGHTPASS? THE LIGHTS WEREN'T EVEN ON.

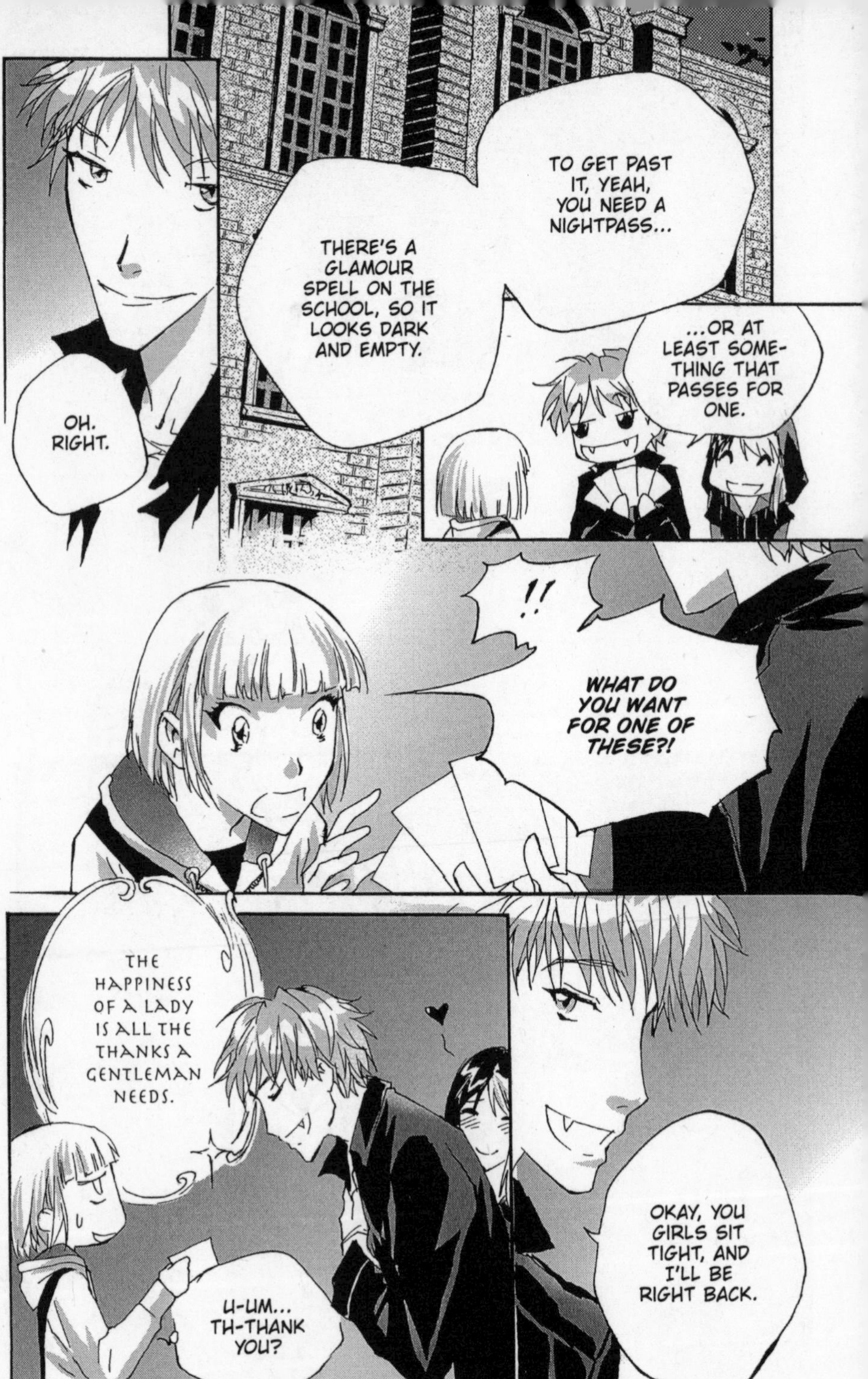
OH. RIGHT.
THERE'S A GLAMOUR SPELL ON THE SCHOOL, SO IT LOOKS DARK AND EMPTY.
TO GET PAST IT, YEAH, YOU NEED A NIGHTPASS...
...OR AT LEAST SOME-THING THAT PASSES FOR ONE.
!!
WHAT DO YOU WANT FOR ONE OF THESE?!
THE HAPPINESS OF A LADY IS ALL THE THANKS A GENTLEMAN NEEDS.
U-UM... TH-THANK YOU?
OKAY, YOU GIRLS SIT TIGHT, AND I'LL BE RIGHT BACK.

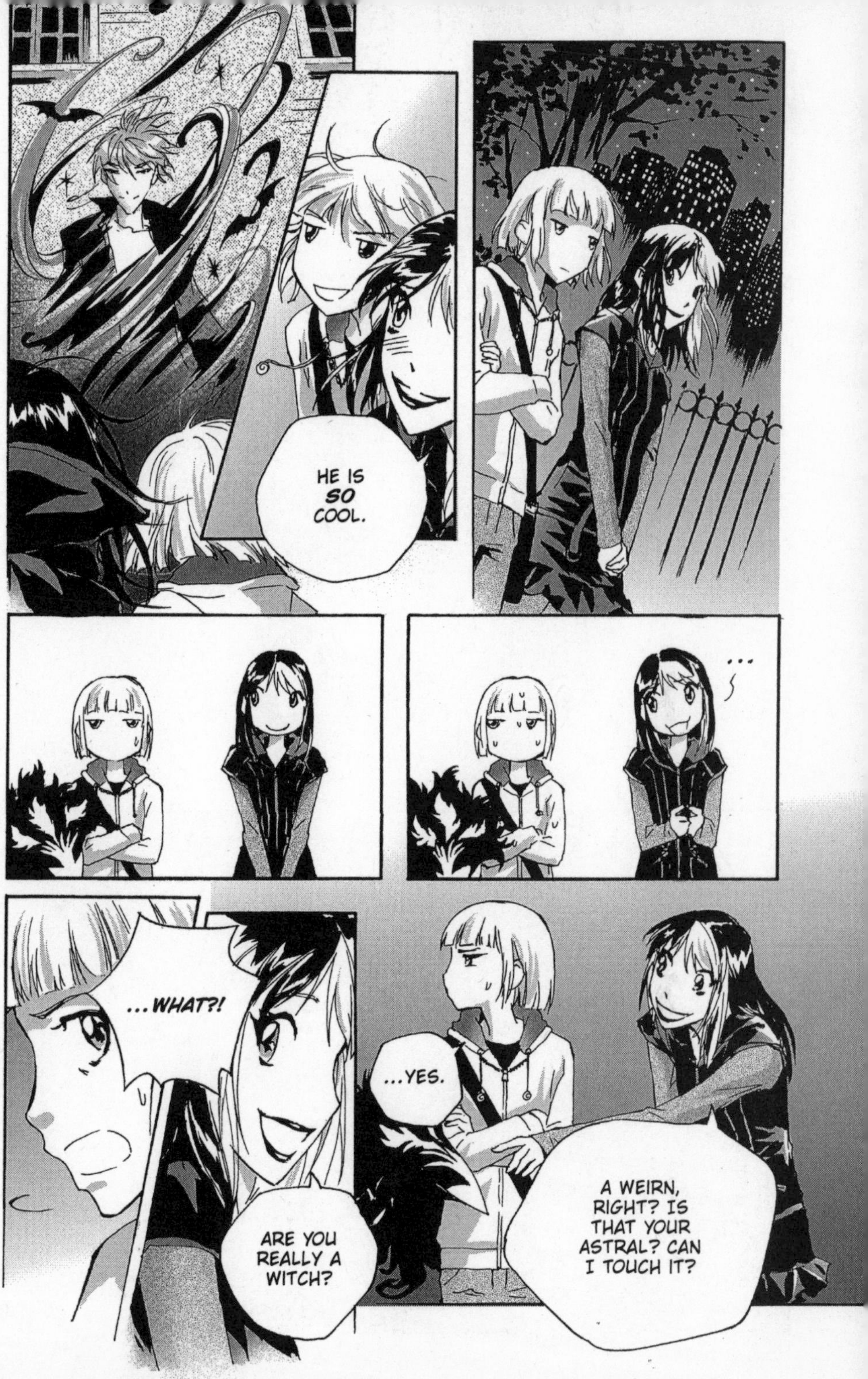
HE IS SO COOL.
...
...WHAT?!
ARE YOU REALLY A WITCH?
...YES.
A WEIRN, RIGHT? IS THAT YOUR ASTRAL? CAN I TOUCH IT?

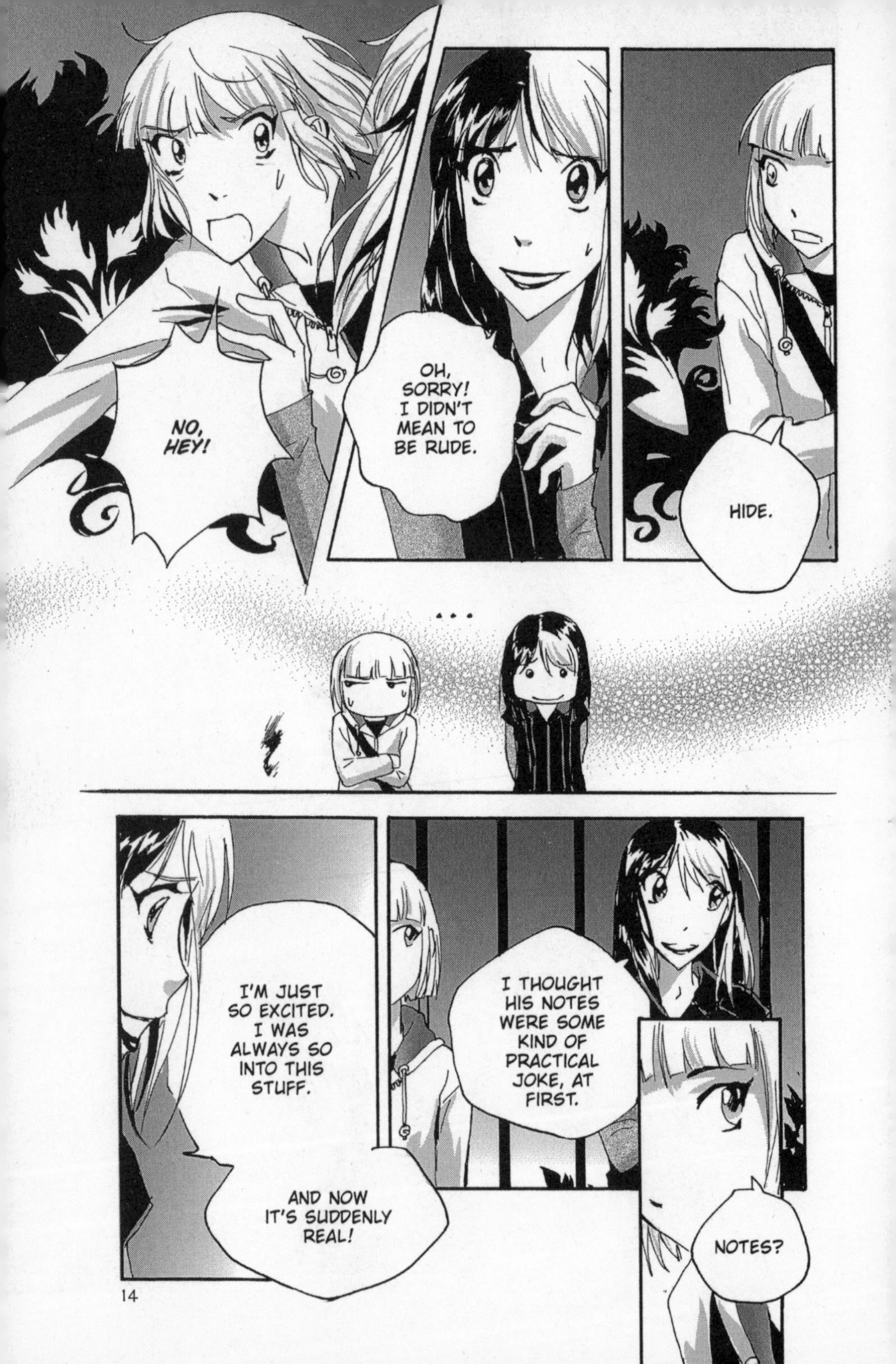
NO, HEY!
OH, SORRY! I DIDN'T MEAN TO BE RUDE.
HIDE.
...
I'M JUST SO EXCITED. I WAS ALWAYS SO INTO THIS STUFF.
AND NOW IT'S SUDDENLY REAL!
I THOUGHT HIS NOTES WERE SOME KIND OF PRACTICAL JOKE, AT FIRST.
NOTES?

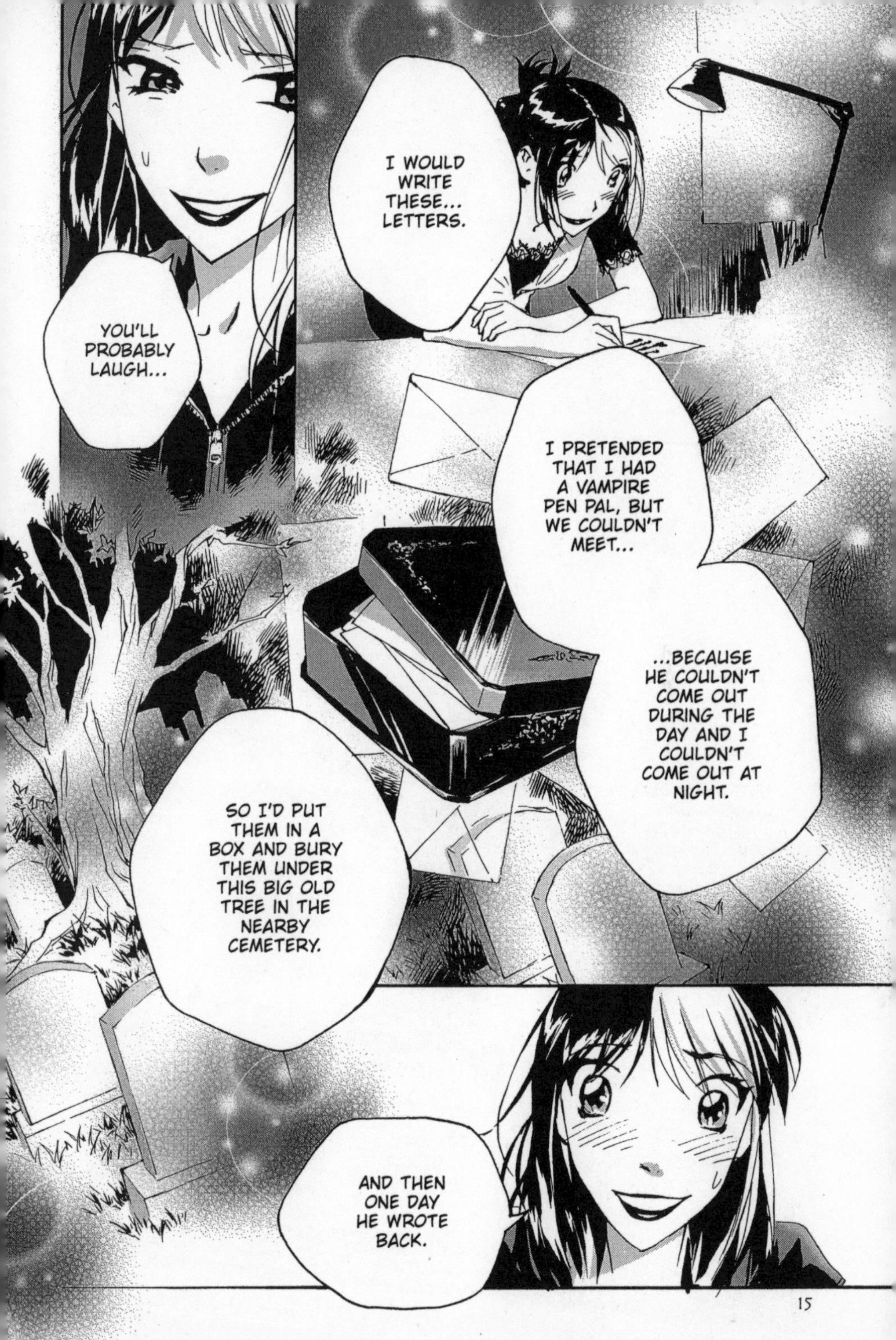
YOU'LL PROBABLY LAUGH...
I WOULD WRITE THESE... LETTERS.
I PRETENDED THAT I HAD A VAMPIRE PEN PAL, BUT WE COULDN'T MEET...
...BECAUSE HE COULDN'T COME OUT DURING THE DAY AND I COULDN'T COME OUT AT NIGHT.
SO I'D PUT THEM IN A BOX AND BURY THEM UNDER THIS BIG OLD TREE IN THE NEARBY CEMETERY.
AND THEN ONE DAY HE WROTE BACK.

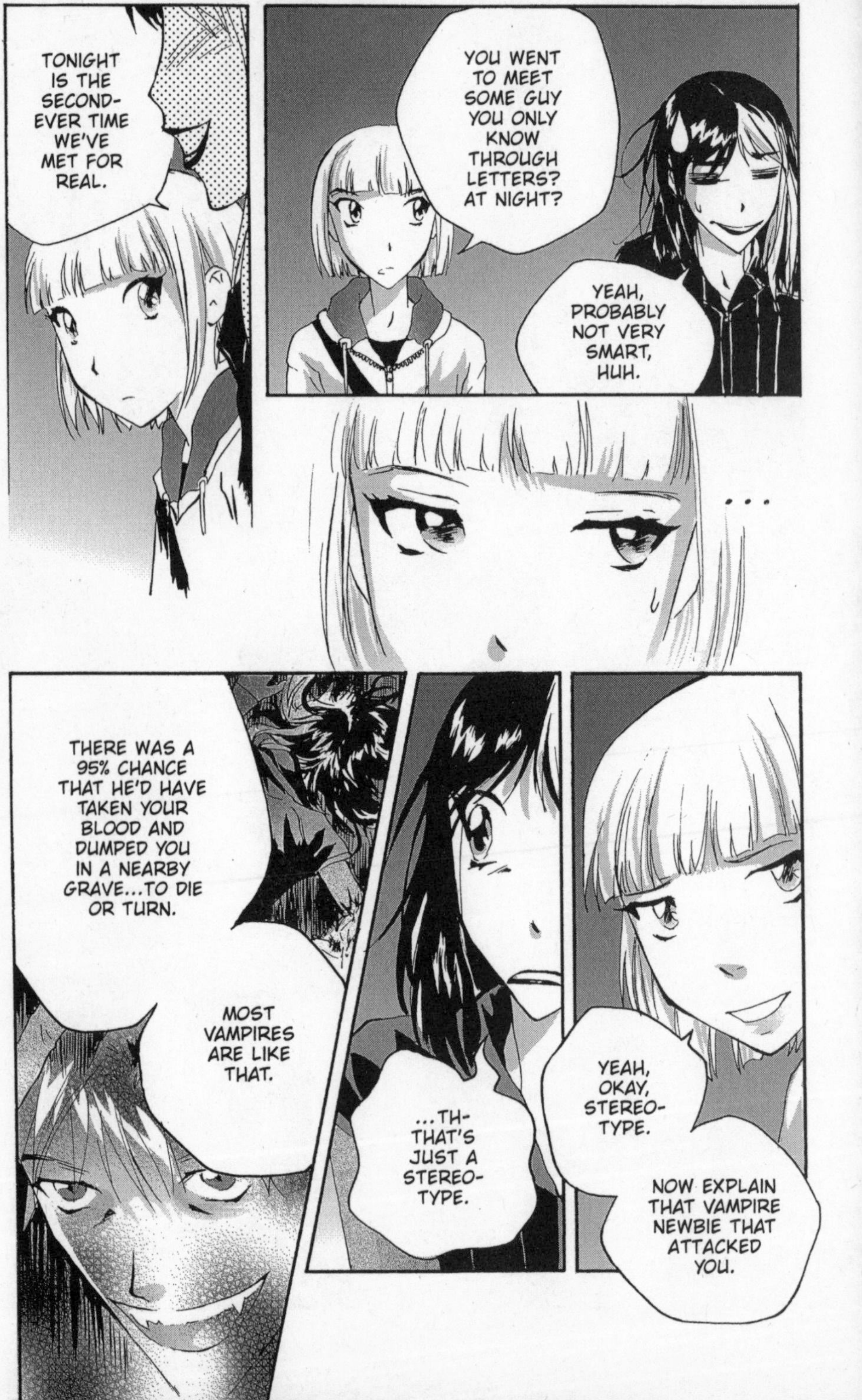
TONIGHT IS THE SECOND-EVER TIME WE'VE MET FOR REAL.
YOU WENT TO MEET SOME GUY YOU ONLY KNOW THROUGH LETTERS? AT NIGHT?
YEAH, PROBABLY NOT VERY SMART, HUH.
...
THERE WAS A 95% CHANCE THAT HE'D HAVE TAKEN YOUR BLOOD AND DUMPED YOU IN A NEARBY GRAVE...TO DIE OR TURN.
MOST VAMPIRES ARE LIKE THAT.
...TH-THAT'S JUST A STEREO-TYPE.
YEAH, OKAY, STEREO-TYPE.
NOW EXPLAIN THAT VAMPIRE NEWBIE THAT ATTACKED YOU.

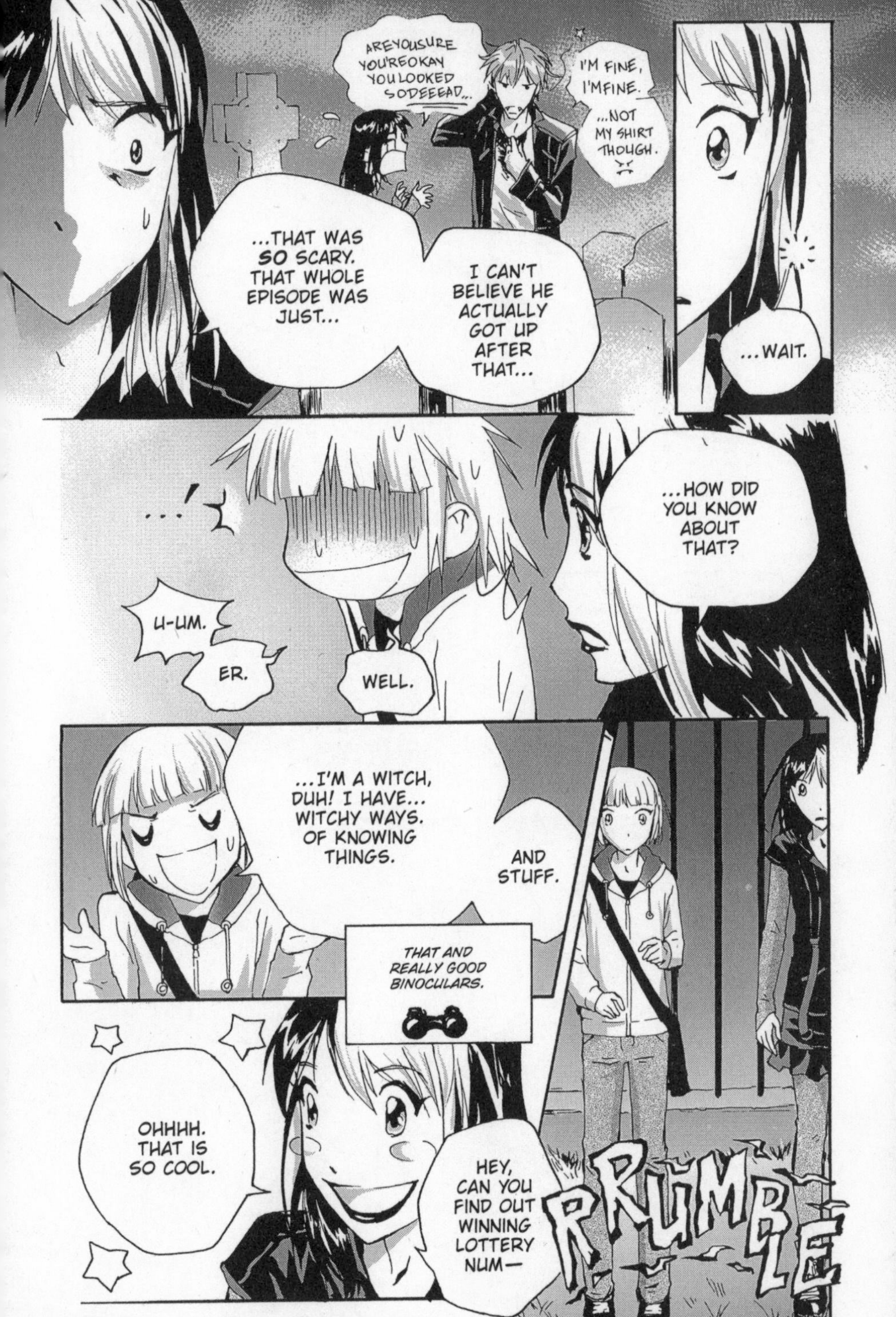
AREYOUSURE YOU'REOKAY YOULOOKED SODEEEEAD...
I'M FINE, I'MFINE.
...NOT MY SHIRT THOUGH.
...THAT WAS SO SCARY. THAT WHOLE EPISODE WAS JUST...
I CAN'T BELIEVE HE ACTUALLY GOT UP AFTER THAT...
...WAIT.
...!
U-UM.
ER.
WELL.
...HOW DID YOU KNOW ABOUT THAT?
...I'M A WITCH, DUH! I HAVE... WITCHY WAYS. OF KNOWING THINGS.
AND STUFF.
THAT AND REALLY GOOD BINOCULARS.
OHHHH. THAT IS SO COOL.
HEY, CAN YOU FIND OUT WINNING LOTTERY NUM—
RRUMBLE

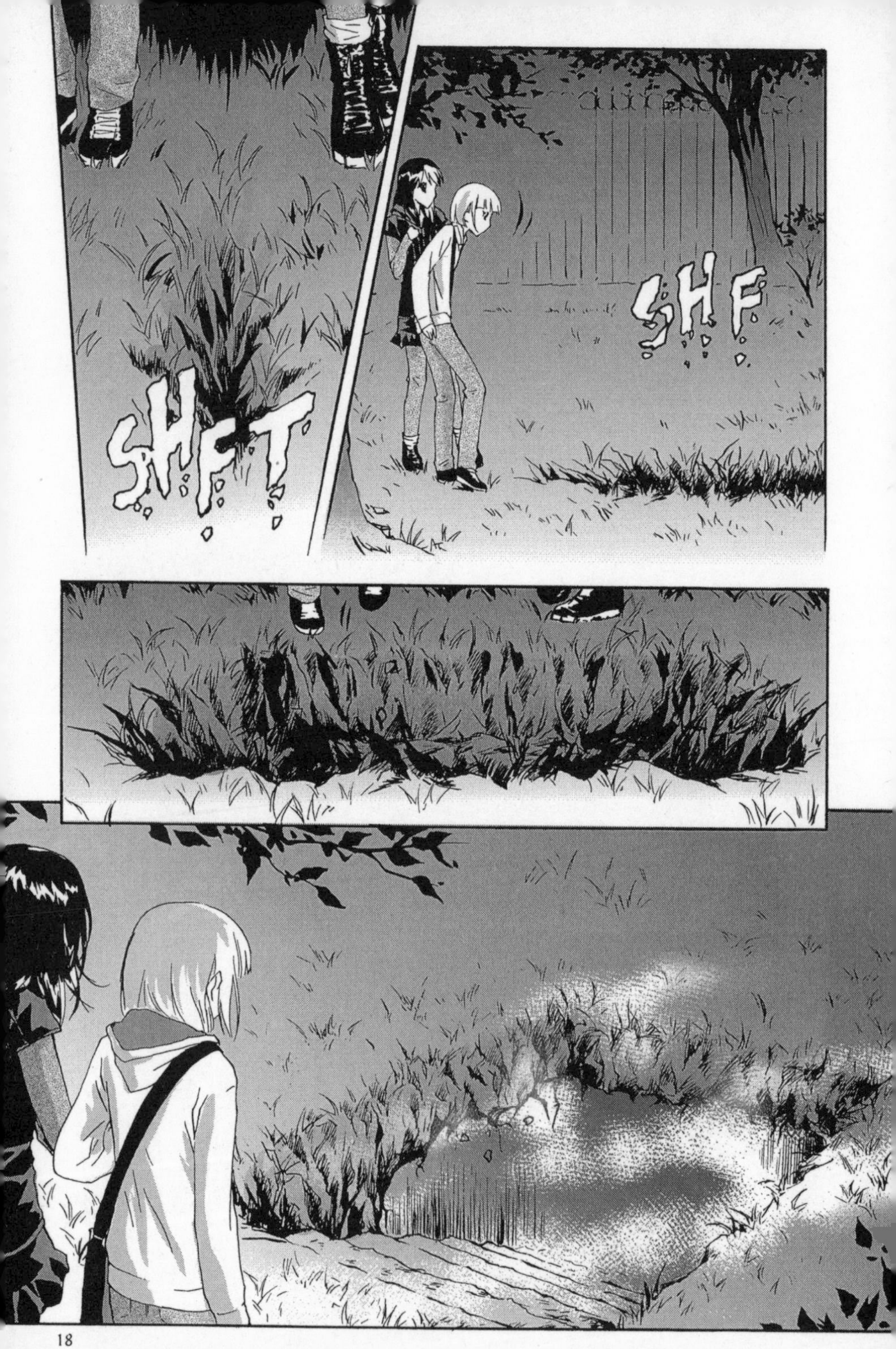
SHFT
SHF

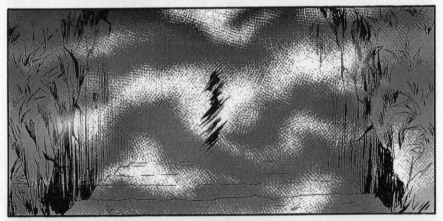

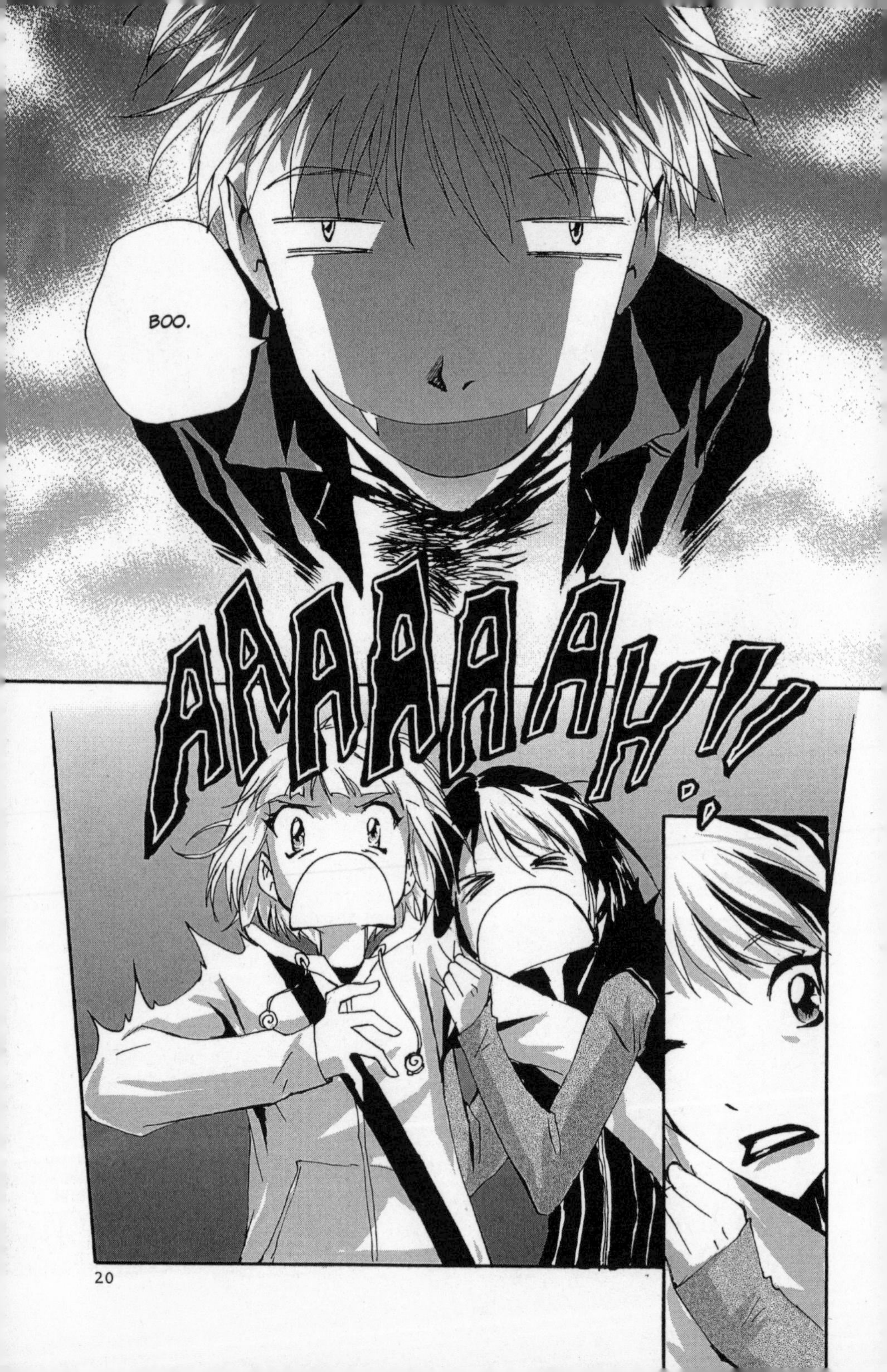
BOO.
AAAAAAH!!

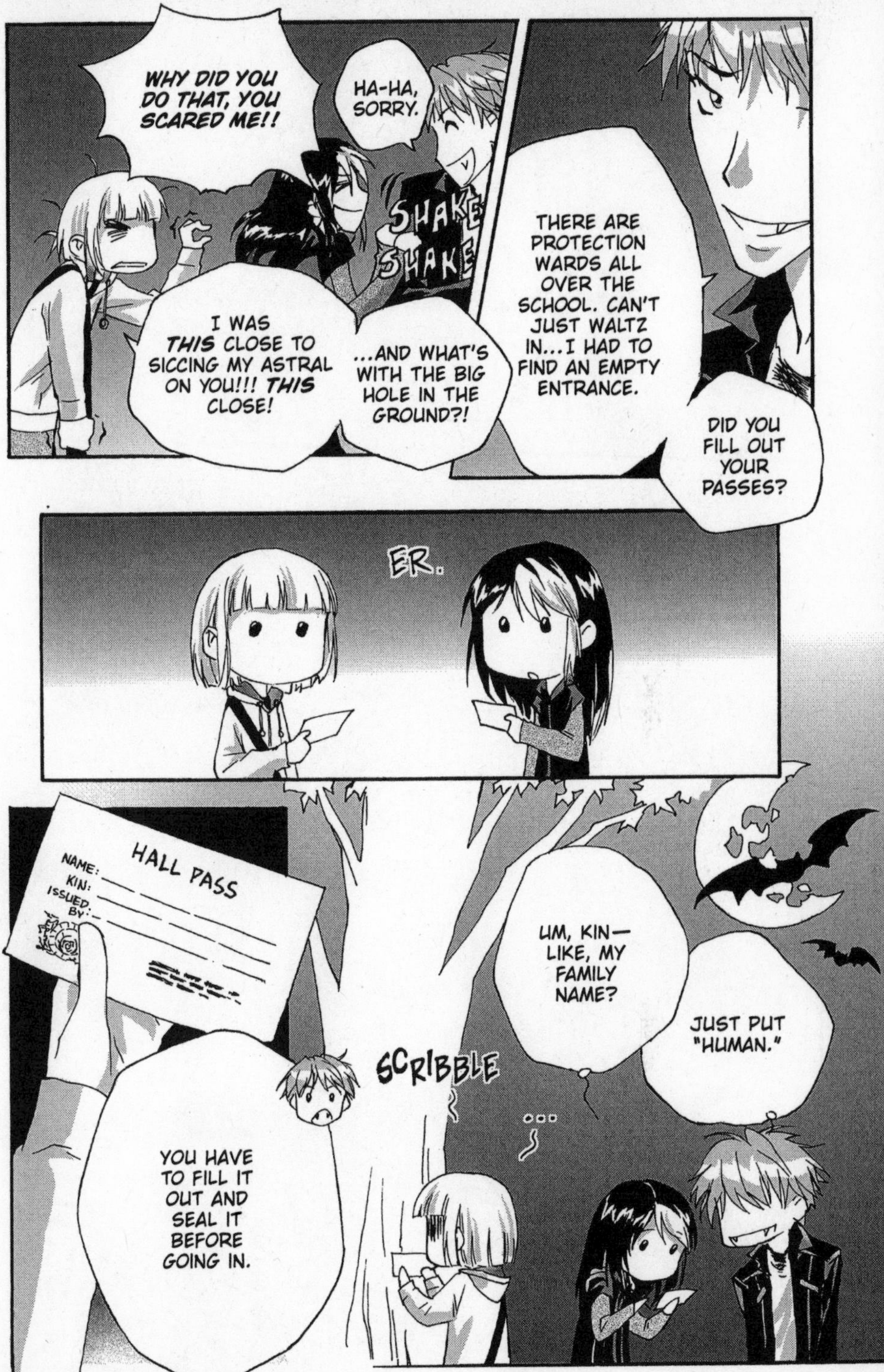
WHY DID YOU DO THAT, YOU SCARED ME!!
HA-HA, SORRY.
SHAKE SHAKE
I WAS THIS CLOSE TO SICCING MY ASTRAL ON YOU!!! THIS CLOSE!
...AND WHAT'S WITH THE BIG HOLE IN THE GROUND?!
THERE ARE PROTECTION WARDS ALL OVER THE SCHOOL. CAN'T JUST WALTZ IN... I HAD TO FIND AN EMPTY ENTRANCE.
DID YOU FILL OUT YOUR PASSES?
ER.
HALL PASS
NAME:
KIN:
ISSUED BY:
YOU HAVE TO FILL IT OUT AND SEAL IT BEFORE GOING IN.
SCRIBBLE
...
UM, KIN— LIKE, MY FAMILY NAME?
JUST PUT "HUMAN."

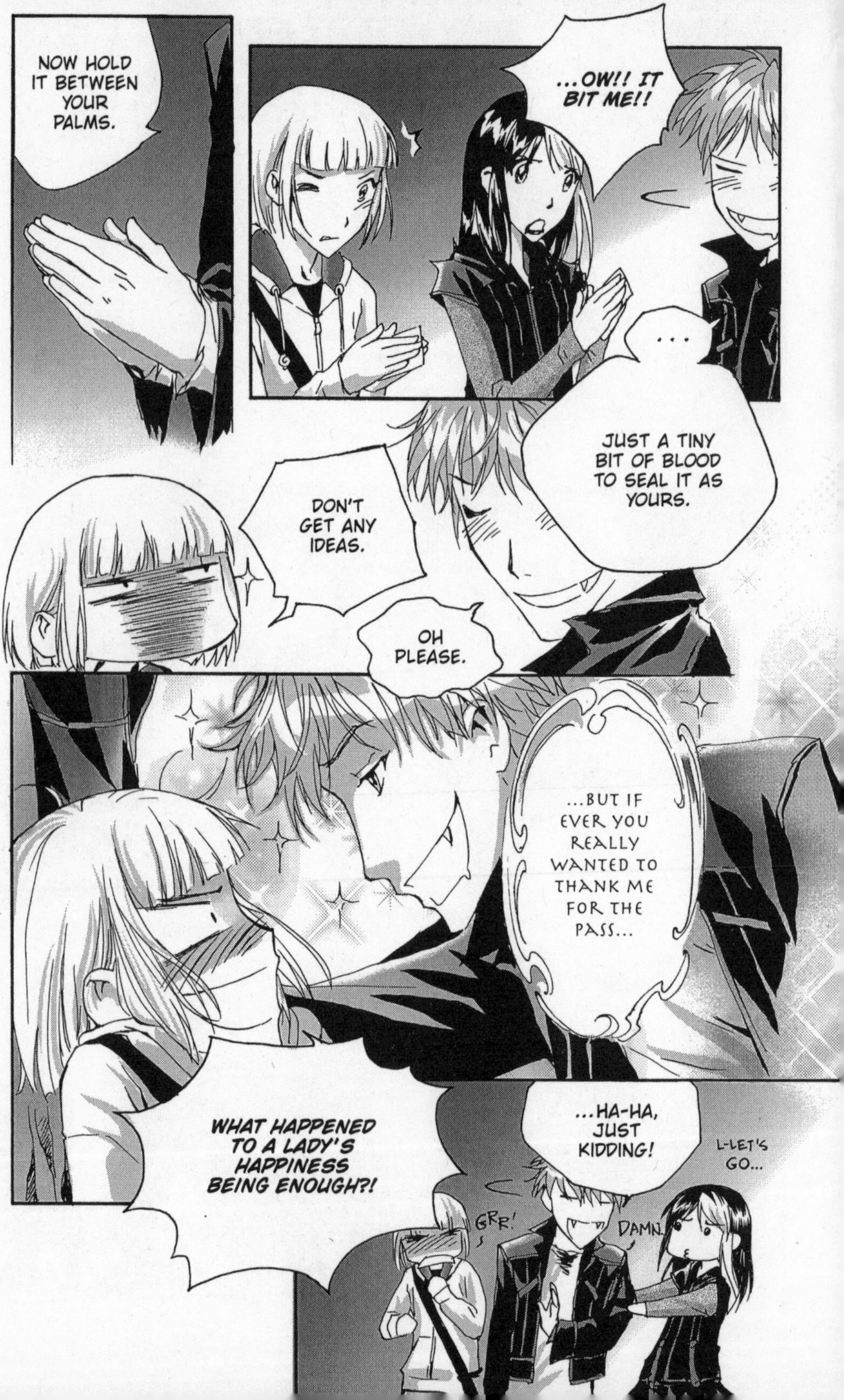
NOW HOLD IT BETWEEN YOUR PALMS.
...OW!! IT BIT ME!!
...
JUST A TINY BIT OF BLOOD TO SEAL IT AS YOURS.
DON'T GET ANY IDEAS.
OH PLEASE.
...BUT IF EVER YOU REALLY WANTED TO THANK ME FOR THE PASS...
WHAT HAPPENED TO A LADY'S HAPPINESS BEING ENOUGH?!
...HA-HA, JUST KIDDING!
L-LET'S GO...
GRR!
DAMN.

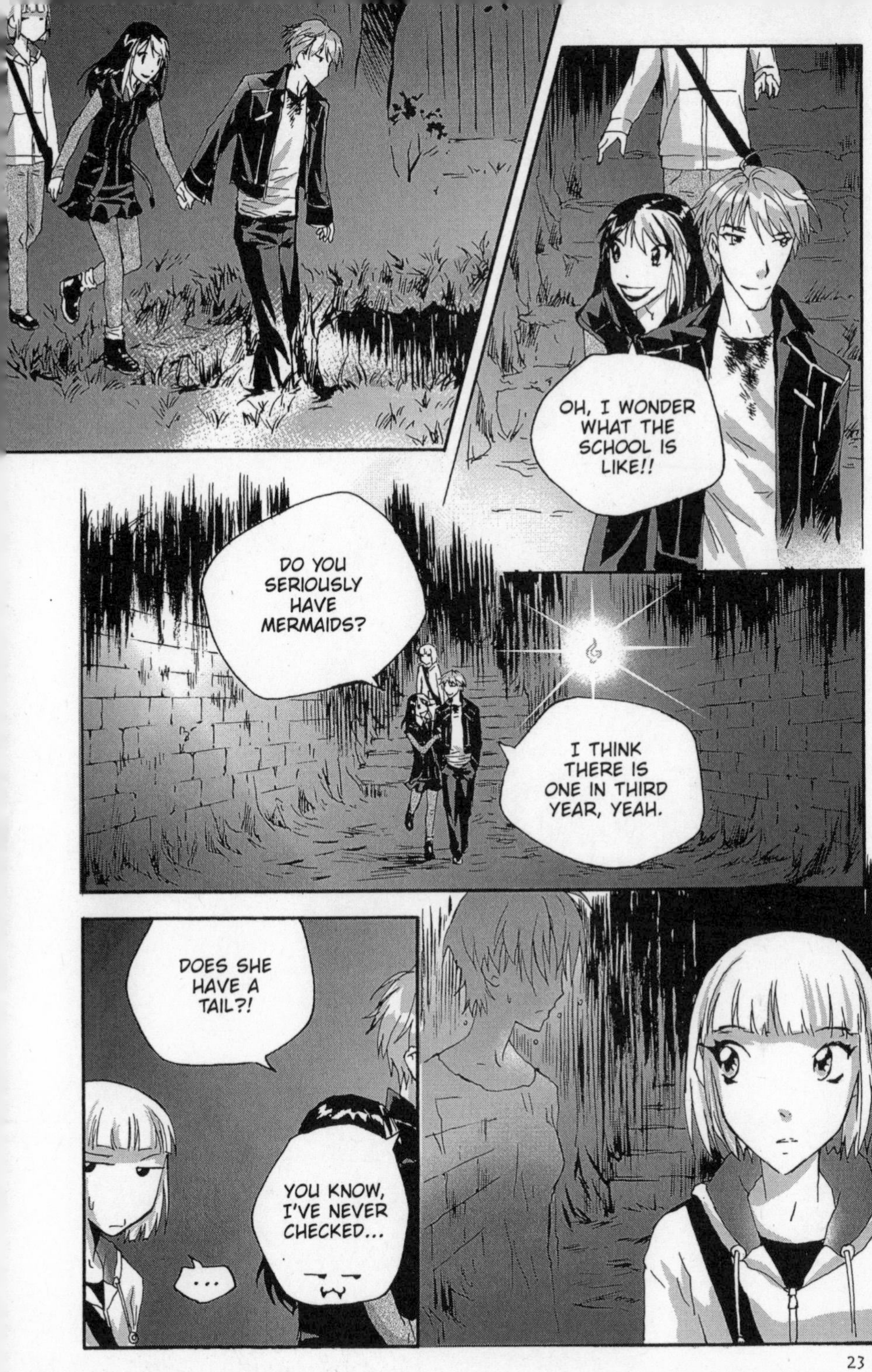
OH, I WONDER WHAT THE SCHOOL IS LIKE!!
DO YOU SERIOUSLY HAVE MERMAIDS?
I THINK THERE IS ONE IN THIRD YEAR, YEAH.
DOES SHE HAVE A TAIL?!
YOU KNOW, I'VE NEVER CHECKED...
...

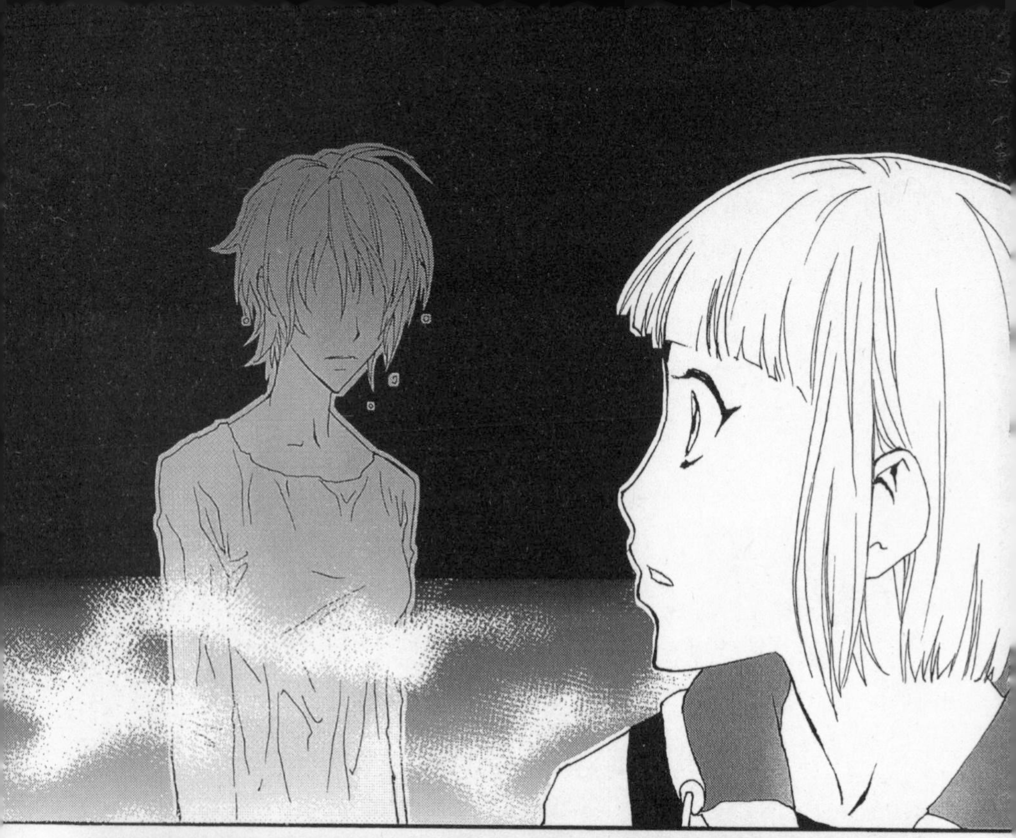

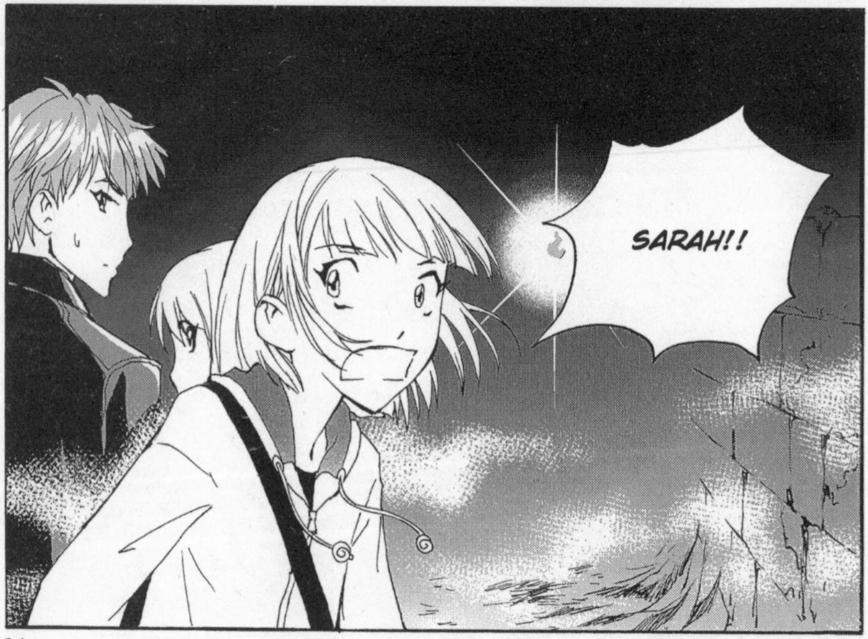
SARAH!!

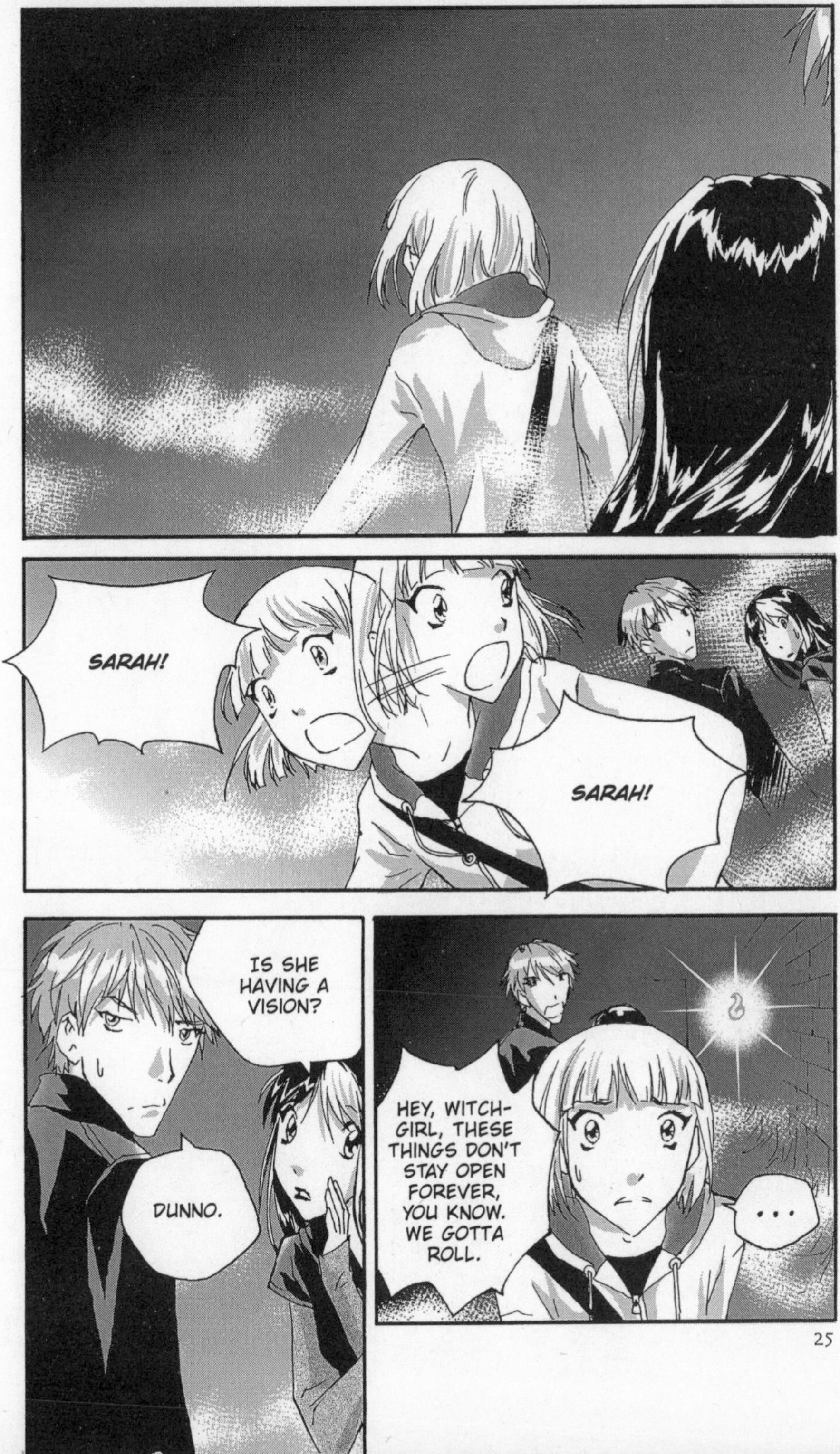
SARAH!
SARAH!
IS SHE HAVING A VISION?
DUNNO.
HEY, WITCH-GIRL, THESE THINGS DON'T STAY OPEN FOREVER, YOU KNOW. WE GOTTA ROLL.
...

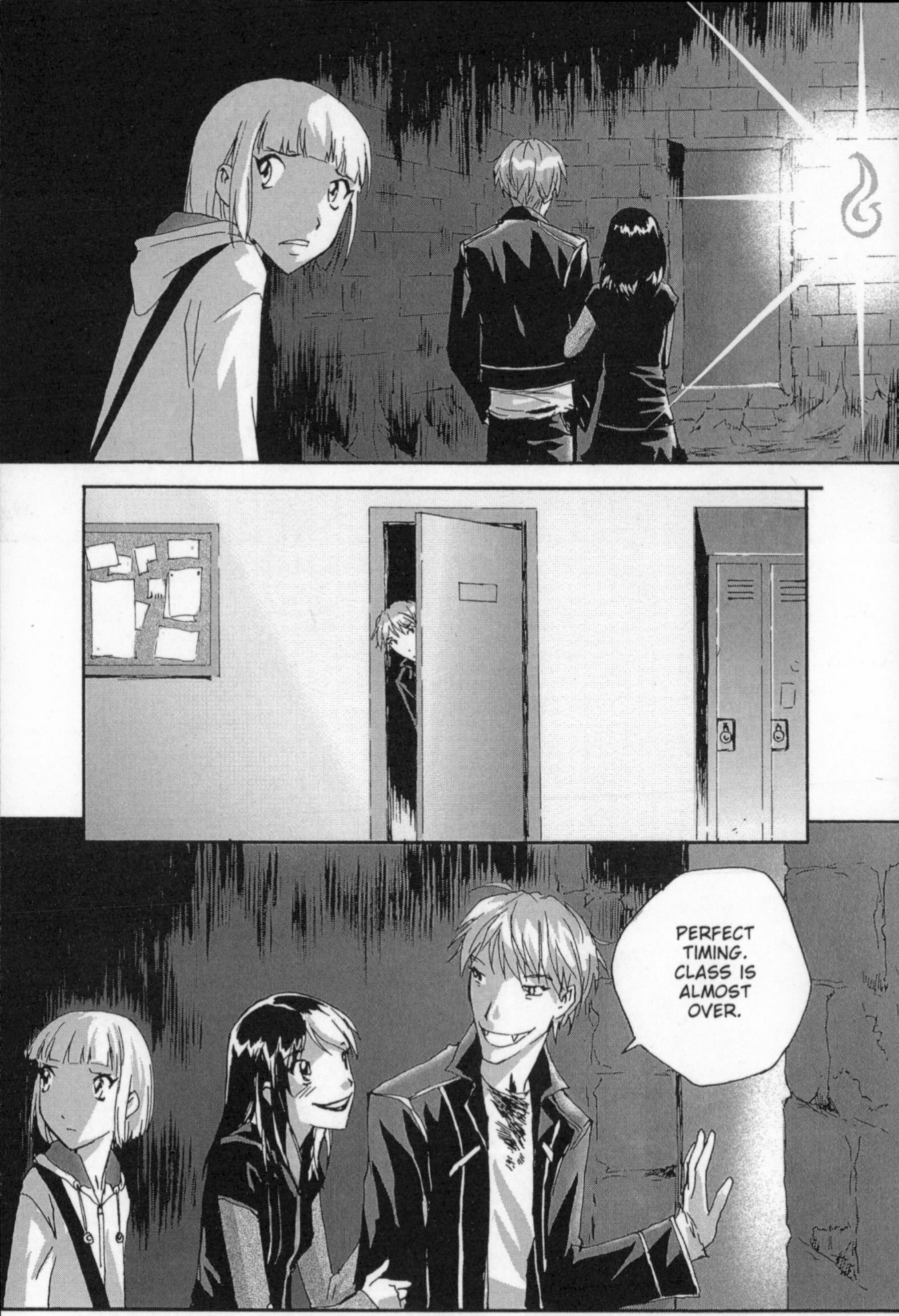
PERFECT TIMING. CLASS IS ALMOST OVER.

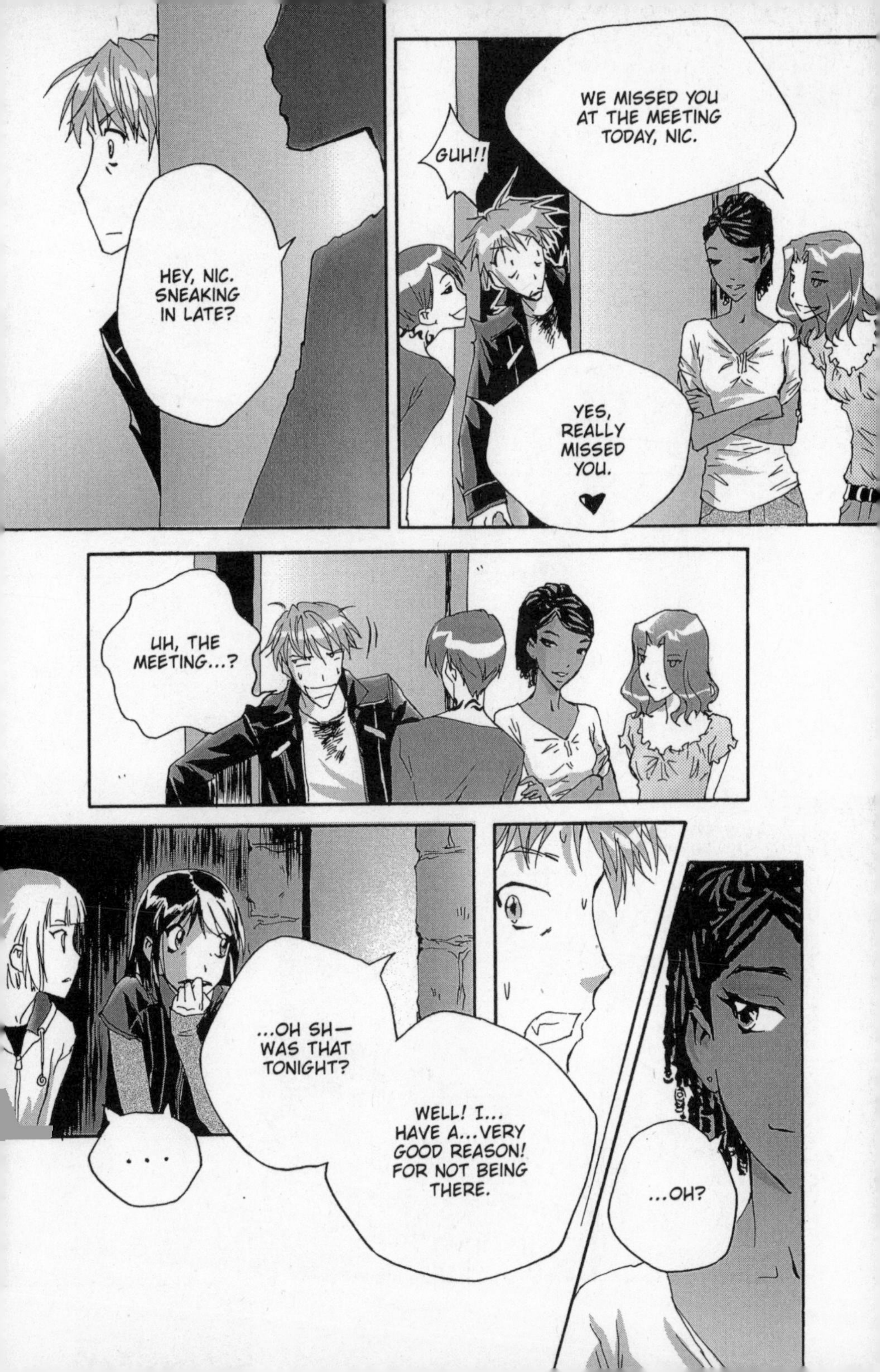
HEY, NIC. SNEAKING IN LATE?
GUH!!
WE MISSED YOU AT THE MEETING TODAY, NIC.
YES, REALLY MISSED YOU.
UH, THE MEETING...?
...OH SH— WAS THAT TONIGHT?
...
WELL! I... HAVE A...VERY GOOD REASON! FOR NOT BEING THERE.
...OH?

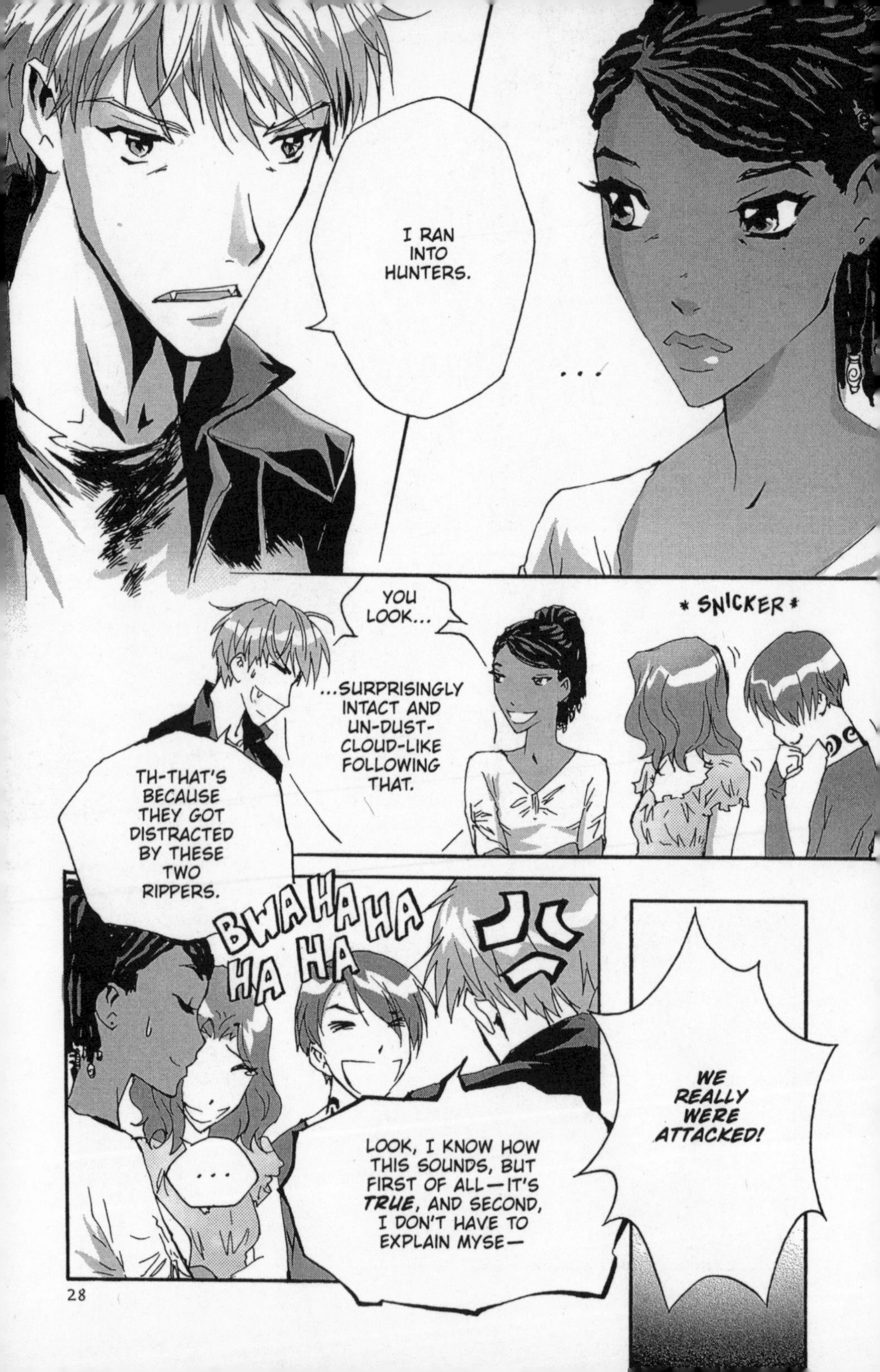
I RAN INTO HUNTERS.
...
YOU LOOK...
...SURPRISINGLY INTACT AND UN-DUST-CLOUD-LIKE FOLLOWING THAT.
SNICKER
TH-THAT'S BECAUSE THEY GOT DISTRACTED BY THESE TWO RIPPERS.
BWAHAHAHA HA HA HA
...
LOOK, I KNOW HOW THIS SOUNDS, BUT FIRST OF ALL—IT'S *TRUE*, AND SECOND, I DON'T HAVE TO EXPLAIN MYSE—
WE REALLY WERE ATTACKED!

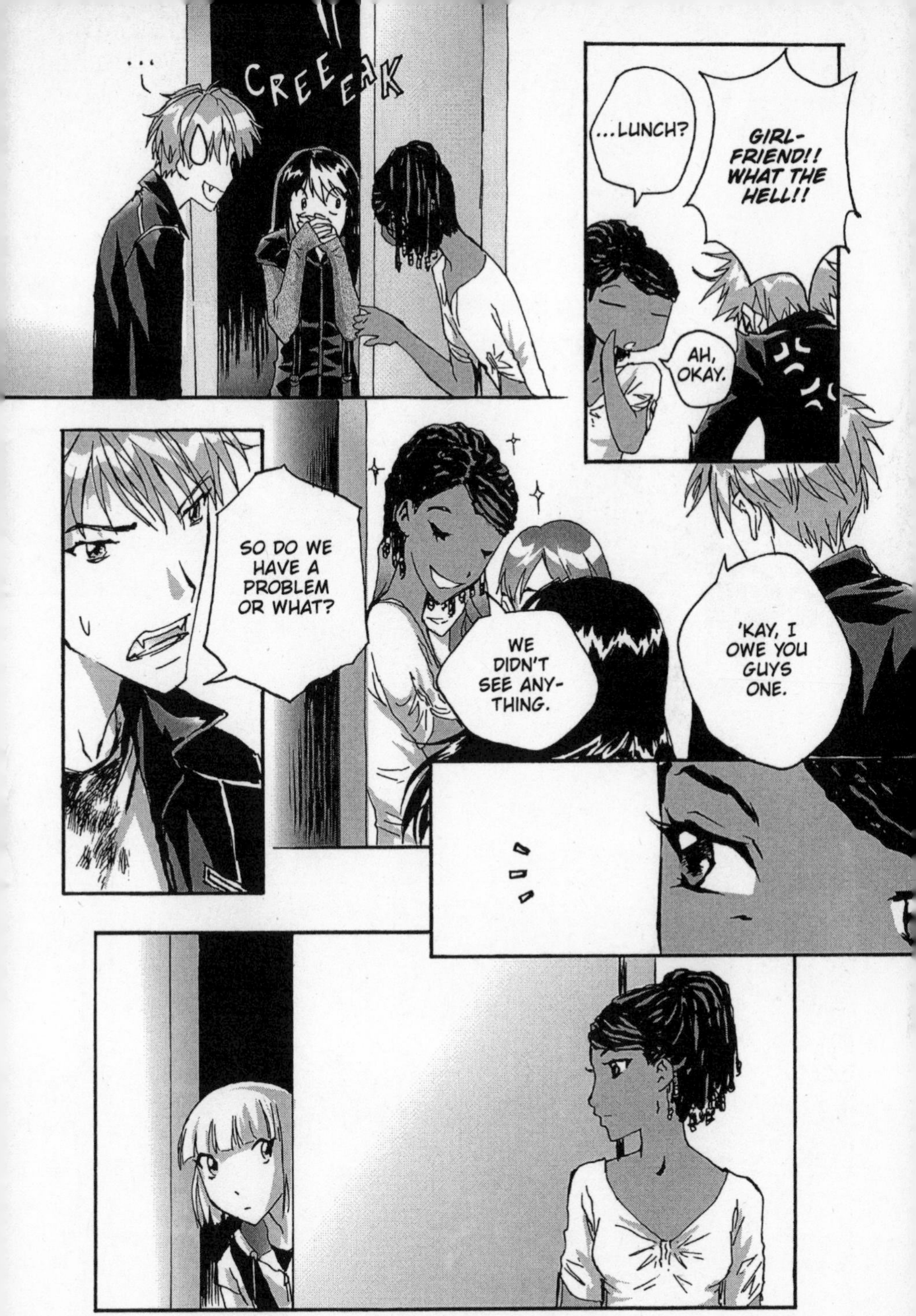
...
CREEEAK
...LUNCH?
GIRL-FRIEND!! WHAT THE HELL!!
AH, OKAY.
SO DO WE HAVE A PROBLEM OR WHAT?
WE DIDN'T SEE ANY-THING.
'KAY, I OWE YOU GUYS ONE.
...

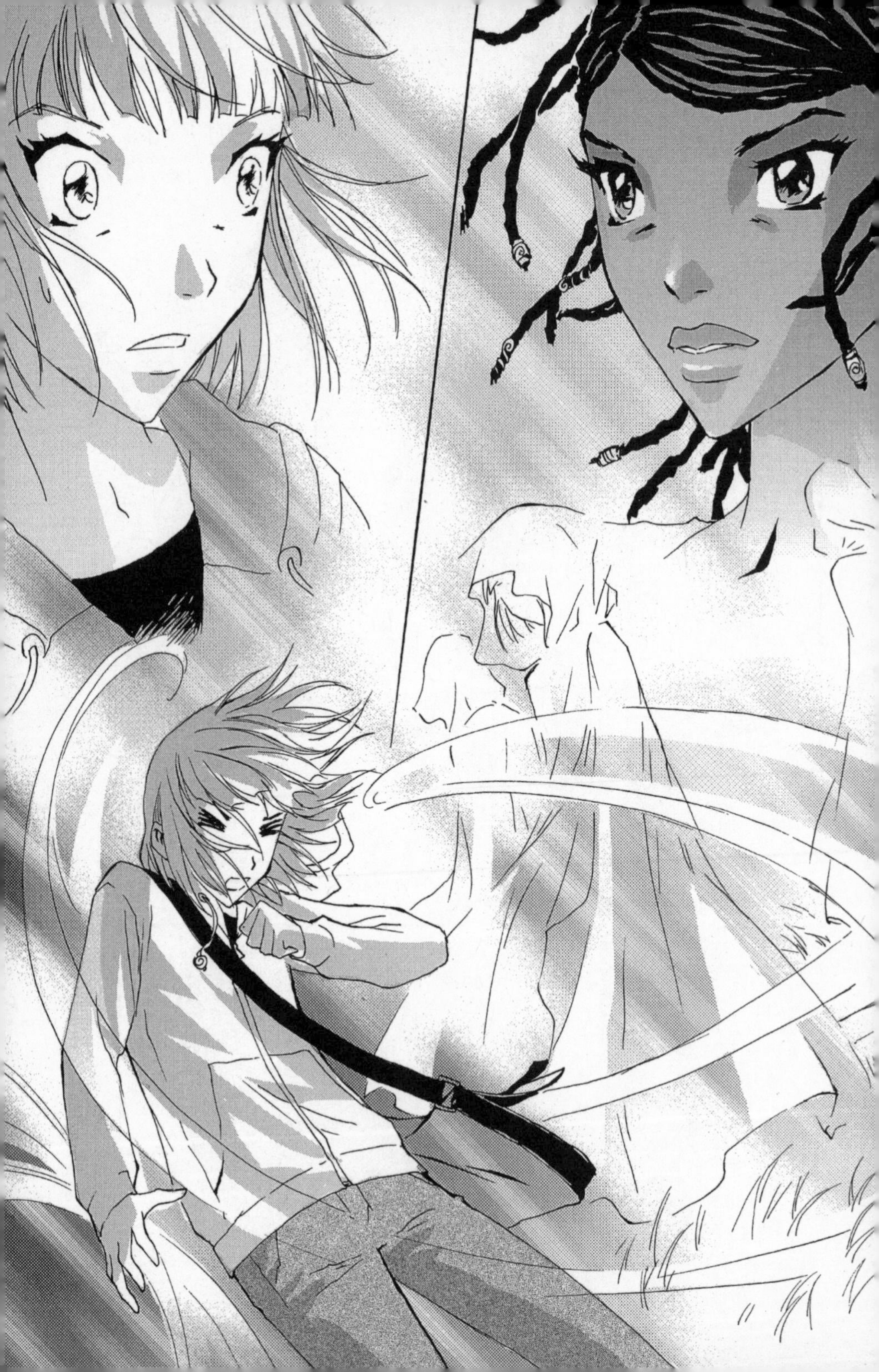

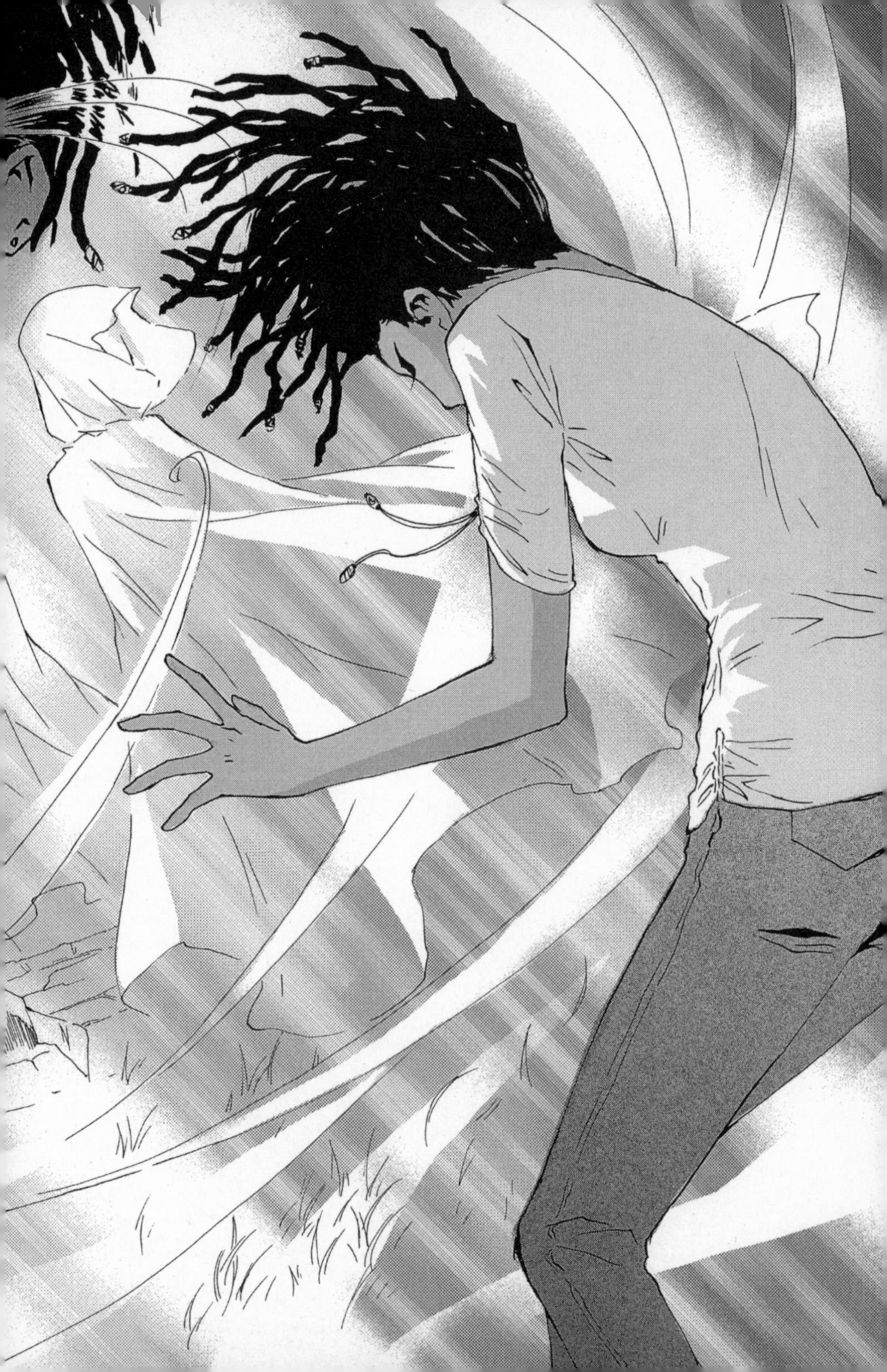

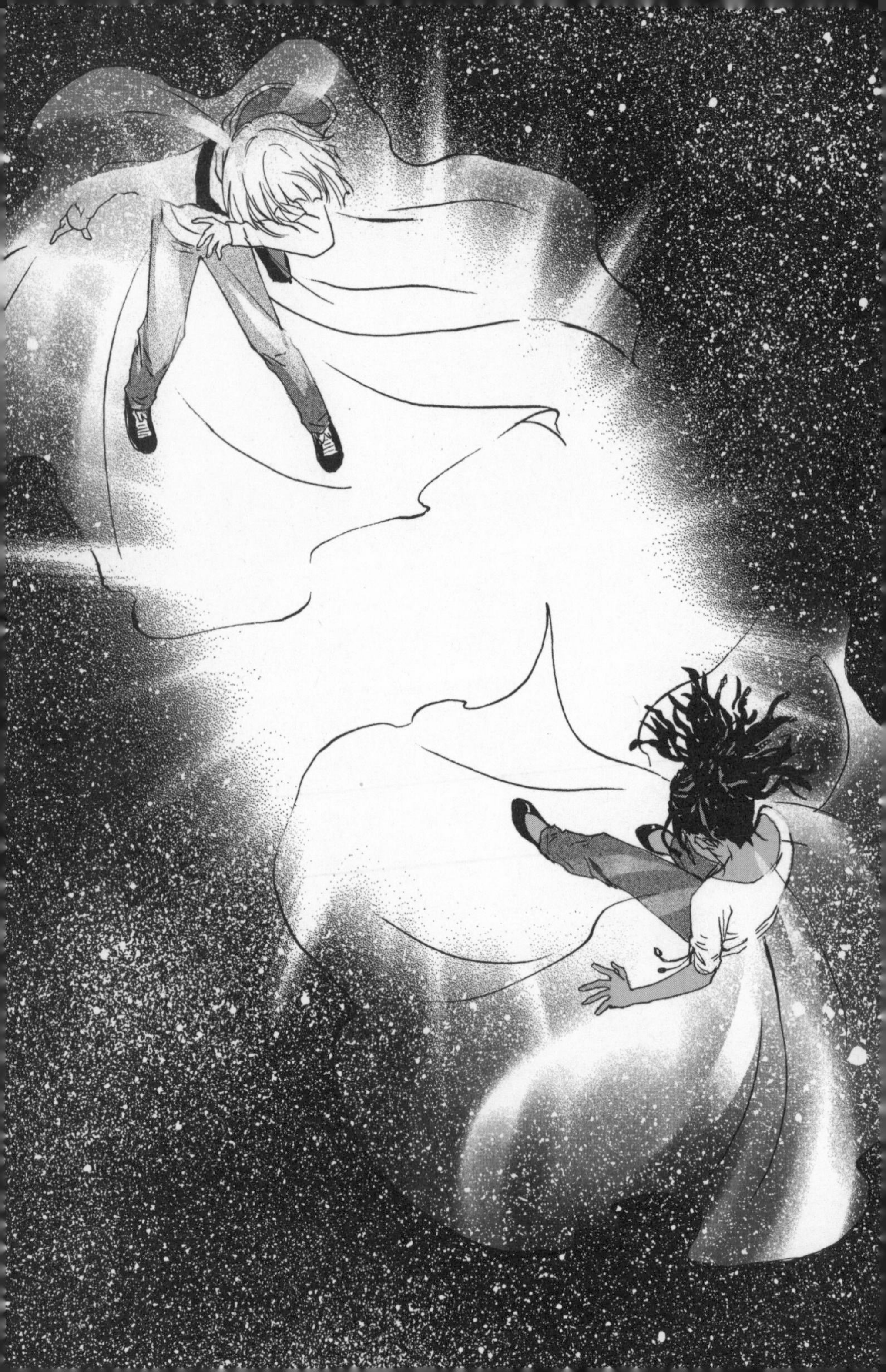

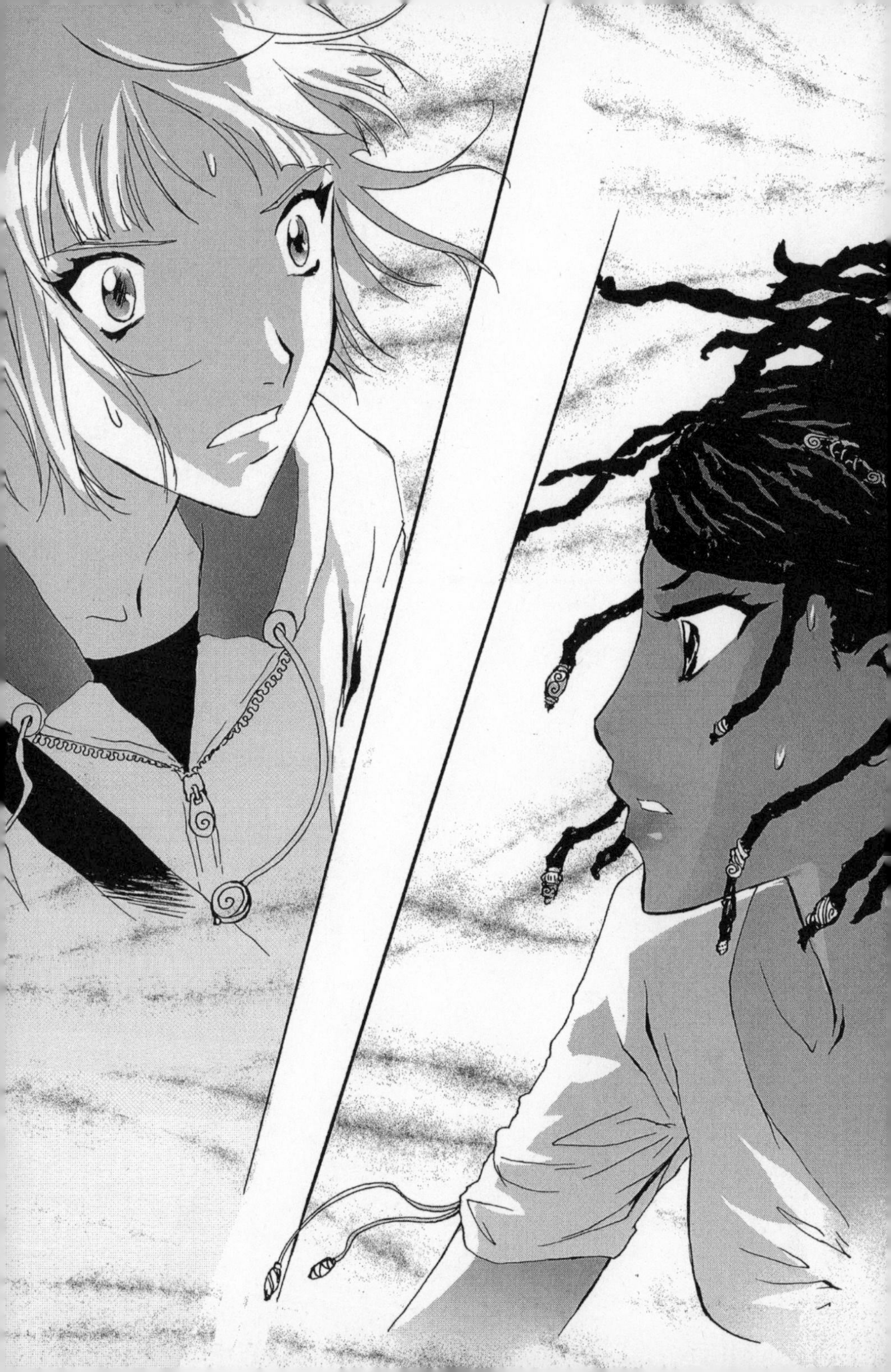

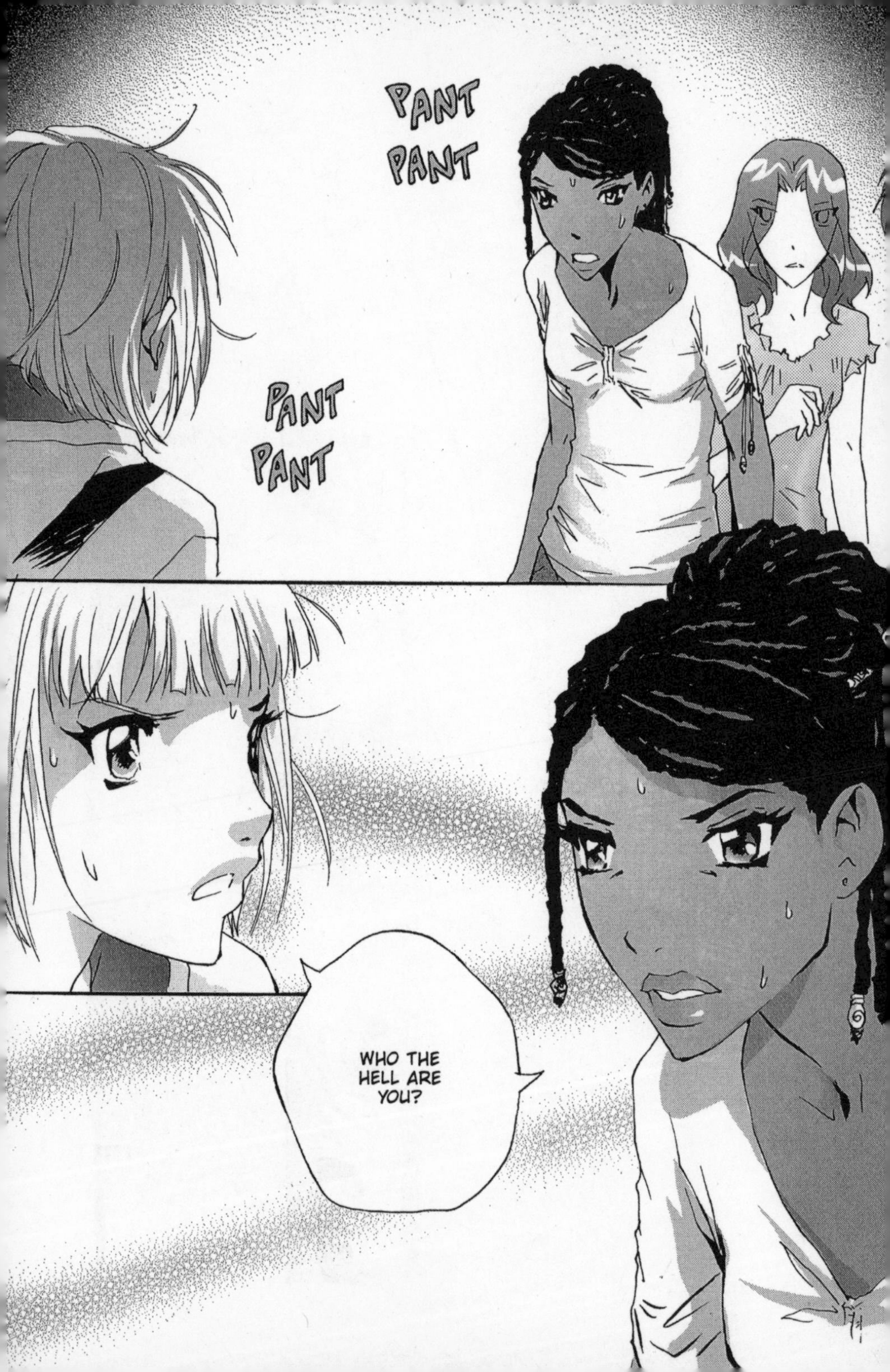
PANT PANT
PANT PANT
WHO THE HELL ARE YOU?

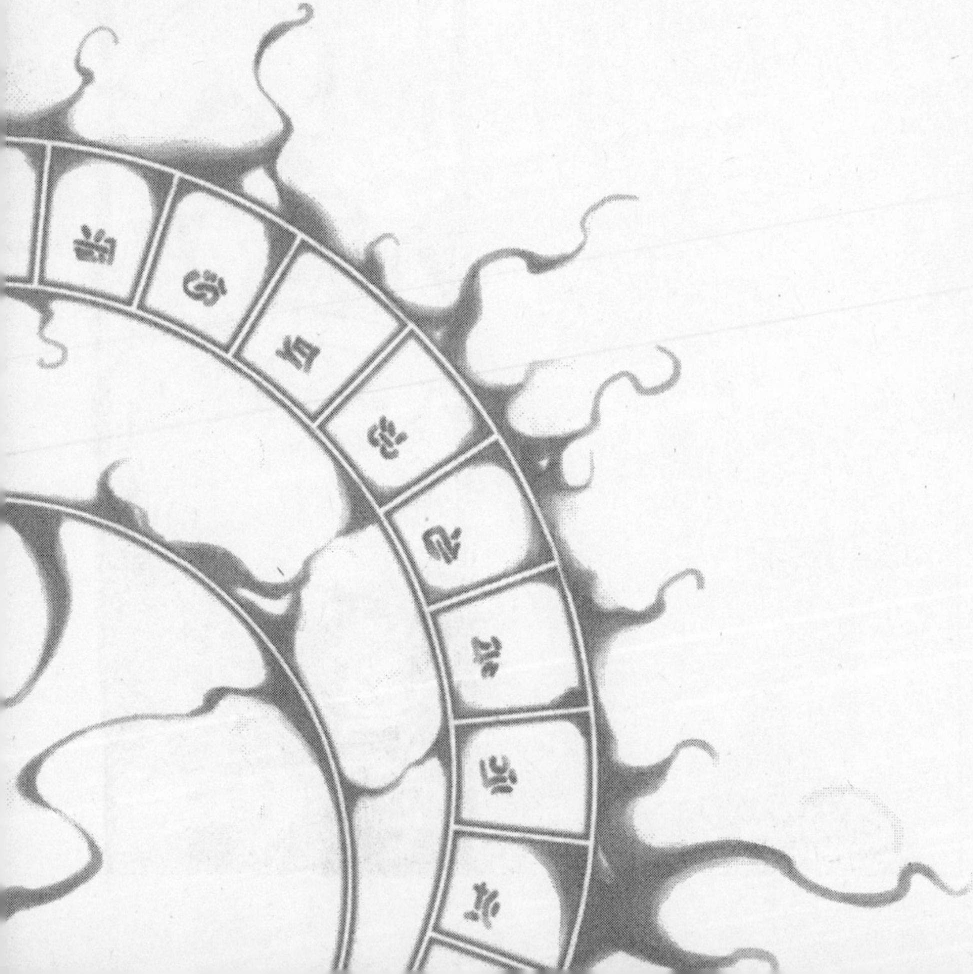

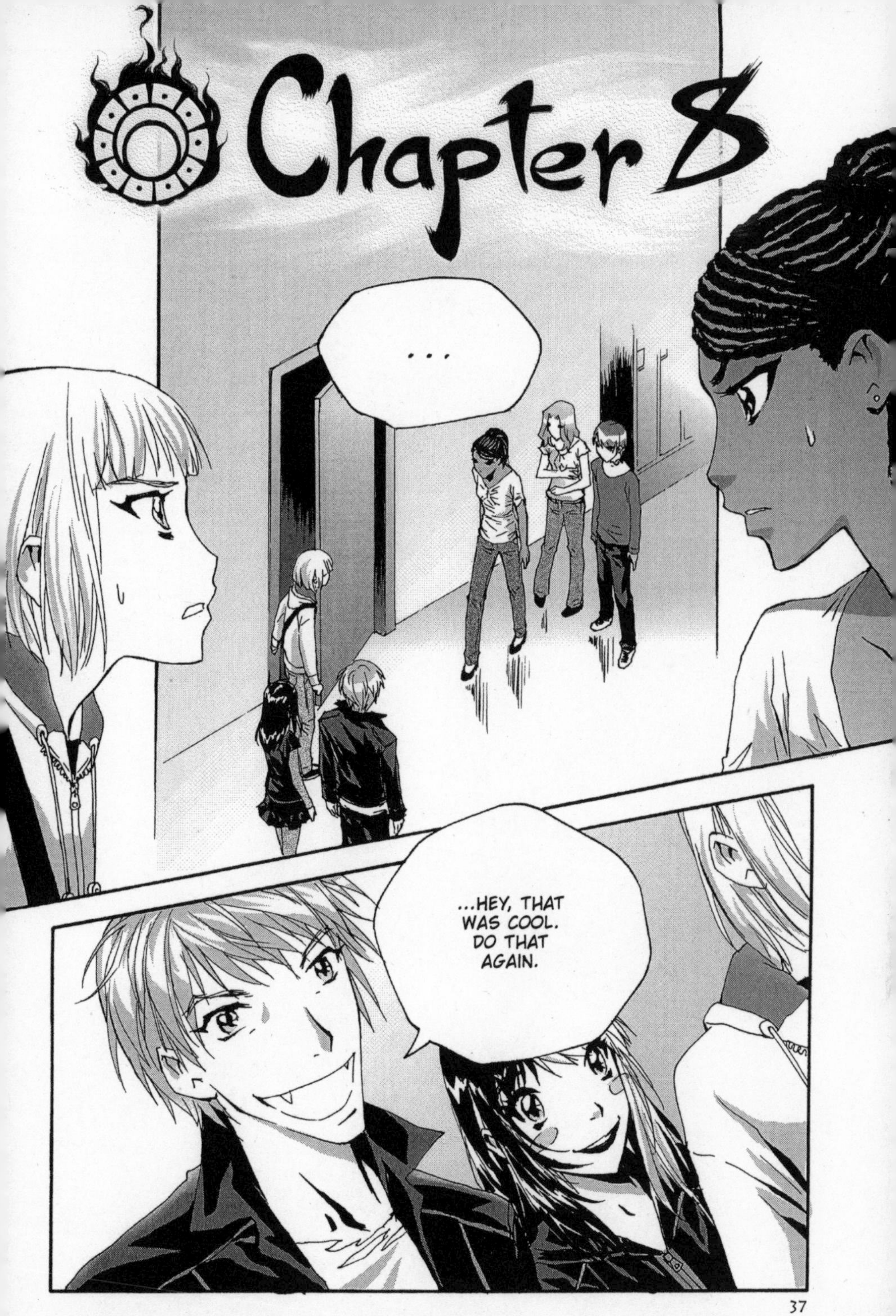
Chapter 8
...
...HEY, THAT WAS COOL. DO THAT AGAIN.

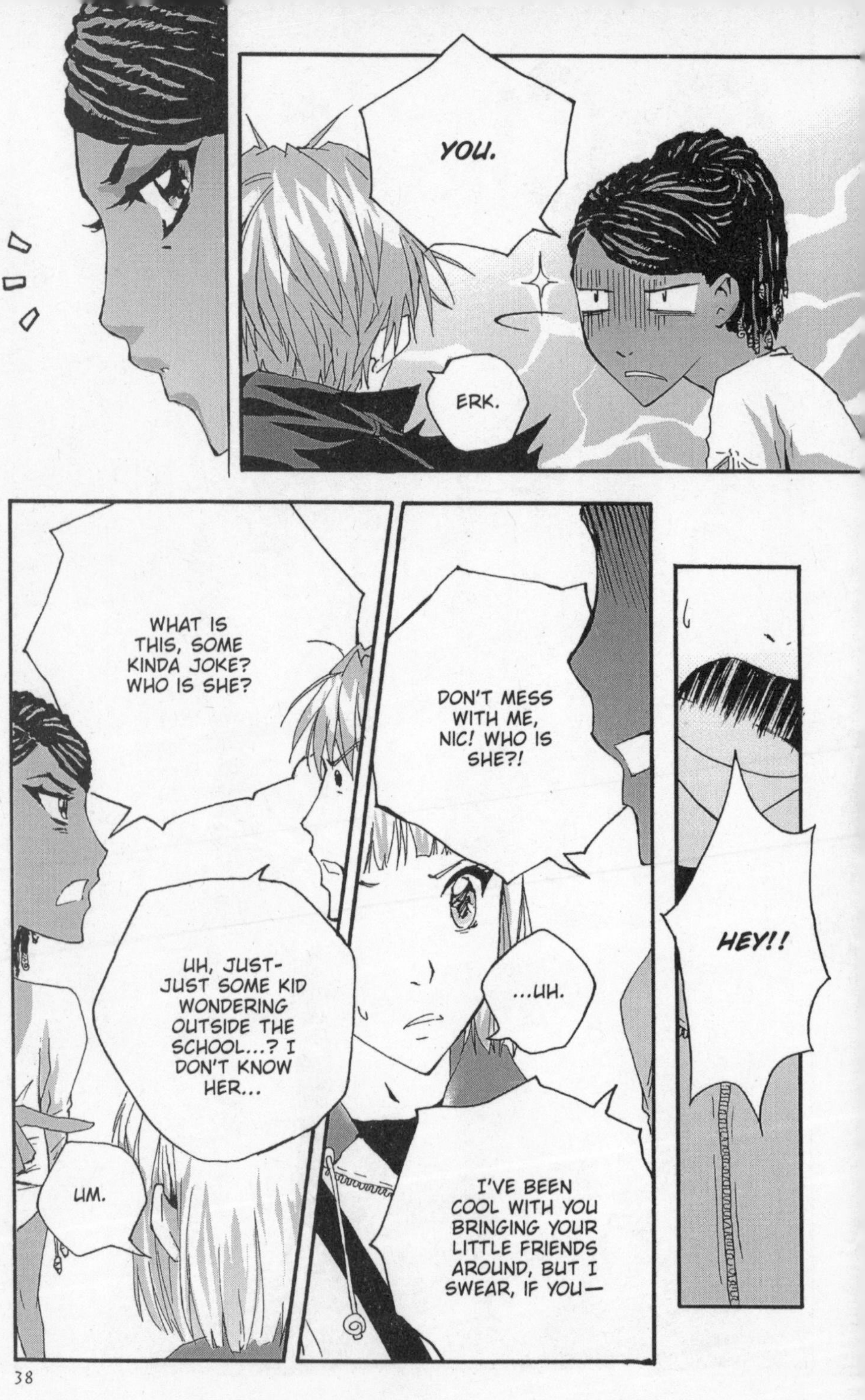
YOU.
ERK.
WHAT IS THIS, SOME KINDA JOKE? WHO IS SHE?
UH, JUST-JUST SOME KID WONDERING OUTSIDE THE SCHOOL...? I DON'T KNOW HER...
UM.
DON'T MESS WITH ME, NIC! WHO IS SHE?!
...UH.
I'VE BEEN COOL WITH YOU BRINGING YOUR LITTLE FRIENDS AROUND, BUT I SWEAR, IF YOU—
HEY!!

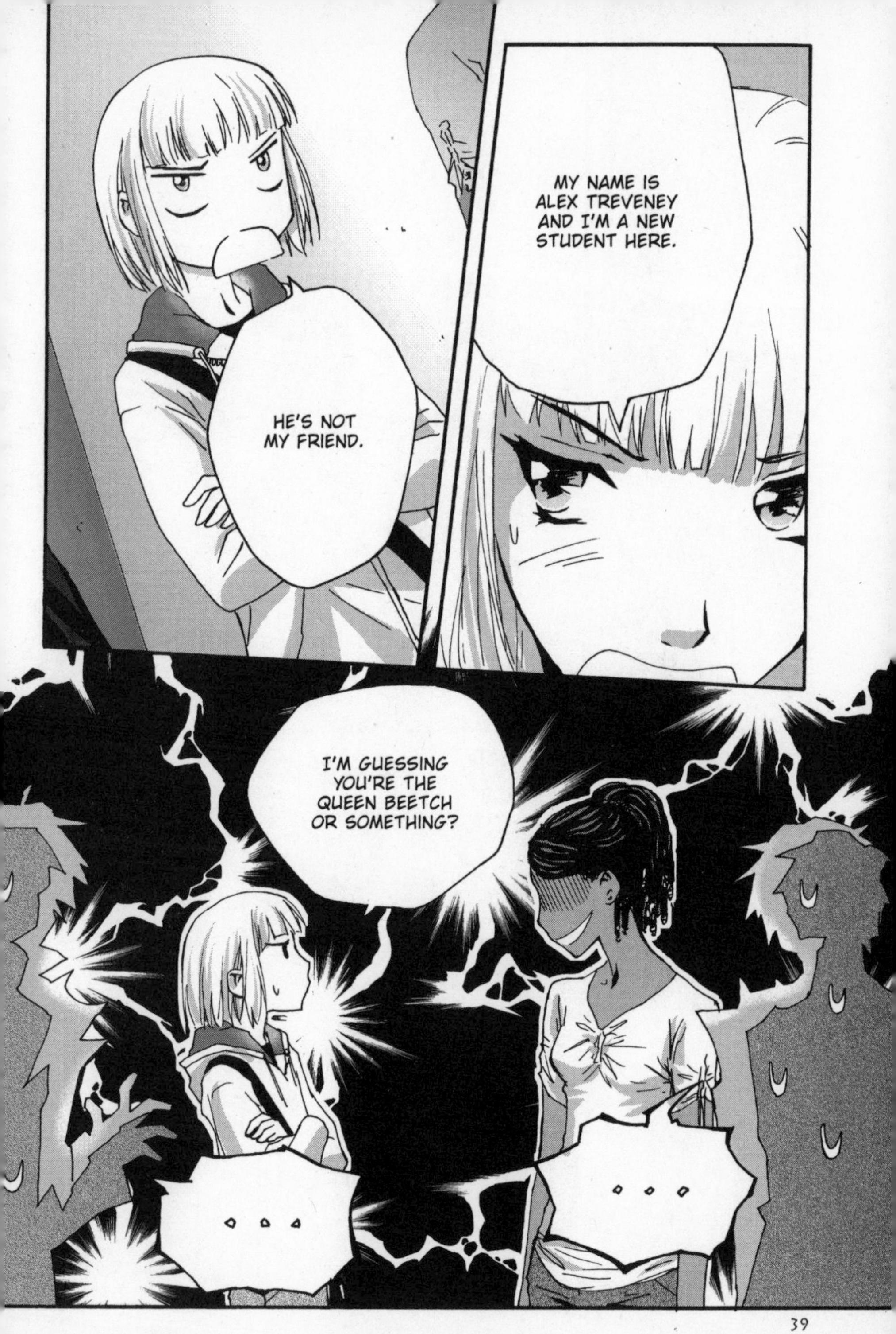
HE'S NOT MY FRIEND.
MY NAME IS ALEX TREVENEY AND I'M A NEW STUDENT HERE.
I'M GUESSING YOU'RE THE QUEEN BEETCH OR SOMETHING?
...
...

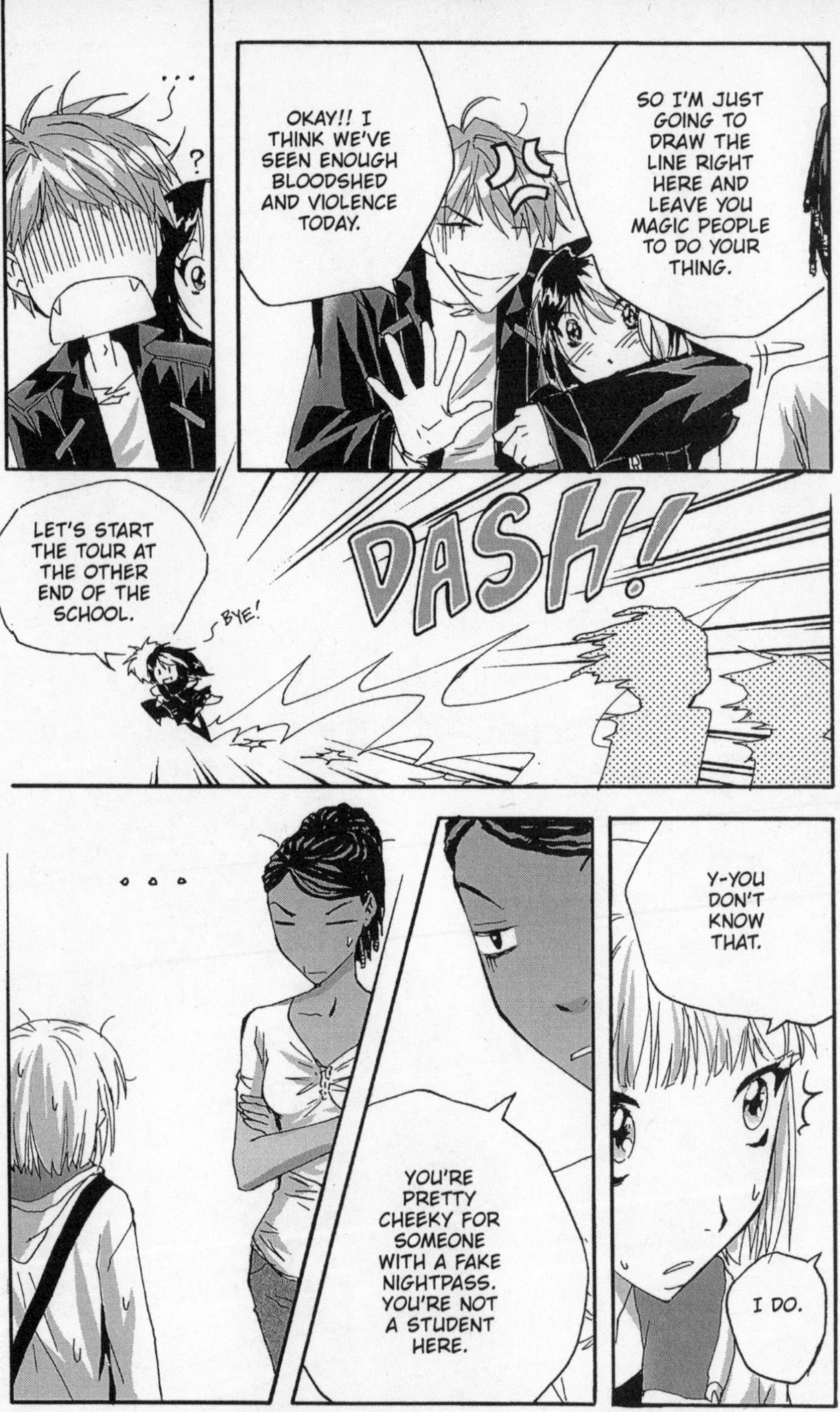
...
?
OKAY!! I THINK WE'VE SEEN ENOUGH BLOODSHED AND VIOLENCE TODAY.
SO I'M JUST GOING TO DRAW THE LINE RIGHT HERE AND LEAVE YOU MAGIC PEOPLE TO DO YOUR THING.
LET'S START THE TOUR AT THE OTHER END OF THE SCHOOL.
BYE!
DASH!
...
YOU'RE PRETTY CHEEKY FOR SOMEONE WITH A FAKE NIGHTPASS. YOU'RE NOT A STUDENT HERE.
Y-YOU DON'T KNOW THAT.
I DO.

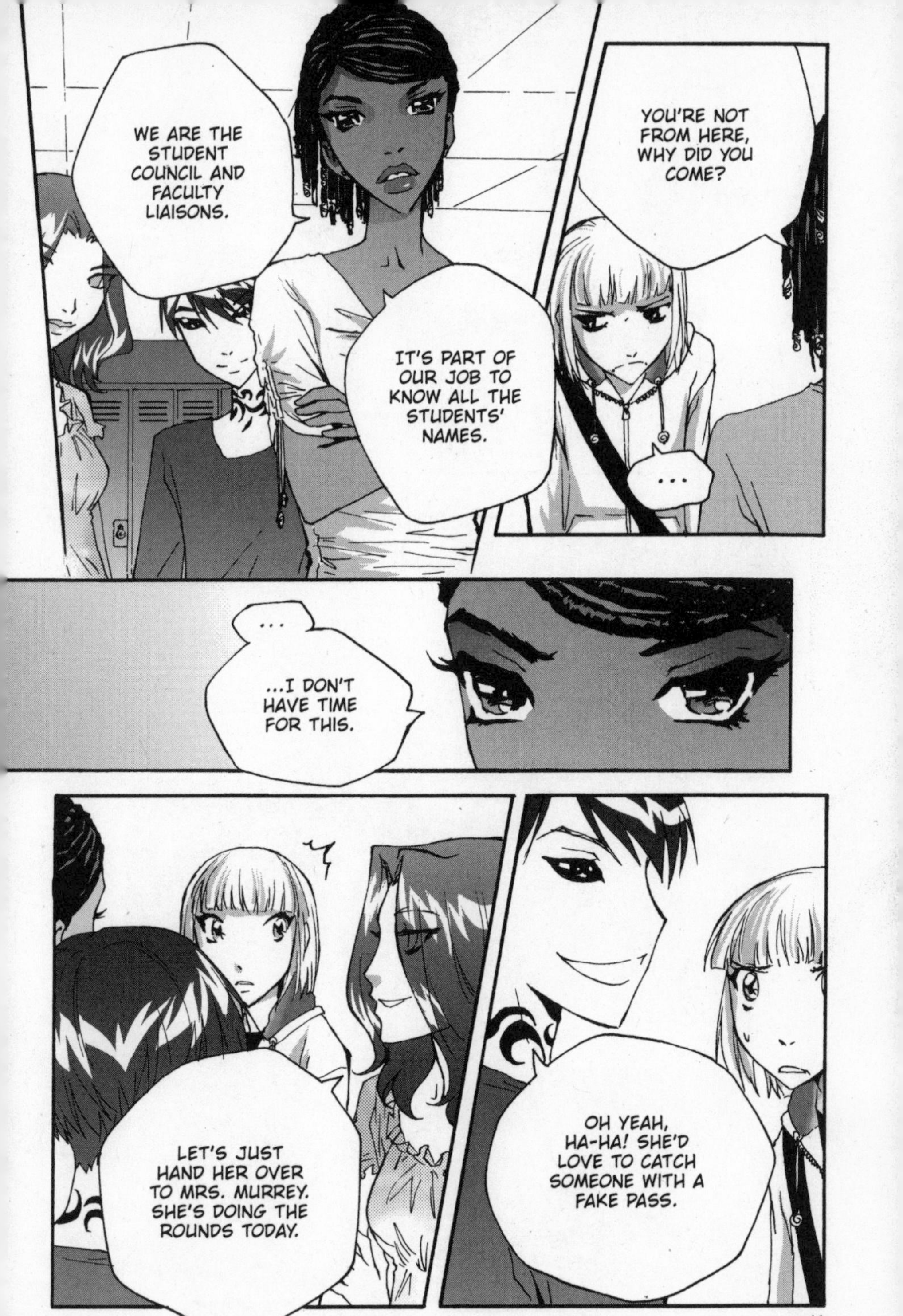
WE ARE THE STUDENT COUNCIL AND FACULTY LIAISONS.
IT'S PART OF OUR JOB TO KNOW ALL THE STUDENTS' NAMES.
YOU'RE NOT FROM HERE, WHY DID YOU COME?
...
...
...I DON'T HAVE TIME FOR THIS.
LET'S JUST HAND HER OVER TO MRS. MURREY. SHE'S DOING THE ROUNDS TODAY.
OH YEAH, HA-HA! SHE'D LOVE TO CATCH SOMEONE WITH A FAKE PASS.

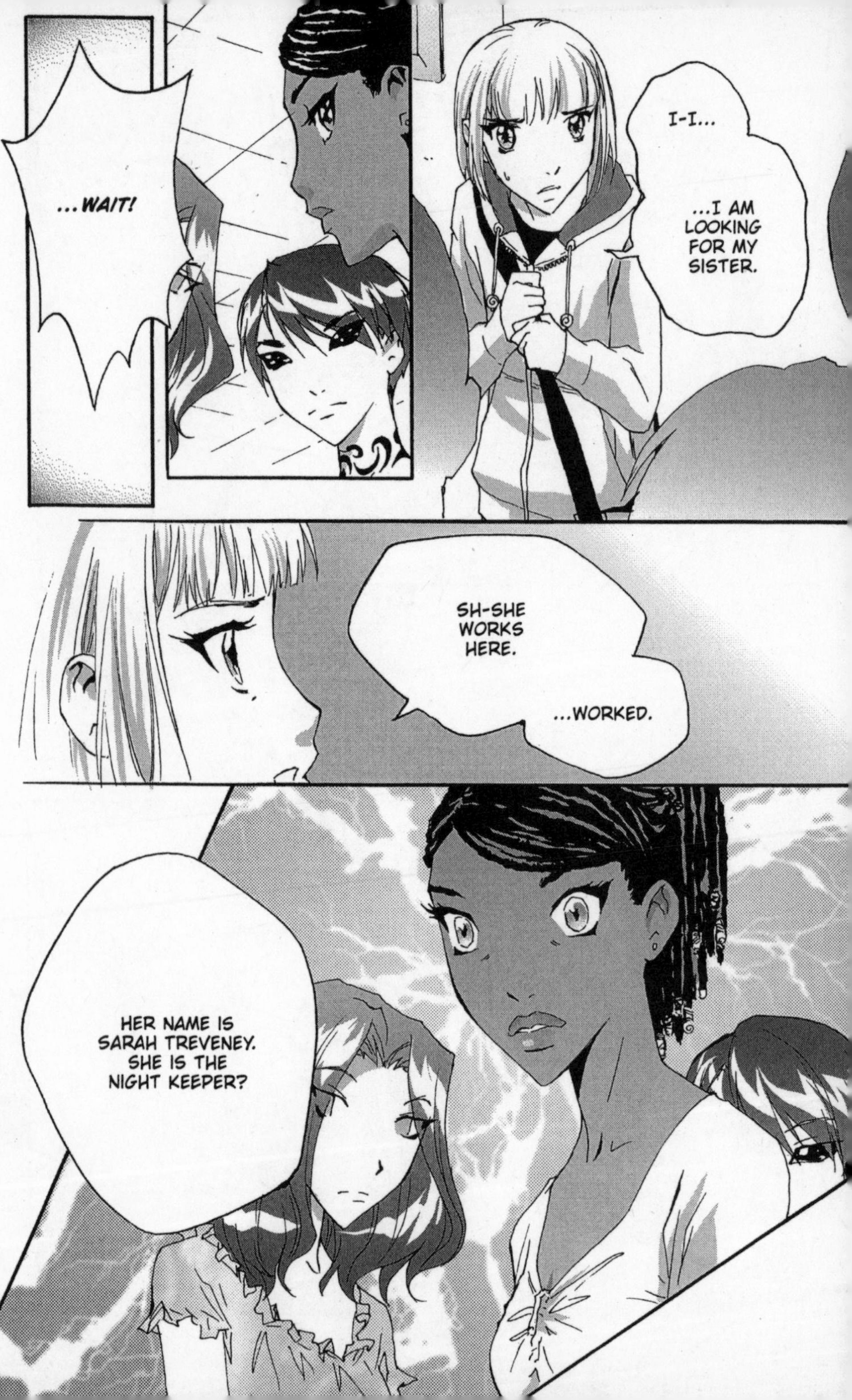
...WAIT!
I-I...
...I AM LOOKING FOR MY SISTER.
SH-SHE WORKS HERE.
...WORKED.
HER NAME IS SARAH TREVENEY. SHE IS THE NIGHT KEEPER?

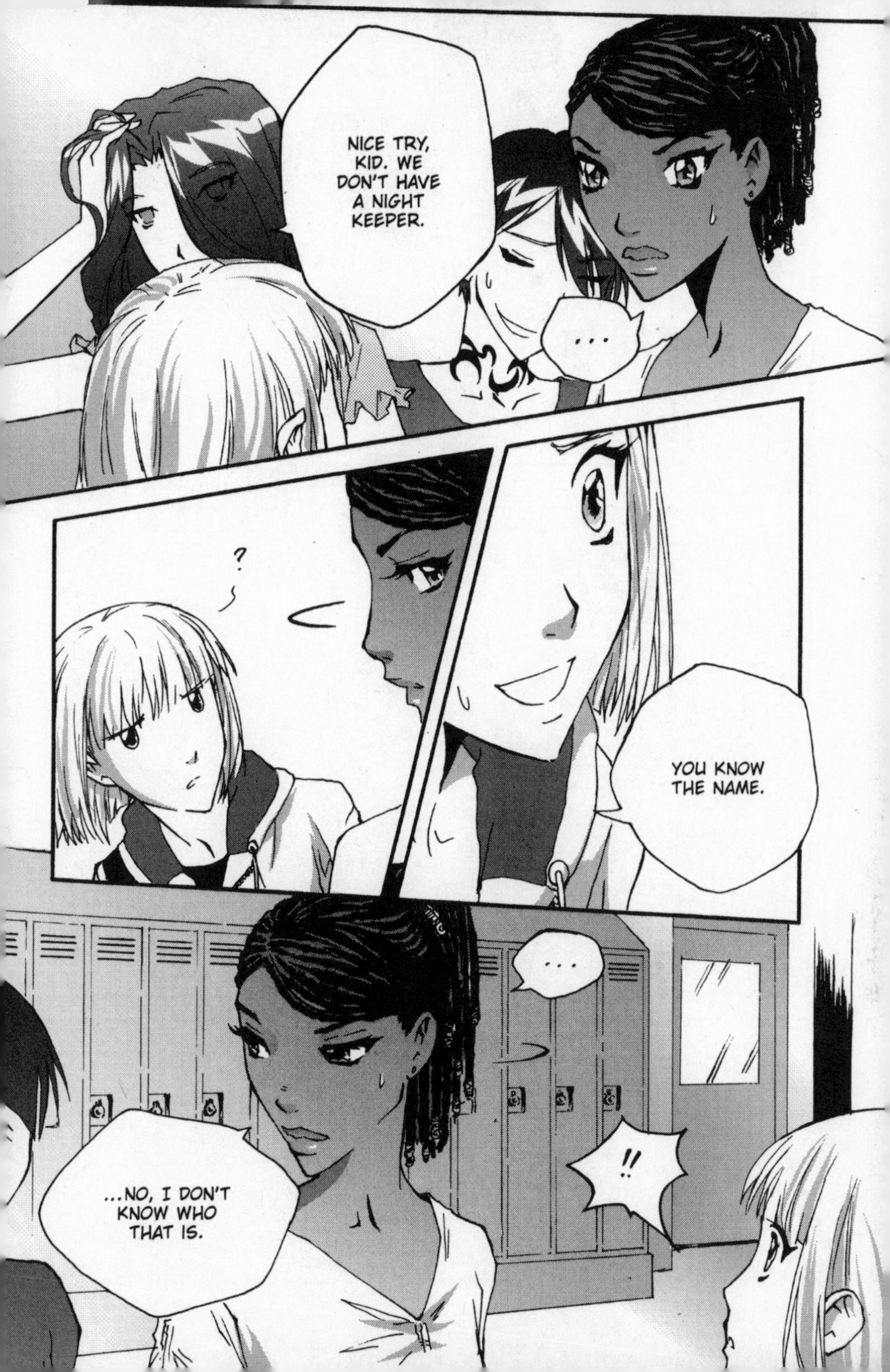
NICE TRY, KID. WE DON'T HAVE A NIGHT KEEPER.
...
?
YOU KNOW THE NAME.
...
...NO, I DON'T KNOW WHO THAT IS.
!!

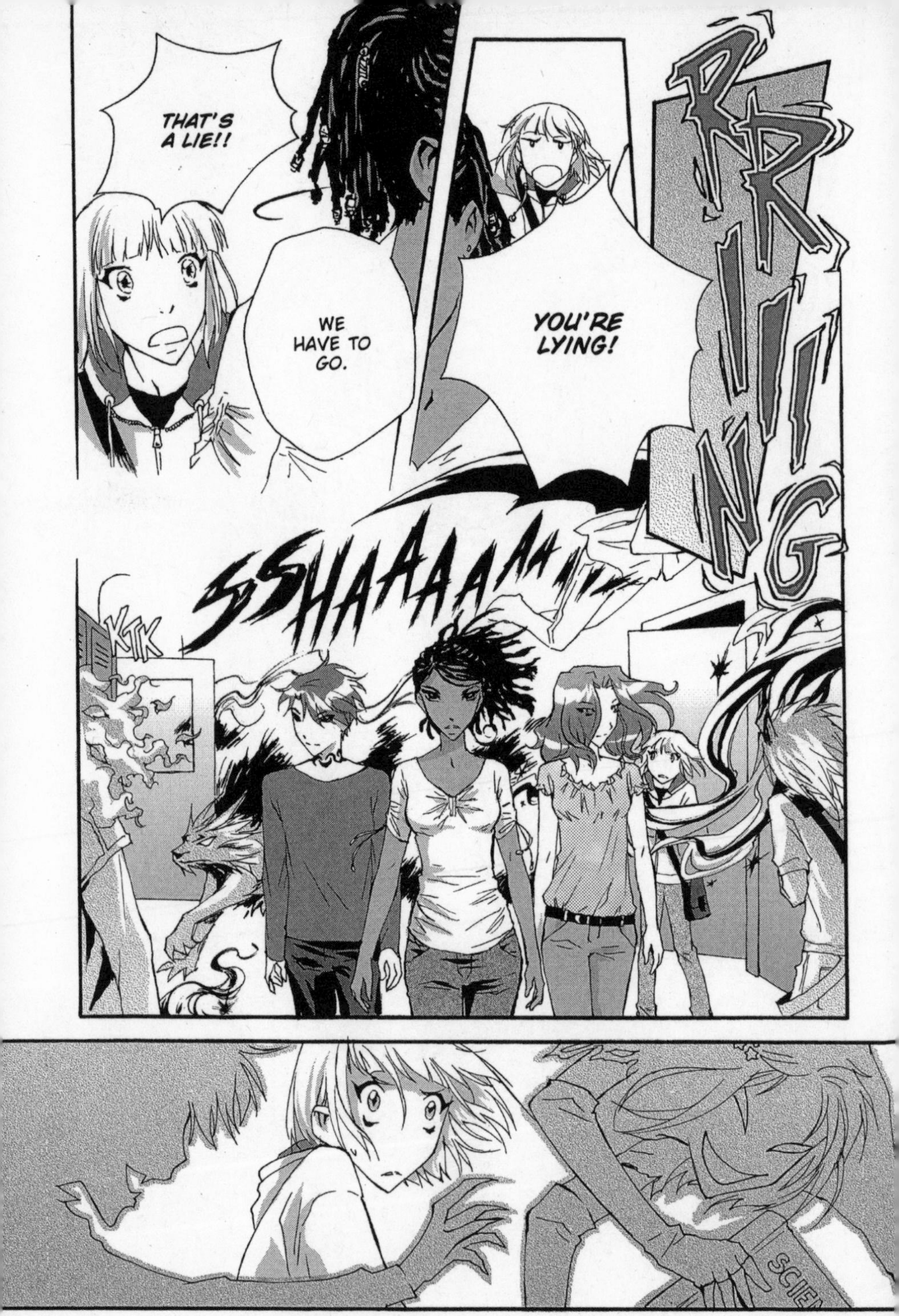

THAT'S A LIE!!
WE HAVE TO GO.
YOU'RE LYING!
RRIIING
SSSHAAAAAA
KTK
SCIEN

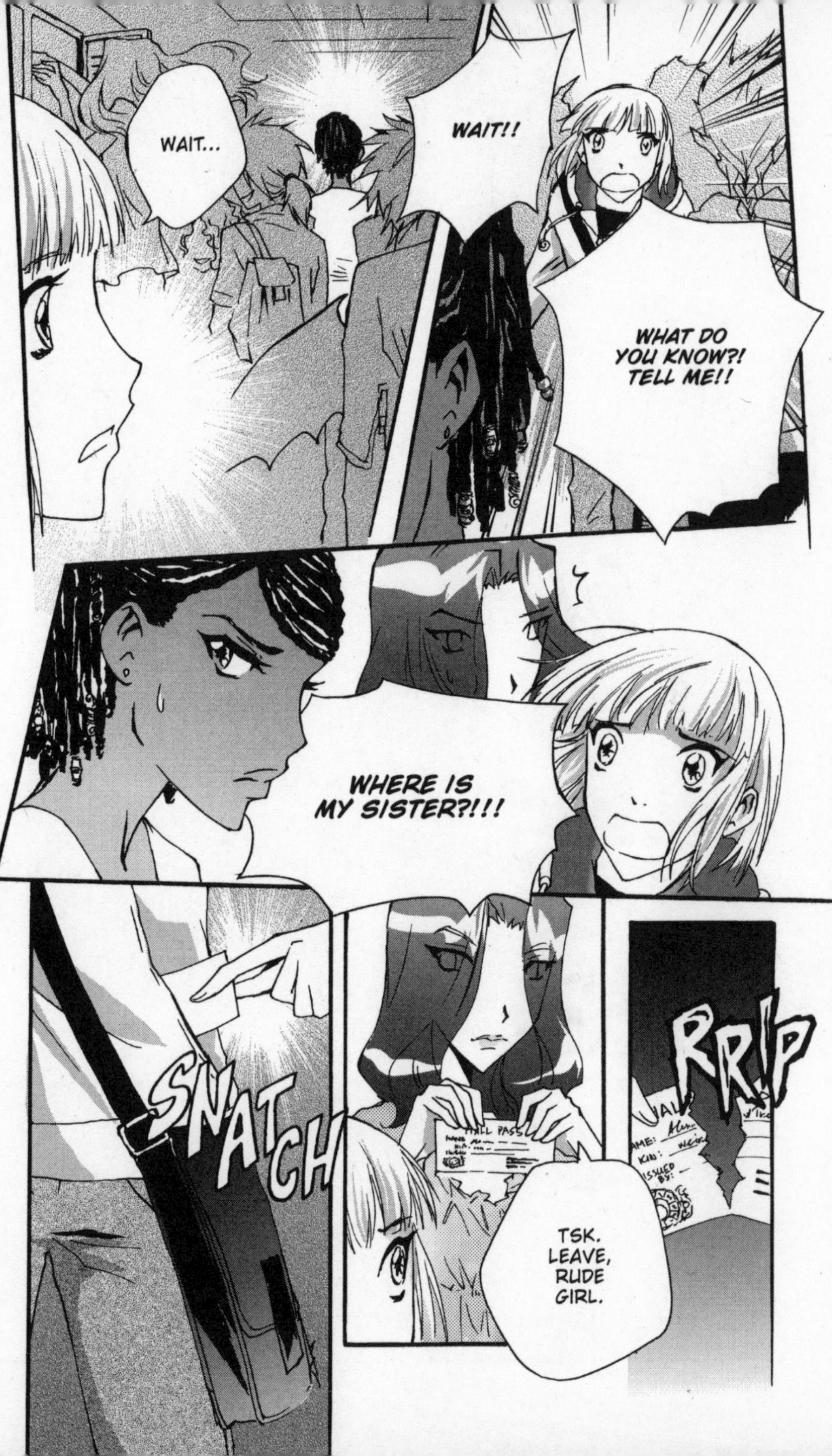
WAIT...
WAIT!!
WHAT DO YOU KNOW?! TELL ME!!
WHERE IS MY SISTER?!!!
SNATCH
TSK. LEAVE, RUDE GIRL.
RRIP

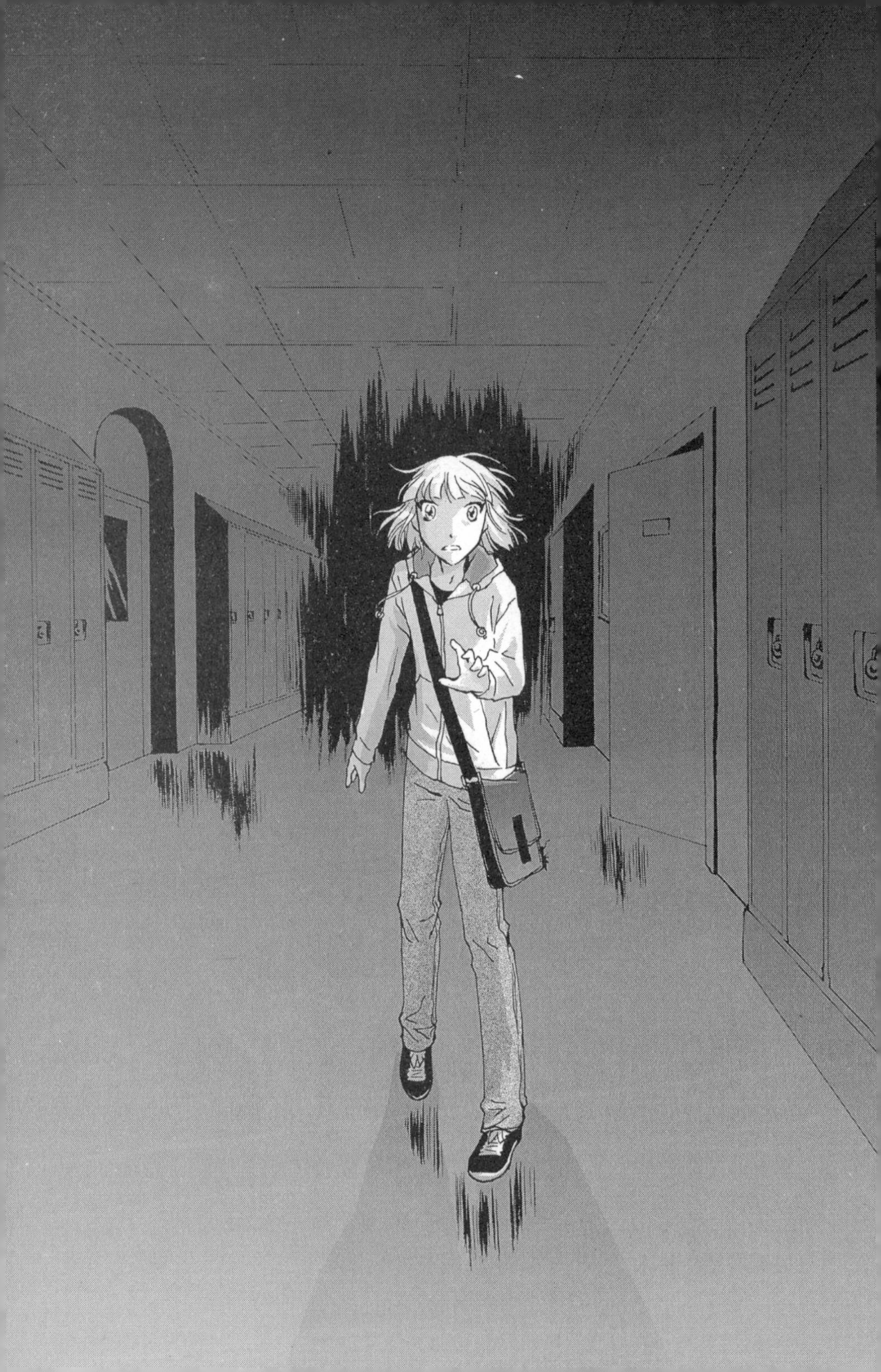

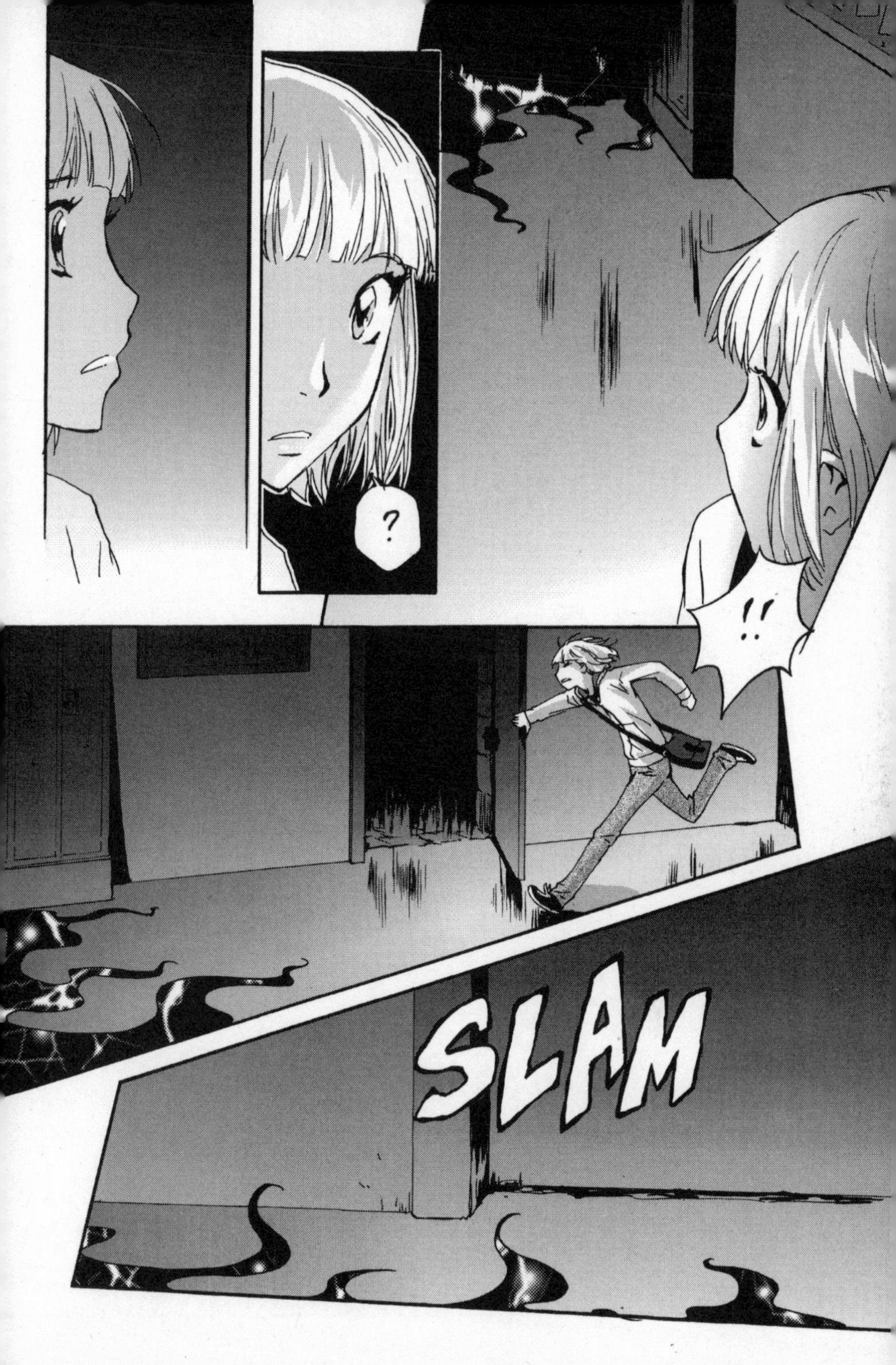
?
!!
SLAM

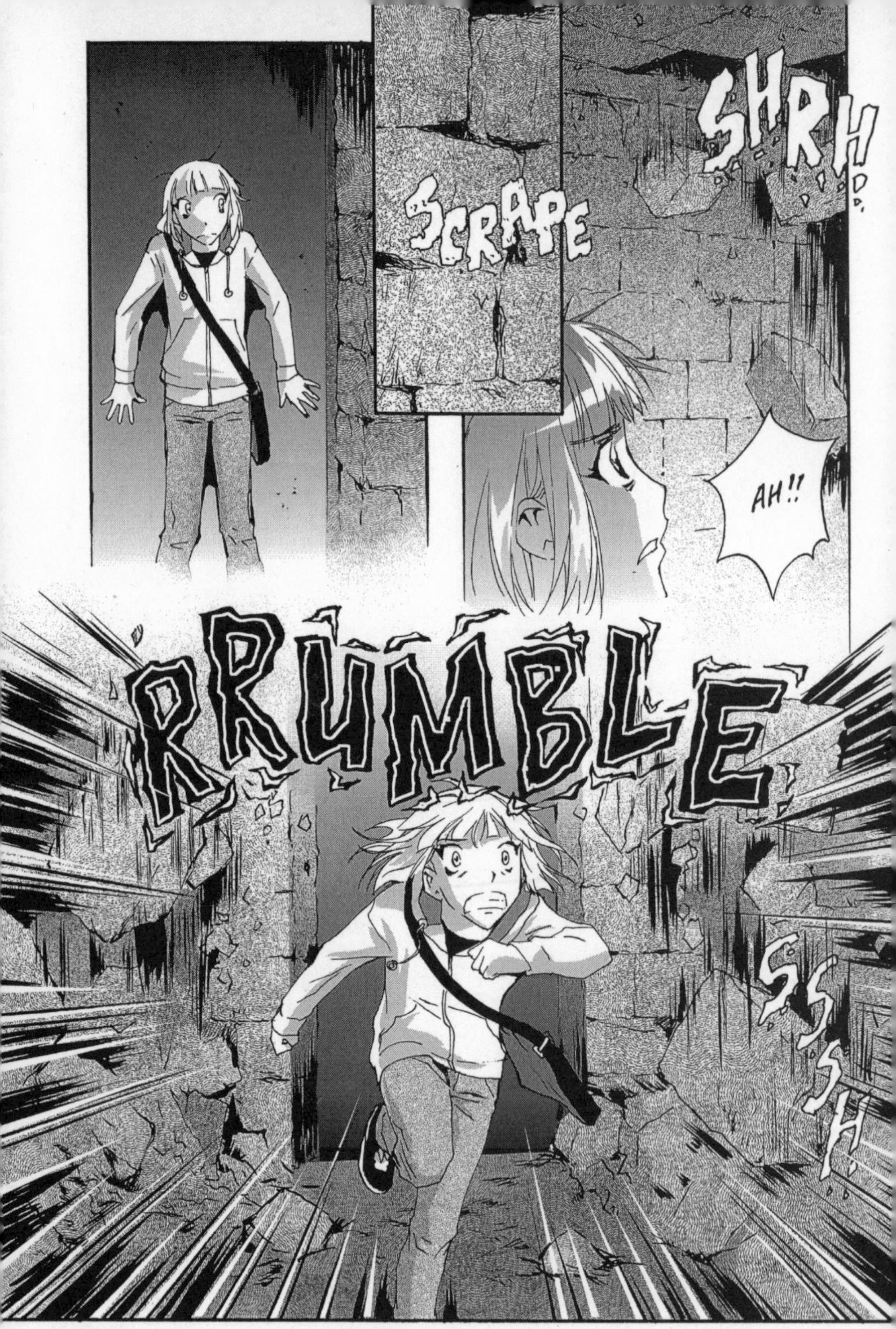
SCRAPE
SHRH
AH!!
RRUMBLE
SSSH

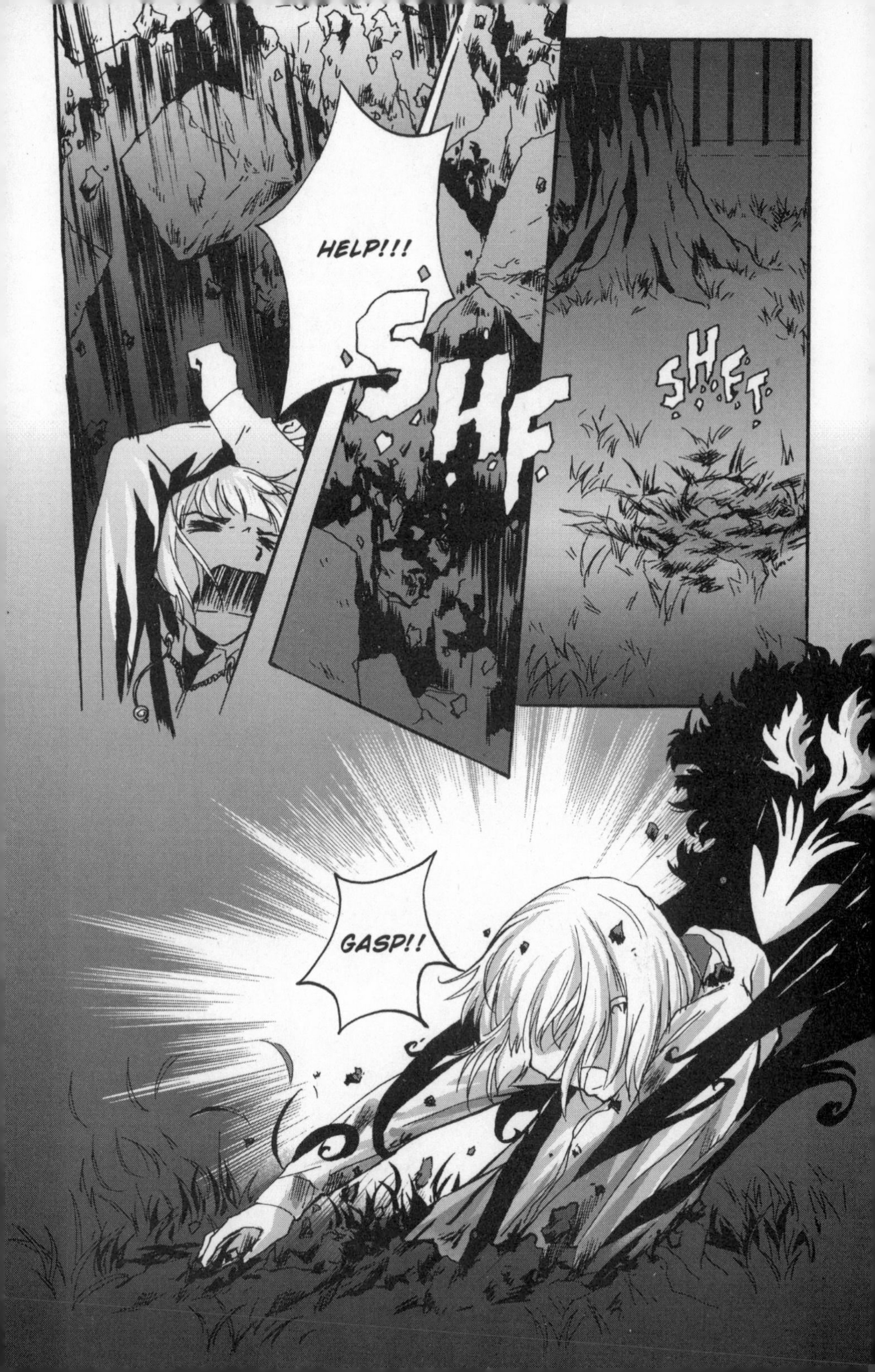

HELP!!!
SHF
SHFT
GASP!!

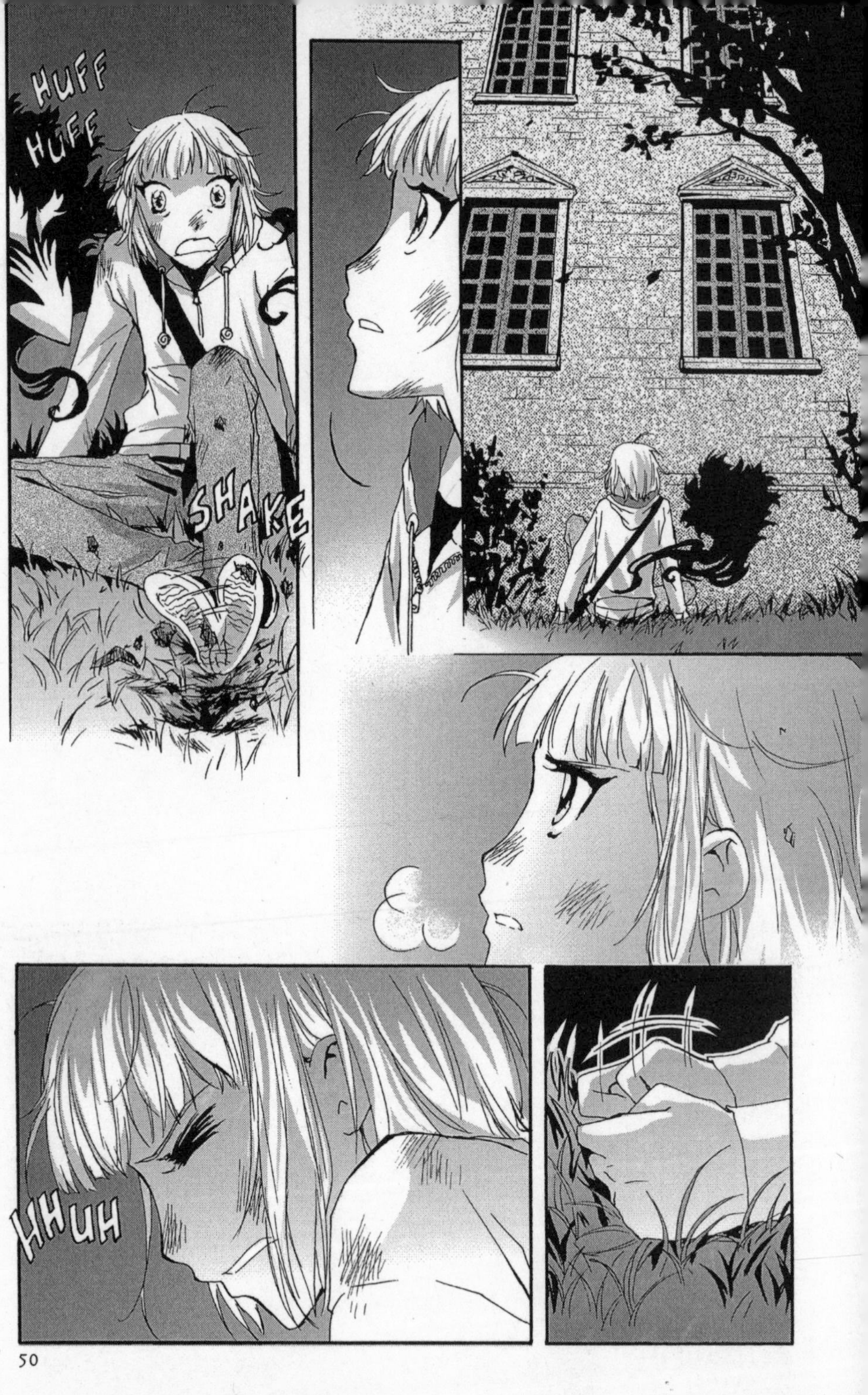
HUFF
HUFF
SHAKE
HHUH

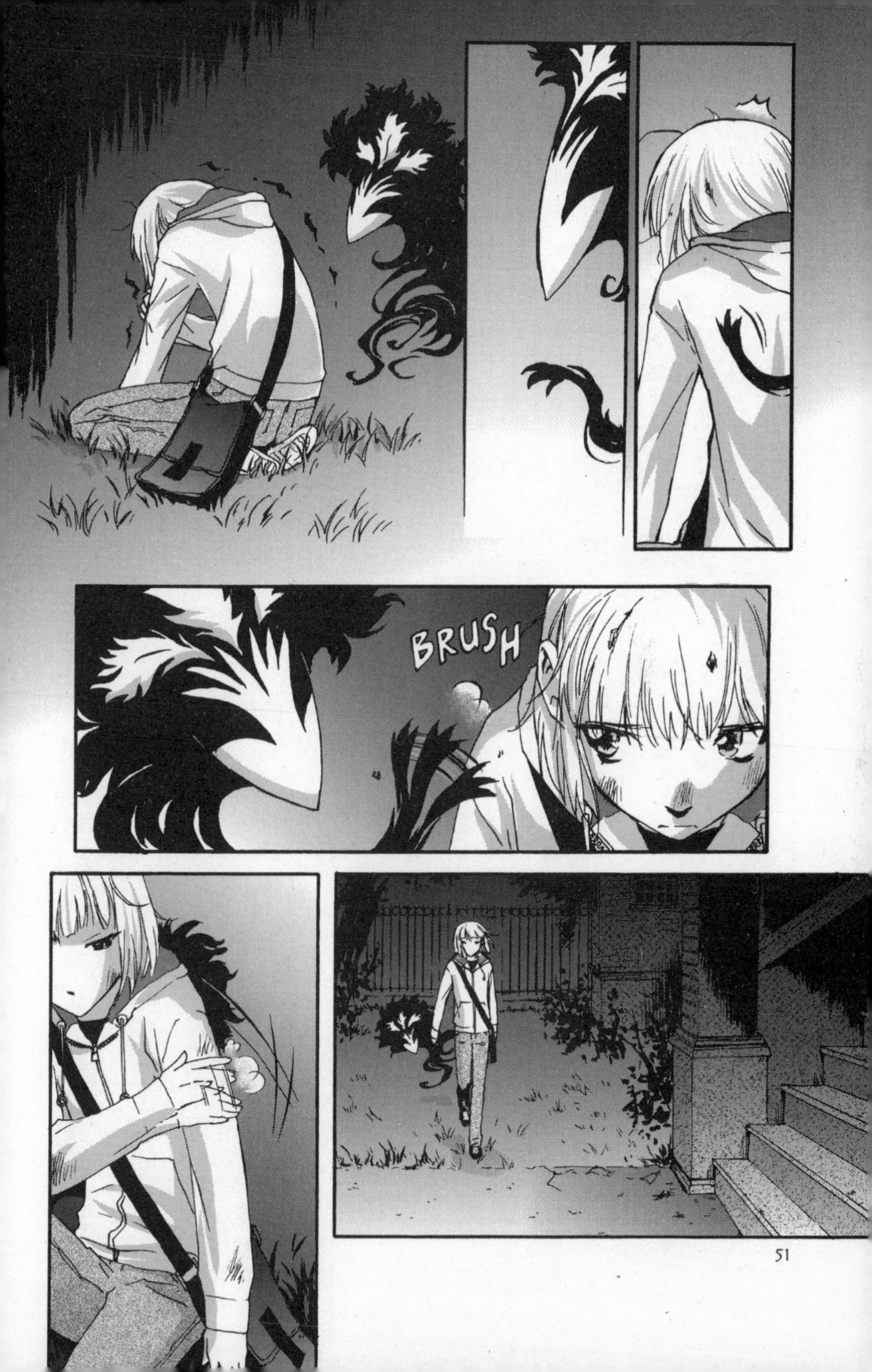
BRUSH

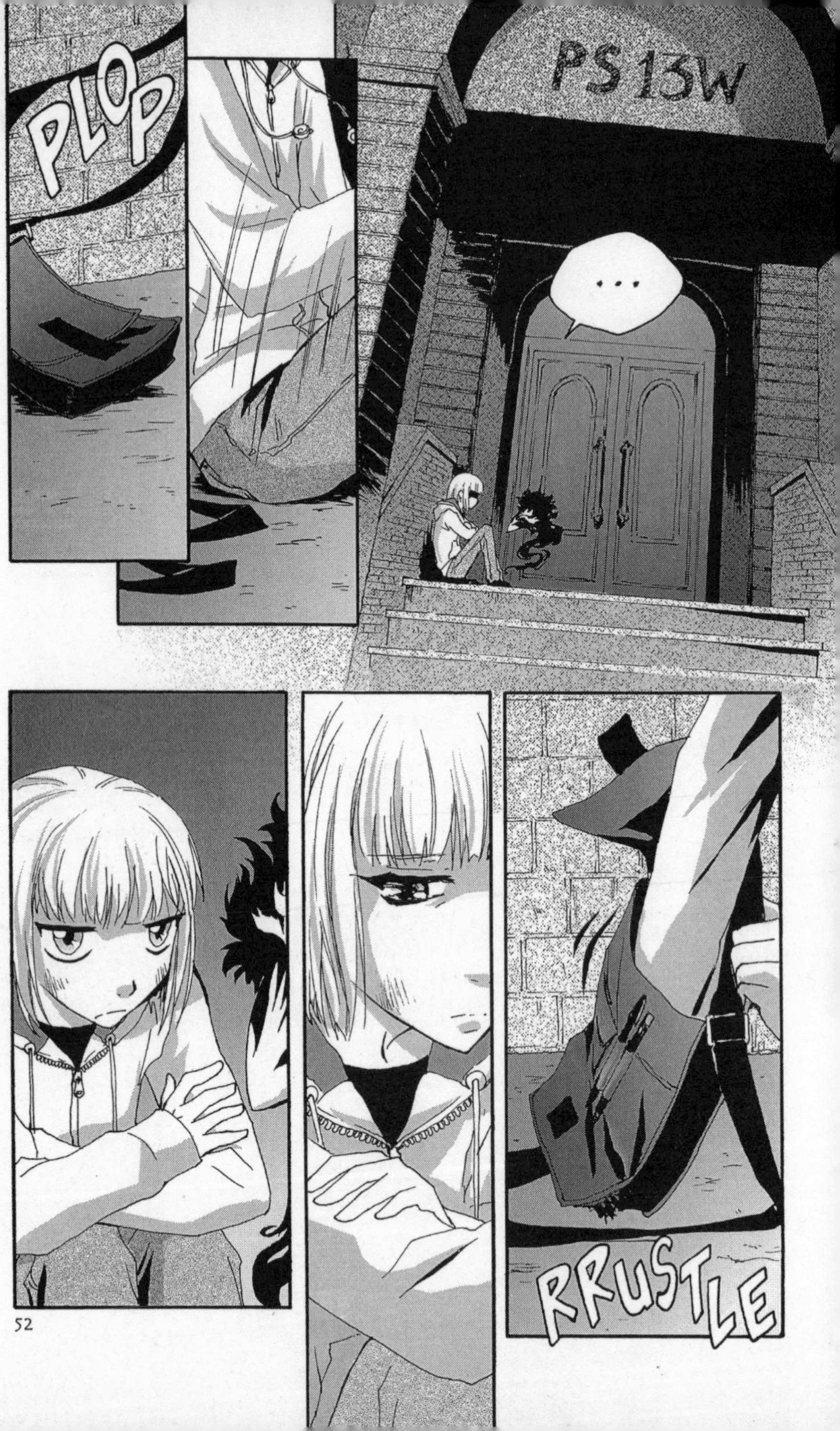
PLOP
PS 13W
...
RRUSTLE

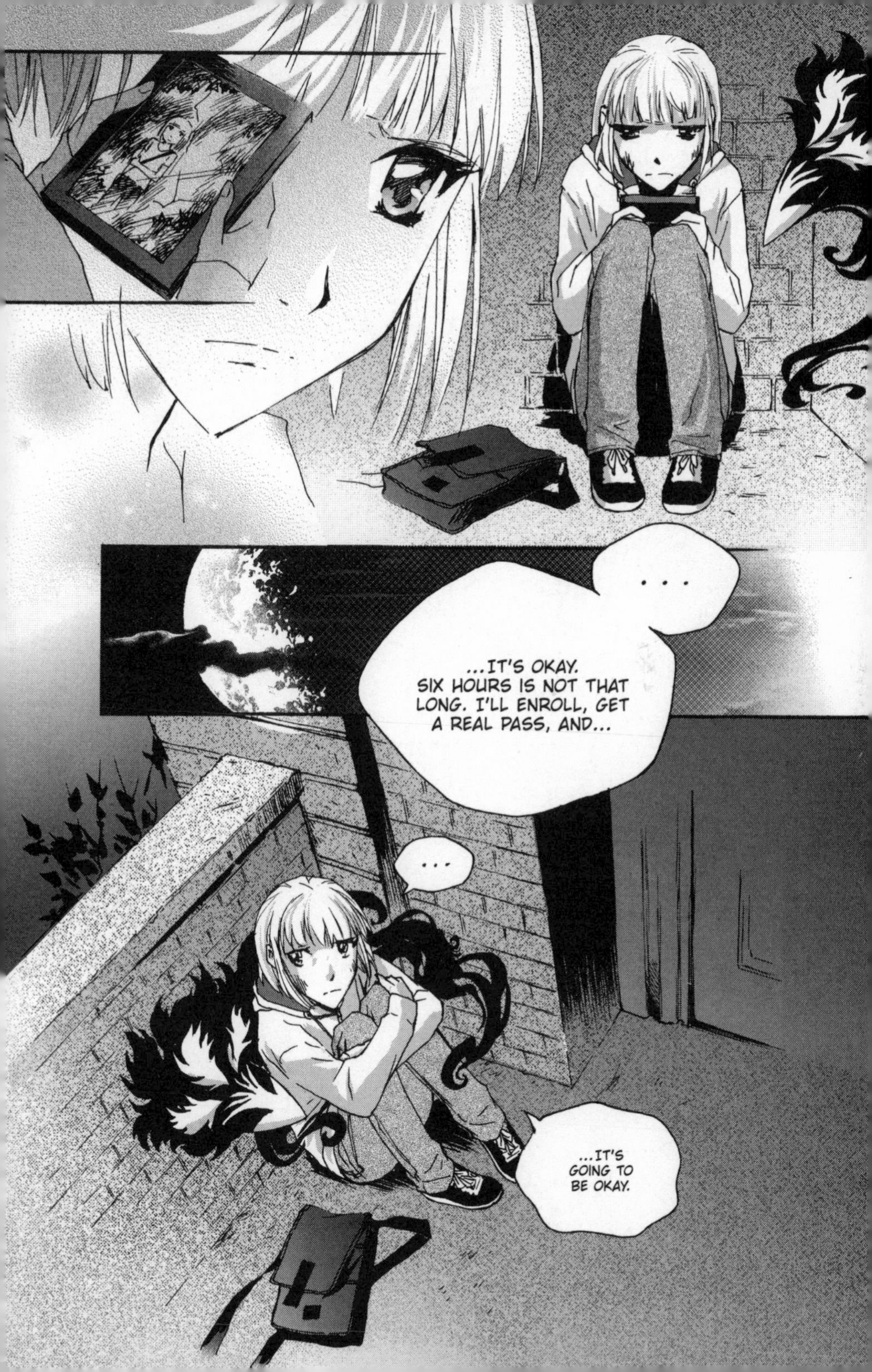
. . .
...IT'S OKAY. SIX HOURS IS NOT THAT LONG. I'LL ENROLL, GET A REAL PASS, AND...
. . .
...IT'S GOING TO BE OKAY.

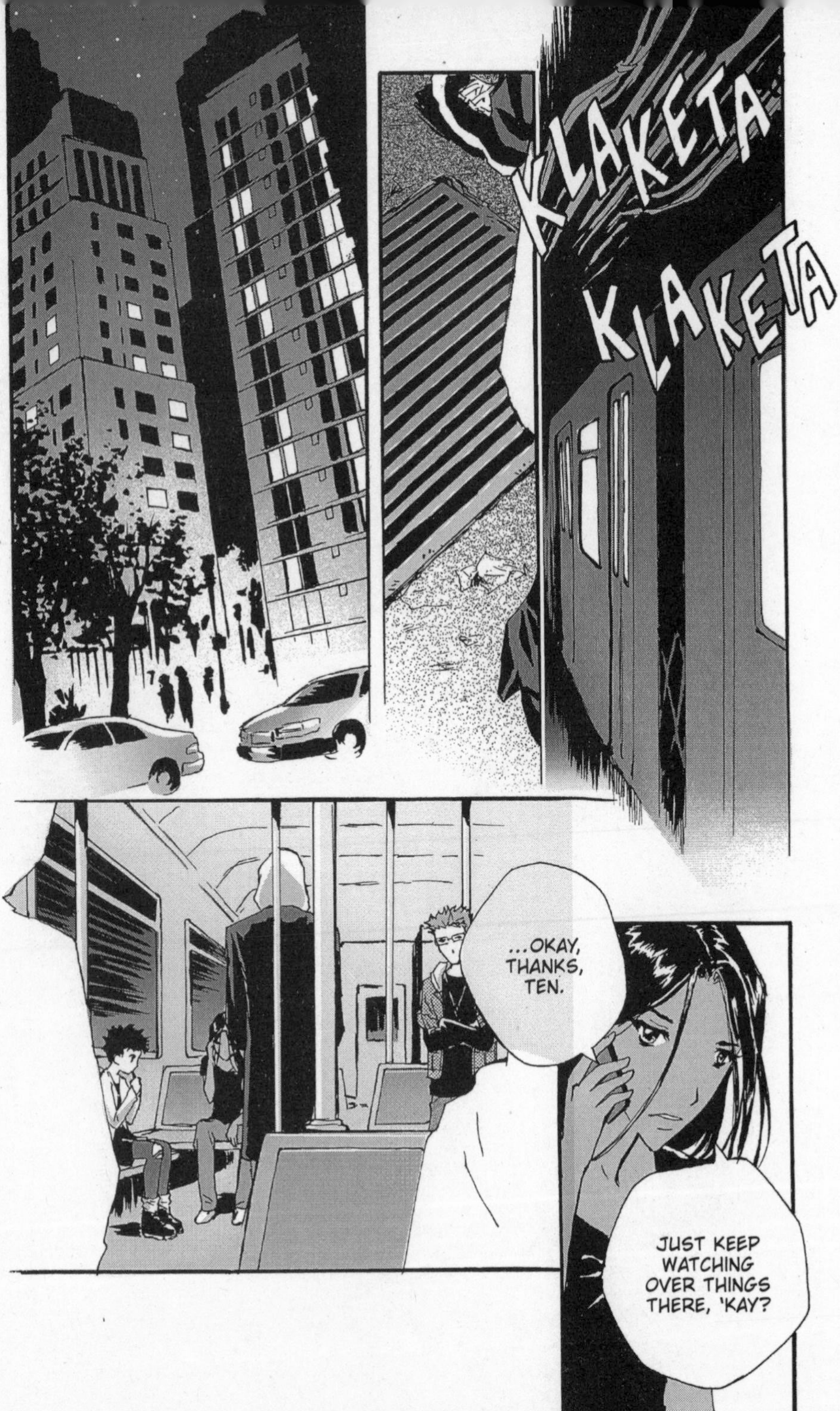
KLAKETA
KLAKETA
...OKAY, THANKS, TEN.
JUST KEEP WATCHING OVER THINGS THERE, 'KAY?

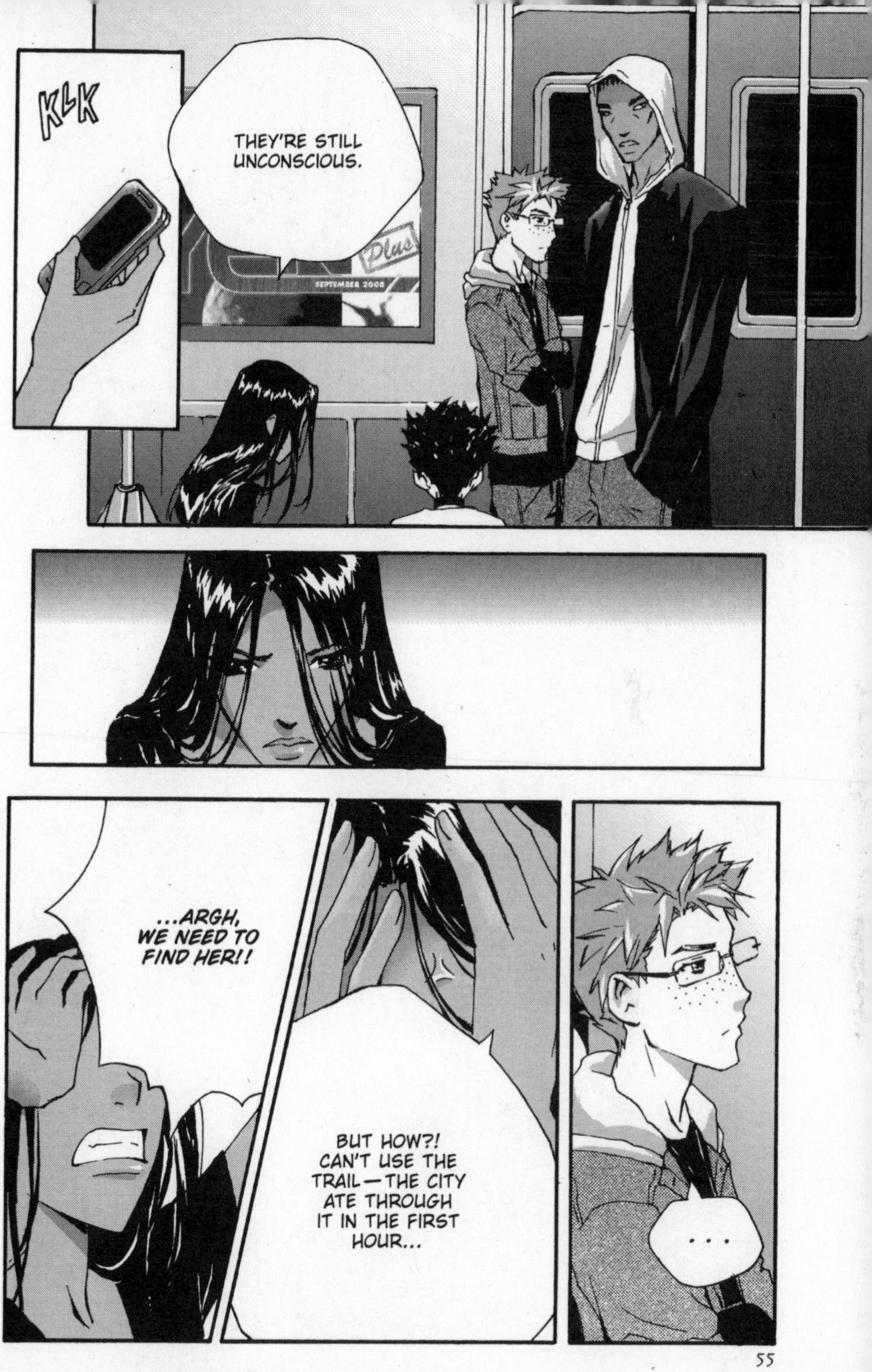
KLK
THEY'RE STILL UNCONSCIOUS.
...ARGH, WE NEED TO FIND HER!!
BUT HOW?! CAN'T USE THE TRAIL—THE CITY ATE THROUGH IT IN THE FIRST HOUR...
...

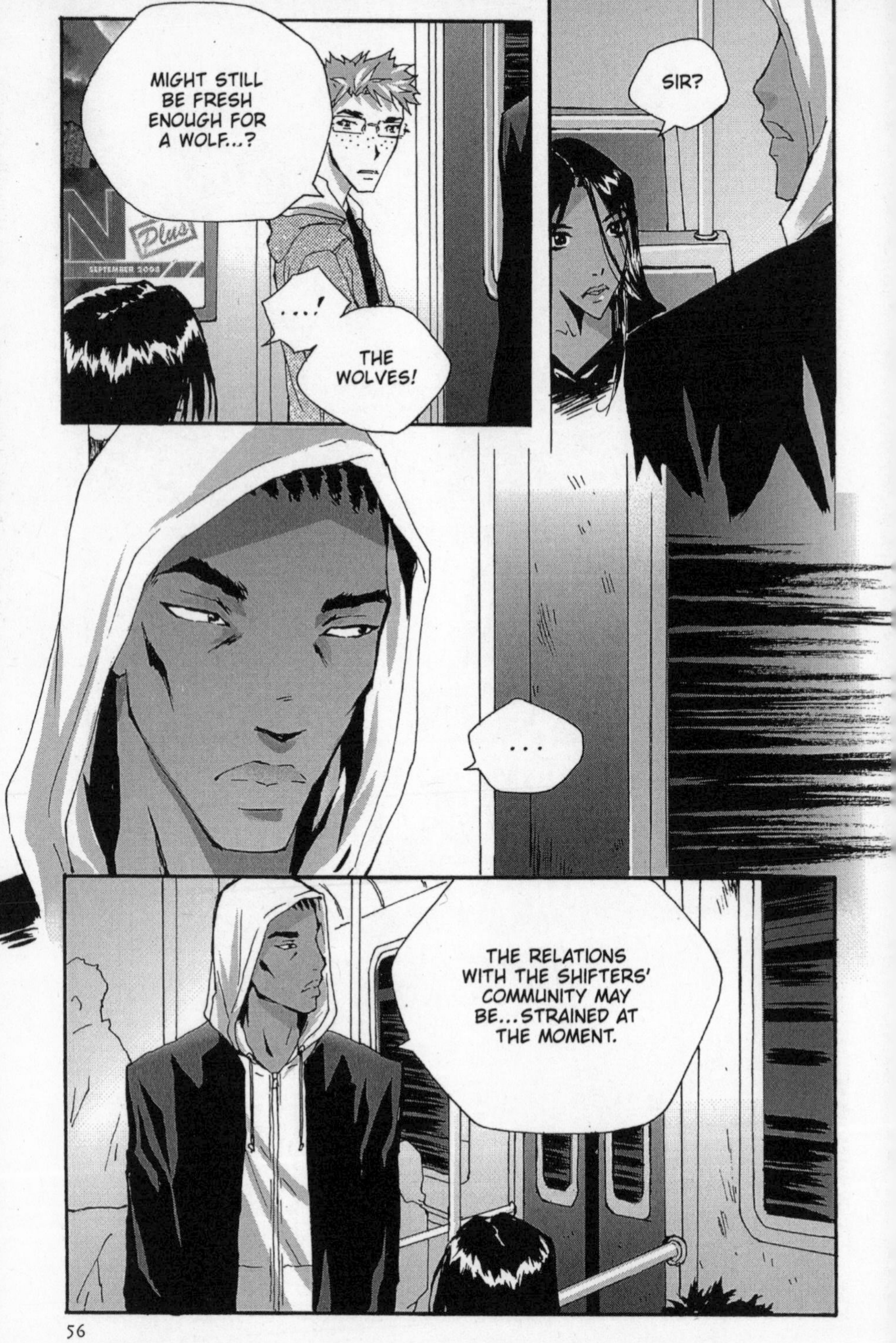
MIGHT STILL BE FRESH ENOUGH FOR A WOLF...?
Plus
....!
THE WOLVES!
SIR?
...
THE RELATIONS WITH THE SHIFTERS' COMMUNITY MAY BE...STRAINED AT THE MOMENT.

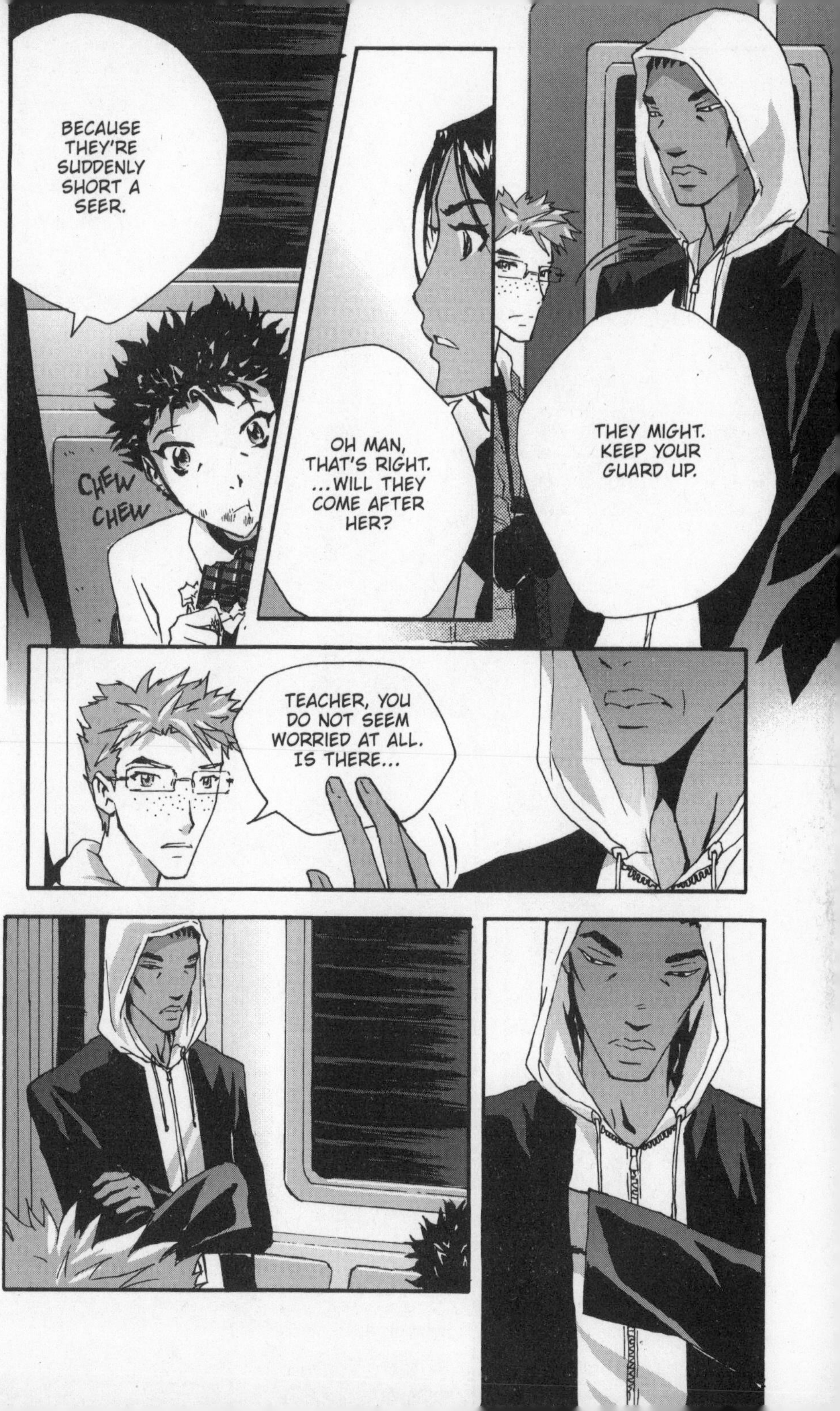
BECAUSE THEY'RE SUDDENLY SHORT A SEER.
CHEW CHEW
OH MAN, THAT'S RIGHT. ...WILL THEY COME AFTER HER?
THEY MIGHT. KEEP YOUR GUARD UP.
TEACHER, YOU DO NOT SEEM WORRIED AT ALL. IS THERE...

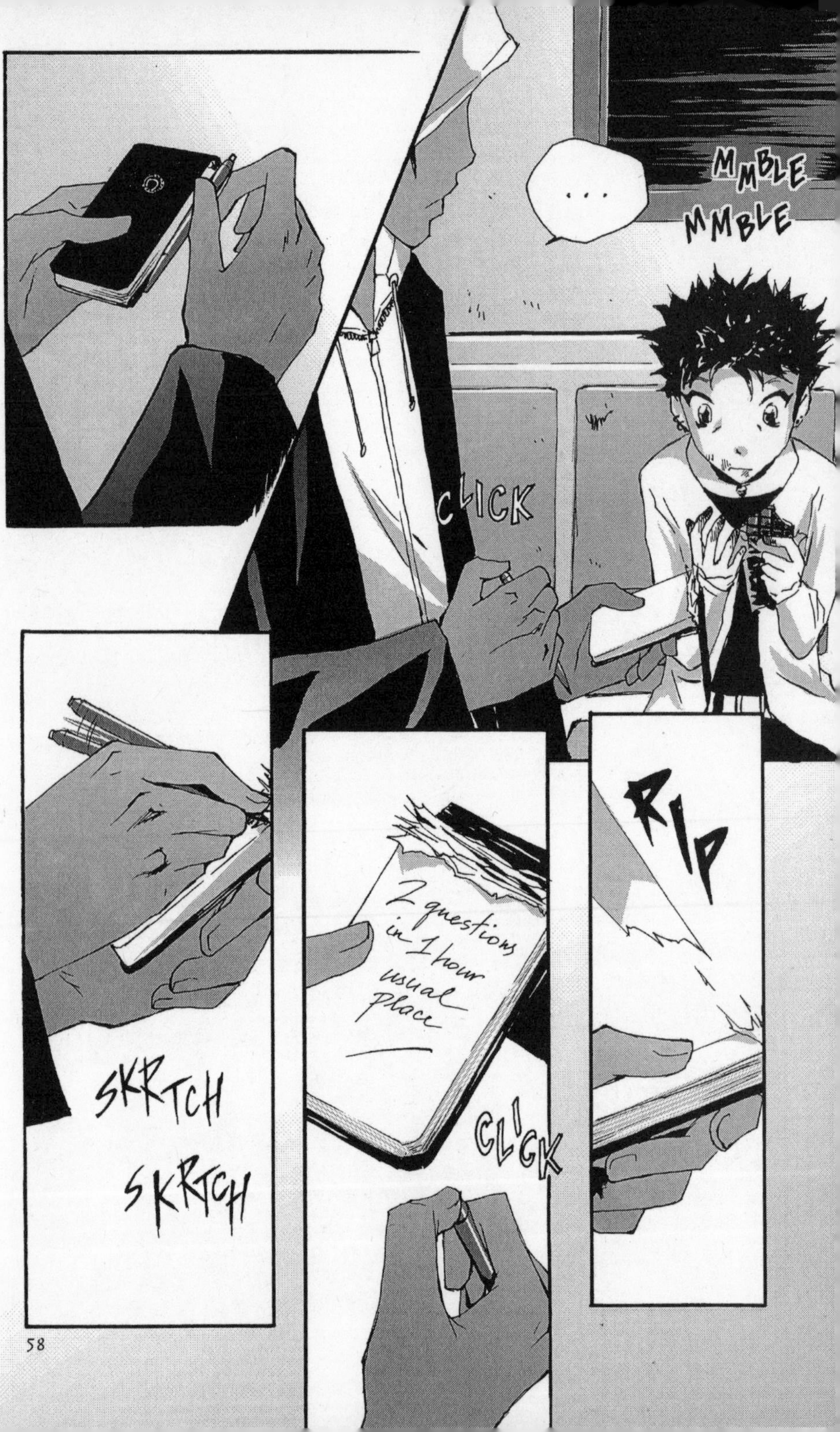
...
MMBLE
MMBLE
CLICK
SKRTCH
SKRTCH
2 questions
in 1 hour
usual
place
CLICK
RIP

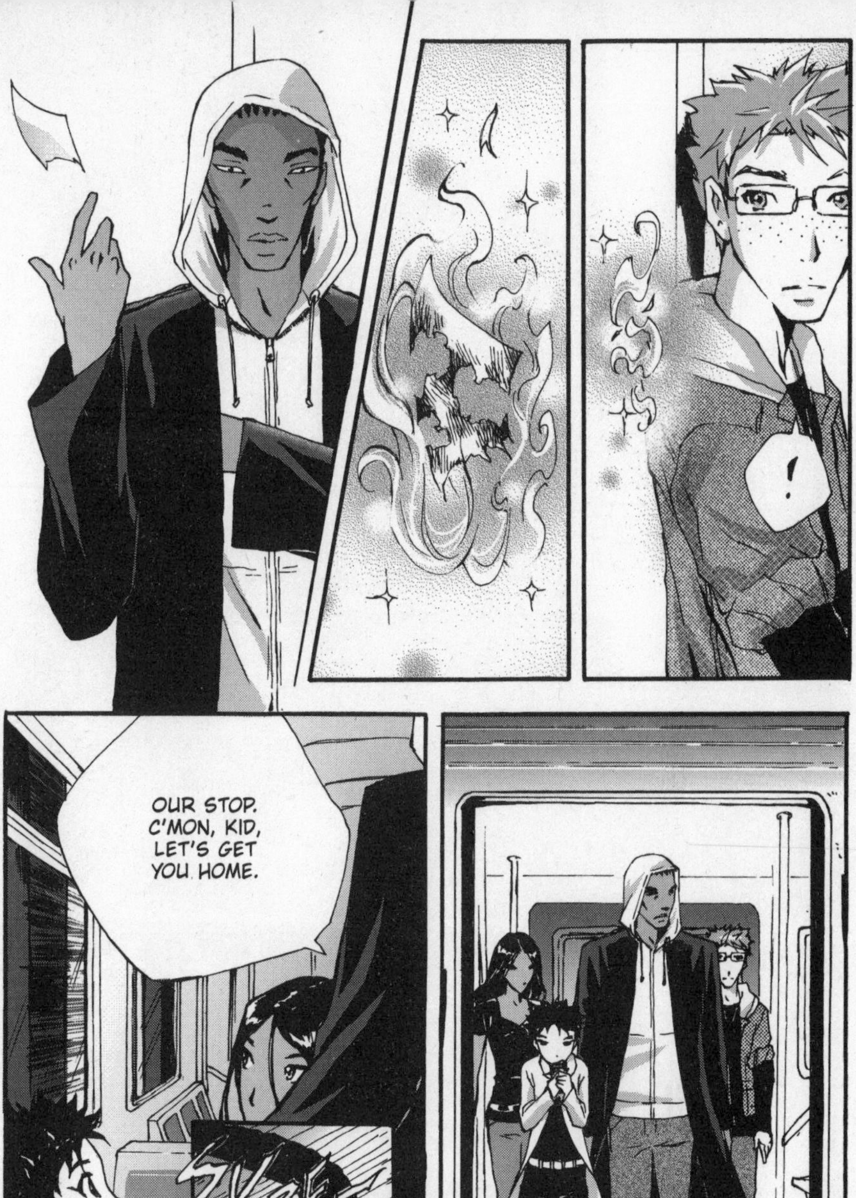
!
OUR STOP. C'MON, KID, LET'S GET YOU HOME.
SKREEE

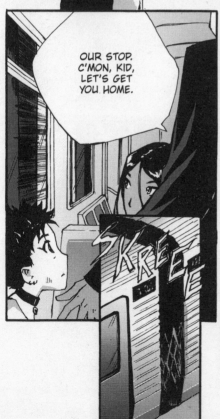

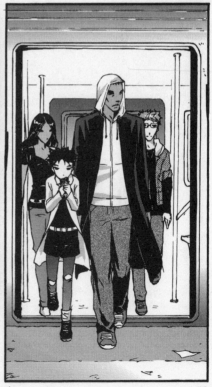

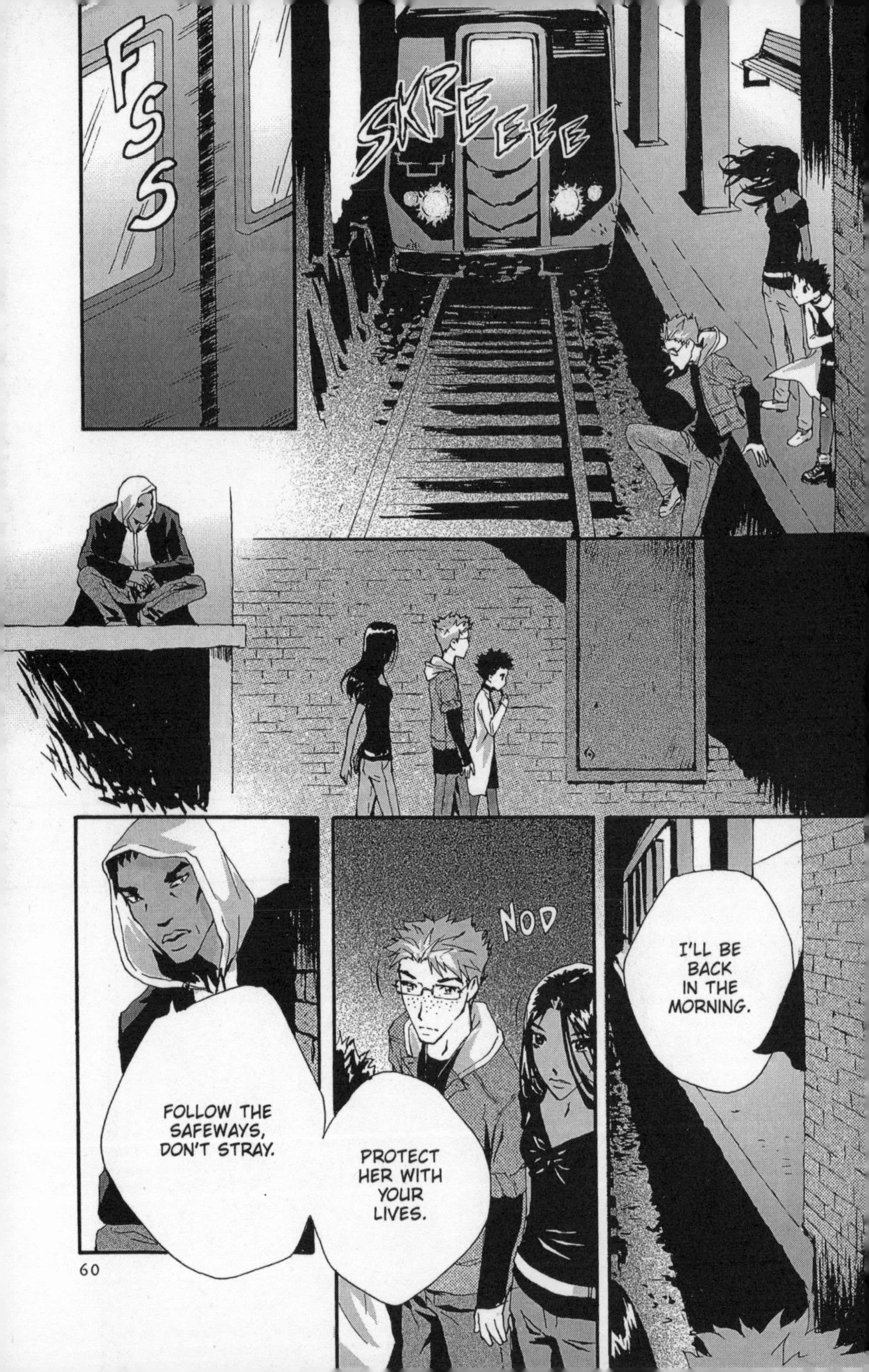
FSS
SKREEEEE
NOD
FOLLOW THE SAFEWAYS, DON'T STRAY.
PROTECT HER WITH YOUR LIVES.
I'LL BE BACK IN THE MORNING.

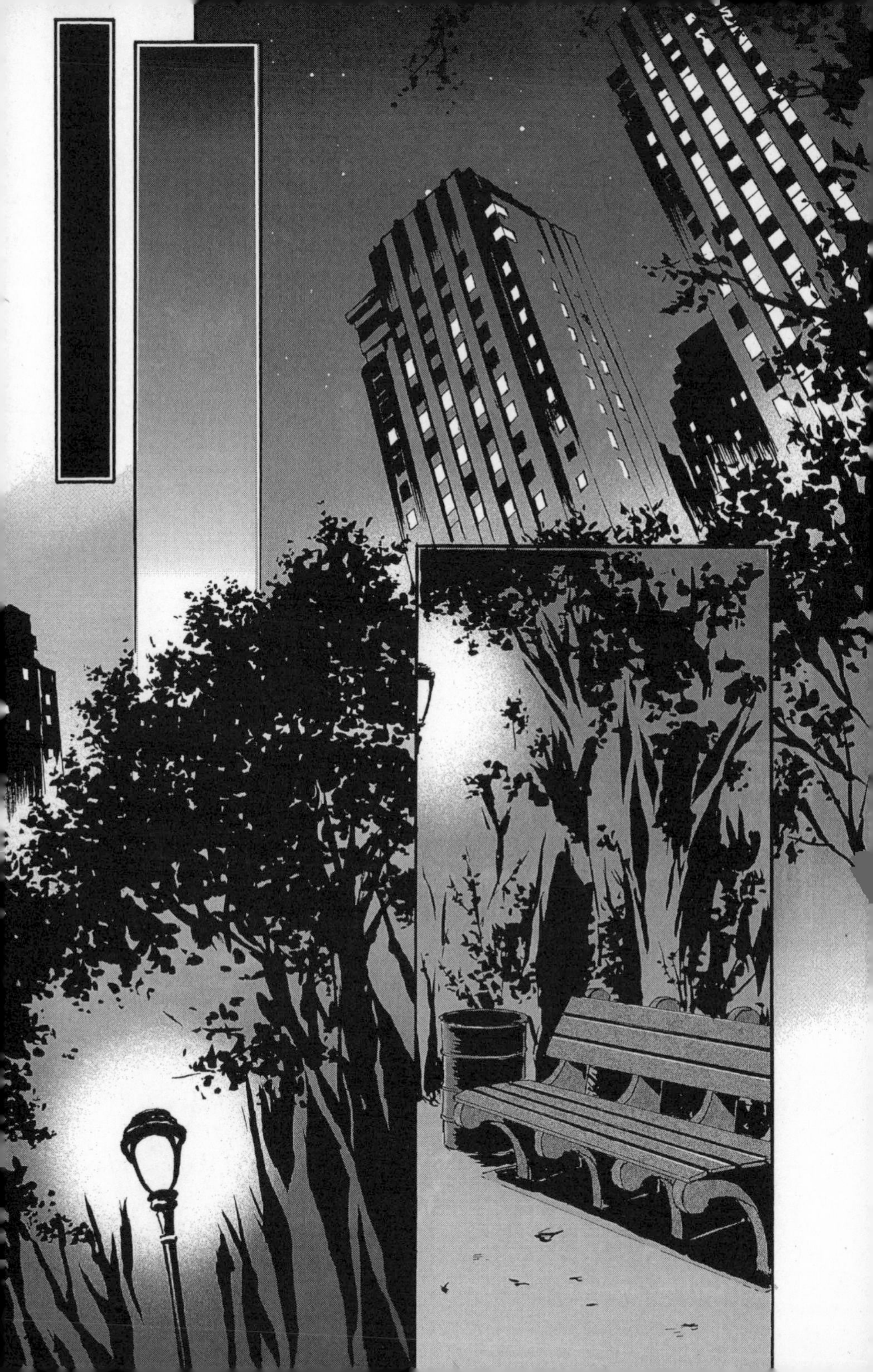

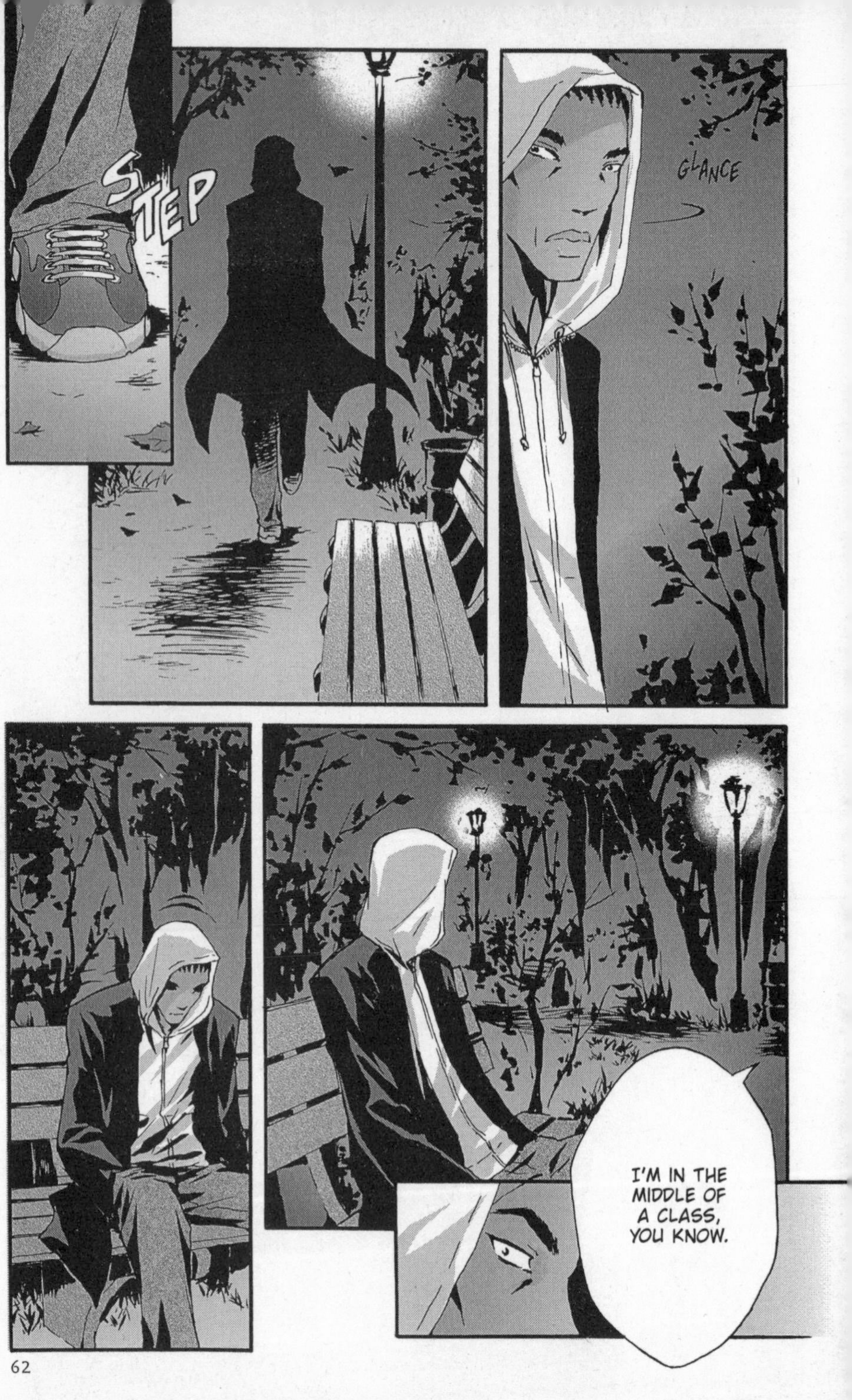
STEP
GLANCE
I'M IN THE MIDDLE OF A CLASS, YOU KNOW.

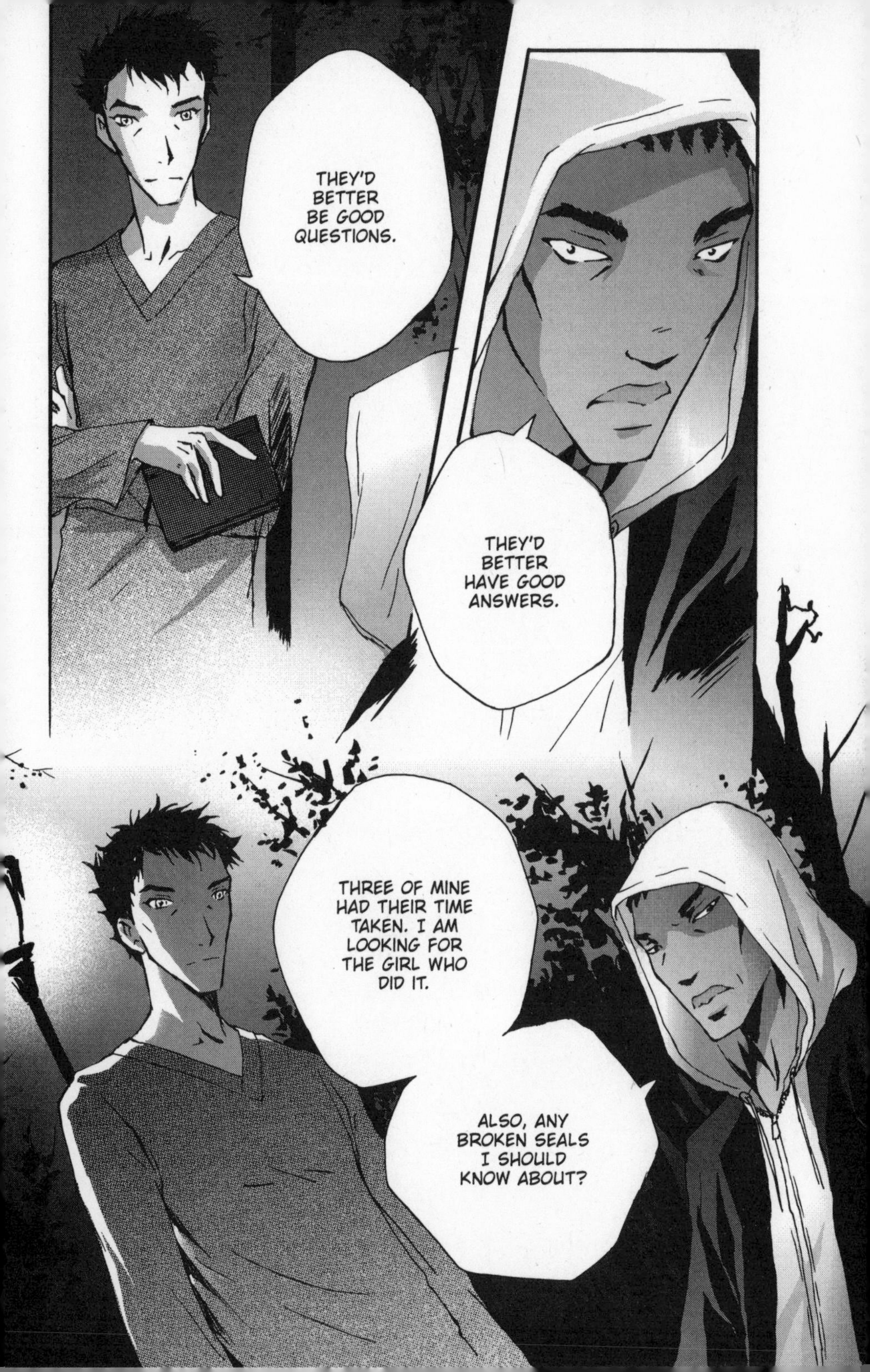
THEY'D BETTER BE GOOD QUESTIONS.
THEY'D BETTER HAVE GOOD ANSWERS.
THREE OF MINE HAD THEIR TIME TAKEN. I AM LOOKING FOR THE GIRL WHO DID IT.
ALSO, ANY BROKEN SEALS I SHOULD KNOW ABOUT?

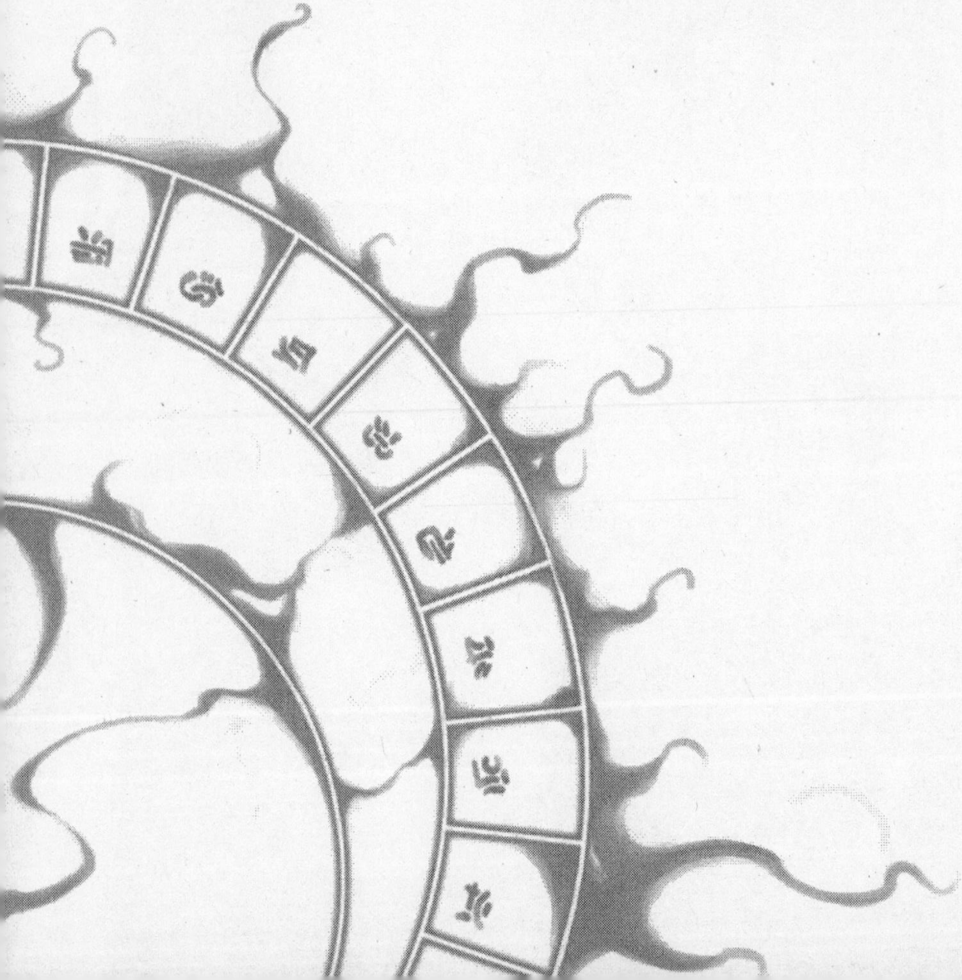

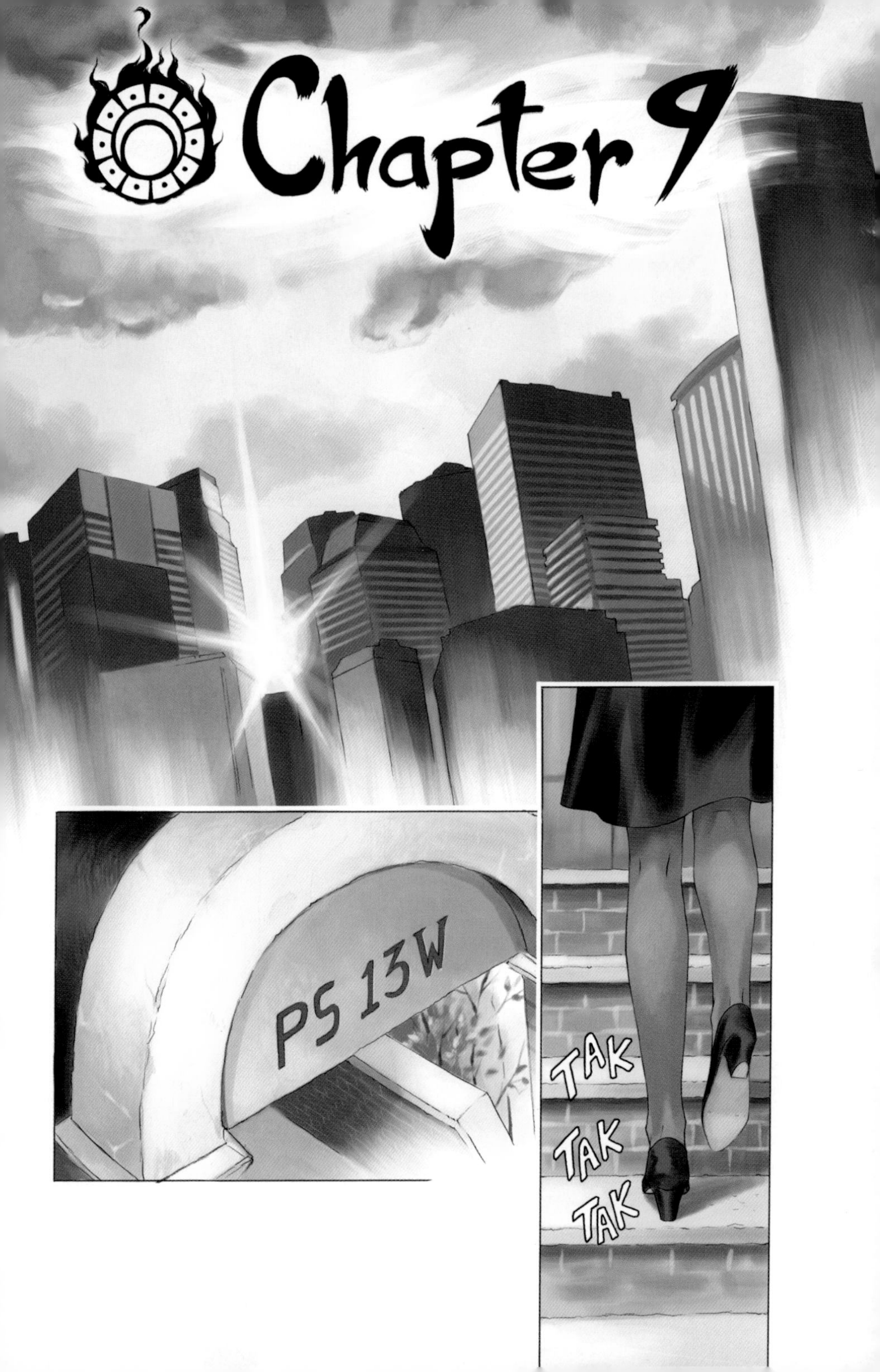
Chapter 9
PS 13W
TAK
TAK
TAK

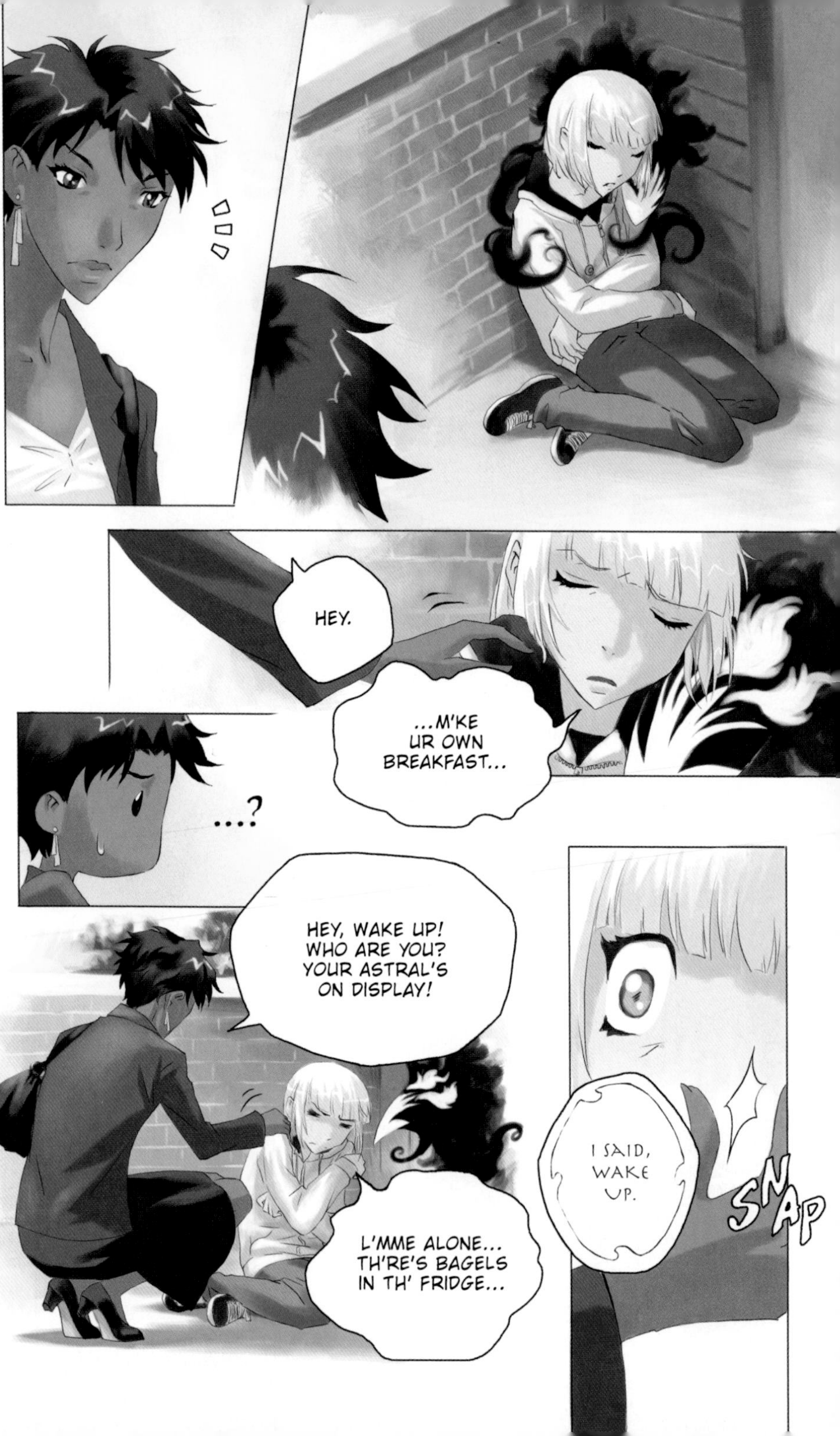
HEY.
...M'KE UR OWN BREAKFAST...
...?
HEY, WAKE UP! WHO ARE YOU? YOUR ASTRAL'S ON DISPLAY!
L'MME ALONE... TH'RE'S BAGELS IN TH' FRIDGE...
I SAID, WAKE UP.
SNAP

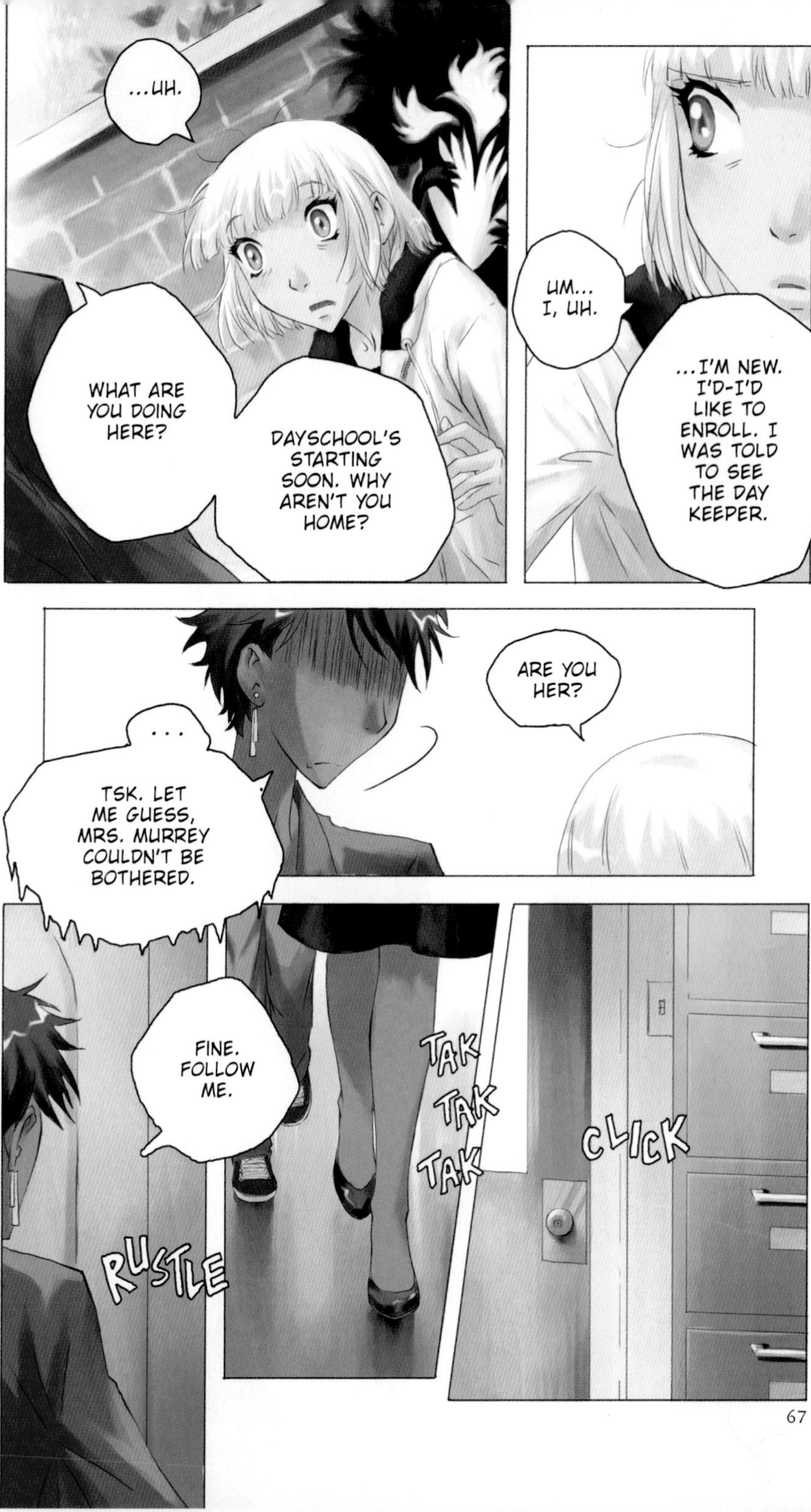
...UH.
WHAT ARE YOU DOING HERE?
DAYSCHOOL'S STARTING SOON. WHY AREN'T YOU HOME?
UM... I, UH.
...I'M NEW. I'D-I'D LIKE TO ENROLL. I WAS TOLD TO SEE THE DAY KEEPER.
ARE YOU HER?
...
TSK. LET ME GUESS, MRS. MURREY COULDN'T BE BOTHERED.
FINE. FOLLOW ME.
RUSTLE
TAK
TAK
TAK
CLICK

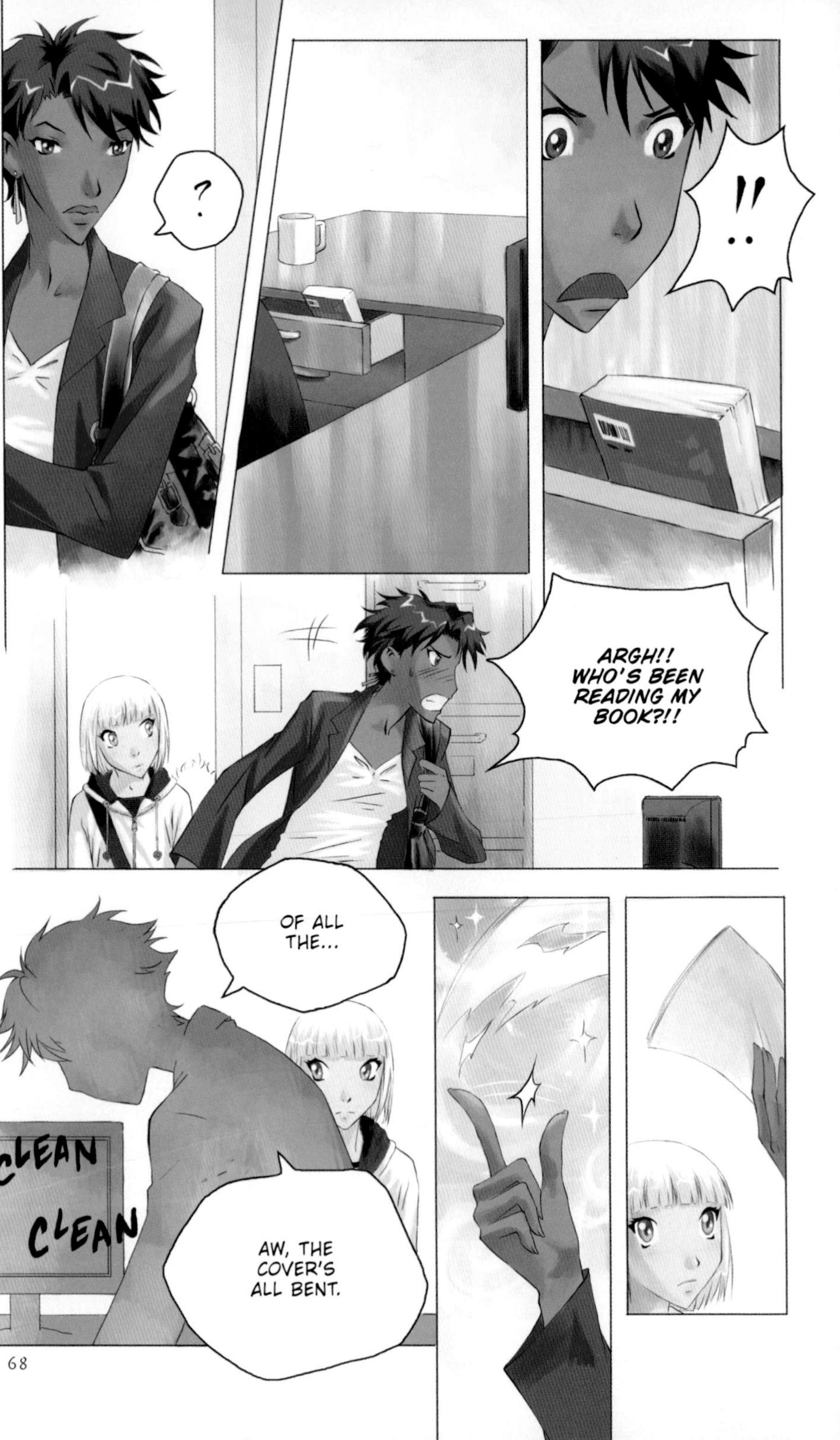
?
!!
ARGH!! WHO'S BEEN READING MY BOOK?!!
OF ALL THE...
CLEAN CLEAN
AW, THE COVER'S ALL BENT.

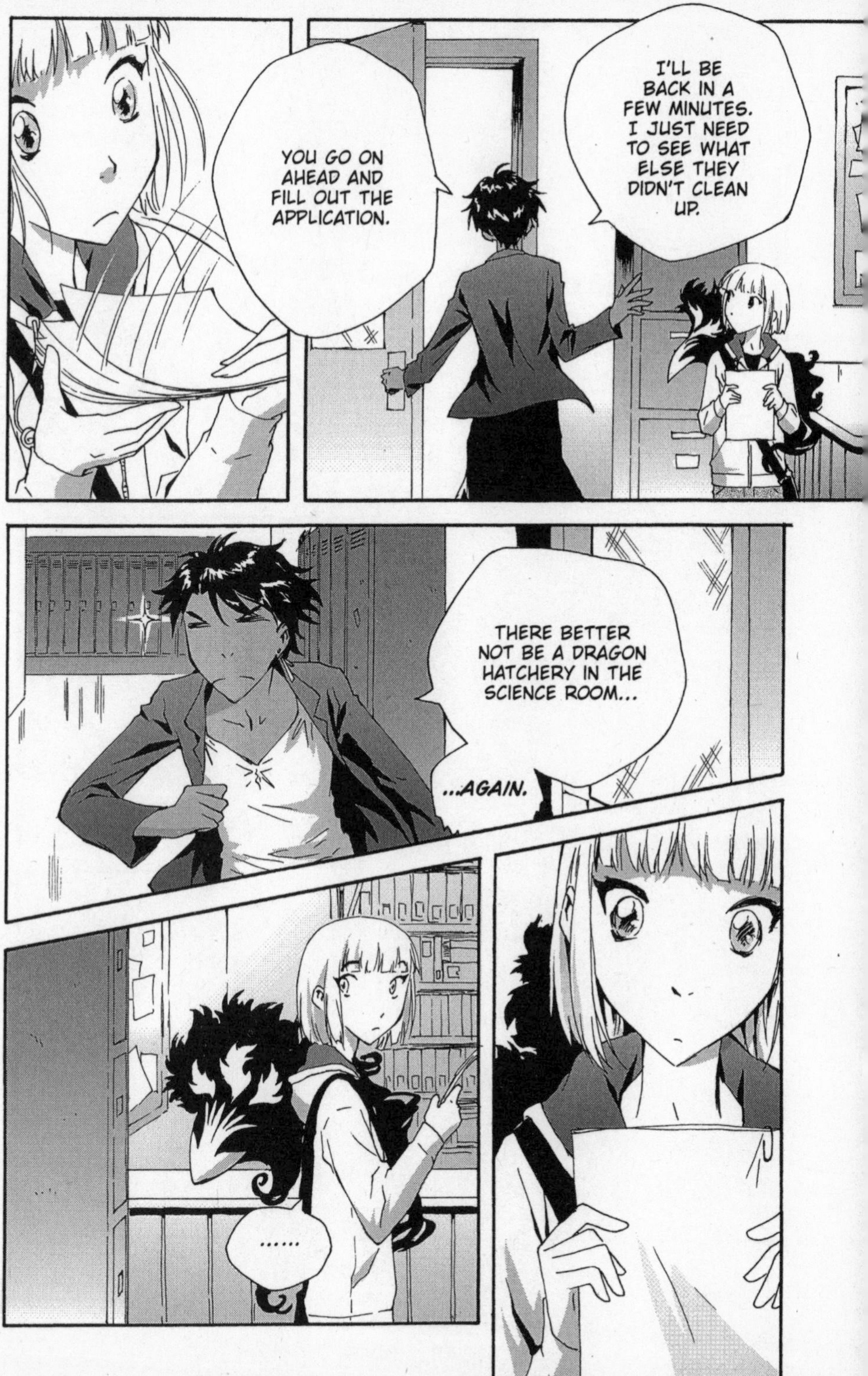
YOU GO ON AHEAD AND FILL OUT THE APPLICATION.
I'LL BE BACK IN A FEW MINUTES. I JUST NEED TO SEE WHAT ELSE THEY DIDN'T CLEAN UP.
THERE BETTER NOT BE A DRAGON HATCHERY IN THE SCIENCE ROOM...
...AGAIN.
......

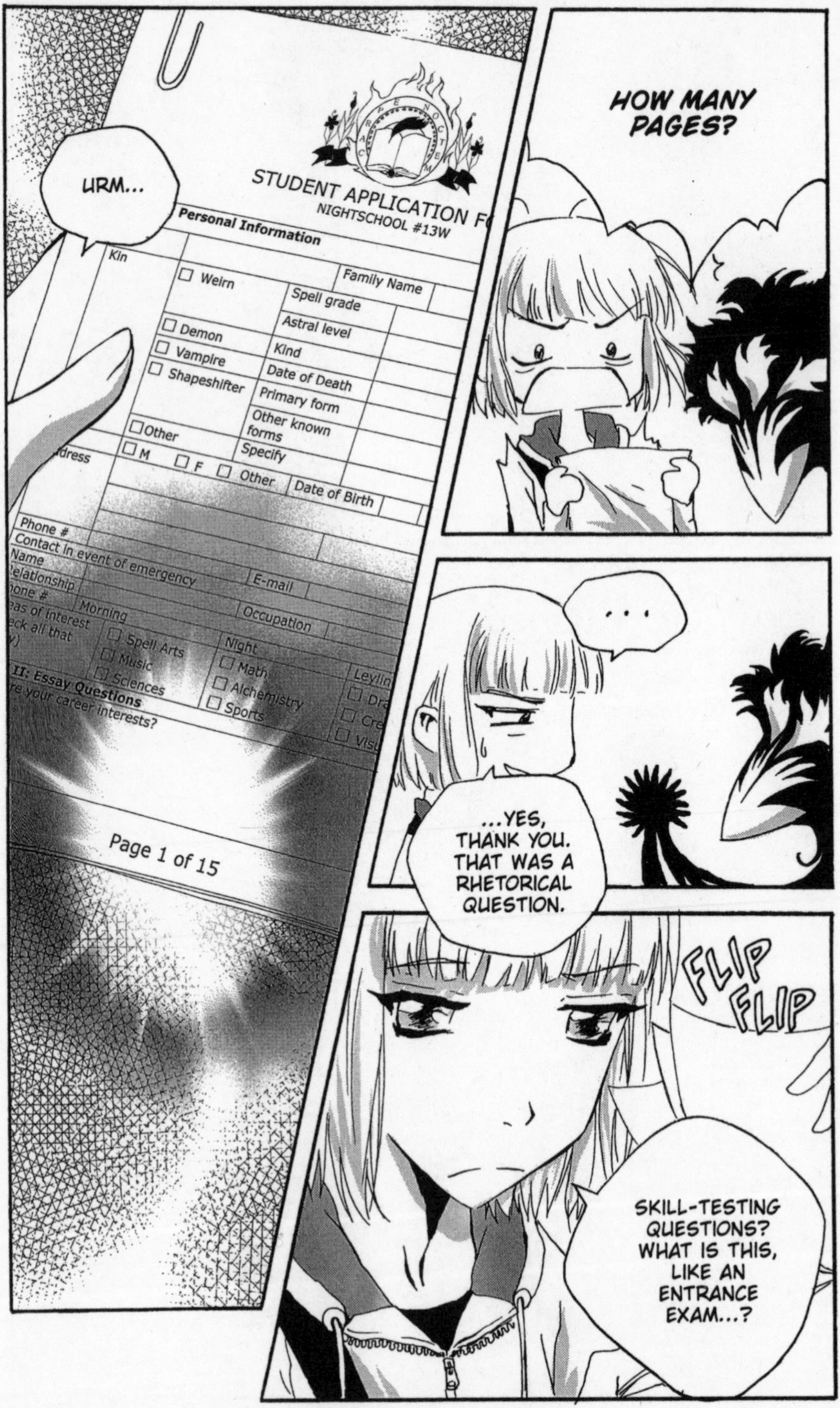
URM...
STUDENT APPLICATION
NIGHTSCHOOL #13W
Personal Information
Kin
Weirn
Family Name
Spell grade
Astral level
Demon
Vampire
Shapeshifter
Kind
Date of Death
Primary form
Other known forms
Other
Specify
M
F
Other
Date of Birth
Phone #
Contact in event of emergency
Name
E-mail
Relationship
Morning
Occupation
Spell Arts
Music
Sciences
Night
Math
Alchemistry
Sports
Essay Questions
Page 1 of 15
HOW MANY PAGES?
...
...YES, THANK YOU. THAT WAS A RHETORICAL QUESTION.
FLIP FLIP
SKILL-TESTING QUESTIONS? WHAT IS THIS, LIKE AN ENTRANCE EXAM...?

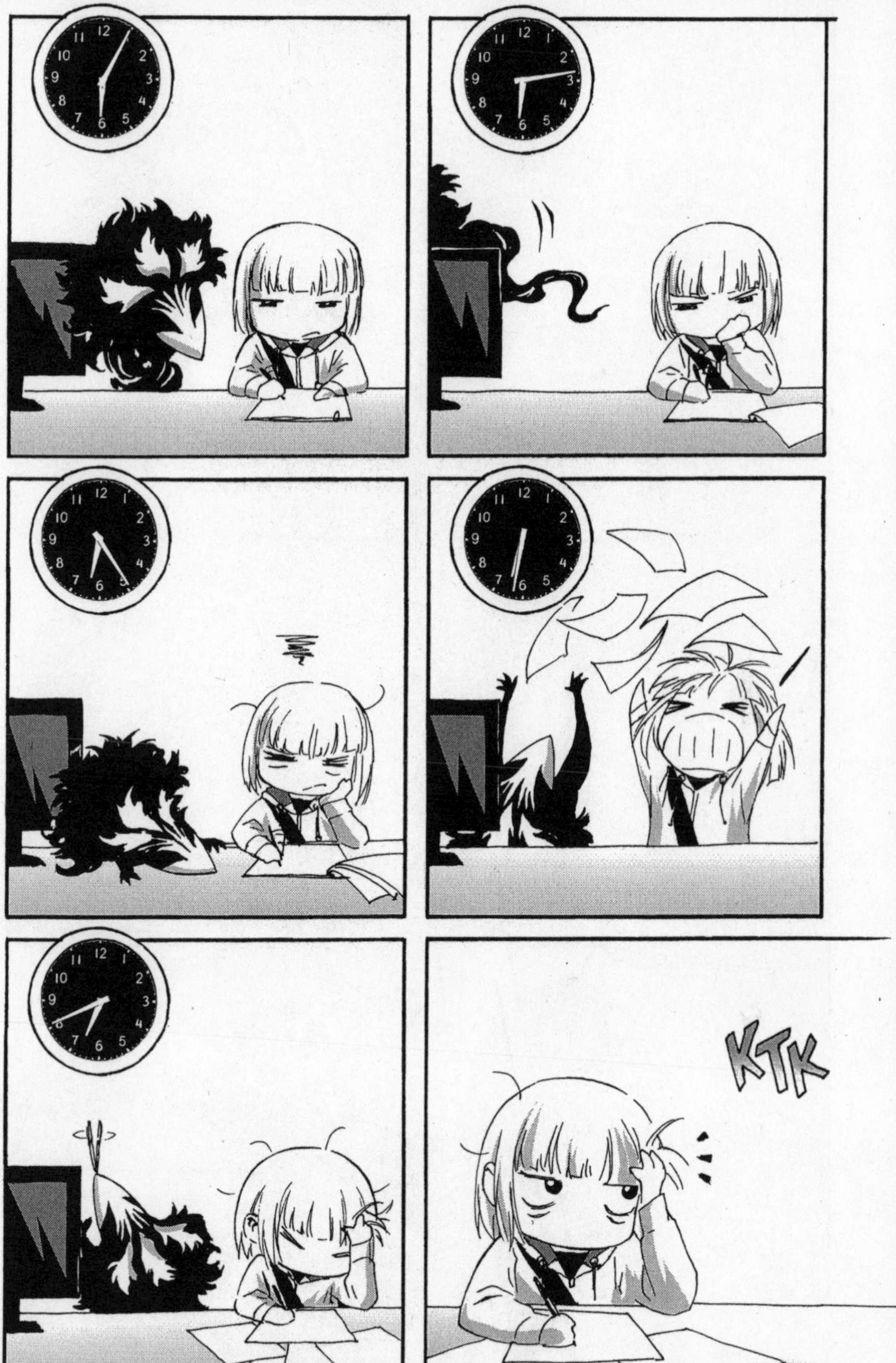
KTK

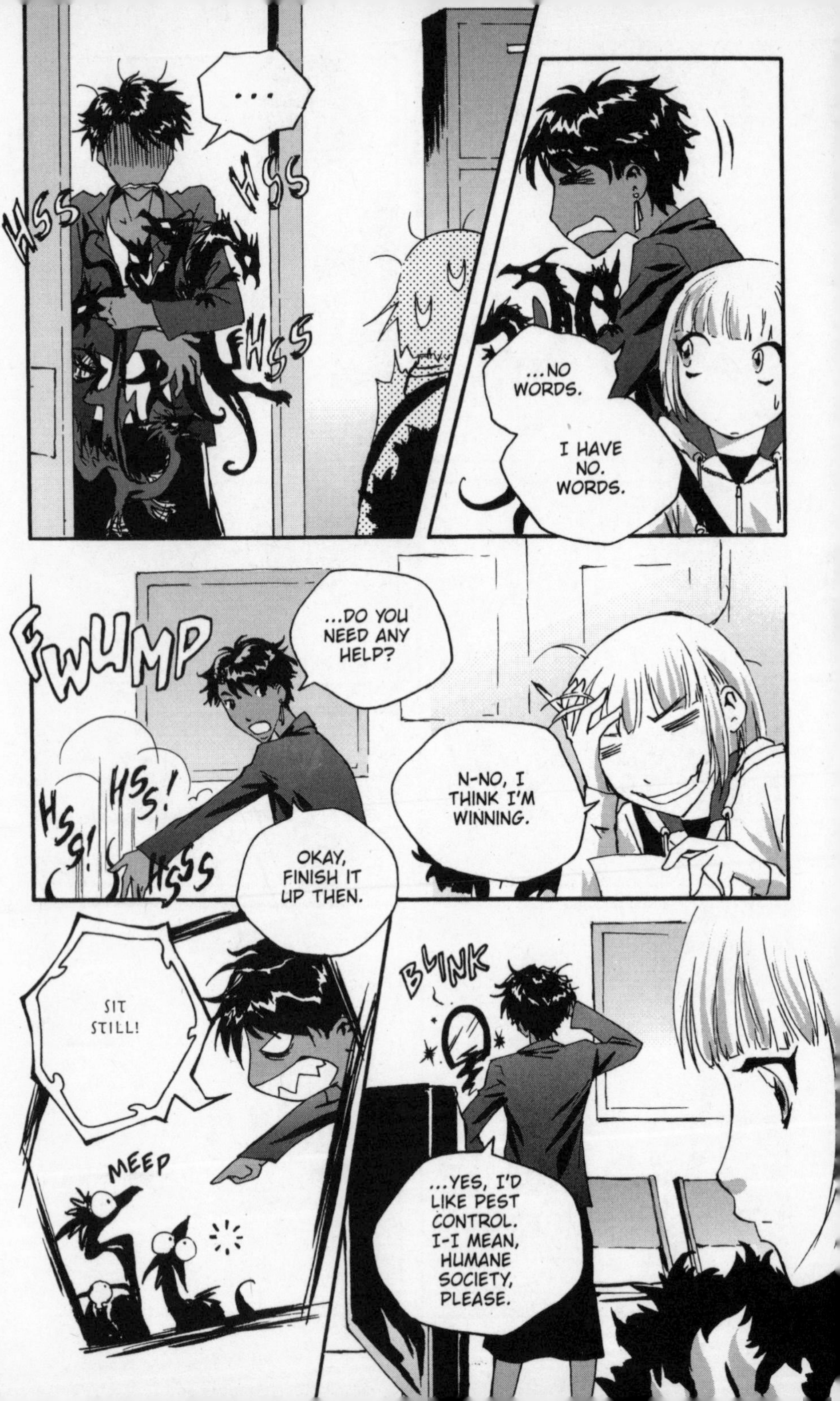
...
HSS
HSS
HSS
...NO WORDS.
I HAVE NO. WORDS.
FWUMP
...DO YOU NEED ANY HELP?
HSS!
HSS!
HSSS
N-NO, I THINK I'M WINNING.
OKAY, FINISH IT UP THEN.
SIT STILL!
MEEP
BLINK
...YES, I'D LIKE PEST CONTROL. I-I MEAN, HUMANE SOCIETY, PLEASE.

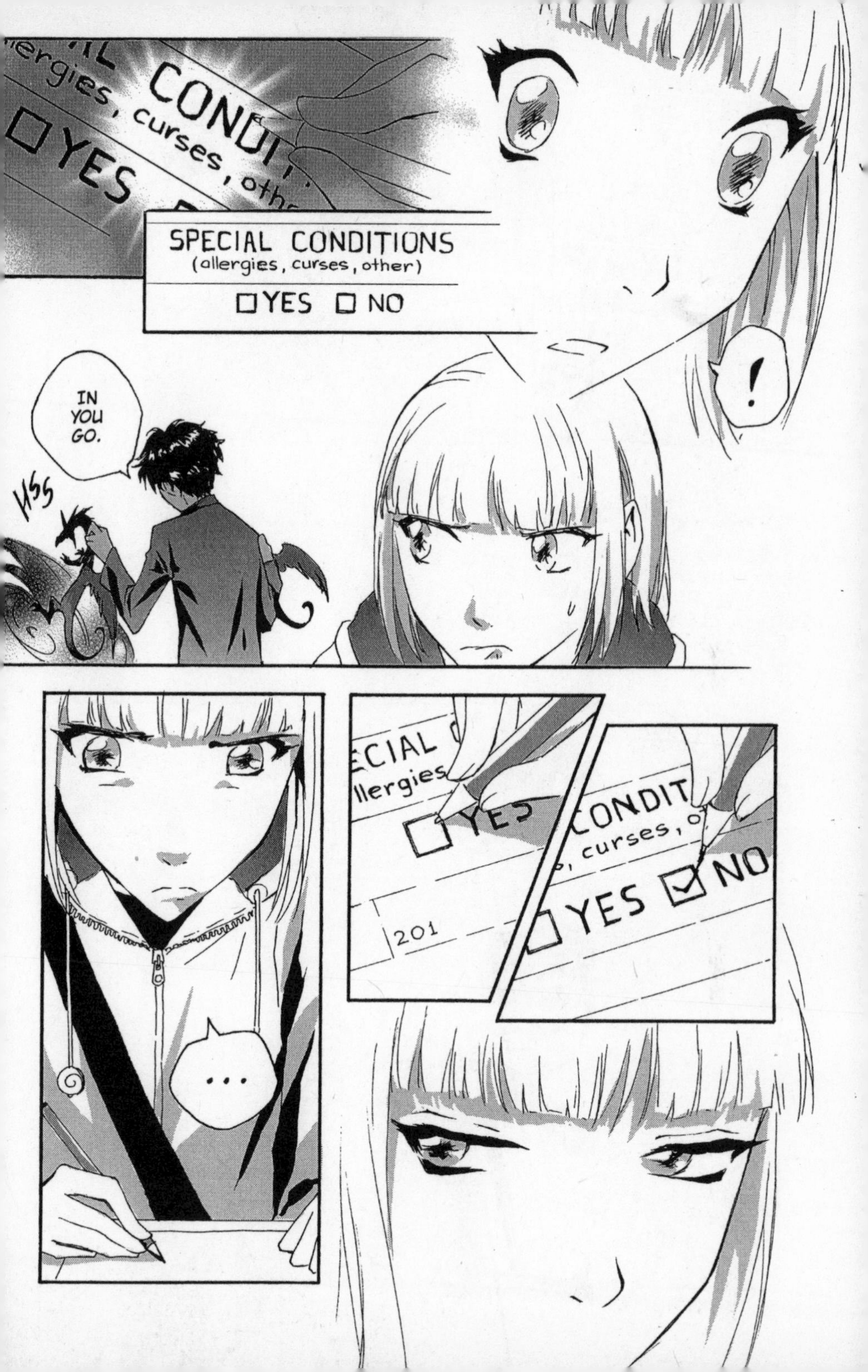
SPECIAL CONDITIONS
(allergies, curses, other)
YES NO
!
IN YOU GO.
HSS
...
YES NO
201

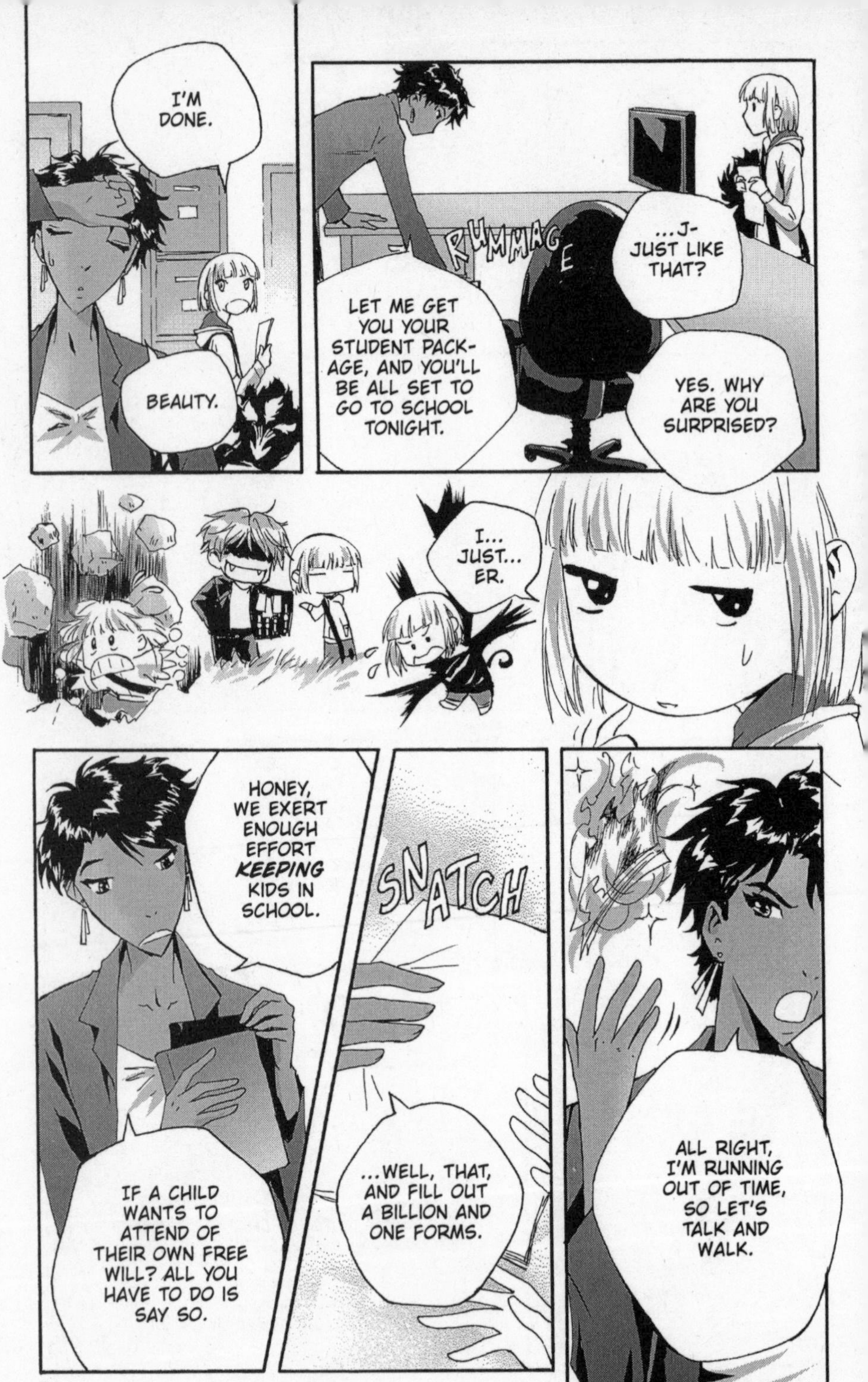
I'M DONE.
BEAUTY.
LET ME GET YOU YOUR STUDENT PACKAGE, AND YOU'LL BE ALL SET TO GO TO SCHOOL TONIGHT.
RUMMAGE
...J- JUST LIKE THAT?
YES. WHY ARE YOU SURPRISED?
I... JUST... ER.
HONEY, WE EXERT ENOUGH EFFORT ***KEEPING*** KIDS IN SCHOOL.
IF A CHILD WANTS TO ATTEND OF THEIR OWN FREE WILL? ALL YOU HAVE TO DO IS SAY SO.
SNATCH
...WELL, THAT, AND FILL OUT A BILLION AND ONE FORMS.
ALL RIGHT, I'M RUNNING OUT OF TIME, SO LET'S TALK AND WALK.

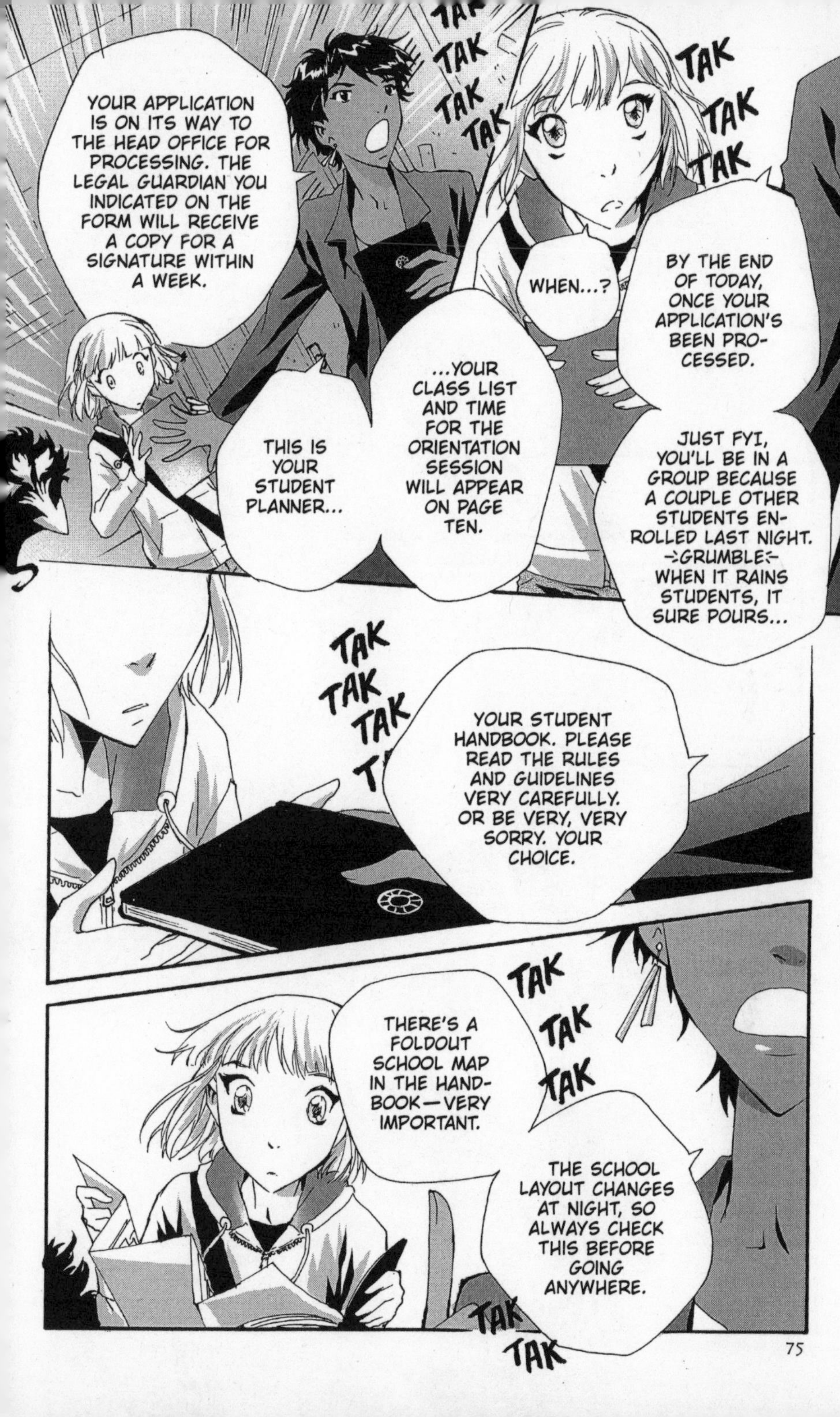
YOUR APPLICATION IS ON ITS WAY TO THE HEAD OFFICE FOR PROCESSING. THE LEGAL GUARDIAN YOU INDICATED ON THE FORM WILL RECEIVE A COPY FOR A SIGNATURE WITHIN A WEEK.
TAK TAK TAK TAK
TAK TAK TAK
WHEN...?
BY THE END OF TODAY, ONCE YOUR APPLICATION'S BEEN PRO-CESSED.
THIS IS YOUR STUDENT PLANNER...
...YOUR CLASS LIST AND TIME FOR THE ORIENTATION SESSION WILL APPEAR ON PAGE TEN.
JUST FYI, YOU'LL BE IN A GROUP BECAUSE A COUPLE OTHER STUDENTS EN-ROLLED LAST NIGHT. ~GRUMBLE~ WHEN IT RAINS STUDENTS, IT SURE POURS...
TAK TAK TAK TAK
YOUR STUDENT HANDBOOK. PLEASE READ THE RULES AND GUIDELINES VERY CAREFULLY. OR BE VERY, VERY SORRY. YOUR CHOICE.
THERE'S A FOLDOUT SCHOOL MAP IN THE HAND-BOOK—VERY IMPORTANT.
TAK TAK TAK
THE SCHOOL LAYOUT CHANGES AT NIGHT, SO ALWAYS CHECK THIS BEFORE GOING ANYWHERE.
TAK TAK

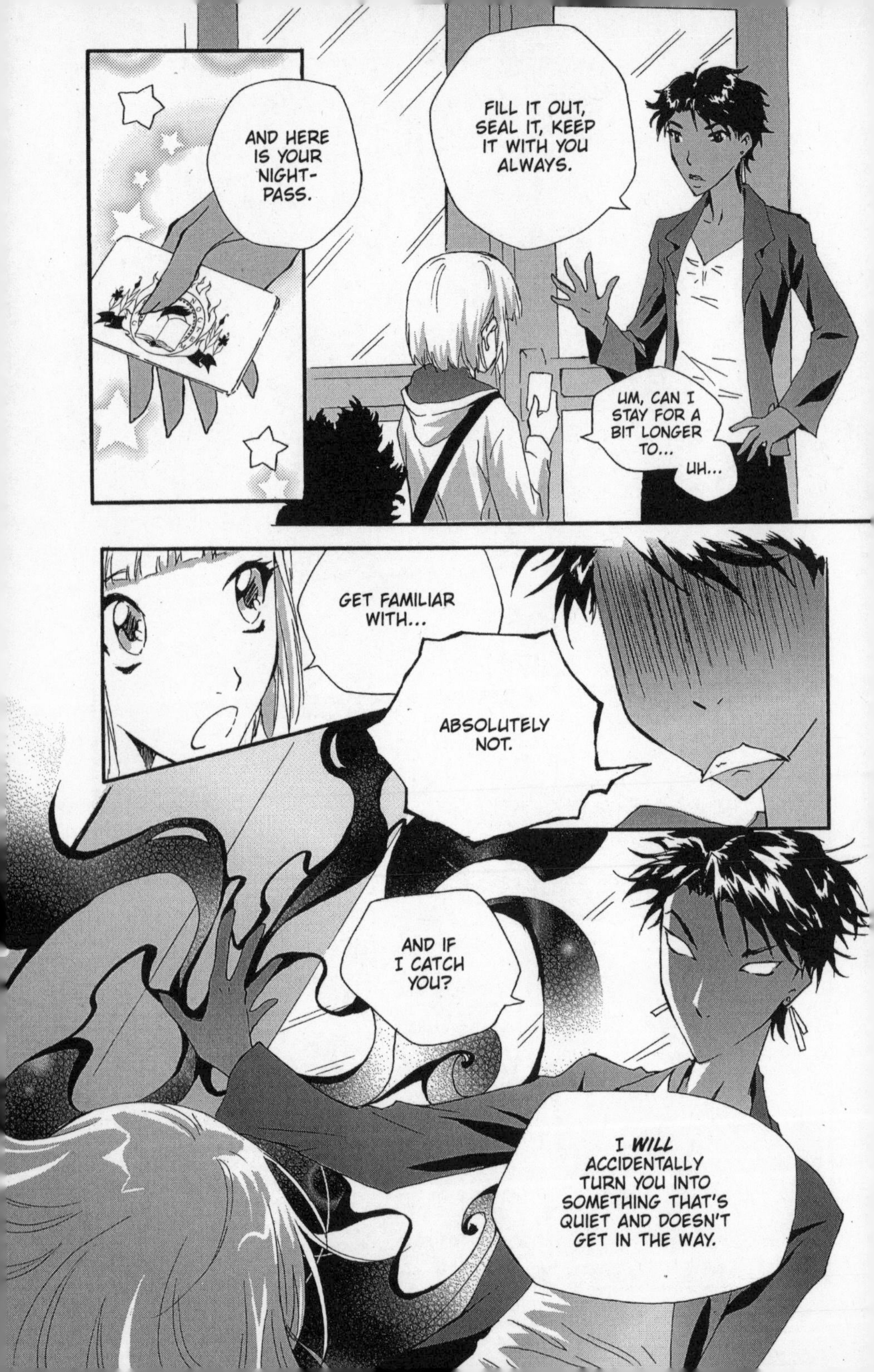
AND HERE IS YOUR NIGHT-PASS.
FILL IT OUT, SEAL IT, KEEP IT WITH YOU ALWAYS.
UM, CAN I STAY FOR A BIT LONGER TO... UH...
GET FAMILIAR WITH...
ABSOLUTELY NOT.
AND IF I CATCH YOU?
I *WILL* ACCIDENTALLY TURN YOU INTO SOMETHING THAT'S QUIET AND DOESN'T GET IN THE WAY.

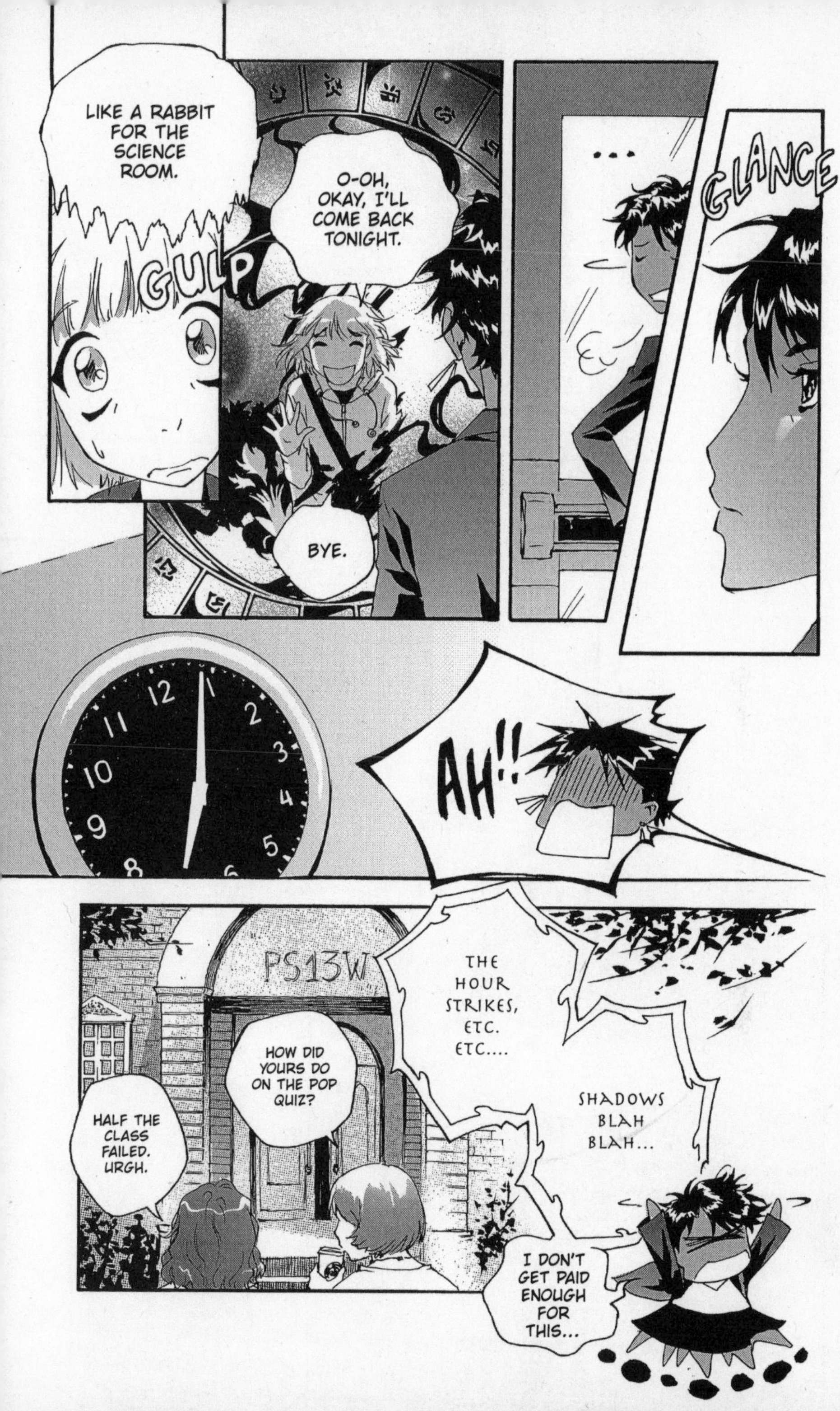
LIKE A RABBIT FOR THE SCIENCE ROOM.
GULP
O-OH, OKAY, I'LL COME BACK TONIGHT.
BYE.
...
GLANCE
12 1 2 3 4 5 6 8 9 10 11
AH!!
PS13W
HOW DID YOURS DO ON THE POP QUIZ?
HALF THE CLASS FAILED. URGH.
THE HOUR STRIKES, ETC. ETC....
SHADOWS BLAH BLAH...
I DON'T GET PAID ENOUGH FOR THIS...

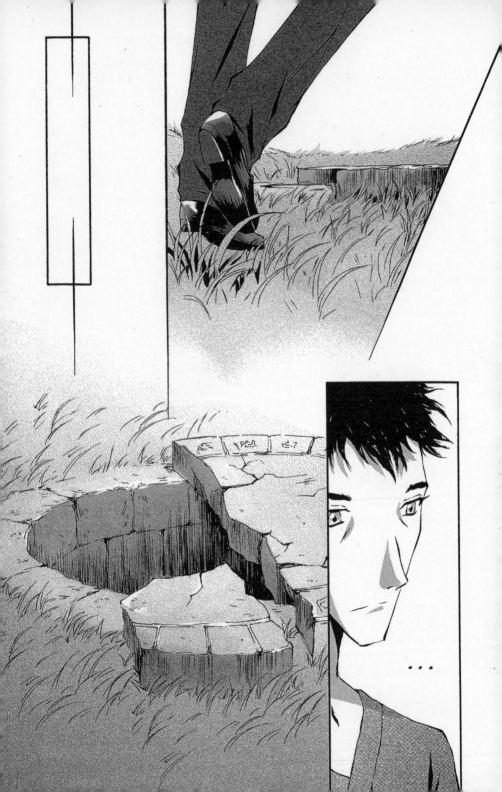

. . .

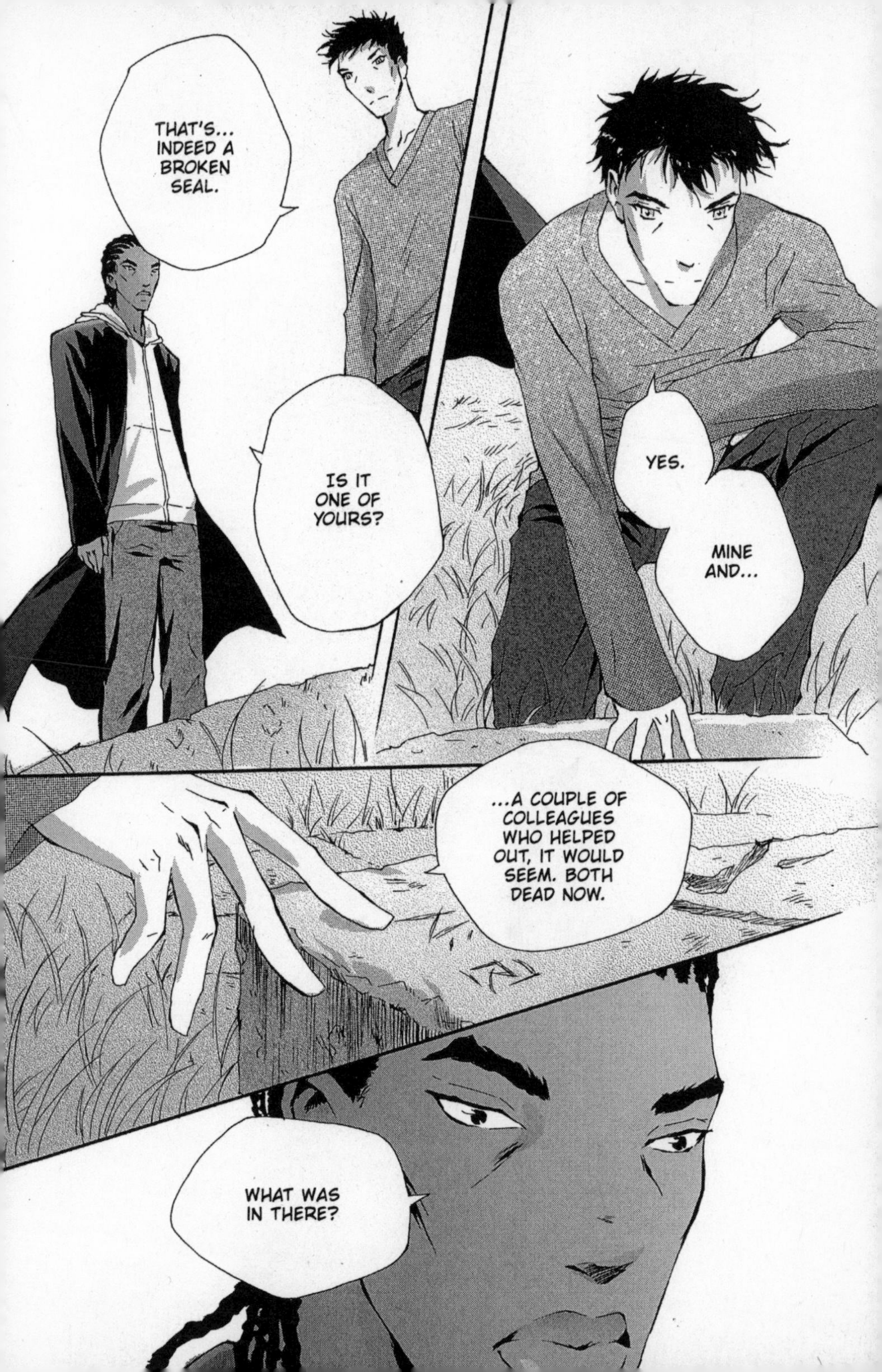
THAT'S... INDEED A BROKEN SEAL.
IS IT ONE OF YOURS?
YES.
MINE AND...
...A COUPLE OF COLLEAGUES WHO HELPED OUT, IT WOULD SEEM. BOTH DEAD NOW.
WHAT WAS IN THERE?

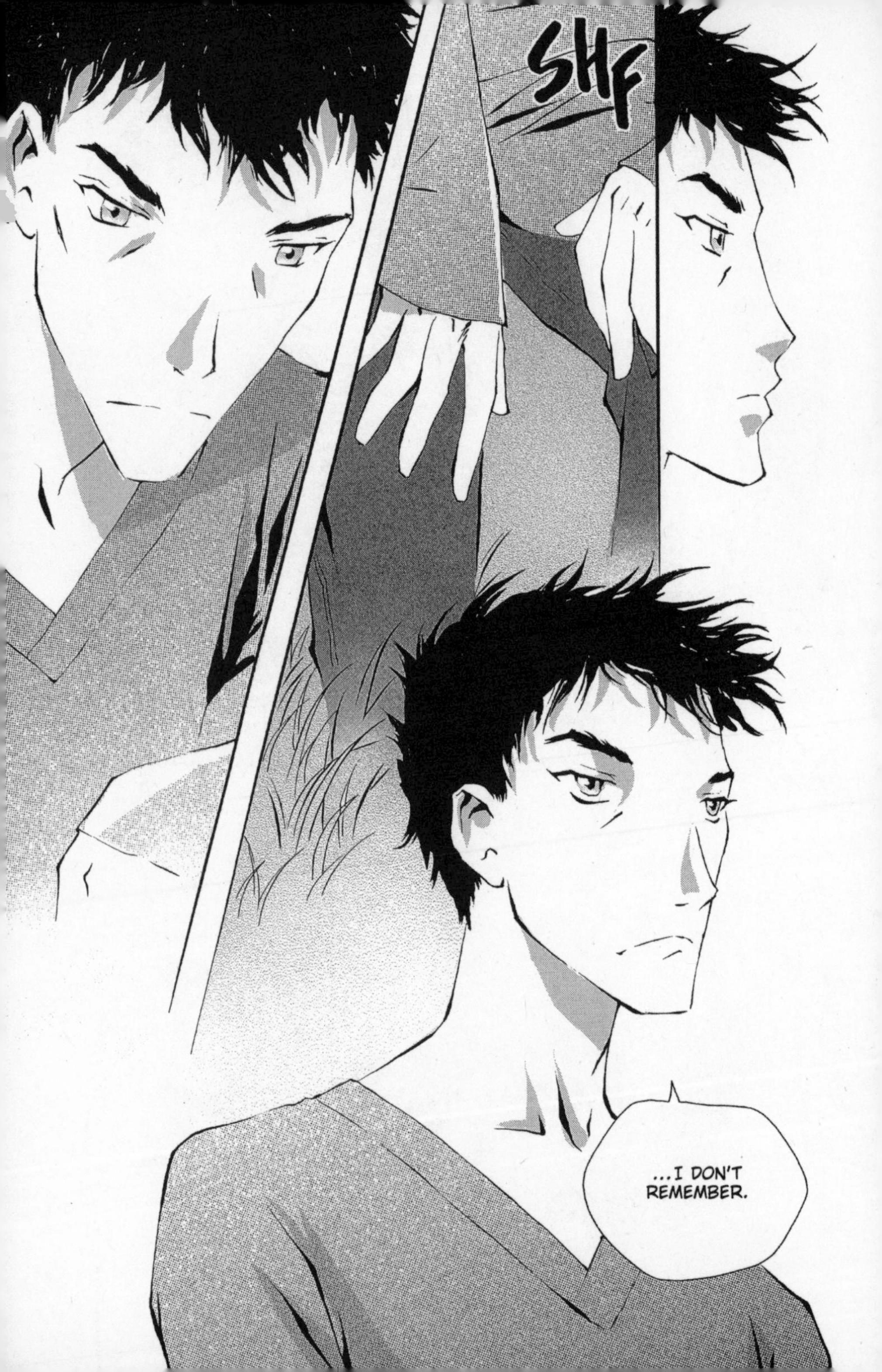
SHF
...I DON'T REMEMBER.

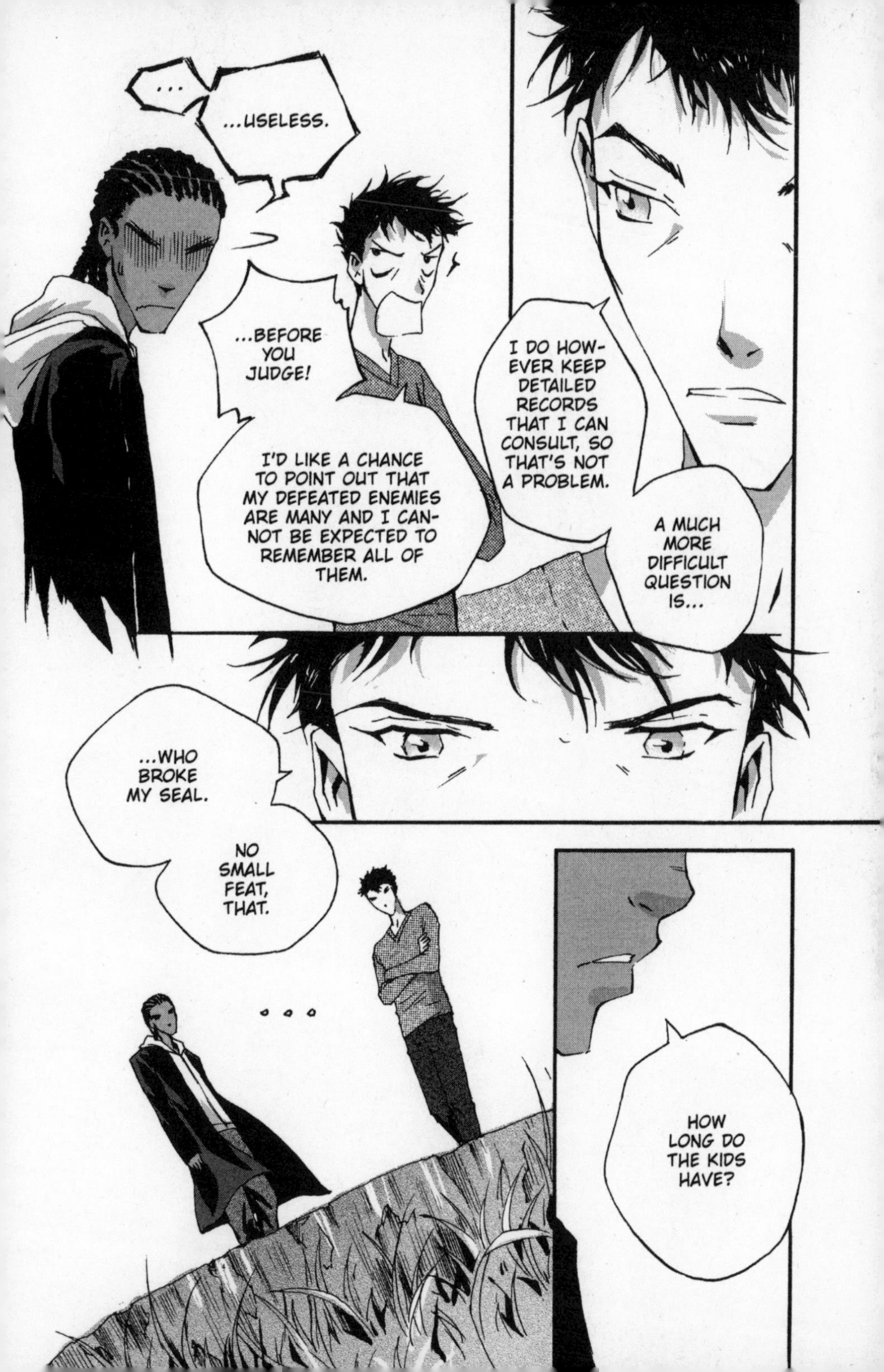
...
...USELESS.
...BEFORE YOU JUDGE!
I'D LIKE A CHANCE TO POINT OUT THAT MY DEFEATED ENEMIES ARE MANY AND I CAN-NOT BE EXPECTED TO REMEMBER ALL OF THEM.
I DO HOW-EVER KEEP DETAILED RECORDS THAT I CAN CONSULT, SO THAT'S NOT A PROBLEM.
A MUCH MORE DIFFICULT QUESTION IS...
...WHO BROKE MY SEAL.
NO SMALL FEAT, THAT.
...
HOW LONG DO THE KIDS HAVE?

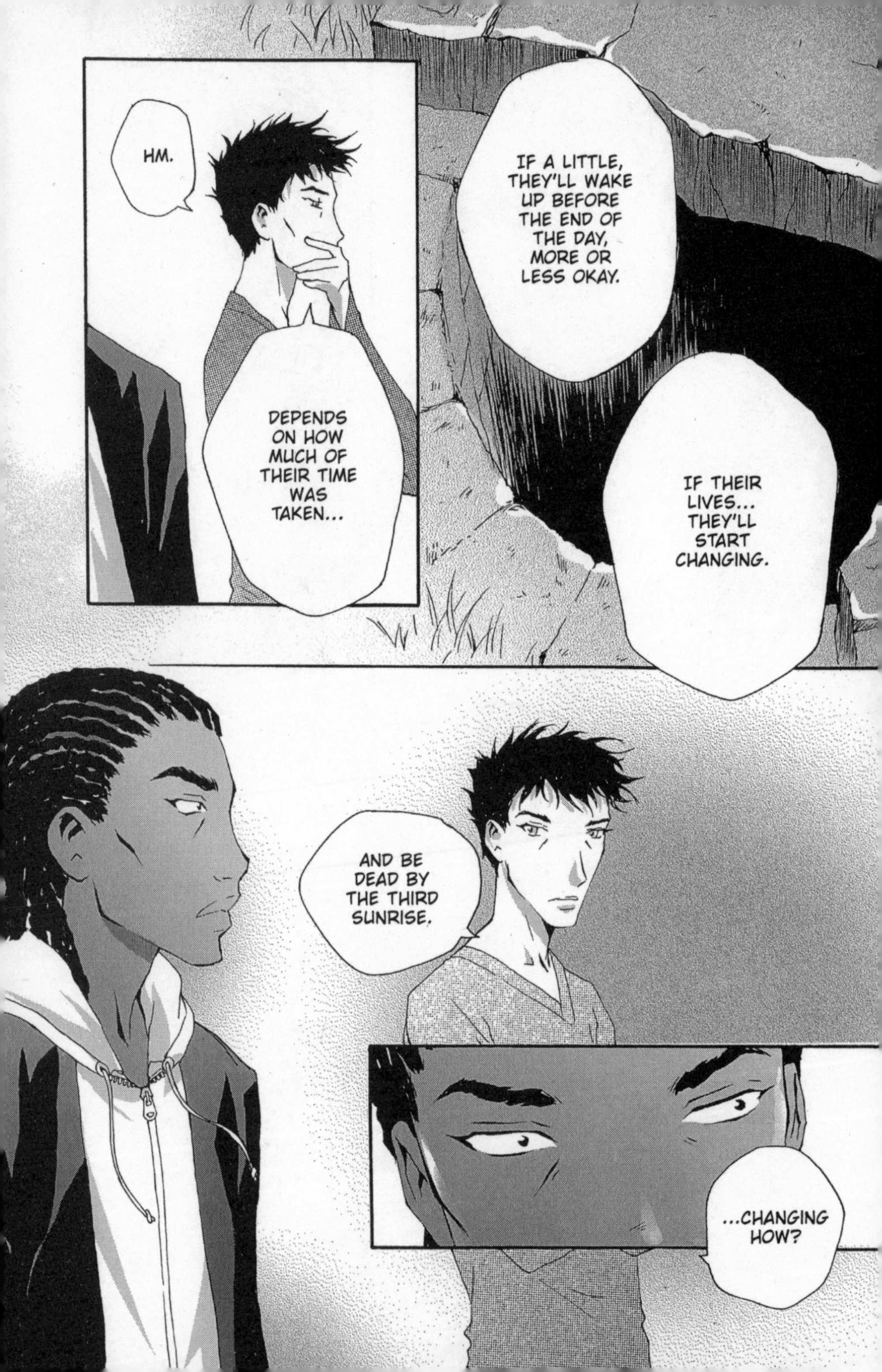
HM.
DEPENDS ON HOW MUCH OF THEIR TIME WAS TAKEN...
IF A LITTLE, THEY'LL WAKE UP BEFORE THE END OF THE DAY, MORE OR LESS OKAY.
IF THEIR LIVES... THEY'LL START CHANGING.
AND BE DEAD BY THE THIRD SUNRISE.
...CHANGING HOW?

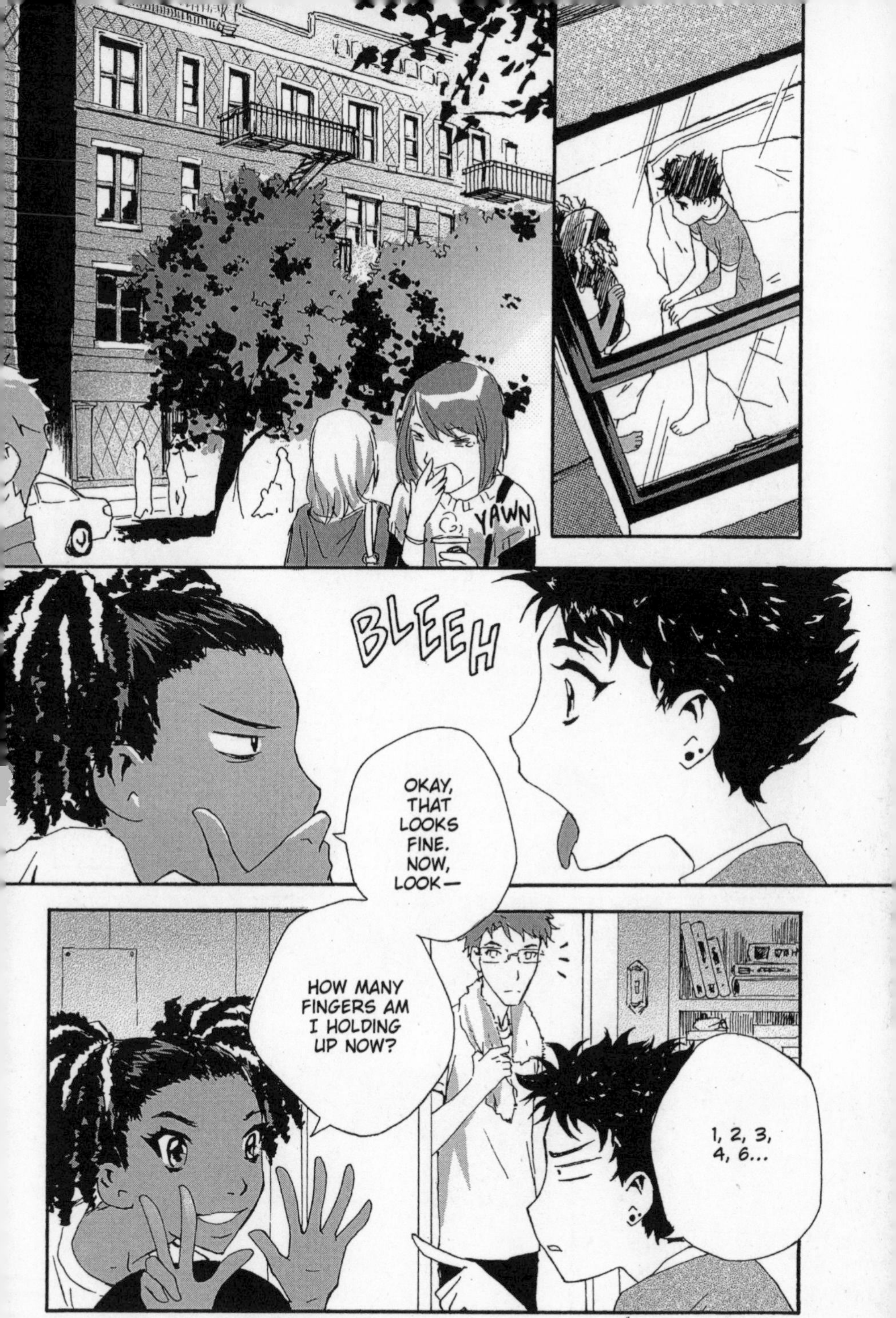
YAWN
BLEEH
OKAY, THAT LOOKS FINE. NOW, LOOK—
HOW MANY FINGERS AM I HOLDING UP NOW?
1, 2, 3, 4, 6...

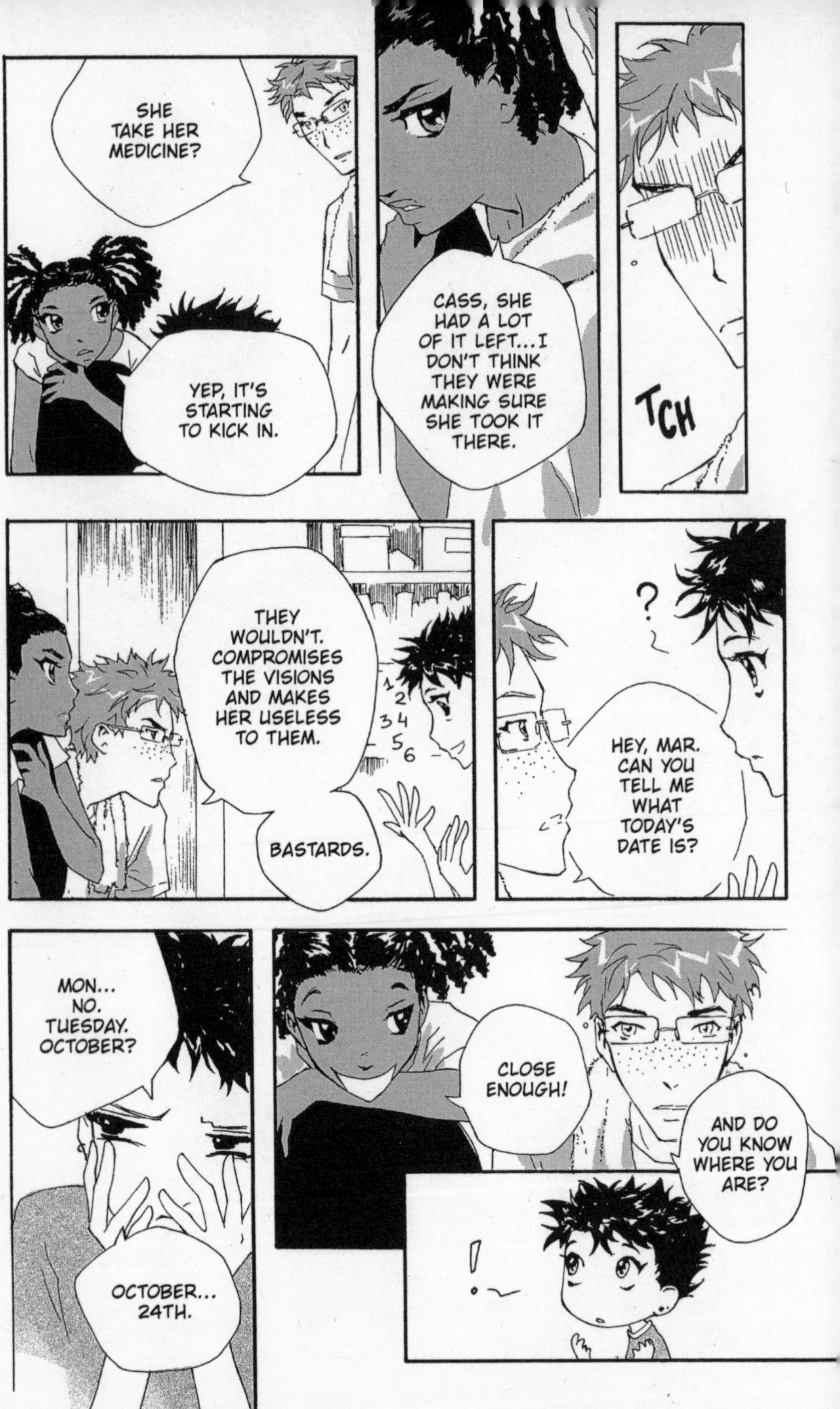
SHE TAKE HER MEDICINE?
YEP, IT'S STARTING TO KICK IN.
CASS, SHE HAD A LOT OF IT LEFT... I DON'T THINK THEY WERE MAKING SURE SHE TOOK IT THERE.
TCH
THEY WOULDN'T. COMPROMISES THE VISIONS AND MAKES HER USELESS TO THEM.
1 2 3 4 5 6
BASTARDS.
HEY, MAR. CAN YOU TELL ME WHAT TODAY'S DATE IS?
MON... NO. TUESDAY. OCTOBER?
OCTOBER... 24TH.
CLOSE ENOUGH!
AND DO YOU KNOW WHERE YOU ARE?

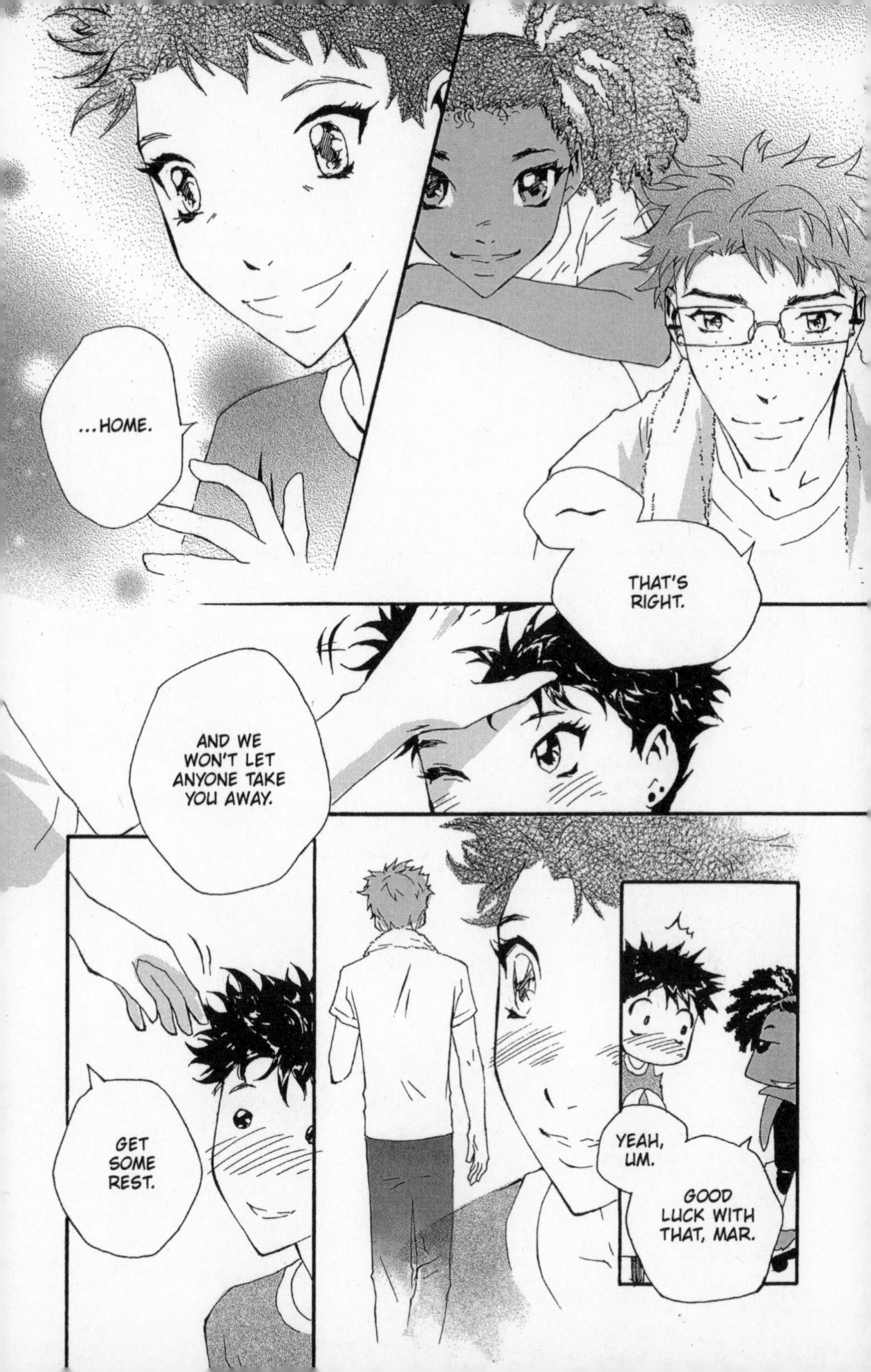
...HOME.
THAT'S RIGHT.
AND WE WON'T LET ANYONE TAKE YOU AWAY.
GET SOME REST.
YEAH, UM.
GOOD LUCK WITH THAT, MAR.

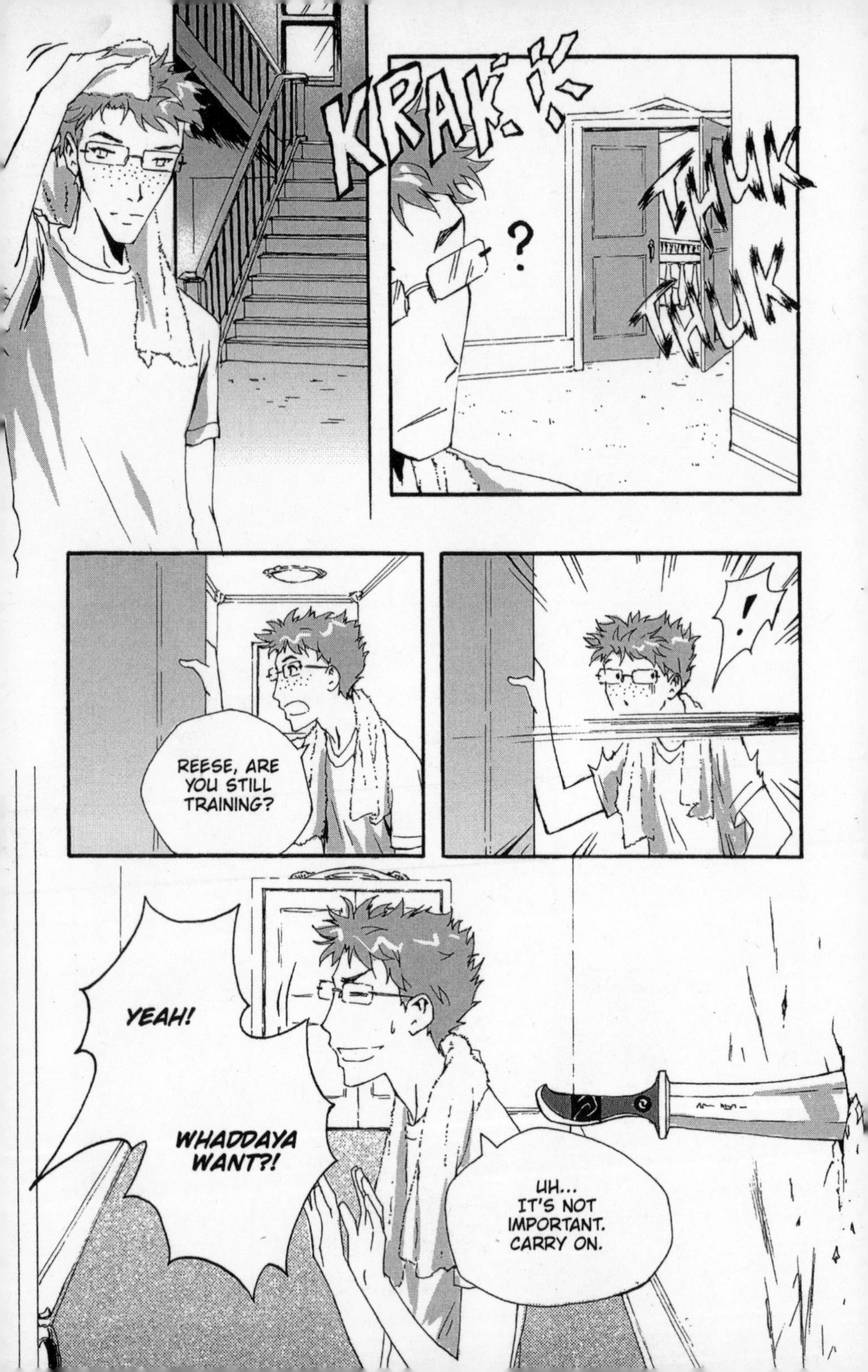
KRAK KRAK
?
THUK THUK
REESE, ARE YOU STILL TRAINING?
!
YEAH!
WHADDAYA WANT?!
UH... IT'S NOT IMPORTANT. CARRY ON.

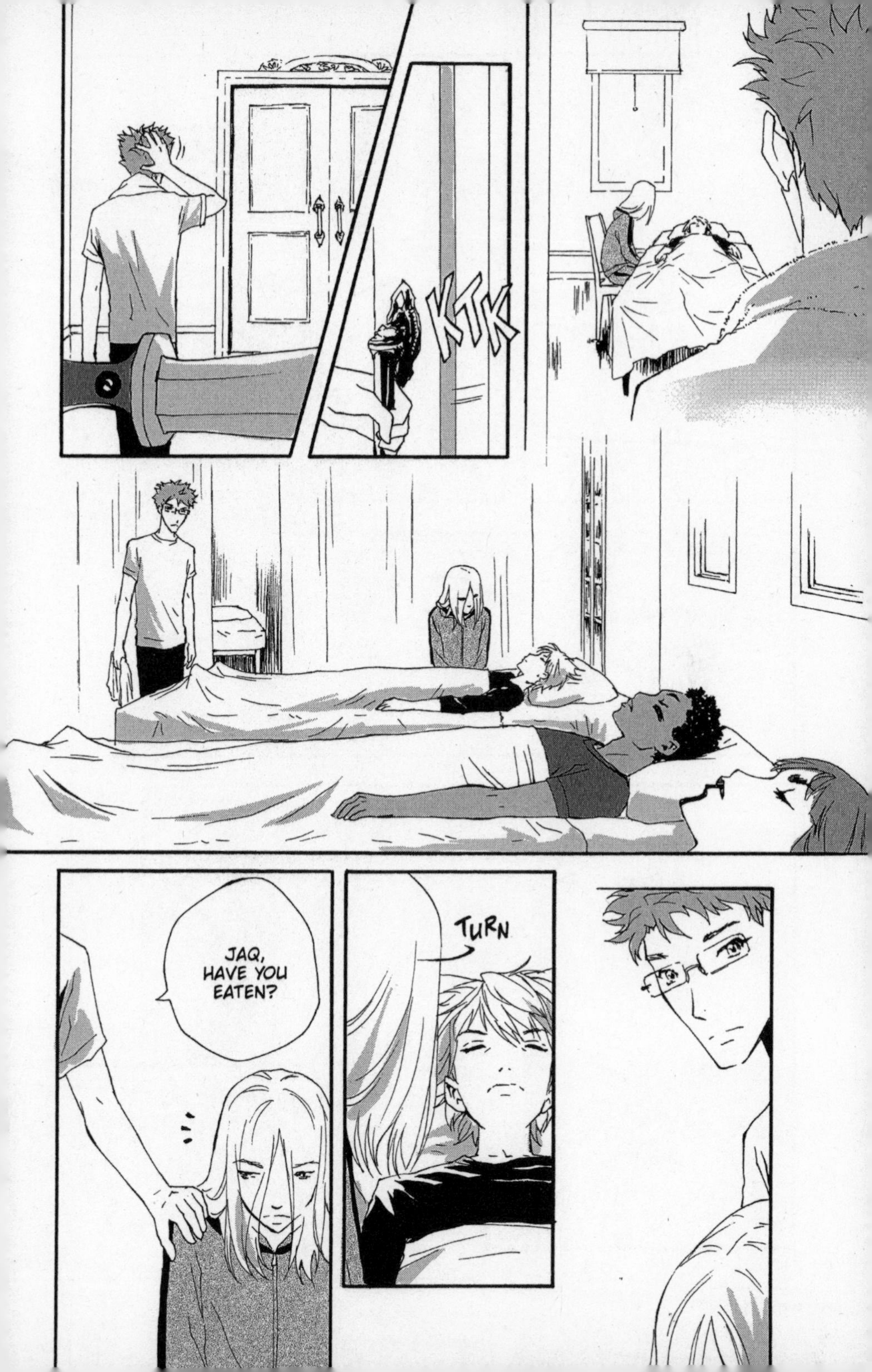
KTK
JAQ, HAVE YOU EATEN?
TURN

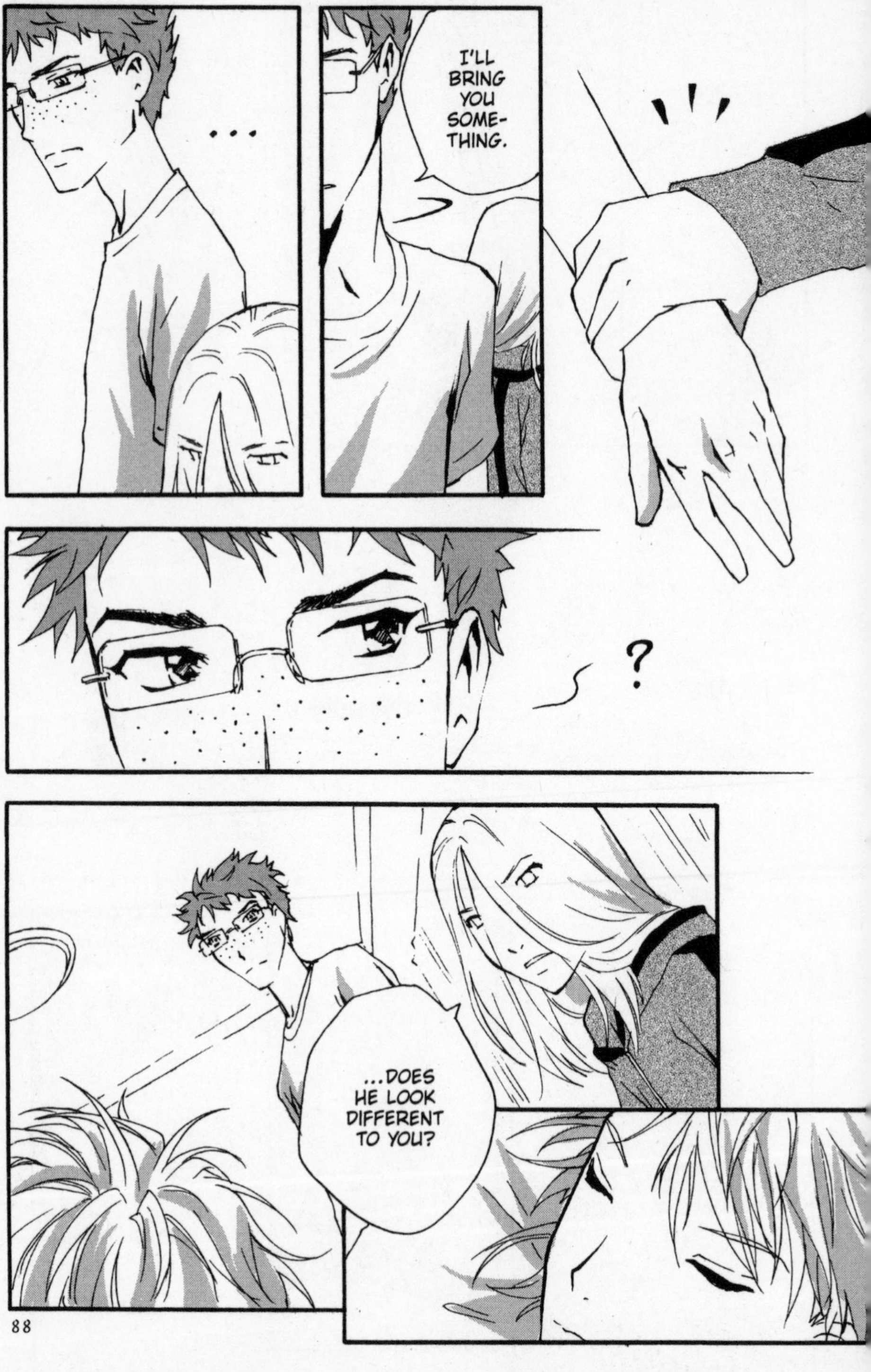
...
I'LL BRING YOU SOME-THING.
?
...DOES HE LOOK DIFFERENT TO YOU?

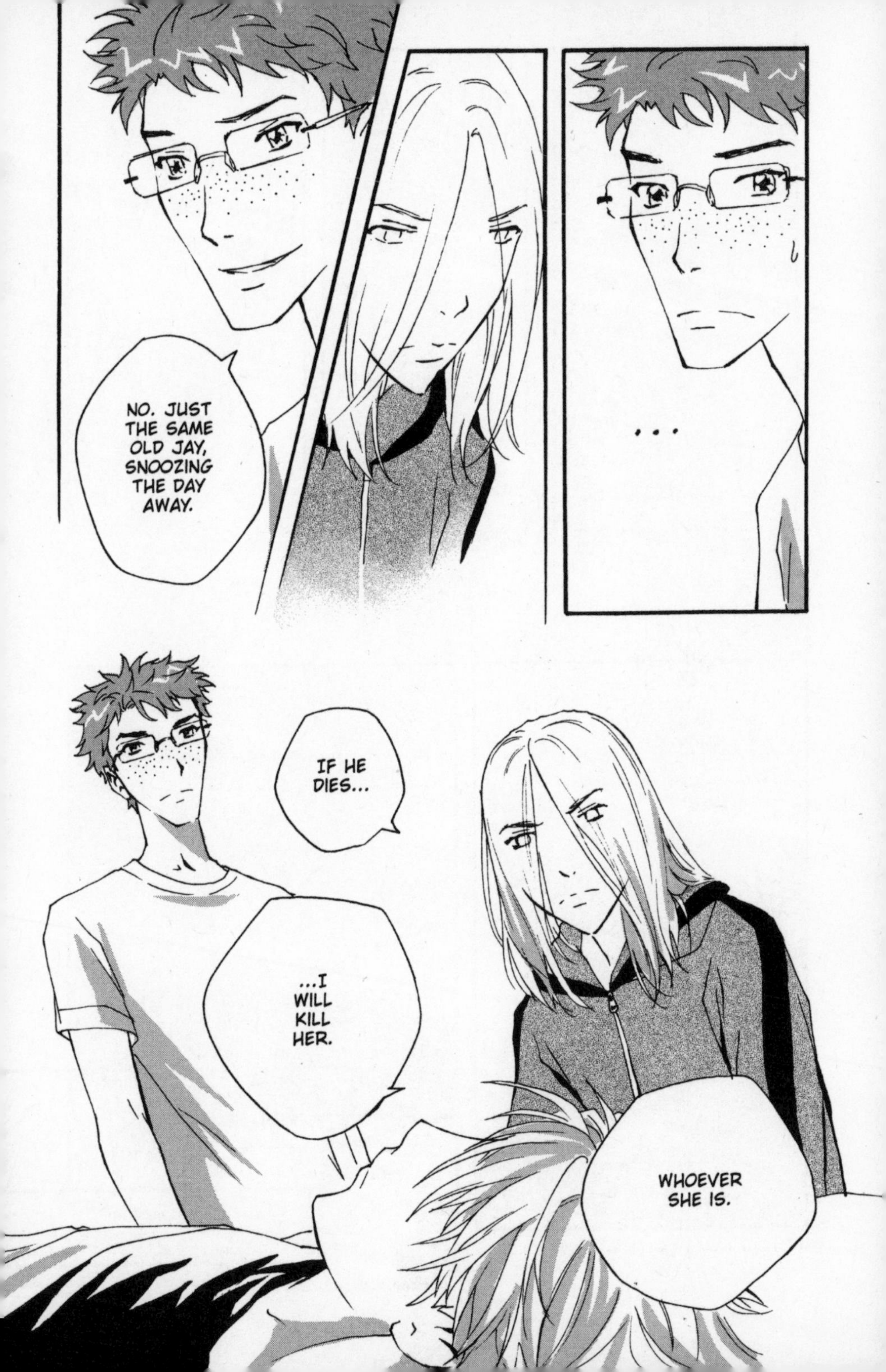
NO. JUST THE SAME OLD JAY, SNOOZING THE DAY AWAY.
...
IF HE DIES...
...I WILL KILL HER.
WHOEVER SHE IS.

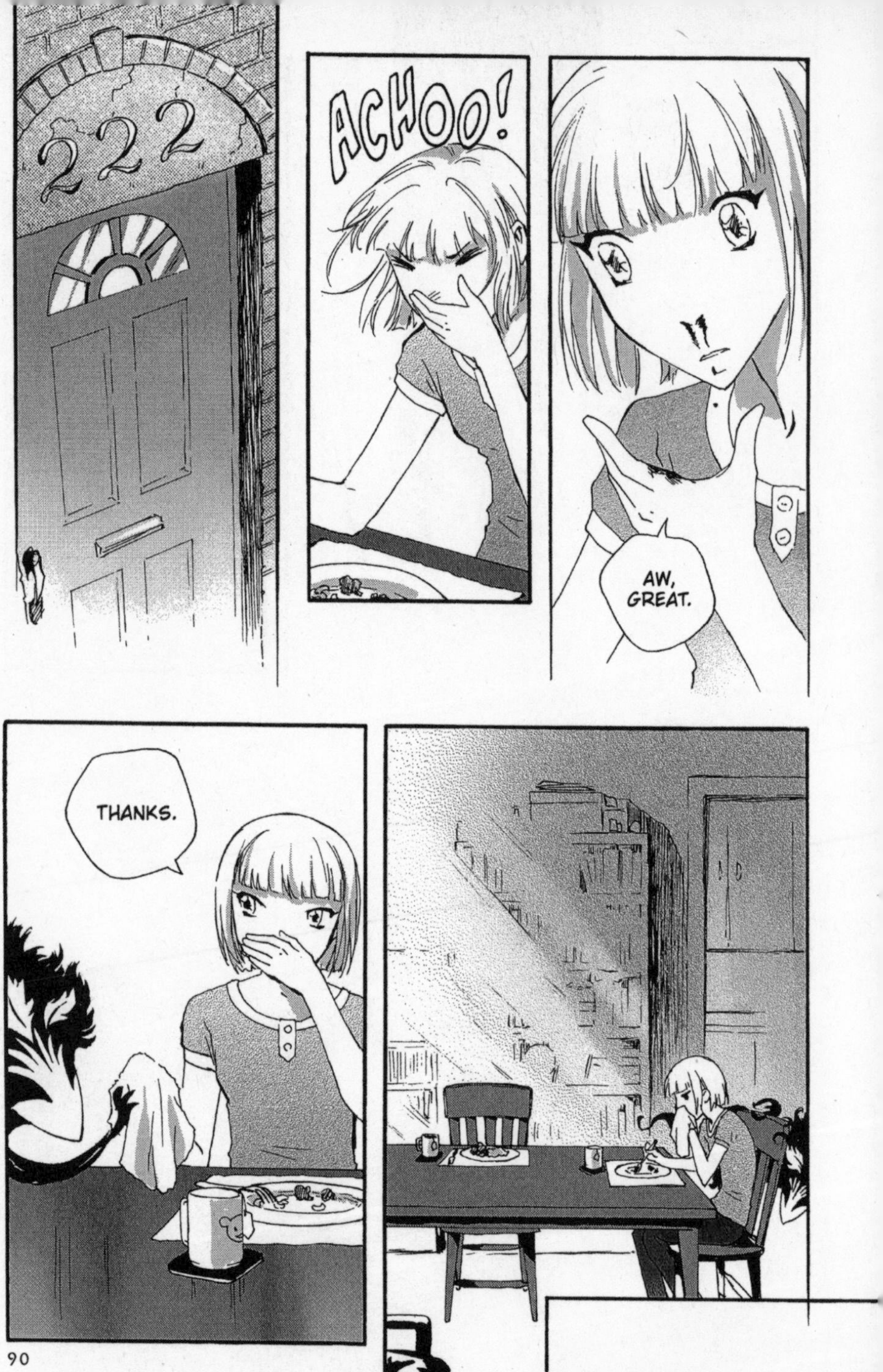
222
ACHOO!
AW, GREAT.
THANKS.

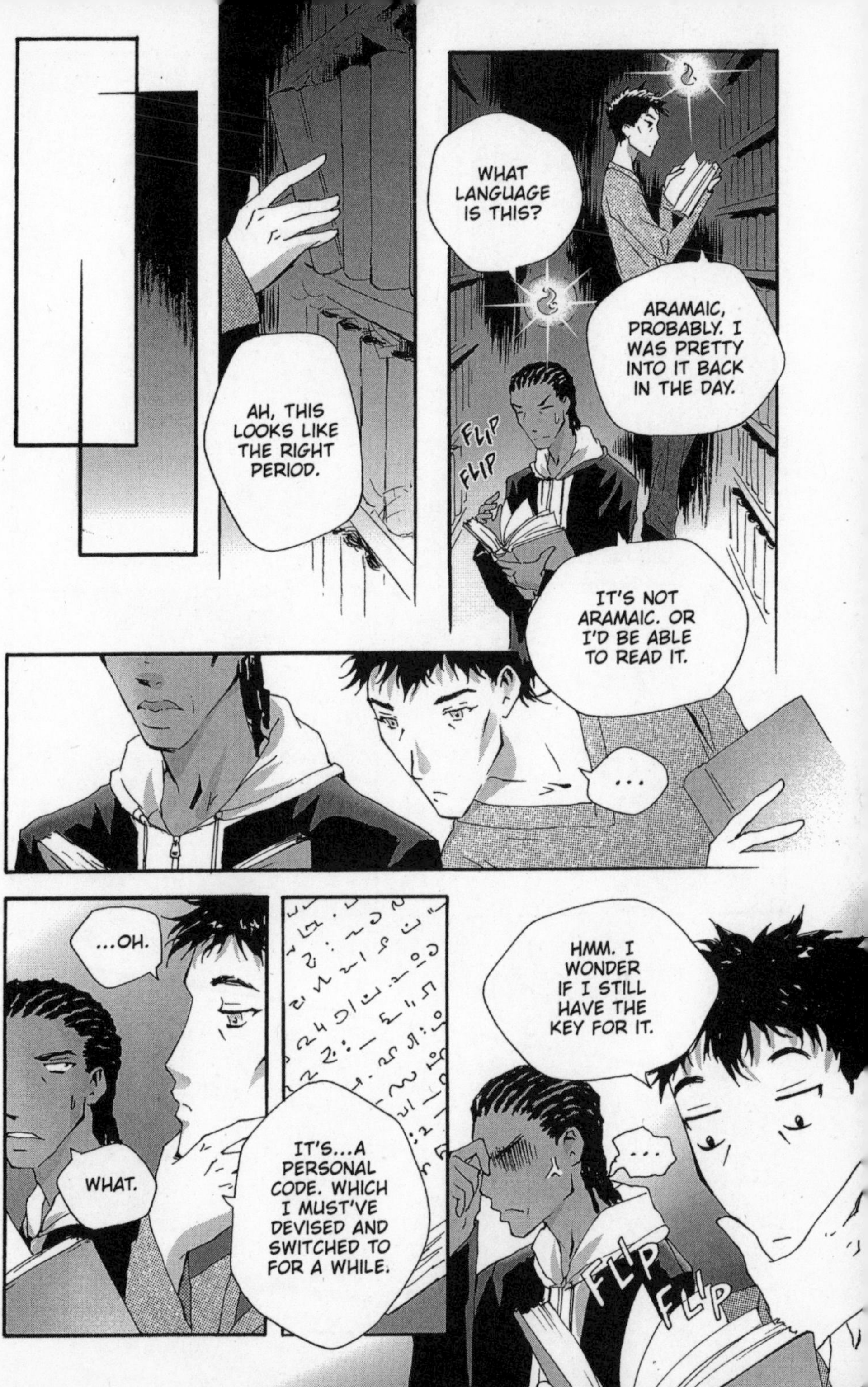

AH, THIS LOOKS LIKE THE RIGHT PERIOD.
WHAT LANGUAGE IS THIS?
ARAMAIC, PROBABLY. I WAS PRETTY INTO IT BACK IN THE DAY.
FLIP
FLIP
IT'S NOT ARAMAIC. OR I'D BE ABLE TO READ IT.
...
...OH.
WHAT.
IT'S...A PERSONAL CODE. WHICH I MUST'VE DEVISED AND SWITCHED TO FOR A WHILE.
HMM. I WONDER IF I STILL HAVE THE KEY FOR IT.
...
FLIP
FLIP

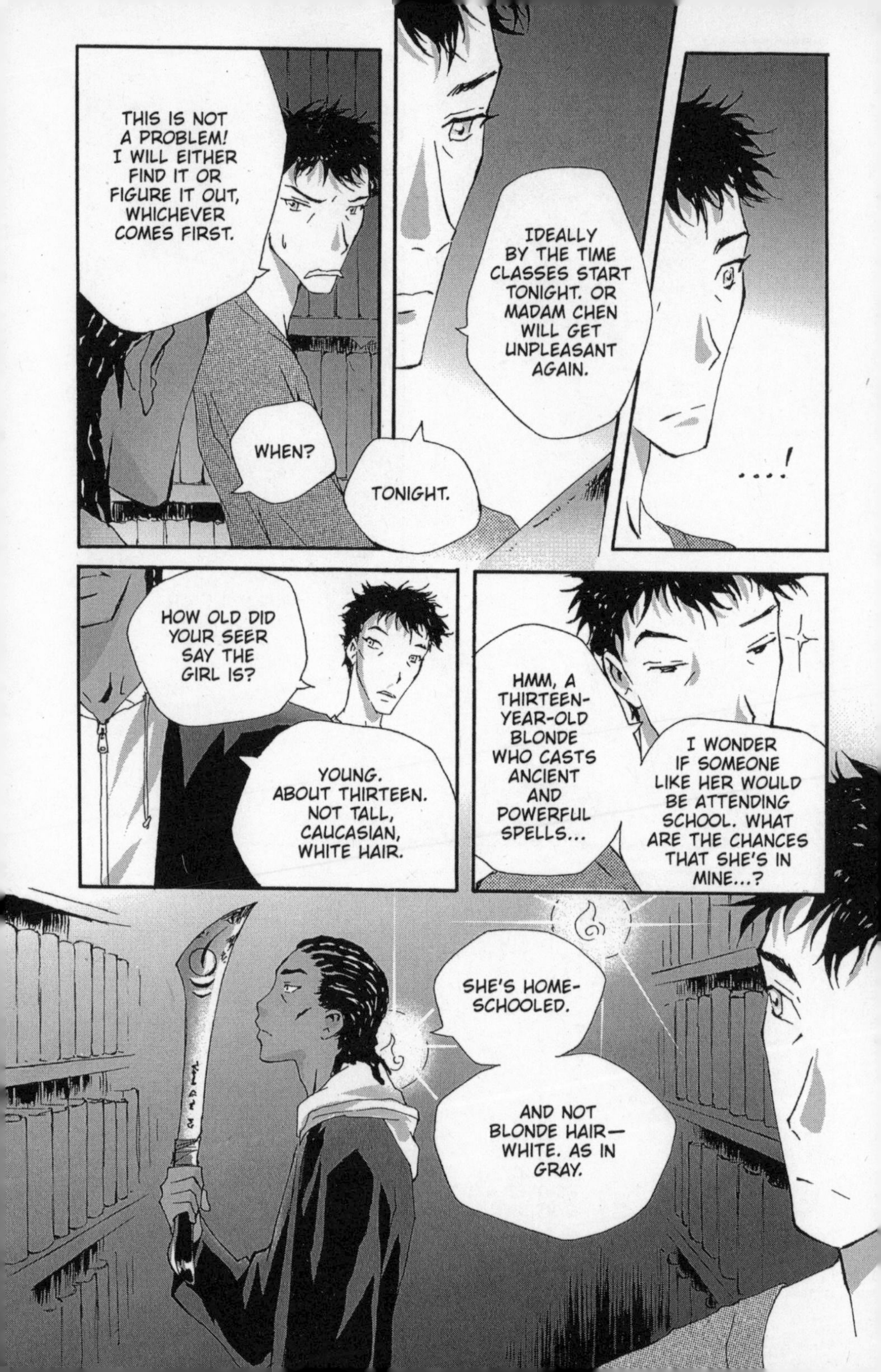
THIS IS NOT A PROBLEM! I WILL EITHER FIND IT OR FIGURE IT OUT, WHICHEVER COMES FIRST.
WHEN?
TONIGHT.
IDEALLY BY THE TIME CLASSES START TONIGHT. OR MADAM CHEN WILL GET UNPLEASANT AGAIN.
...!
HOW OLD DID YOUR SEER SAY THE GIRL IS?
YOUNG. ABOUT THIRTEEN. NOT TALL, CAUCASIAN, WHITE HAIR.
HMM, A THIRTEEN-YEAR-OLD BLONDE WHO CASTS ANCIENT AND POWERFUL SPELLS...
I WONDER IF SOMEONE LIKE HER WOULD BE ATTENDING SCHOOL. WHAT ARE THE CHANCES THAT SHE'S IN MINE...?
SHE'S HOME-SCHOOLED.
AND NOT BLONDE HAIR— WHITE. AS IN GRAY.

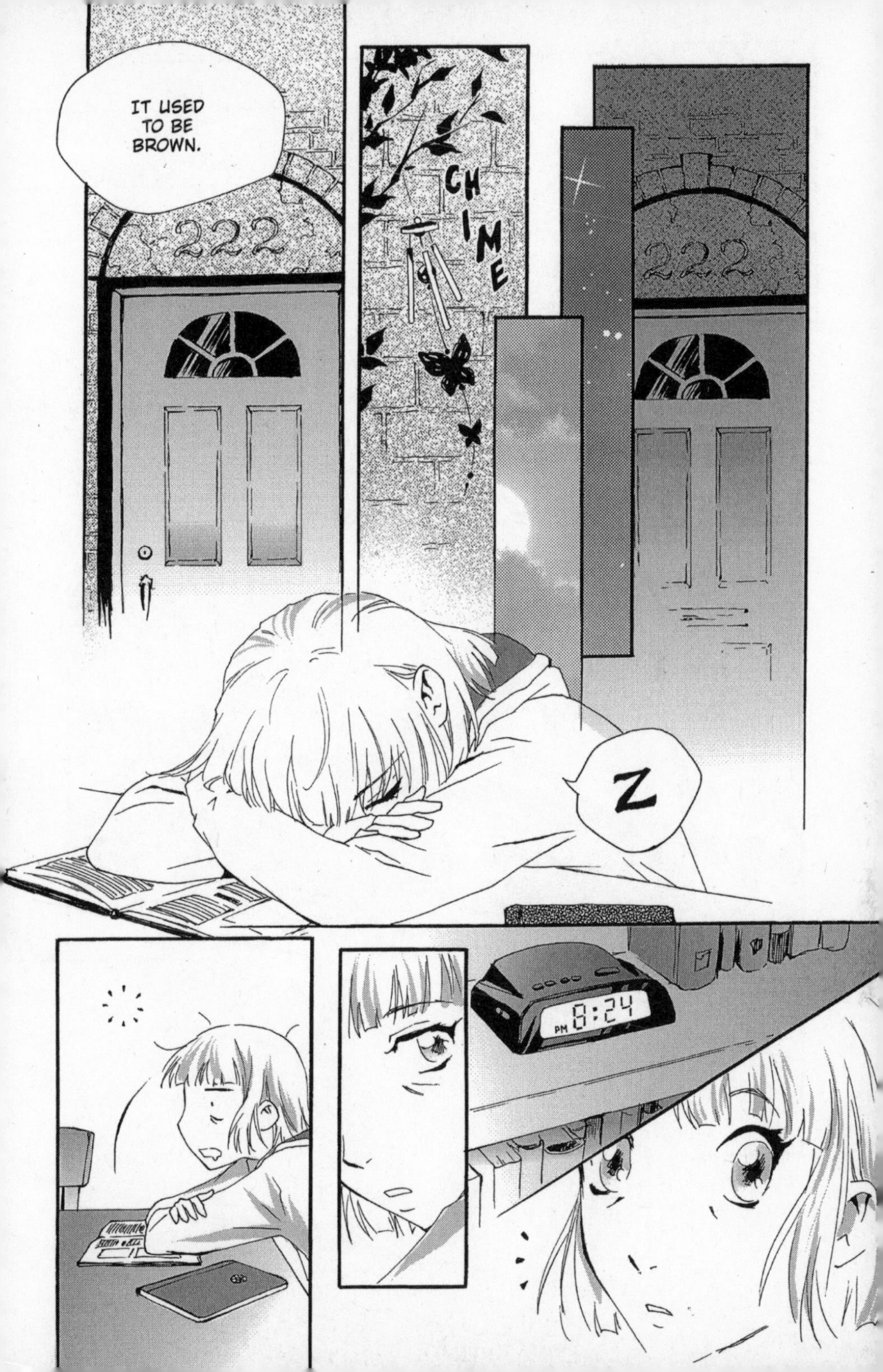
IT USED TO BE BROWN.
CHIME
Z
PM 8:24

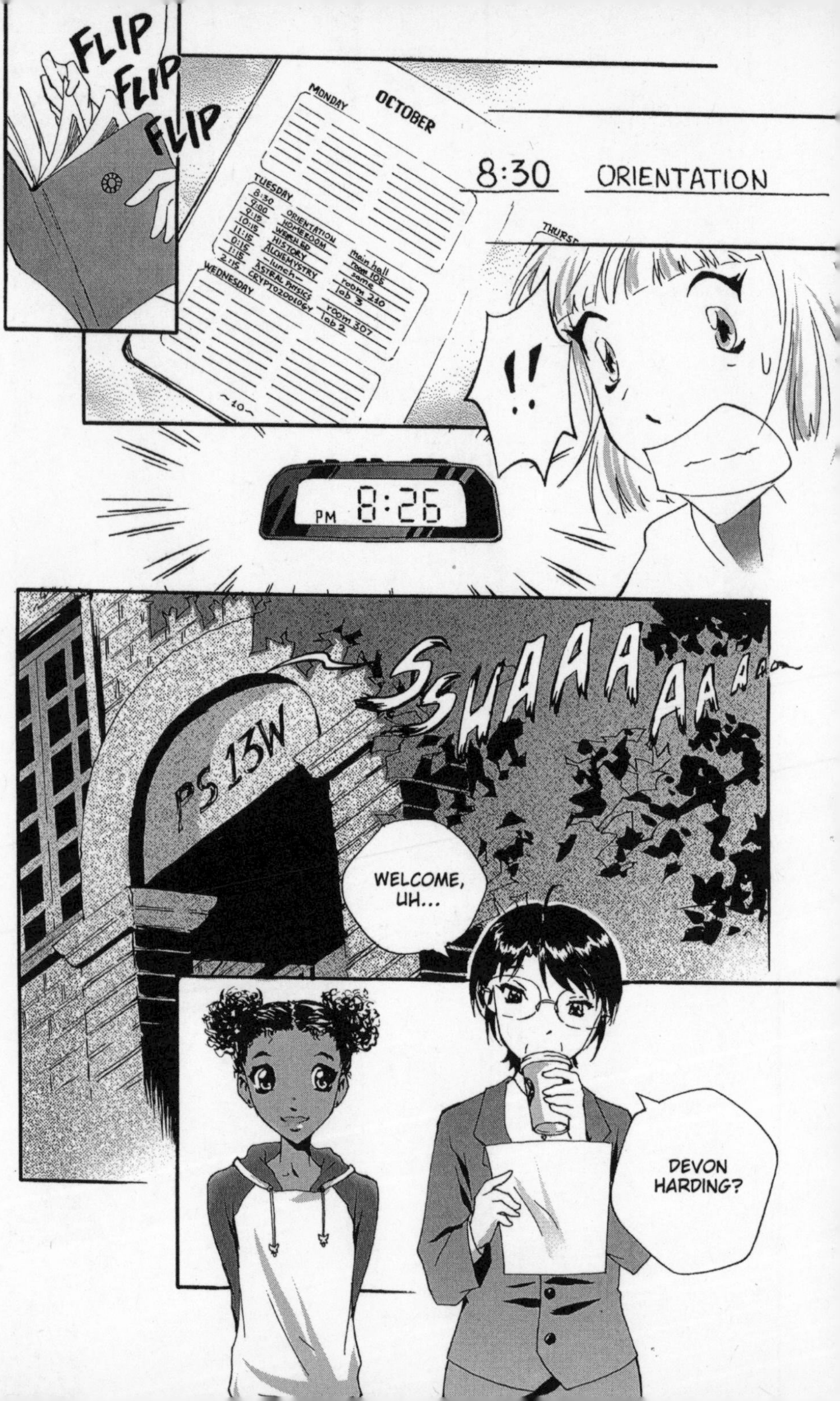

FLIP
FLIP
FLIP
MONDAY
OCTOBER
TUESDAY
8:30 ORIENTATION main hall
9:00 HOMEROOM room 105
10:15 HISTORY room 210
11:15 ALCHEMYSTRY lab 3
0:15 -lunch-
1:15 ASTRAL PHYSICS room 307
2:15 CRYPTOZOOLOGY lab 2
WEDNESDAY
~10~
8:30
ORIENTATION
!!
PM 8:26
PS 13W
SSHAAAAAAA
WELCOME, UH...
DEVON HARDING?

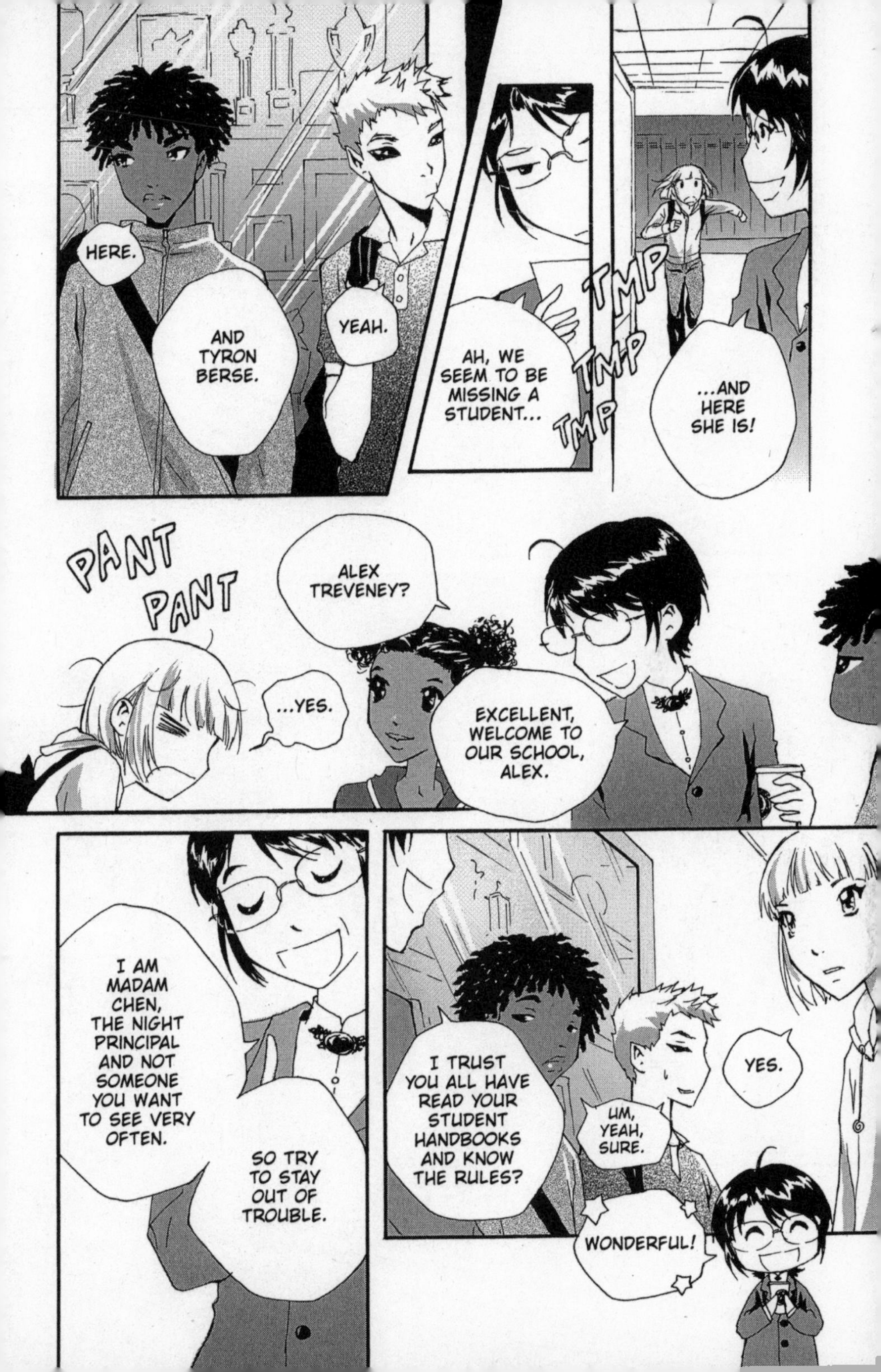
HERE.
AND TYRON BERSE.
YEAH.
AH, WE SEEM TO BE MISSING A STUDENT...
TMP TMP TMP
...AND HERE SHE IS!
PANT PANT
ALEX TREVENEY?
...YES.
EXCELLENT, WELCOME TO OUR SCHOOL, ALEX.
I AM MADAM CHEN, THE NIGHT PRINCIPAL AND NOT SOMEONE YOU WANT TO SEE VERY OFTEN.
SO TRY TO STAY OUT OF TROUBLE.
I TRUST YOU ALL HAVE READ YOUR STUDENT HANDBOOKS AND KNOW THE RULES?
YES.
UM, YEAH, SURE.
WONDERFUL!

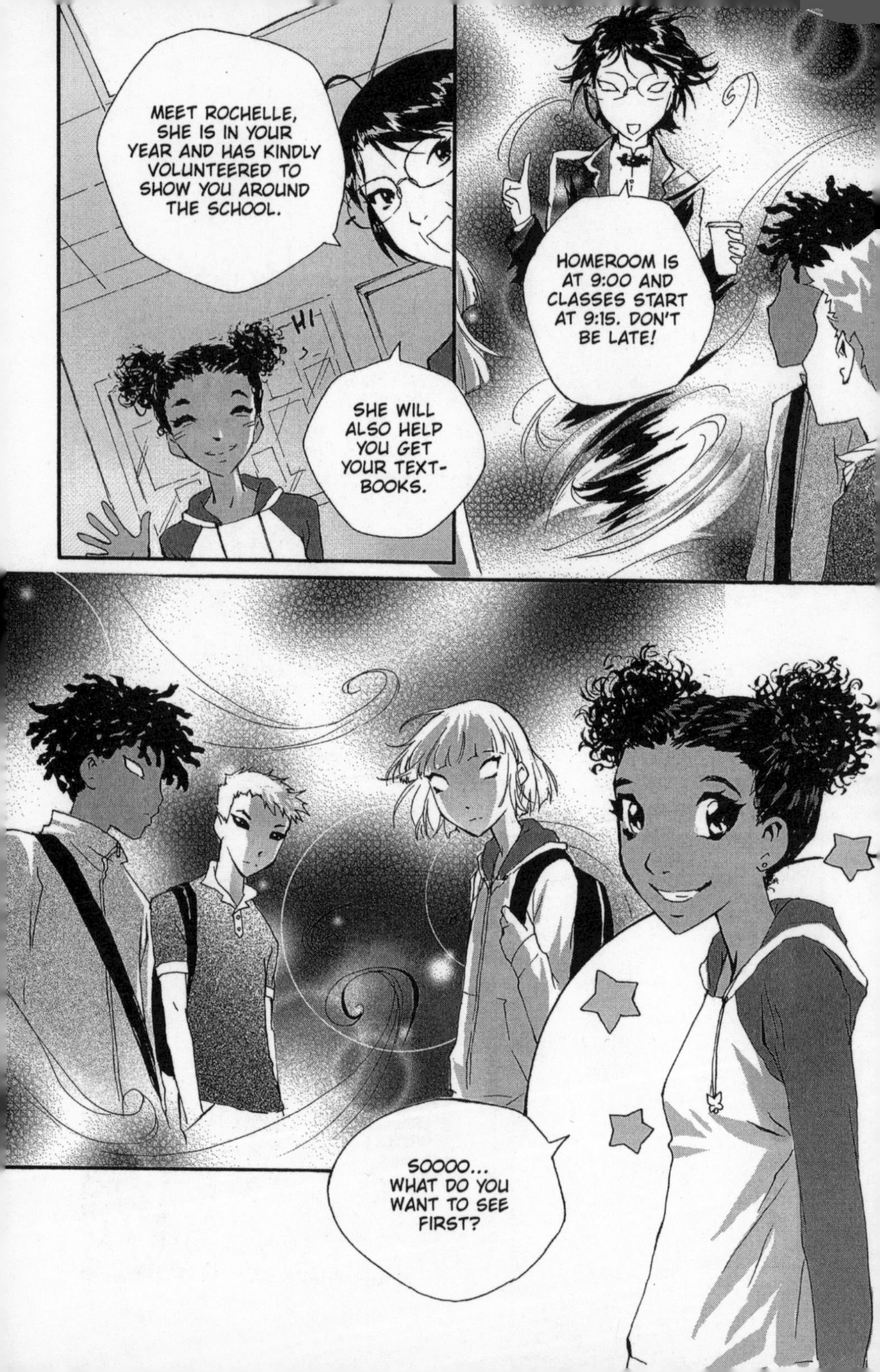
MEET ROCHELLE, SHE IS IN YOUR YEAR AND HAS KINDLY VOLUNTEERED TO SHOW YOU AROUND THE SCHOOL.
HI
SHE WILL ALSO HELP YOU GET YOUR TEXT-BOOKS.
HOMEROOM IS AT 9:00 AND CLASSES START AT 9:15. DON'T BE LATE!
SOOOO... WHAT DO YOU WANT TO SEE FIRST?

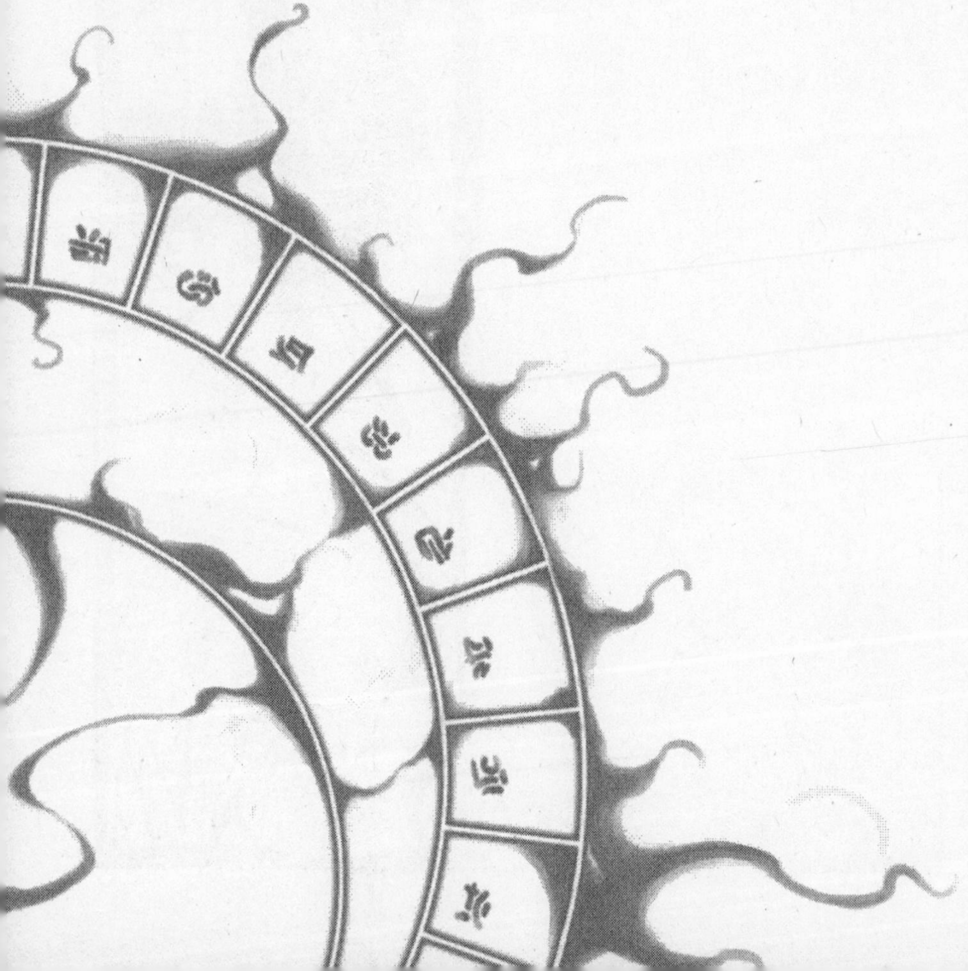

Chapter 10

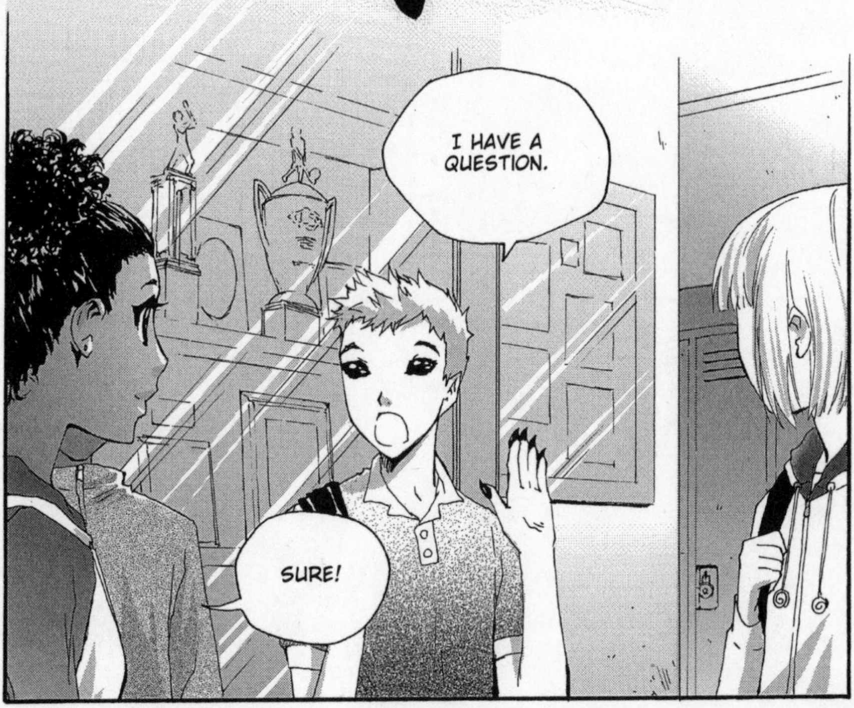
I HAVE A QUESTION.
SURE!

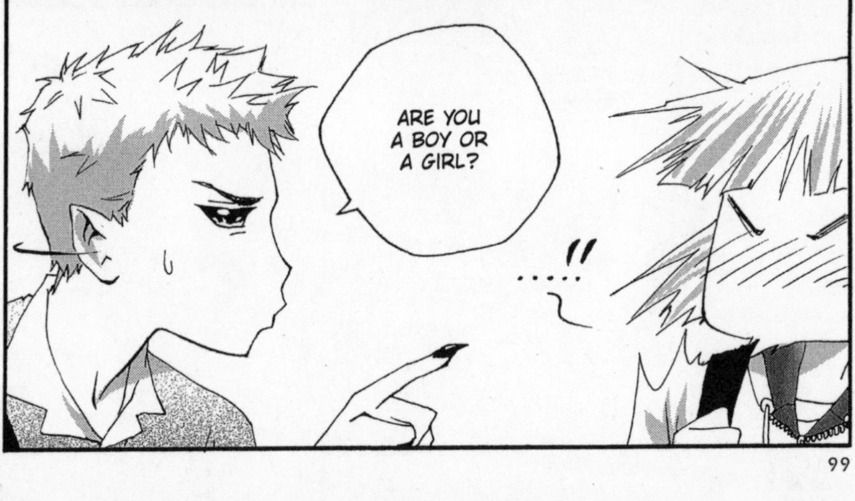
ARE YOU A BOY OR A GIRL?
.....!!

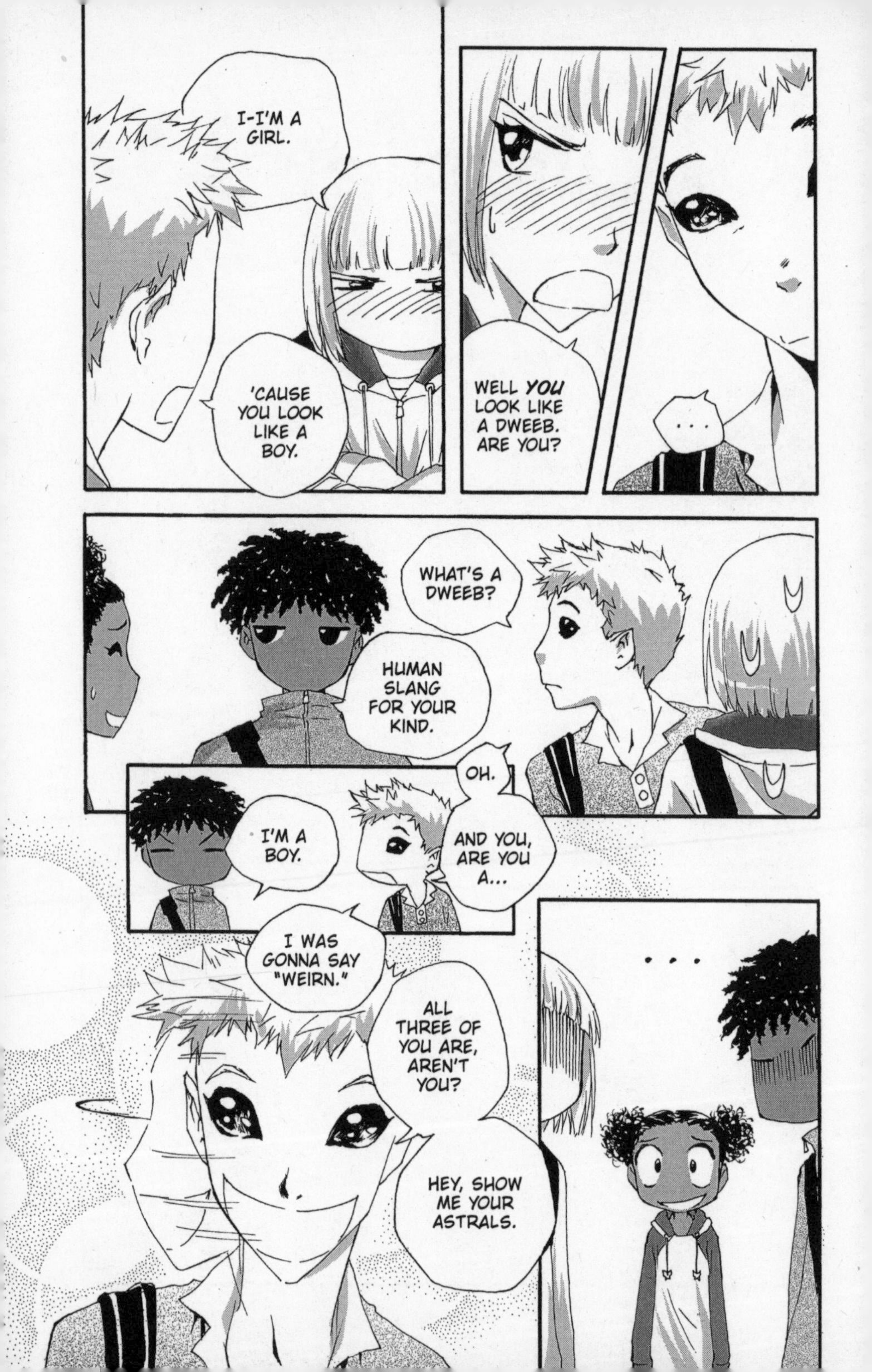
I-I'M A GIRL.
'CAUSE YOU LOOK LIKE A BOY.
WELL *YOU* LOOK LIKE A DWEEB. ARE YOU?
...
WHAT'S A DWEEB?
HUMAN SLANG FOR YOUR KIND.
OH.
I'M A BOY.
AND YOU, ARE YOU A...
I WAS GONNA SAY "WEIRN."
ALL THREE OF YOU ARE, AREN'T YOU?
HEY, SHOW ME YOUR ASTRALS.
...

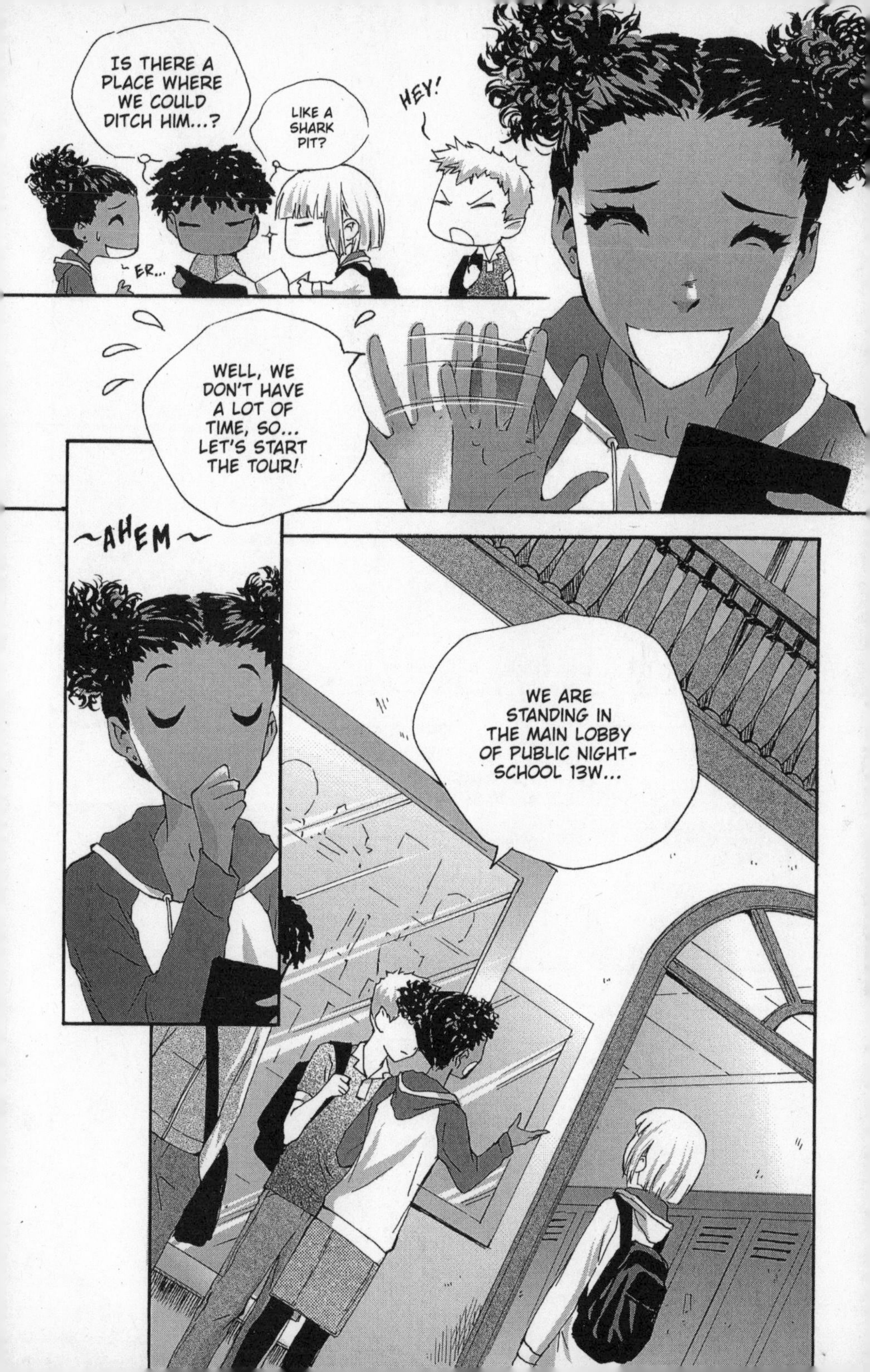
IS THERE A PLACE WHERE WE COULD DITCH HIM...?
LIKE A SHARK PIT?
HEY!
ER...
WELL, WE DON'T HAVE A LOT OF TIME, SO... LET'S START THE TOUR!
~AHEM~
WE ARE STANDING IN THE MAIN LOBBY OF PUBLIC NIGHT-SCHOOL 13W...

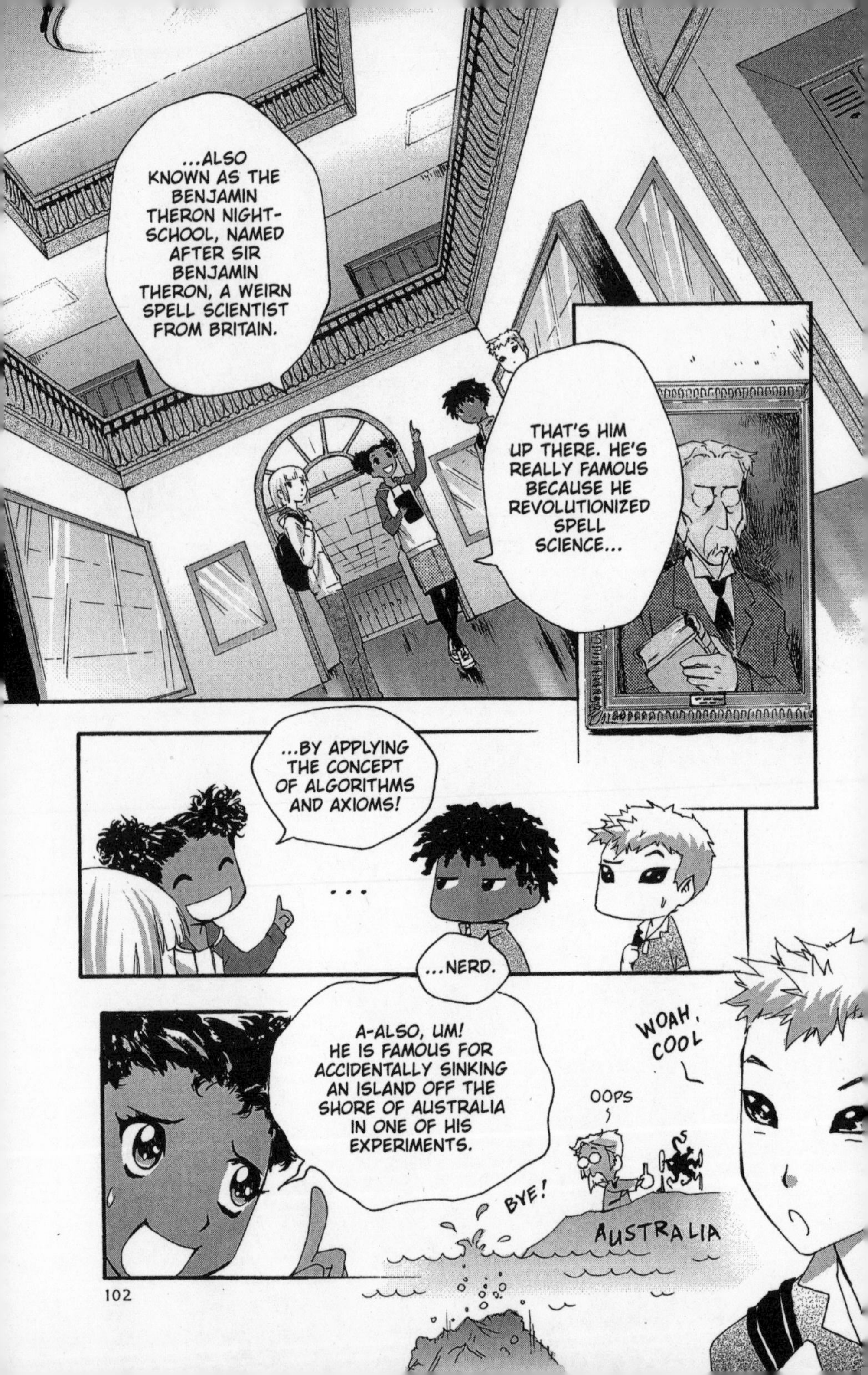

...ALSO KNOWN AS THE BENJAMIN THERON NIGHT-SCHOOL, NAMED AFTER SIR BENJAMIN THERON, A WEIRN SPELL SCIENTIST FROM BRITAIN.
THAT'S HIM UP THERE. HE'S REALLY FAMOUS BECAUSE HE REVOLUTIONIZED SPELL SCIENCE...
...BY APPLYING THE CONCEPT OF ALGORITHMS AND AXIOMS!
...
...NERD.
A-ALSO, UM! HE IS FAMOUS FOR ACCIDENTALLY SINKING AN ISLAND OFF THE SHORE OF AUSTRALIA IN ONE OF HIS EXPERIMENTS.
WOAH, COOL
OOPS
BYE!
AUSTRALIA

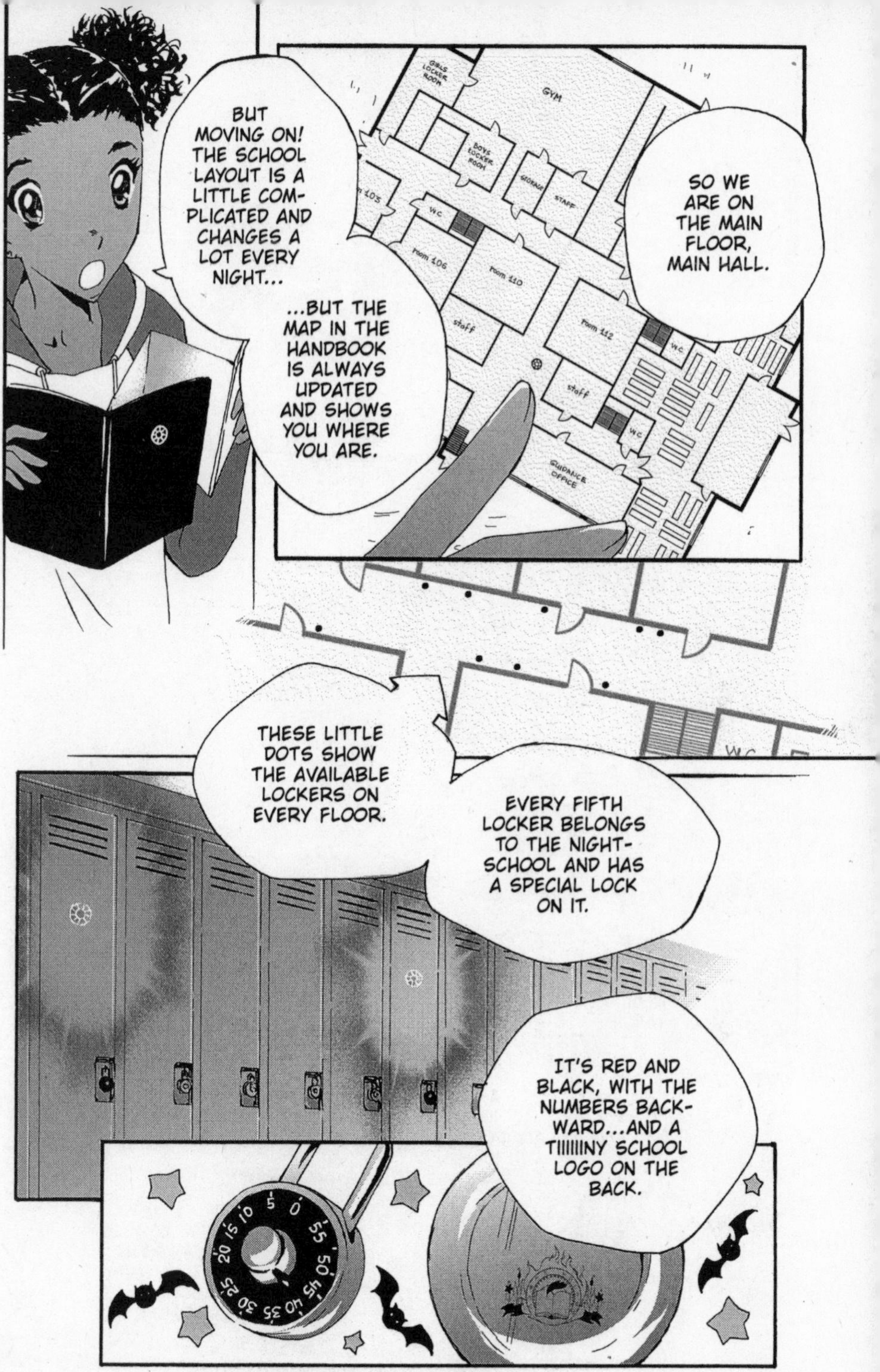
BUT MOVING ON! THE SCHOOL LAYOUT IS A LITTLE COMPLICATED AND CHANGES A LOT EVERY NIGHT...
...BUT THE MAP IN THE HANDBOOK IS ALWAYS UPDATED AND SHOWS YOU WHERE YOU ARE.
SO WE ARE ON THE MAIN FLOOR, MAIN HALL.
GIRLS LOCKER ROOM
GYM
BOYS LOCKER ROOM
STORAGE
STAFF
room 105
W.C.
room 106
room 110
staff
room 112
staff
W.C.
W.C.
GUIDANCE OFFICE
THESE LITTLE DOTS SHOW THE AVAILABLE LOCKERS ON EVERY FLOOR.
EVERY FIFTH LOCKER BELONGS TO THE NIGHT-SCHOOL AND HAS A SPECIAL LOCK ON IT.
IT'S RED AND BLACK, WITH THE NUMBERS BACKWARD...AND A TIIIIIINY SCHOOL LOGO ON THE BACK.

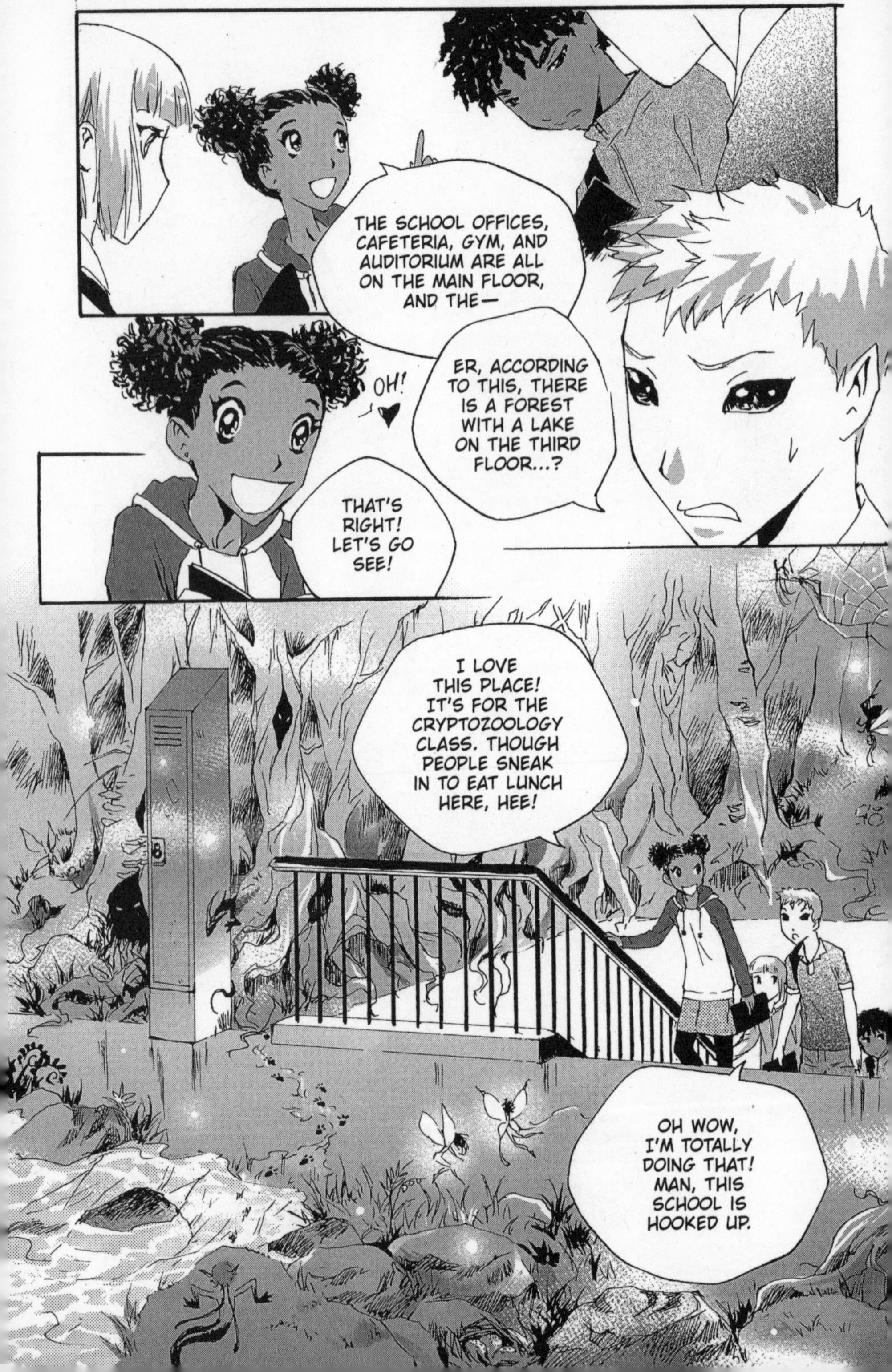
THE SCHOOL OFFICES, CAFETERIA, GYM, AND AUDITORIUM ARE ALL ON THE MAIN FLOOR, AND THE—
OH!
ER, ACCORDING TO THIS, THERE IS A FOREST WITH A LAKE ON THE THIRD FLOOR...?
THAT'S RIGHT! LET'S GO SEE!
I LOVE THIS PLACE! IT'S FOR THE CRYPTOZOOLOGY CLASS. THOUGH PEOPLE SNEAK IN TO EAT LUNCH HERE, HEE!
OH WOW, I'M TOTALLY DOING THAT! MAN, THIS SCHOOL IS HOOKED UP.

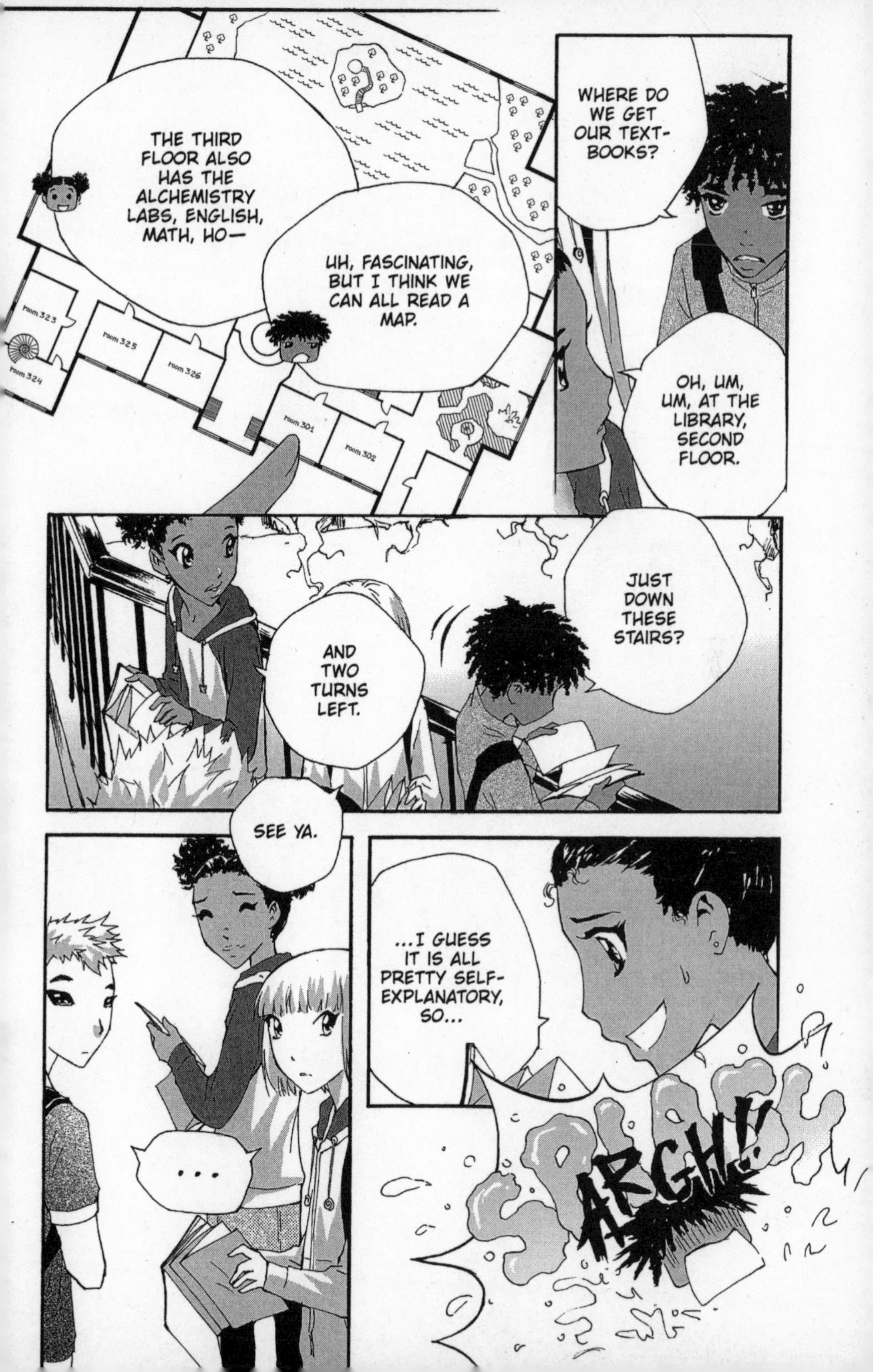
THE THIRD FLOOR ALSO HAS THE ALCHEMISTRY LABS, ENGLISH, MATH, HO—
room 323
room 325
room 326
room 324
room 301
room 302
UH, FASCINATING, BUT I THINK WE CAN ALL READ A MAP.
WHERE DO WE GET OUR TEXT-BOOKS?
OH, UM, UM, AT THE LIBRARY, SECOND FLOOR.
JUST DOWN THESE STAIRS?
AND TWO TURNS LEFT.
SEE YA.
...
...I GUESS IT IS ALL PRETTY SELF-EXPLANATORY, SO...
ARGH!!

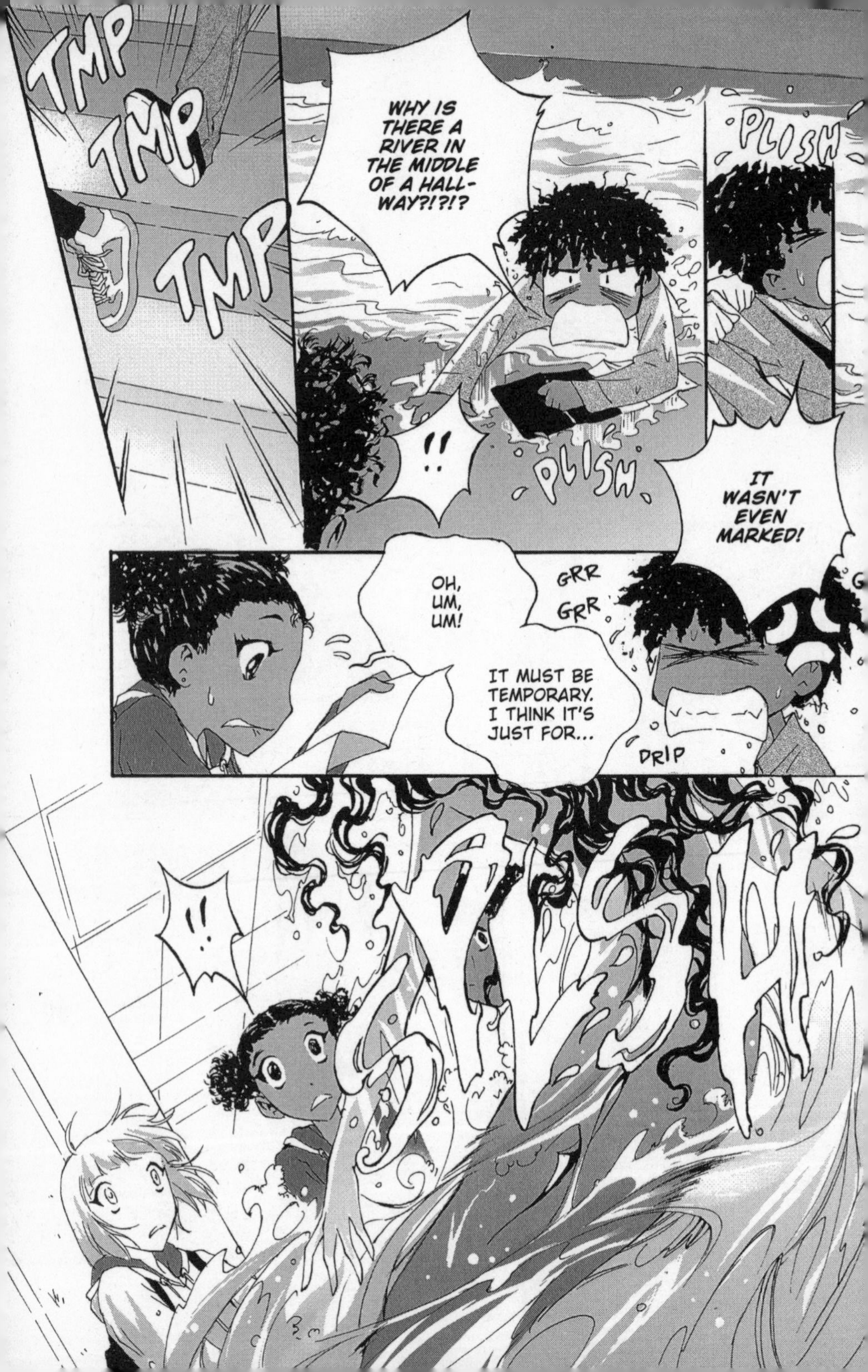
TMP
TMP
TMP
WHY IS THERE A RIVER IN THE MIDDLE OF A HALL-WAY?!?!?
!!
PLISH
PLISH
IT WASN'T EVEN MARKED!
OH, UM, UM!
GRR
GRR
IT MUST BE TEMPORARY. I THINK IT'S JUST FOR...
DRIP
!!

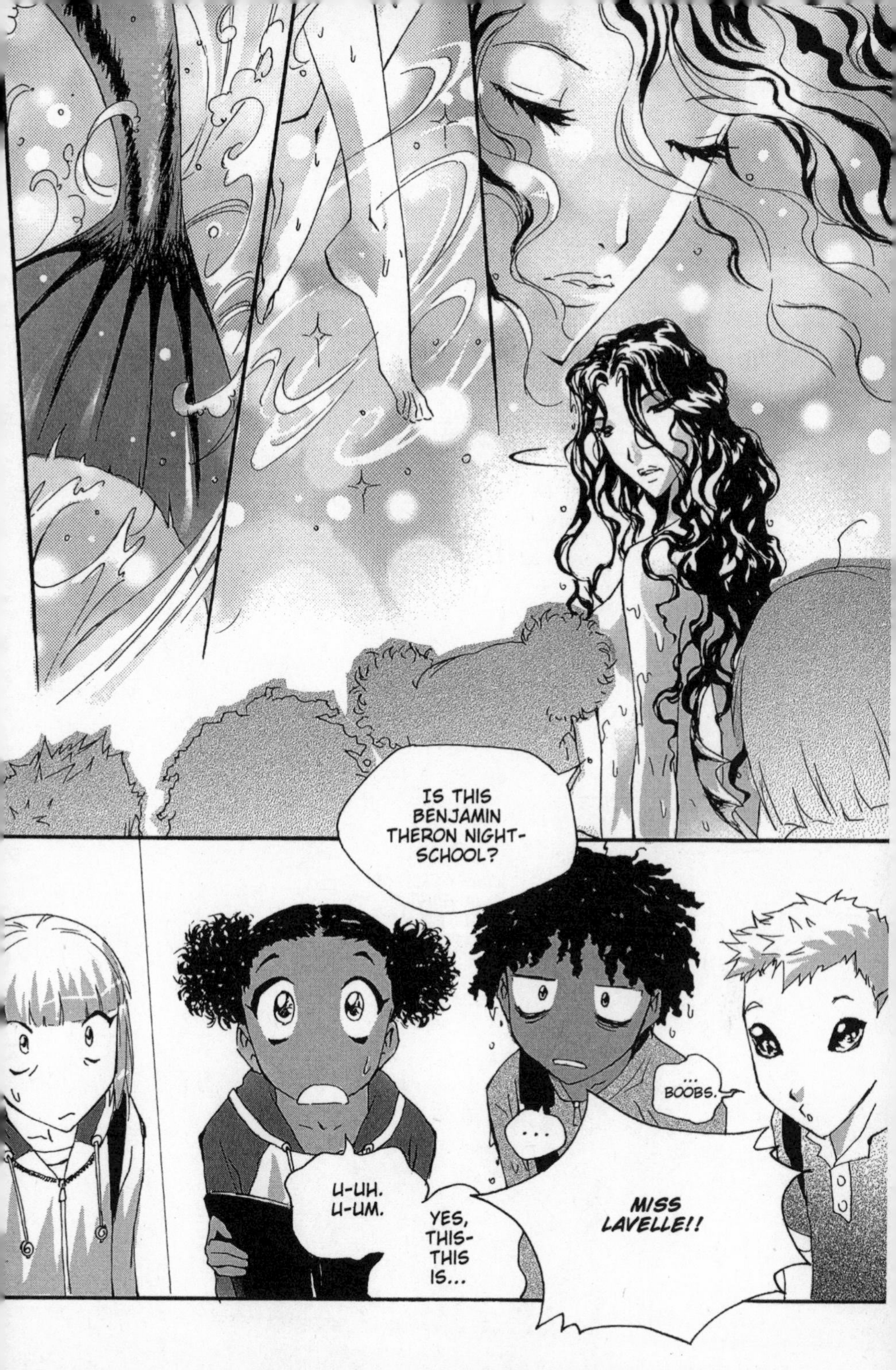

IS THIS BENJAMIN THERON NIGHT-SCHOOL?
U-UH. U-UM.
YES, THIS- THIS IS...
...
MISS LAVELLE!!
... BOOBS.

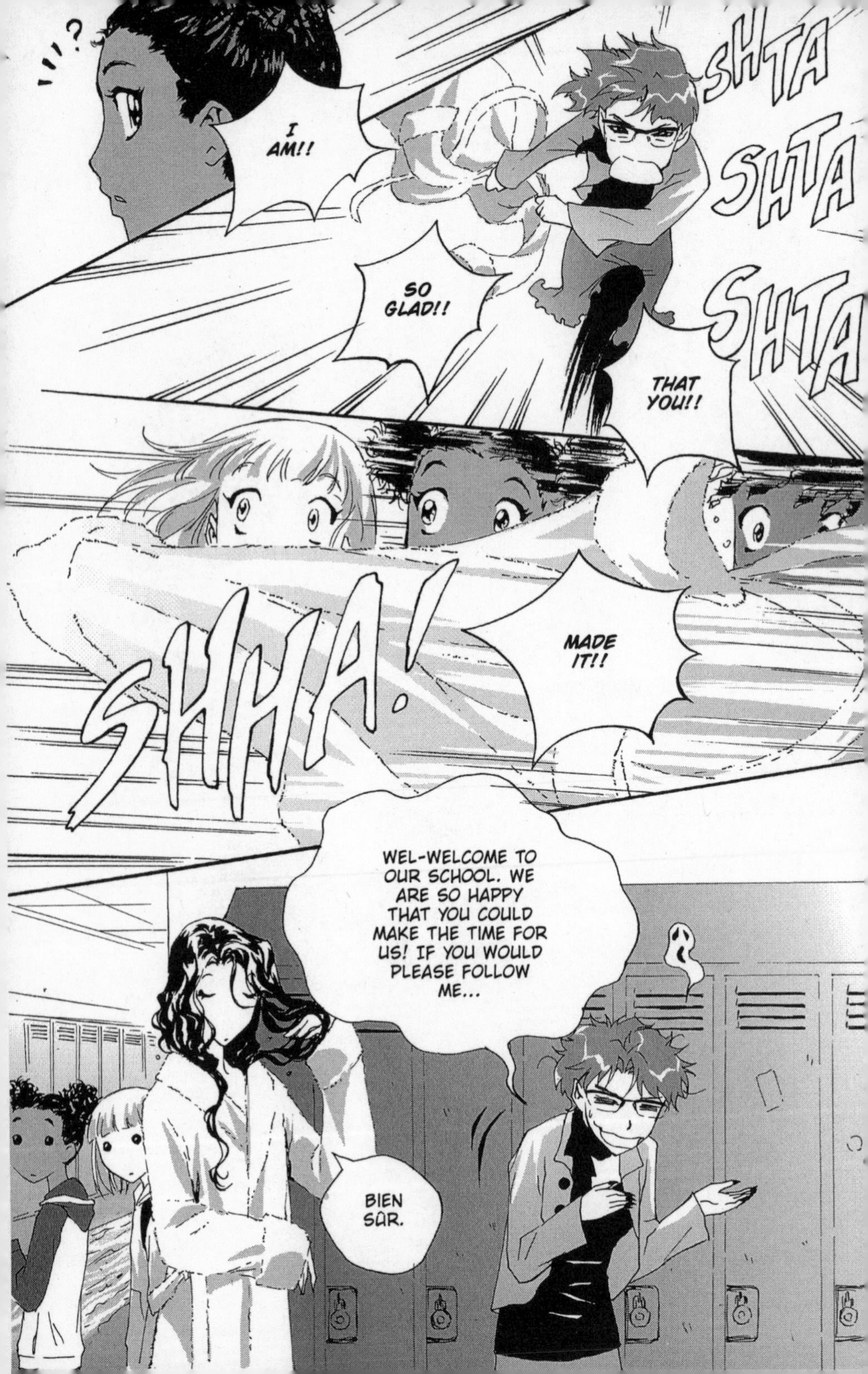

?
I AM!!
SHTA
SHTA
SO GLAD!!
SHTA
THAT YOU!!
SHHA!
MADE IT!!
WEL-WELCOME TO OUR SCHOOL. WE ARE SO HAPPY THAT YOU COULD MAKE THE TIME FOR US! IF YOU WOULD PLEASE FOLLOW ME...
BIEN SÛR.

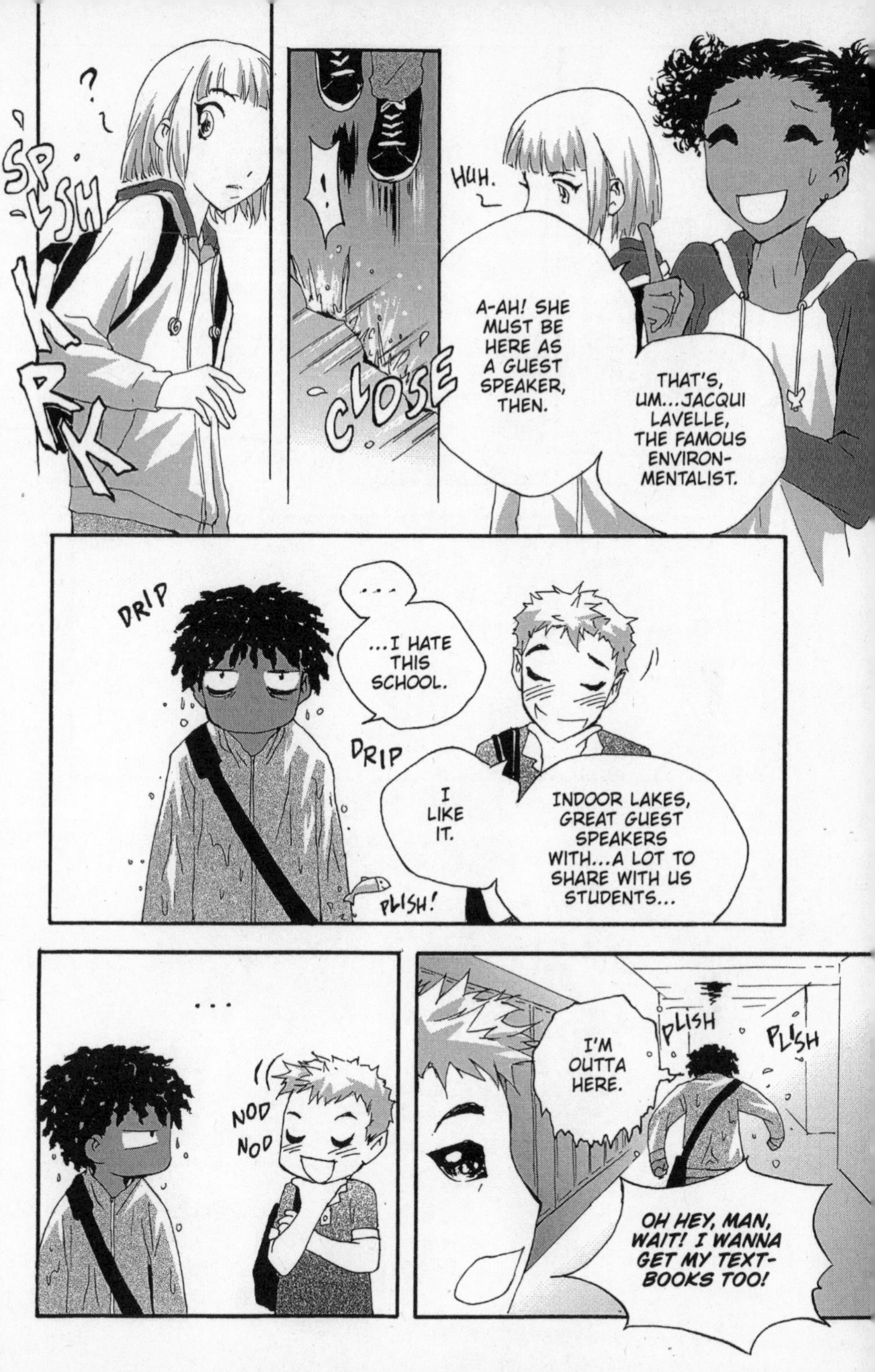
SPLSH
KRRK
!
CLOSE
HUH.
A-AH! SHE MUST BE HERE AS A GUEST SPEAKER, THEN.
THAT'S, UM...JACQUI LAVELLE, THE FAMOUS ENVIRON-MENTALIST.
DRIP
...
...I HATE THIS SCHOOL.
DRIP
I LIKE IT.
INDOOR LAKES, GREAT GUEST SPEAKERS WITH...A LOT TO SHARE WITH US STUDENTS...
PLISH!
...
NOD NOD
I'M OUTTA HERE.
PLISH
PLISH
OH HEY, MAN, WAIT! I WANNA GET MY TEXT-BOOKS TOO!

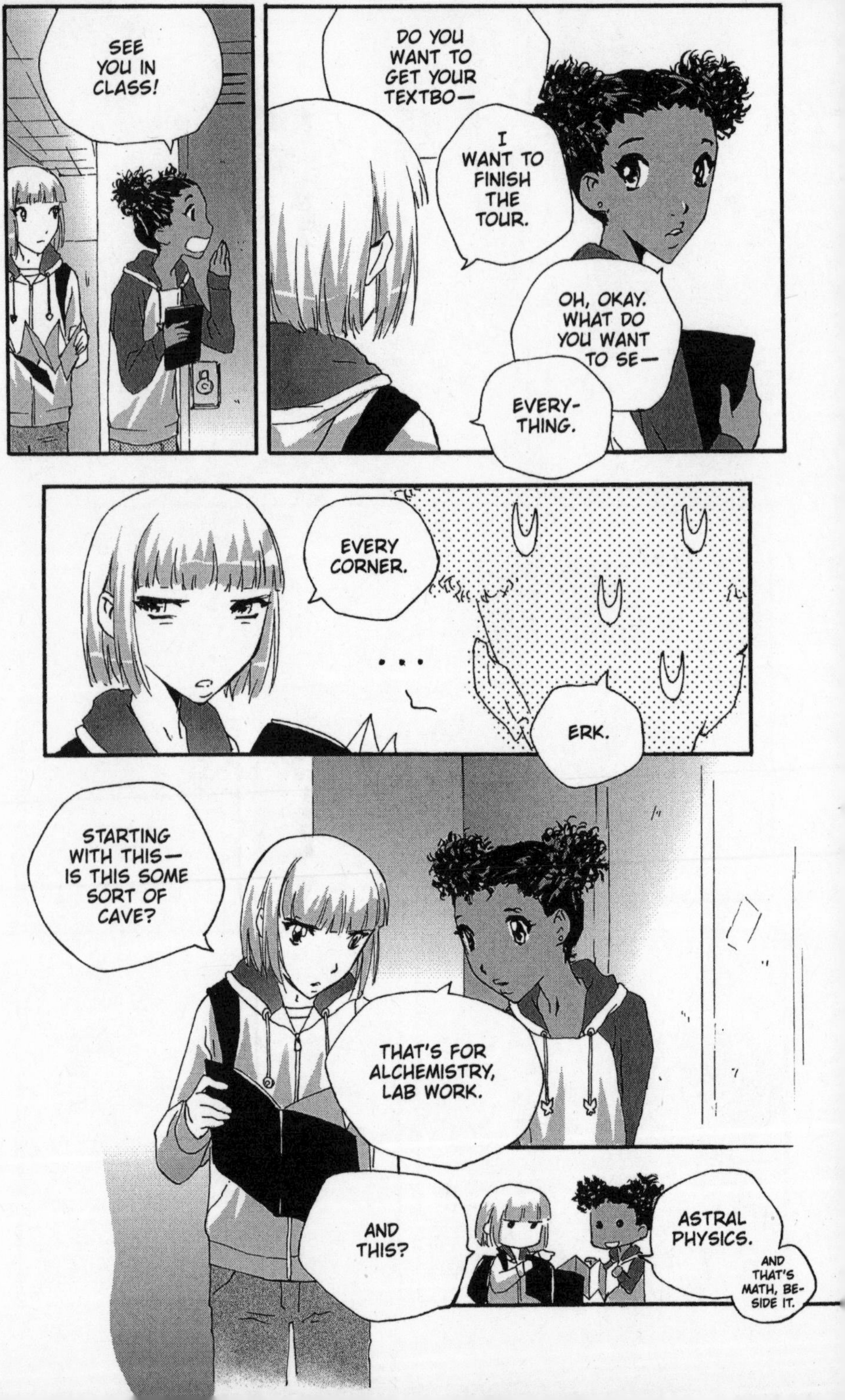
SEE YOU IN CLASS!
DO YOU WANT TO GET YOUR TEXTBO—
I WANT TO FINISH THE TOUR.
OH, OKAY. WHAT DO YOU WANT TO SE—
EVERY-THING.
EVERY CORNER.
...
ERK.
STARTING WITH THIS— IS THIS SOME SORT OF CAVE?
THAT'S FOR ALCHEMISTRY, LAB WORK.
AND THIS?
ASTRAL PHYSICS.
AND THAT'S MATH, BE-SIDE IT.

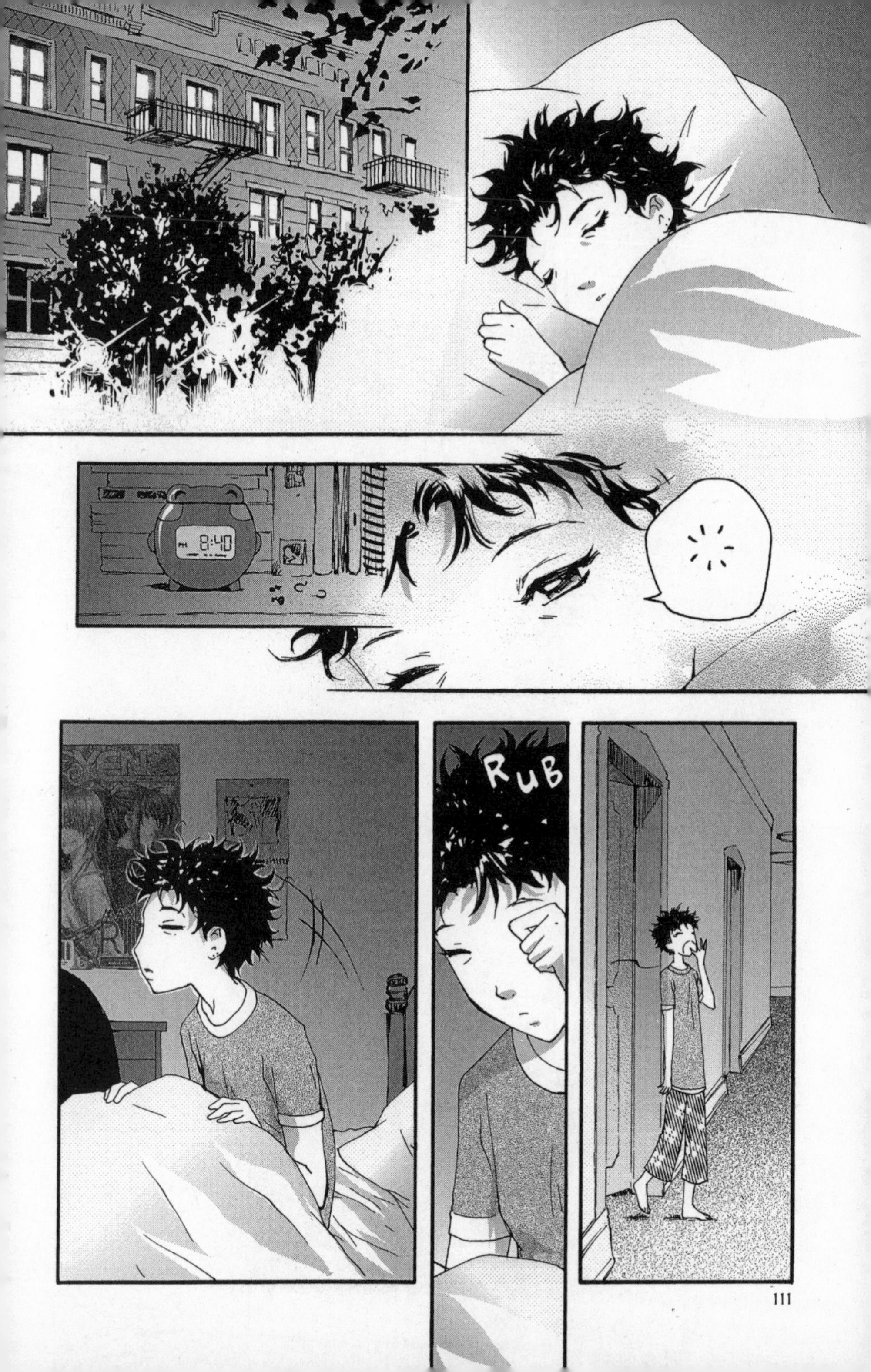
8:40
RUB

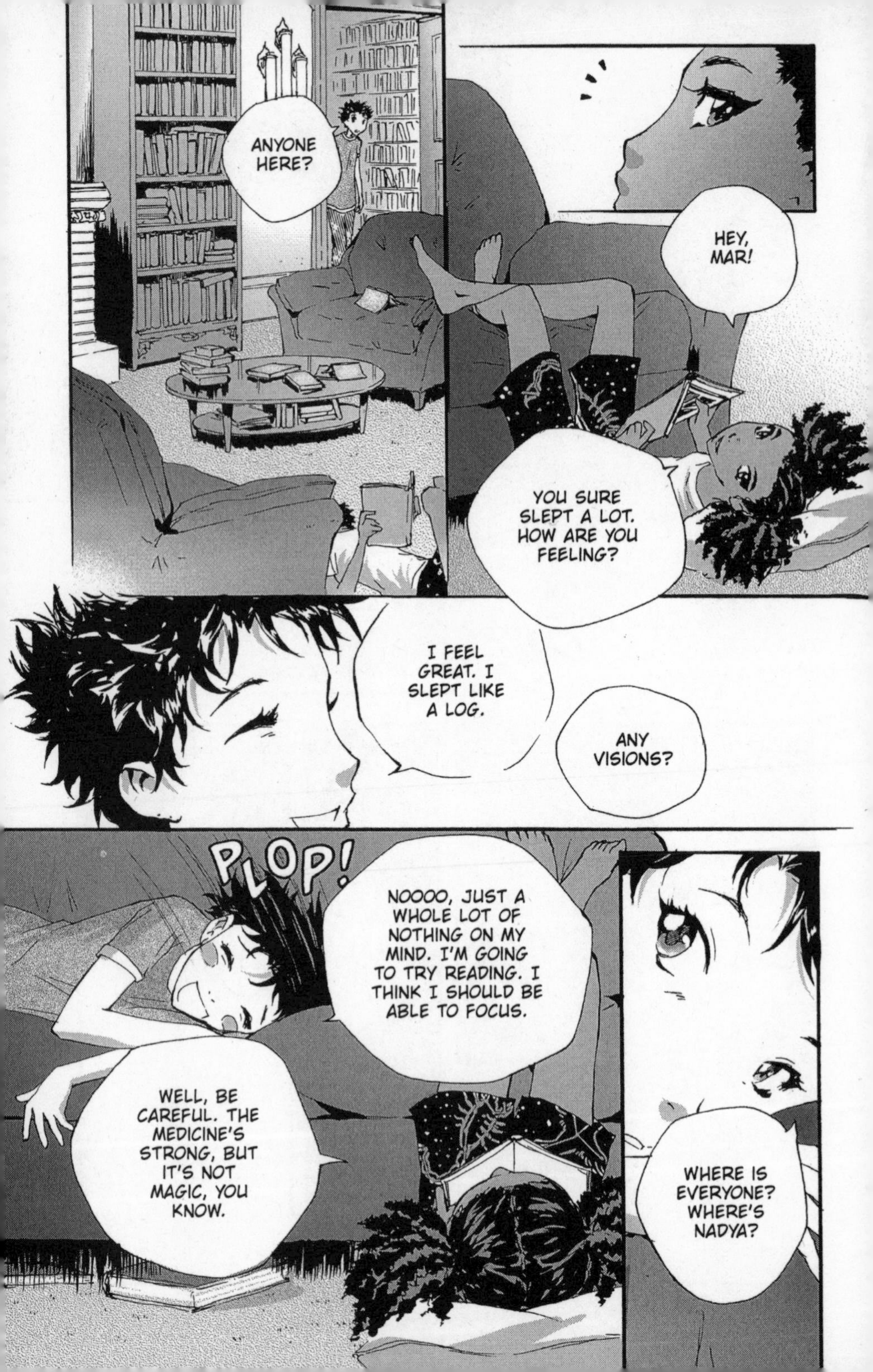
ANYONE HERE?
HEY, MAR!
YOU SURE SLEPT A LOT. HOW ARE YOU FEELING?
I FEEL GREAT. I SLEPT LIKE A LOG.
ANY VISIONS?
PLOP!
NOOOO, JUST A WHOLE LOT OF NOTHING ON MY MIND. I'M GOING TO TRY READING. I THINK I SHOULD BE ABLE TO FOCUS.
WELL, BE CAREFUL. THE MEDICINE'S STRONG, BUT IT'S NOT MAGIC, YOU KNOW.
WHERE IS EVERYONE? WHERE'S NADYA?

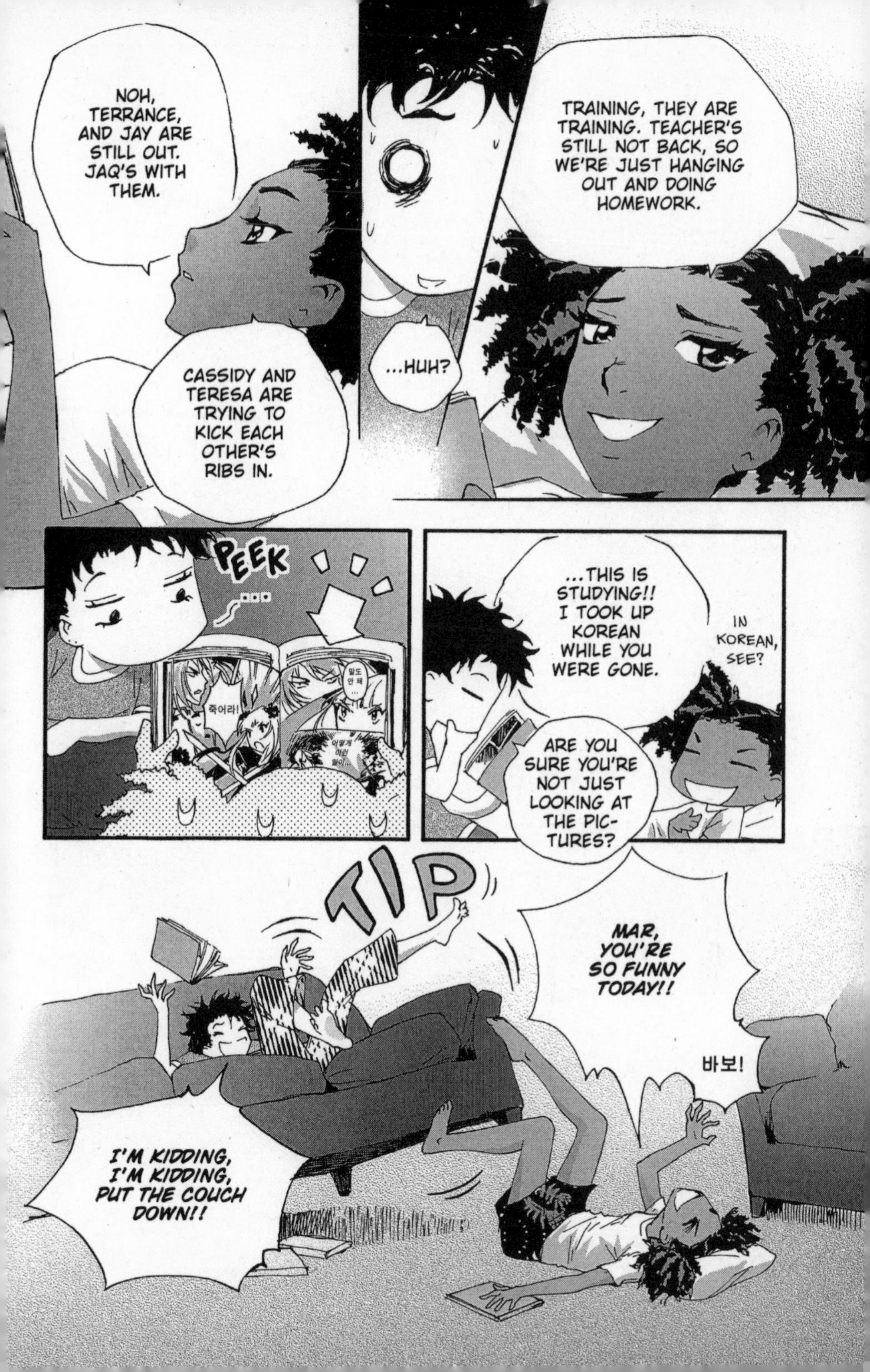

NOH, TERRANCE, AND JAY ARE STILL OUT. JAQ'S WITH THEM.
CASSIDY AND TERESA ARE TRYING TO KICK EACH OTHER'S RIBS IN.
...HUH?
TRAINING, THEY ARE TRAINING. TEACHER'S STILL NOT BACK, SO WE'RE JUST HANGING OUT AND DOING HOMEWORK.
PEEK
죽어라!
...THIS IS STUDYING!! I TOOK UP KOREAN WHILE YOU WERE GONE.
IN KOREAN, SEE?
ARE YOU SURE YOU'RE NOT JUST LOOKING AT THE PIC-TURES?
TIP
MAR, YOU'RE SO FUNNY TODAY!!
바보!
I'M KIDDING, I'M KIDDING, PUT THE COUCH DOWN!!

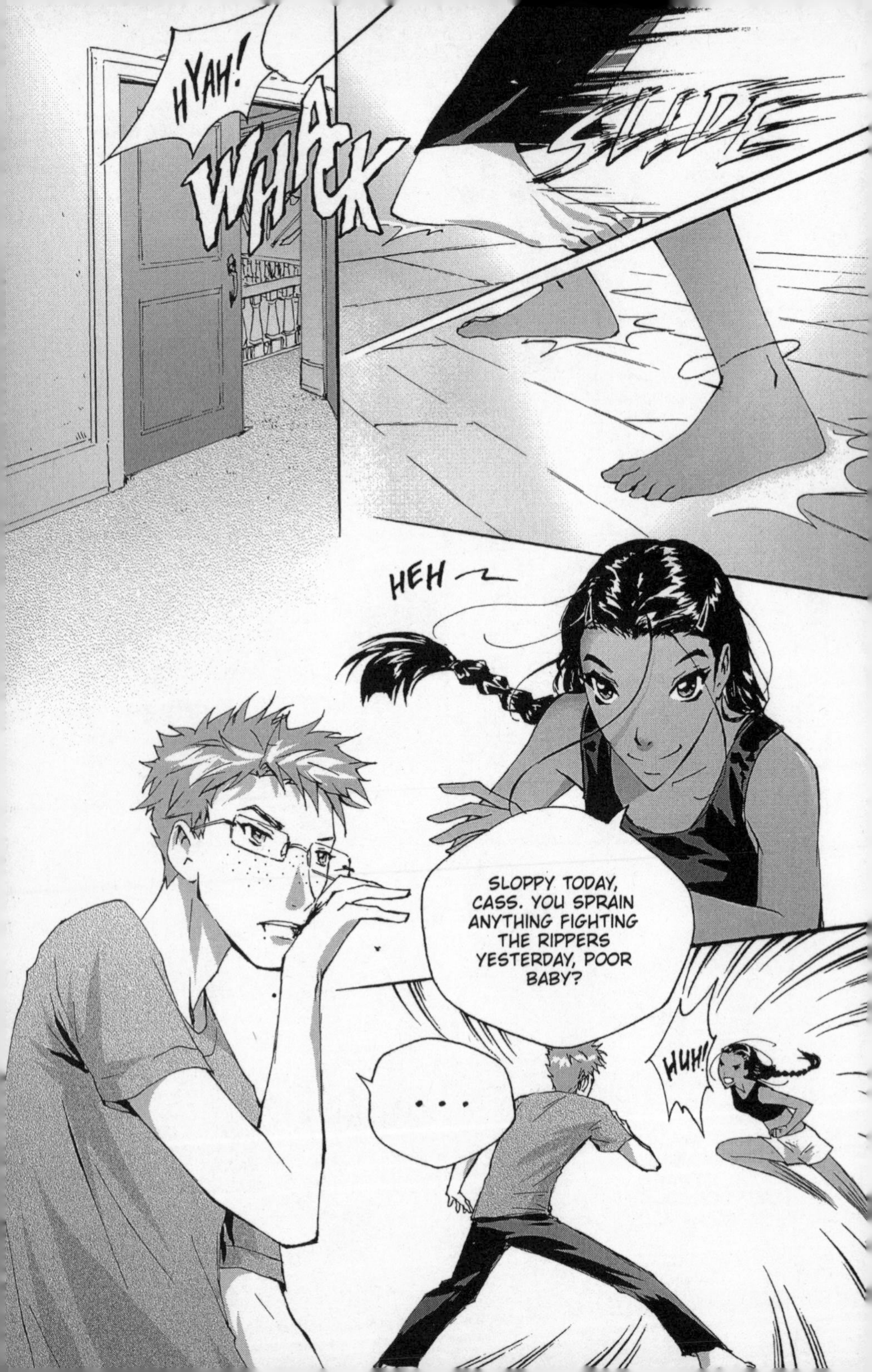
HYAH!
WHACK
SLIDE
HEH~
SLOPPY TODAY, CASS. YOU SPRAIN ANYTHING FIGHTING THE RIPPERS YESTERDAY, POOR BABY?
...
HUH!

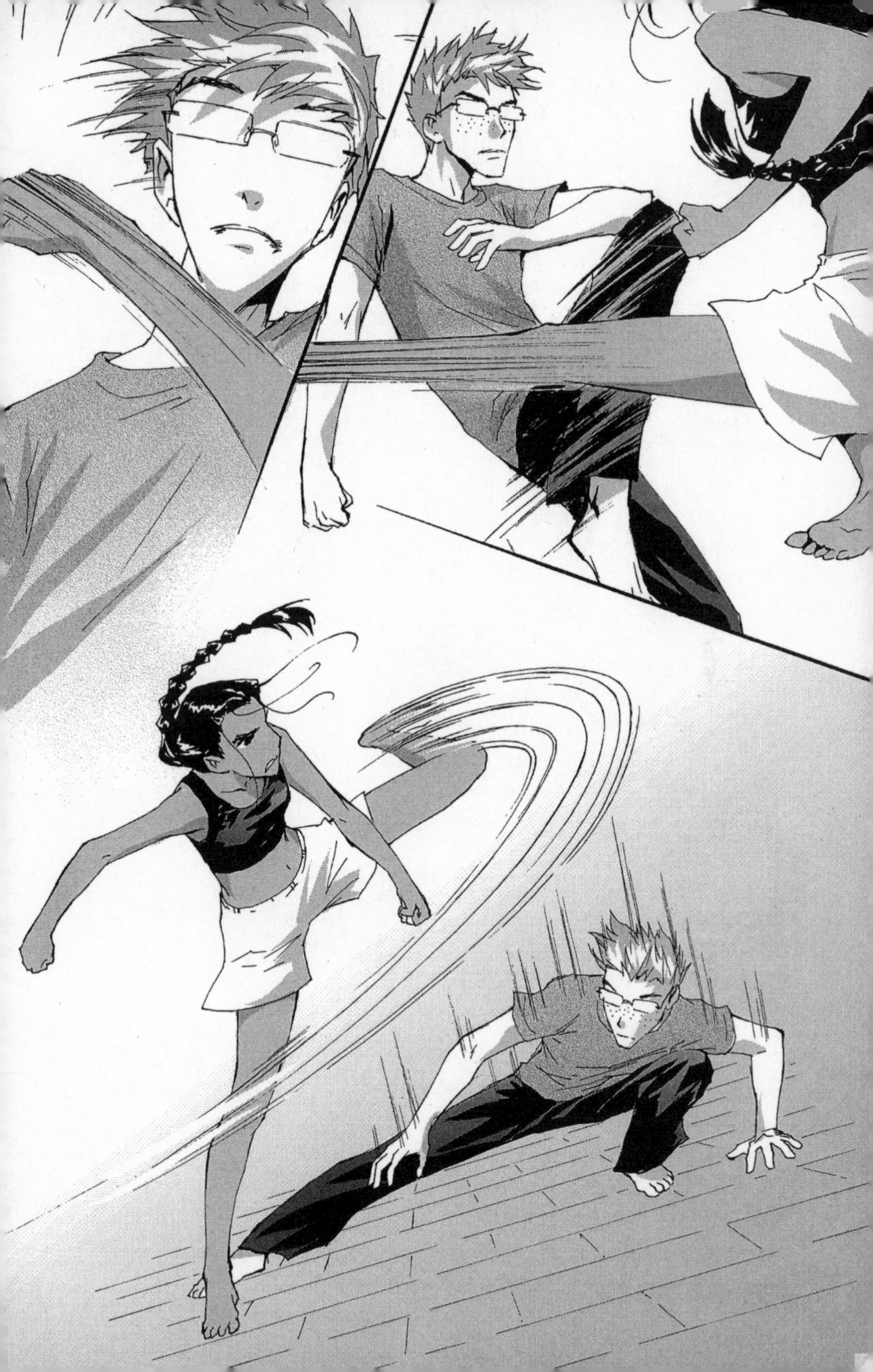

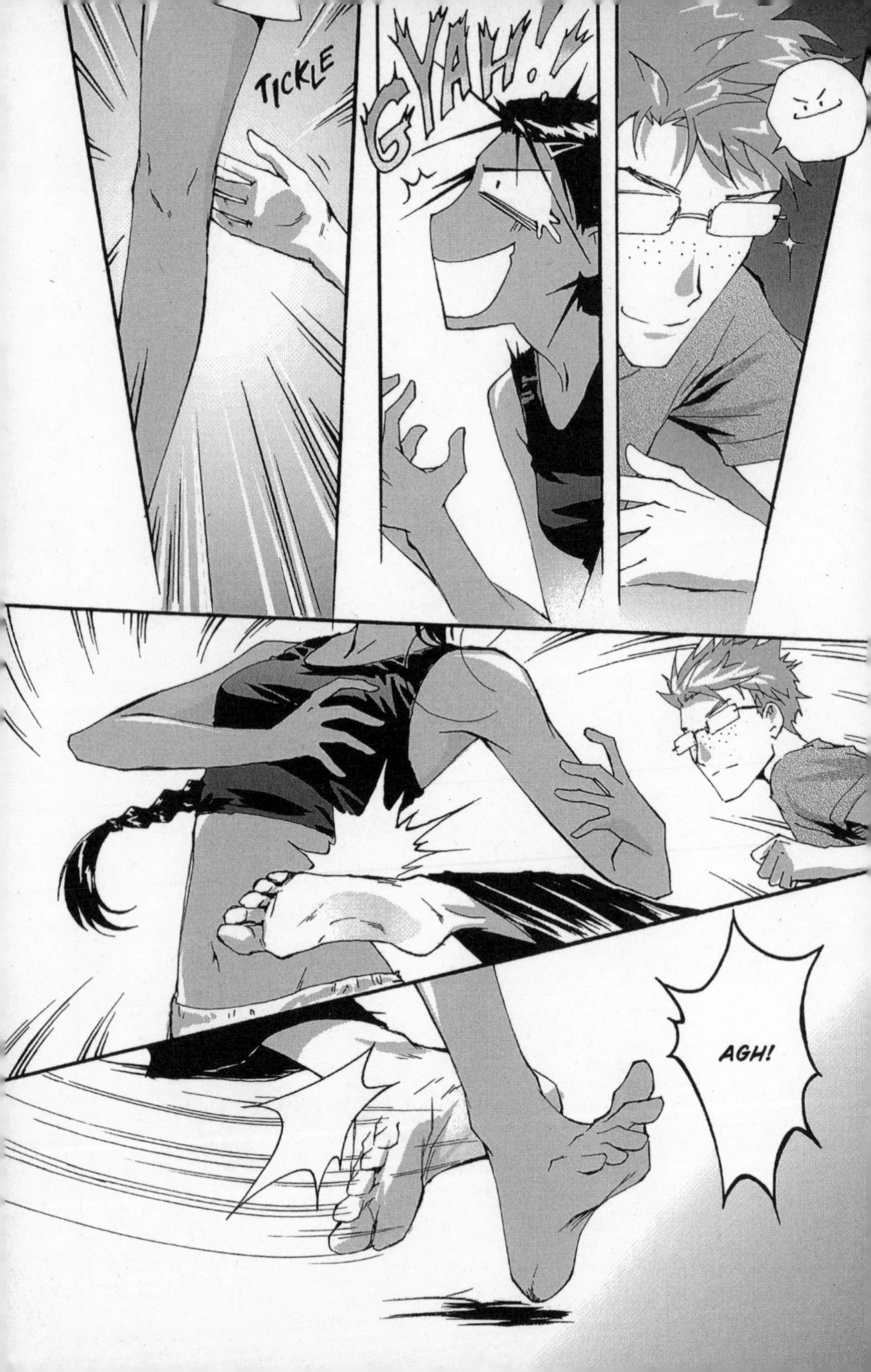
TICKLE
GYAH!!
AGH!

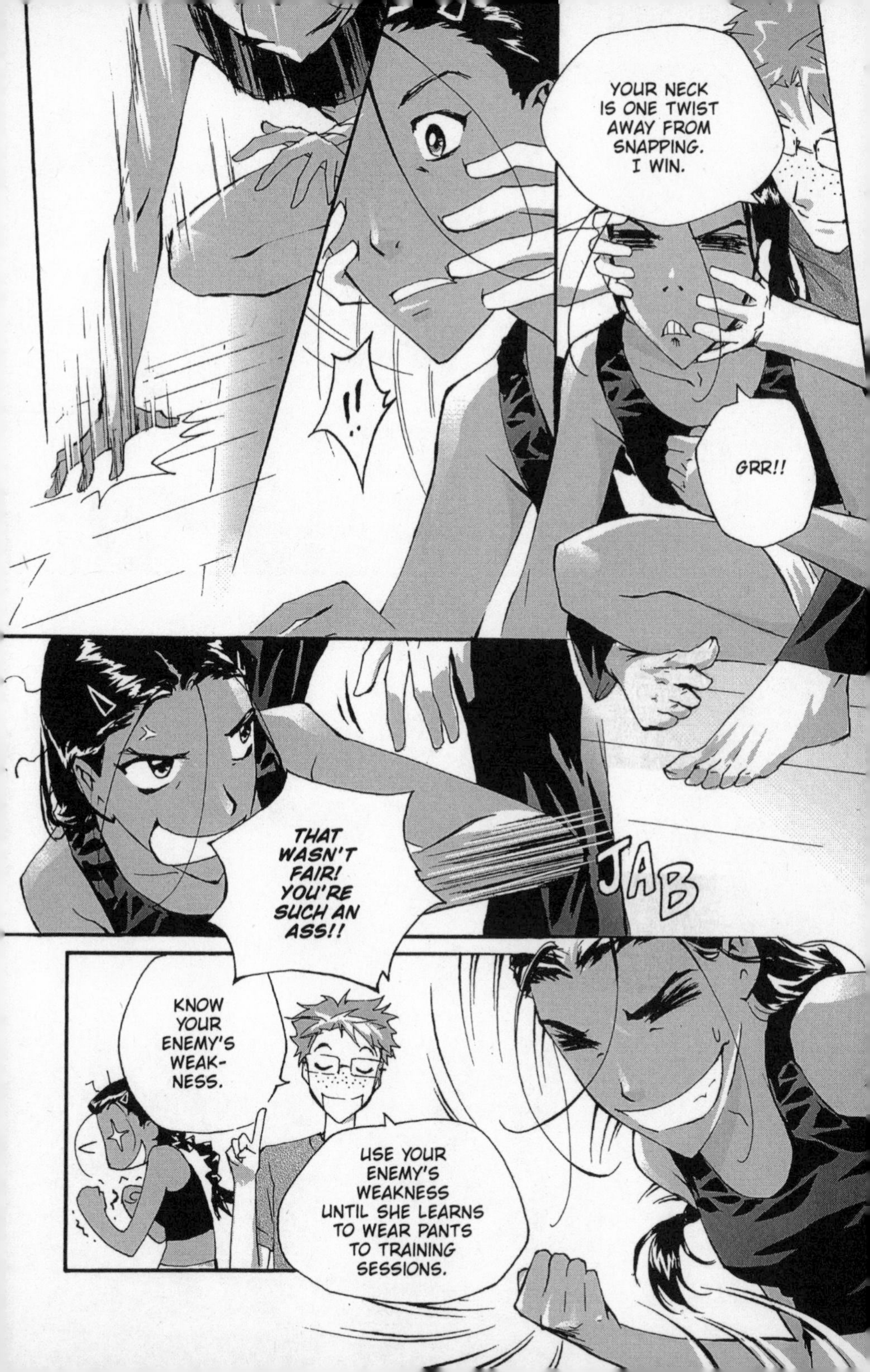
!!
YOUR NECK IS ONE TWIST AWAY FROM SNAPPING. I WIN.
GRR!!
THAT WASN'T FAIR! YOU'RE SUCH AN ASS!!
JAB
KNOW YOUR ENEMY'S WEAK-NESS.
USE YOUR ENEMY'S WEAKNESS UNTIL SHE LEARNS TO WEAR PANTS TO TRAINING SESSIONS.

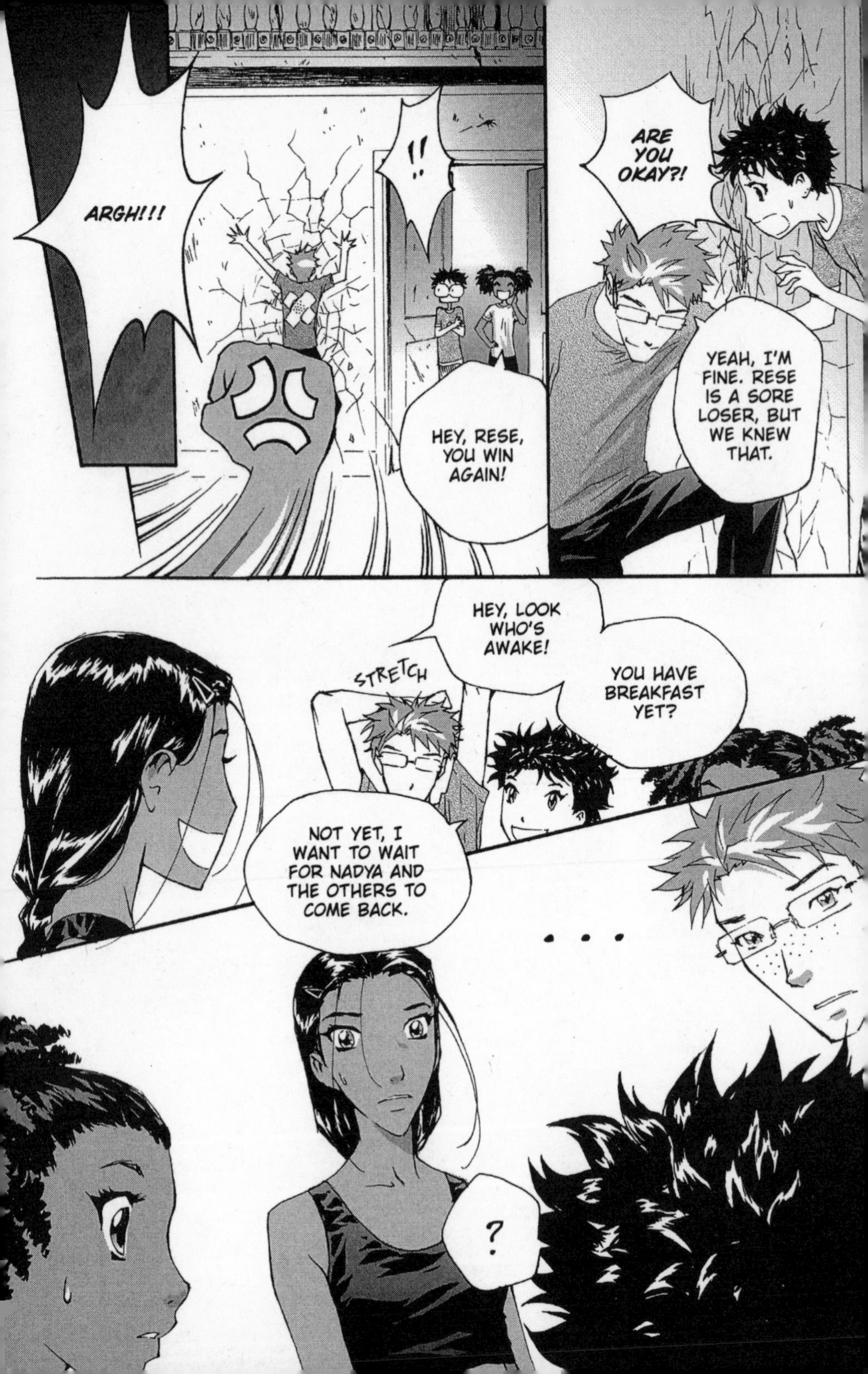
ARGH!!!
!!
HEY, RESE, YOU WIN AGAIN!
ARE YOU OKAY?!
YEAH, I'M FINE. RESE IS A SORE LOSER, BUT WE KNEW THAT.
HEY, LOOK WHO'S AWAKE!
STRETCH
YOU HAVE BREAKFAST YET?
NOT YET, I WANT TO WAIT FOR NADYA AND THE OTHERS TO COME BACK.
...
?

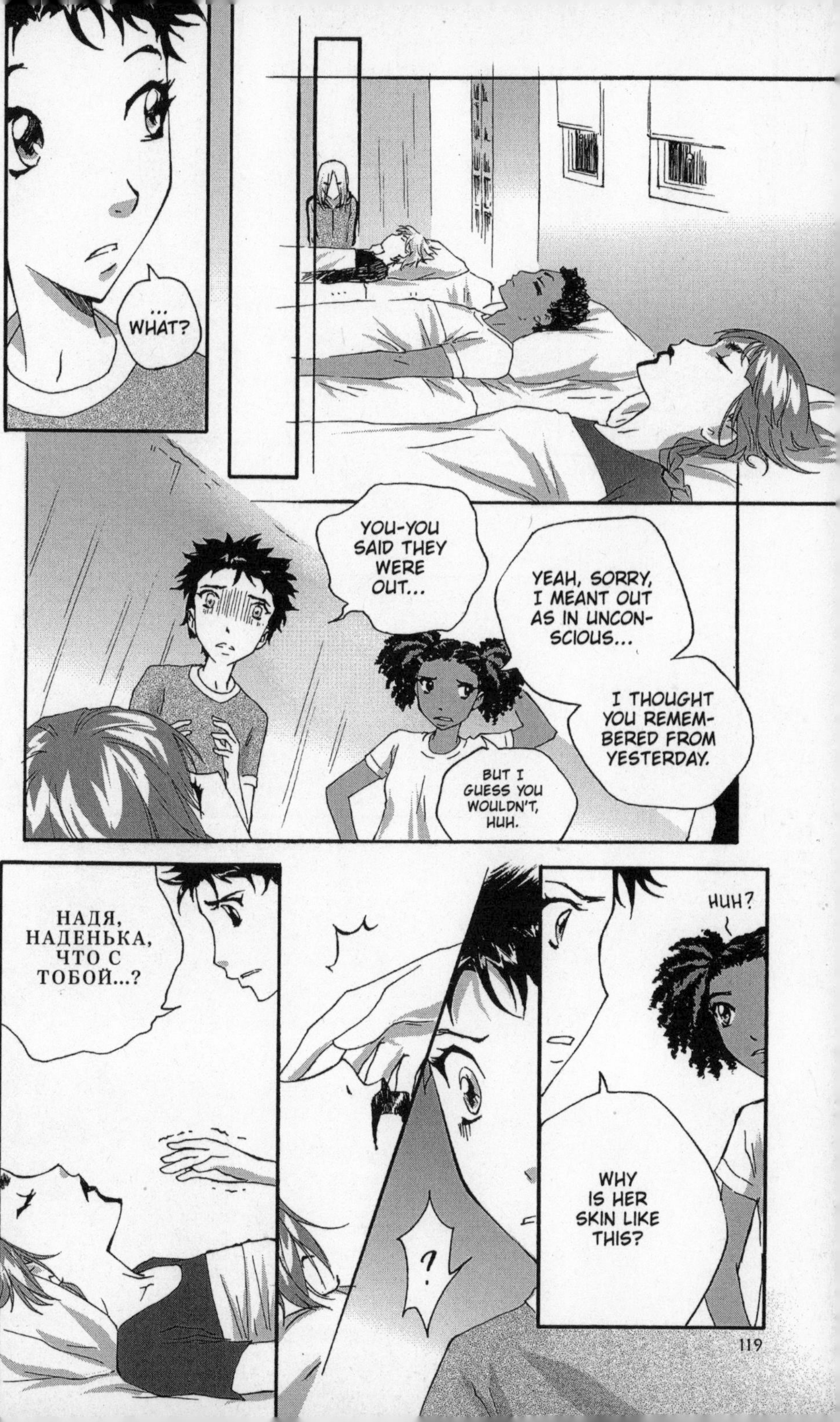
... WHAT?
YOU-YOU SAID THEY WERE OUT...
YEAH, SORRY, I MEANT OUT AS IN UNCON-SCIOUS...
I THOUGHT YOU REMEM-BERED FROM YESTERDAY.
BUT I GUESS YOU WOULDN'T, HUH.
НАДЯ, НАДЕНЬКА, ЧТО С ТОБОЙ...?
?
HUH?
WHY IS HER SKIN LIKE THIS?

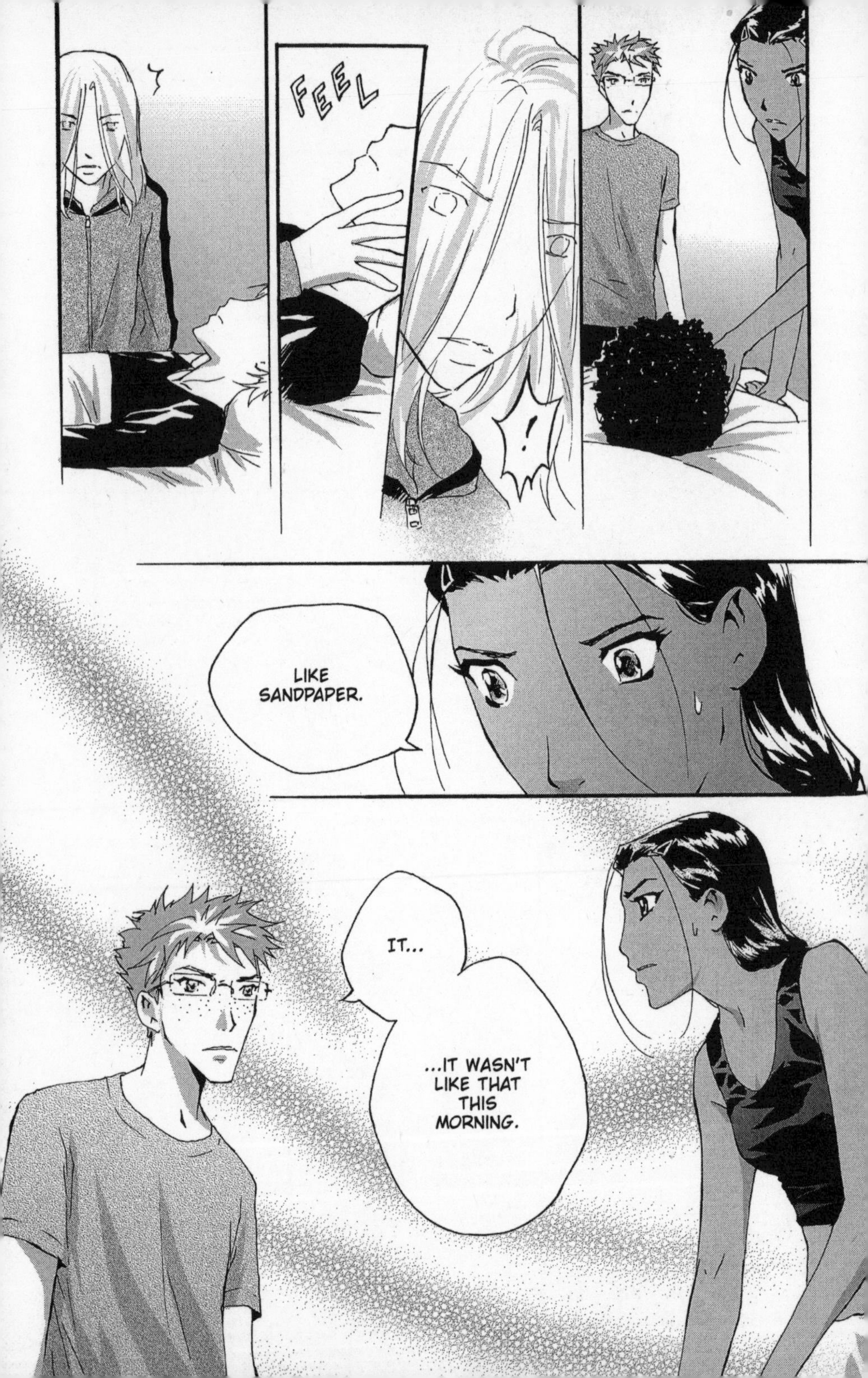
FEEL
!
LIKE SANDPAPER.
IT...
...IT WASN'T LIKE THAT THIS MORNING.

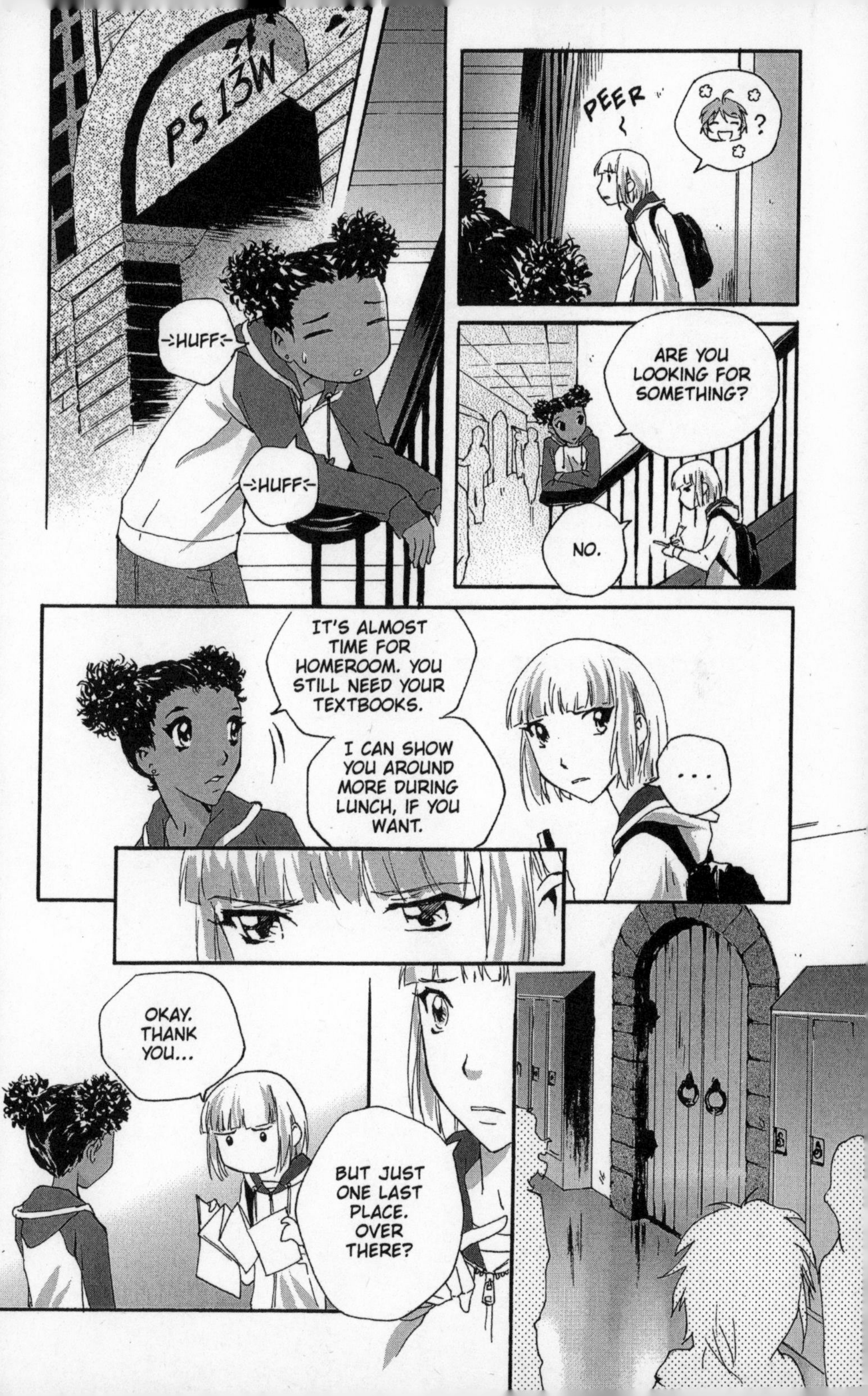
PS 13W
HUFF
HUFF
PEER
?
ARE YOU LOOKING FOR SOMETHING?
NO.
IT'S ALMOST TIME FOR HOMEROOM. YOU STILL NEED YOUR TEXTBOOKS.
I CAN SHOW YOU AROUND MORE DURING LUNCH, IF YOU WANT.
...
OKAY. THANK YOU...
BUT JUST ONE LAST PLACE. OVER THERE?

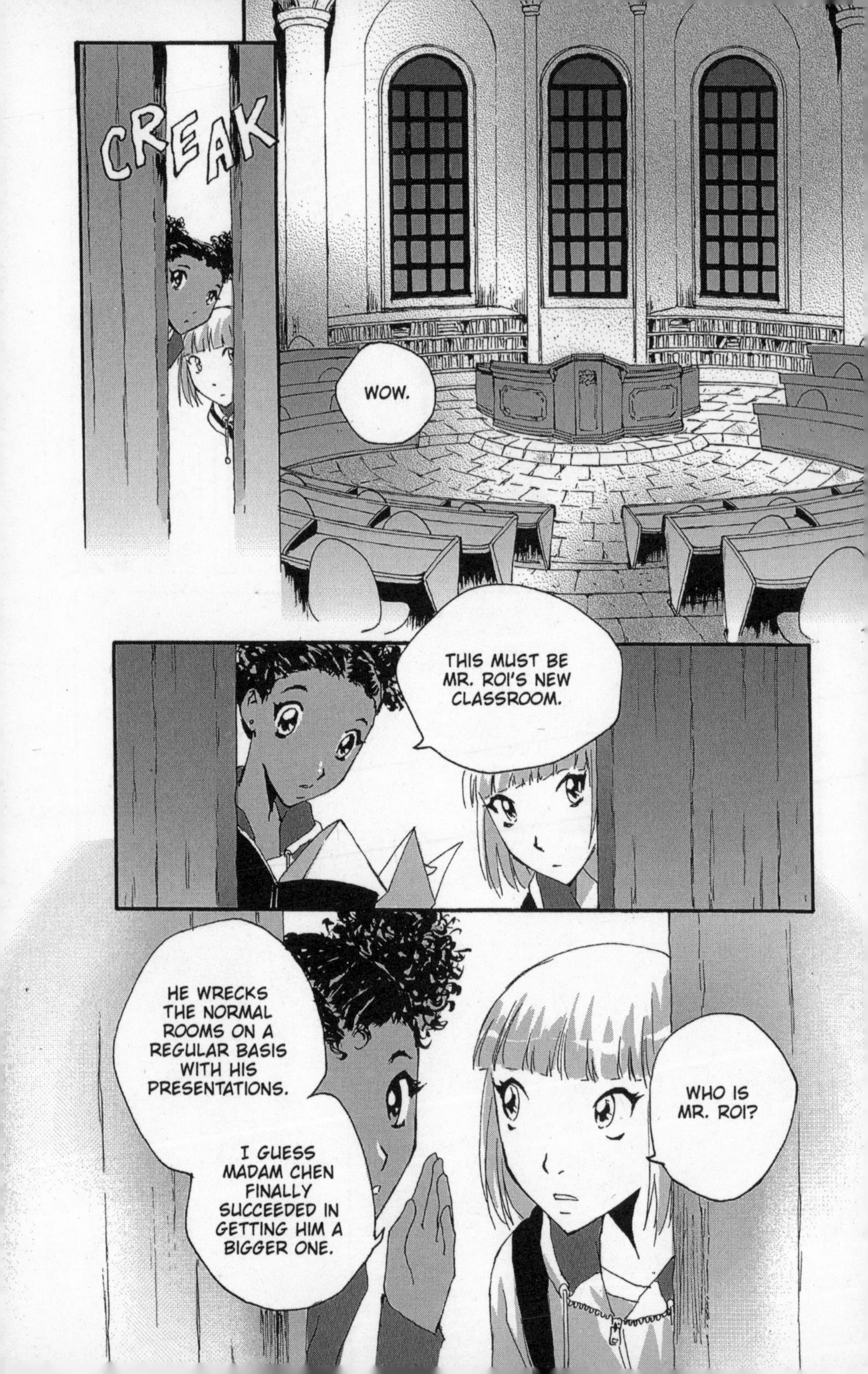
CREAK
WOW.
THIS MUST BE MR. ROI'S NEW CLASSROOM.
HE WRECKS THE NORMAL ROOMS ON A REGULAR BASIS WITH HIS PRESENTATIONS.
I GUESS MADAM CHEN FINALLY SUCCEEDED IN GETTING HIM A BIGGER ONE.
WHO IS MR. ROI?

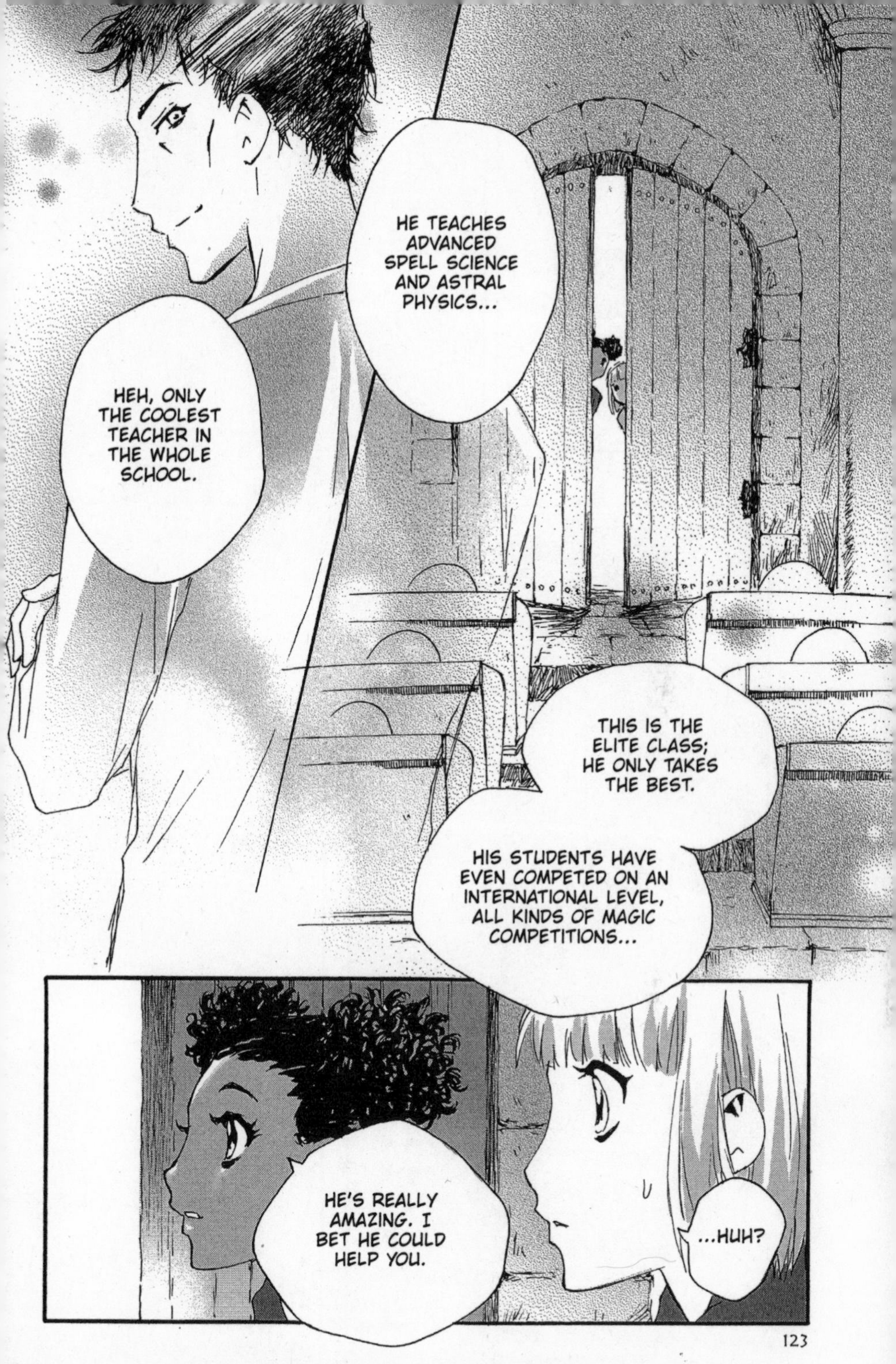
HE TEACHES ADVANCED SPELL SCIENCE AND ASTRAL PHYSICS...
HEH, ONLY THE COOLEST TEACHER IN THE WHOLE SCHOOL.
THIS IS THE ELITE CLASS; HE ONLY TAKES THE BEST.
HIS STUDENTS HAVE EVEN COMPETED ON AN INTERNATIONAL LEVEL, ALL KINDS OF MAGIC COMPETITIONS...
HE'S REALLY AMAZING. I BET HE COULD HELP YOU.
...HUH?

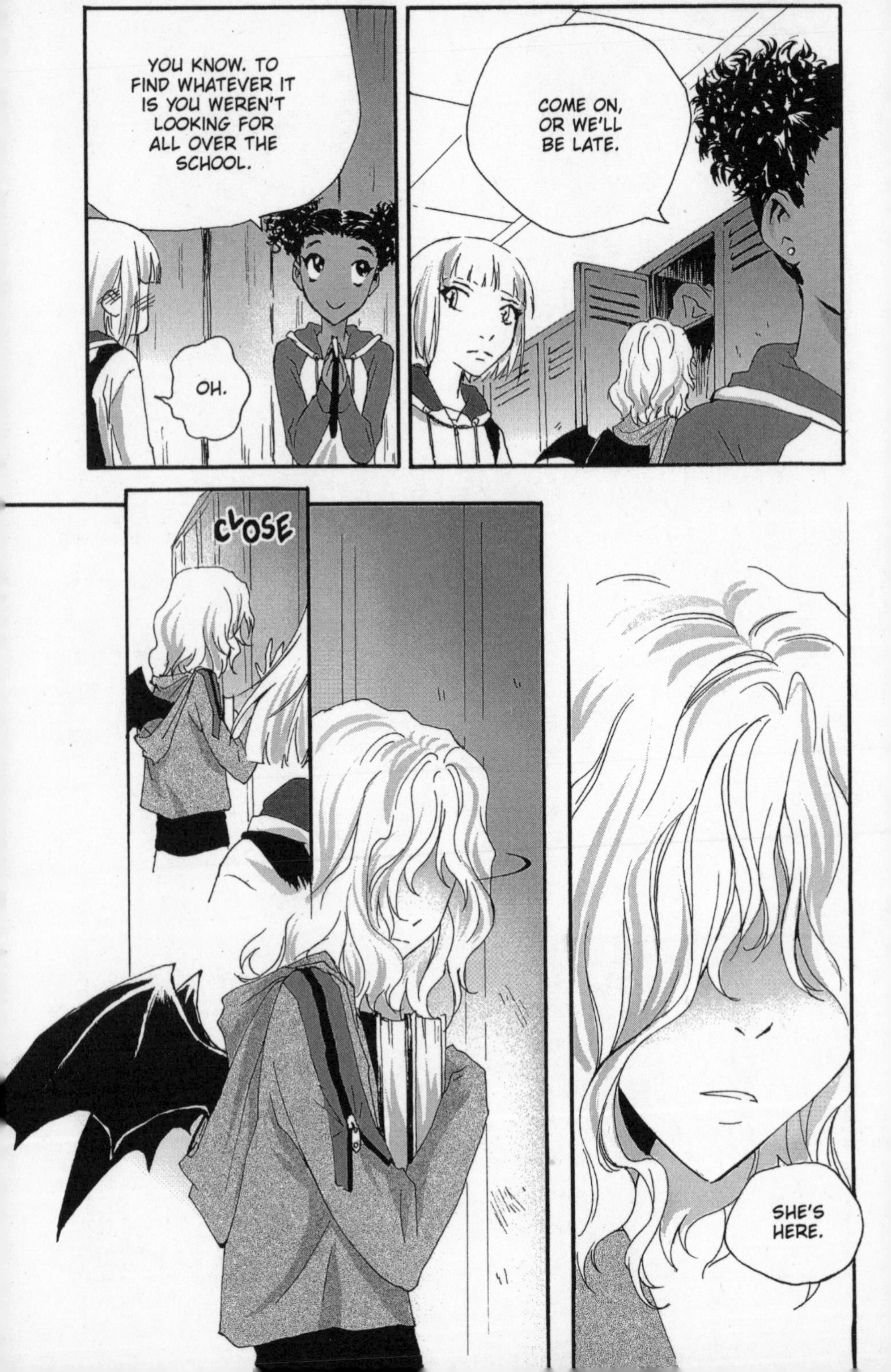
YOU KNOW. TO FIND WHATEVER IT IS YOU WEREN'T LOOKING FOR ALL OVER THE SCHOOL.
OH.
COME ON, OR WE'LL BE LATE.
CLOSE
SHE'S HERE.

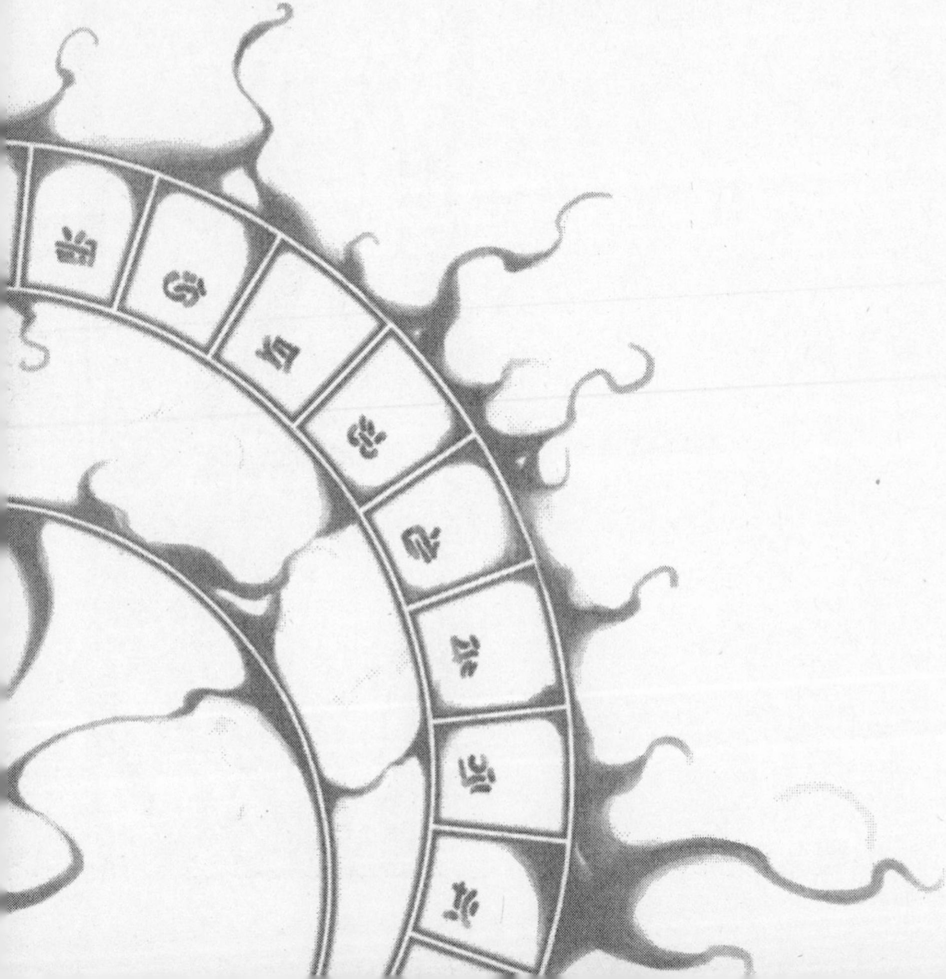

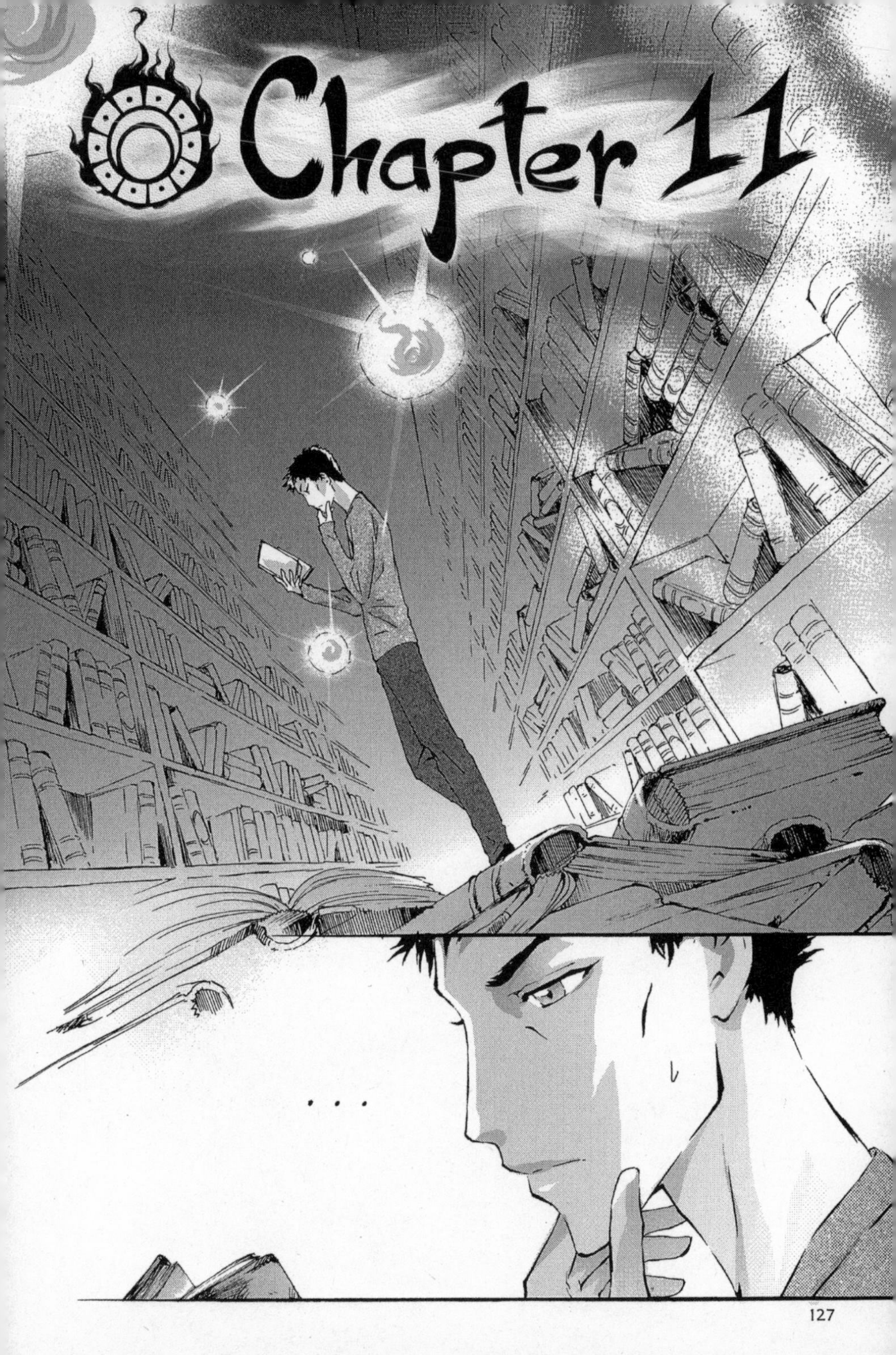
Chapter 11
. . .

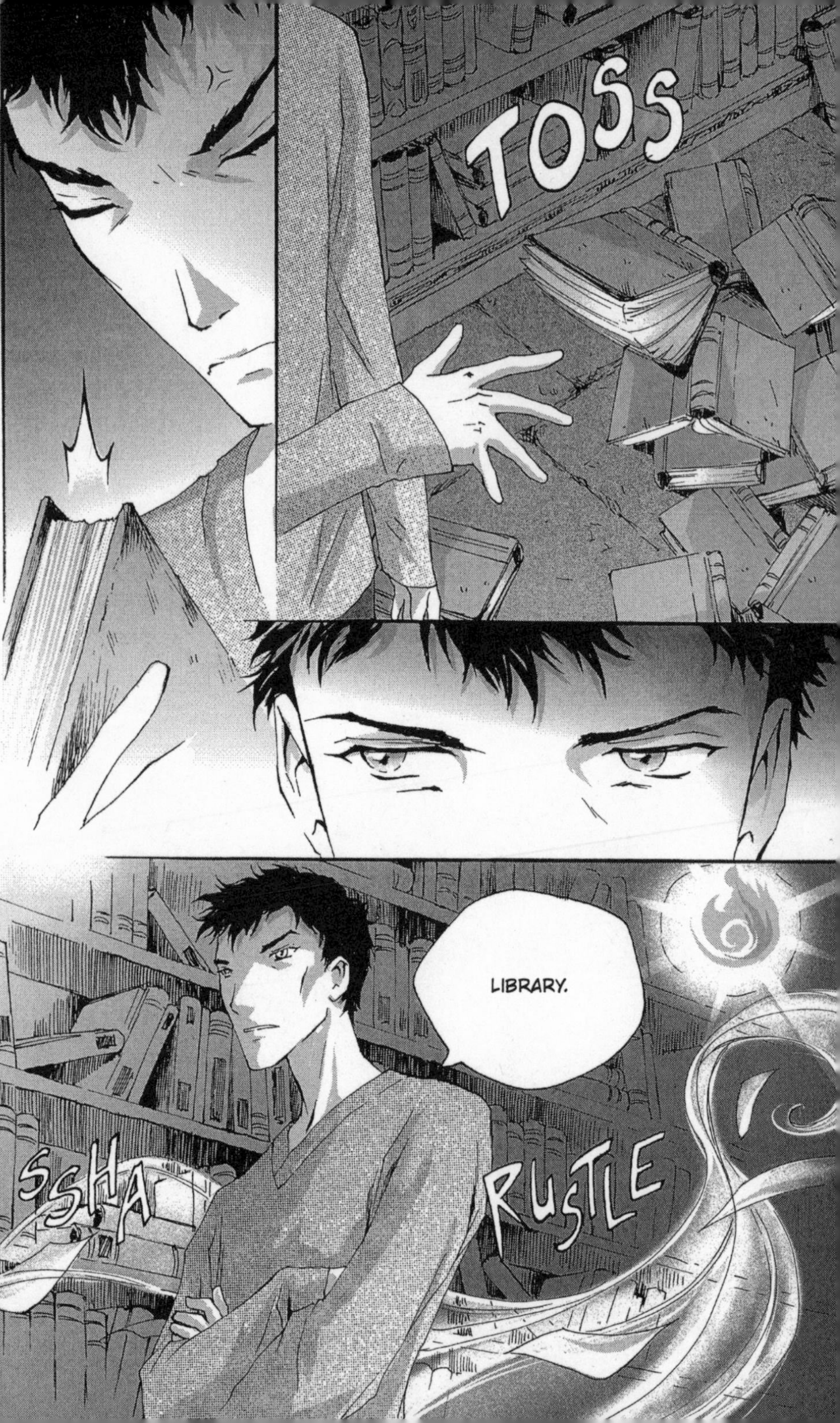
TOSS
LIBRARY.
SSHA
RUSTLE

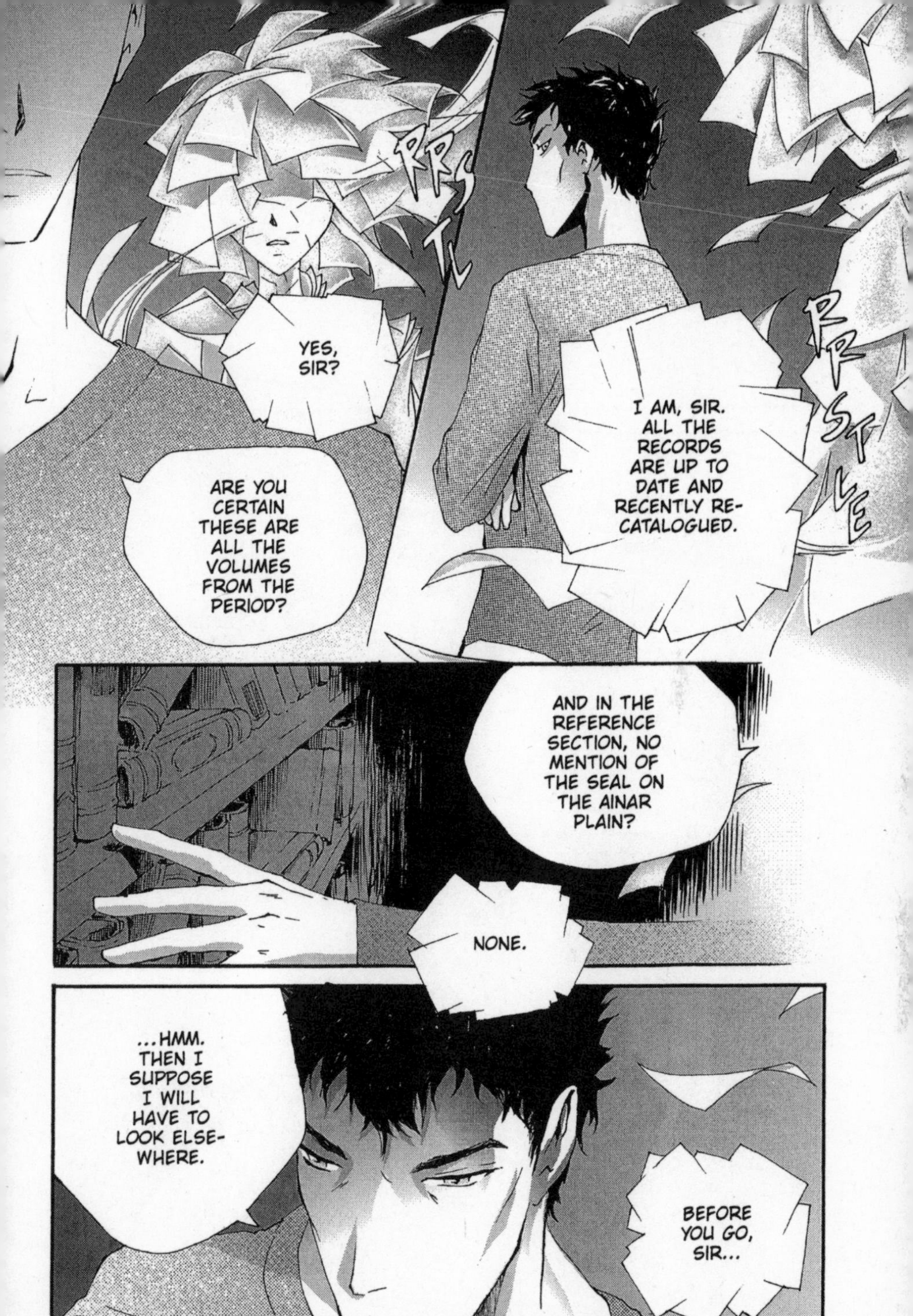
YES, SIR?
ARE YOU CERTAIN THESE ARE ALL THE VOLUMES FROM THE PERIOD?
RRSTL
I AM, SIR. ALL THE RECORDS ARE UP TO DATE AND RECENTLY RE-CATALOGUED.
RRRSTLE
AND IN THE REFERENCE SECTION, NO MENTION OF THE SEAL ON THE AINAR PLAIN?
NONE.
...HMM. THEN I SUPPOSE I WILL HAVE TO LOOK ELSE-WHERE.
BEFORE YOU GO, SIR...

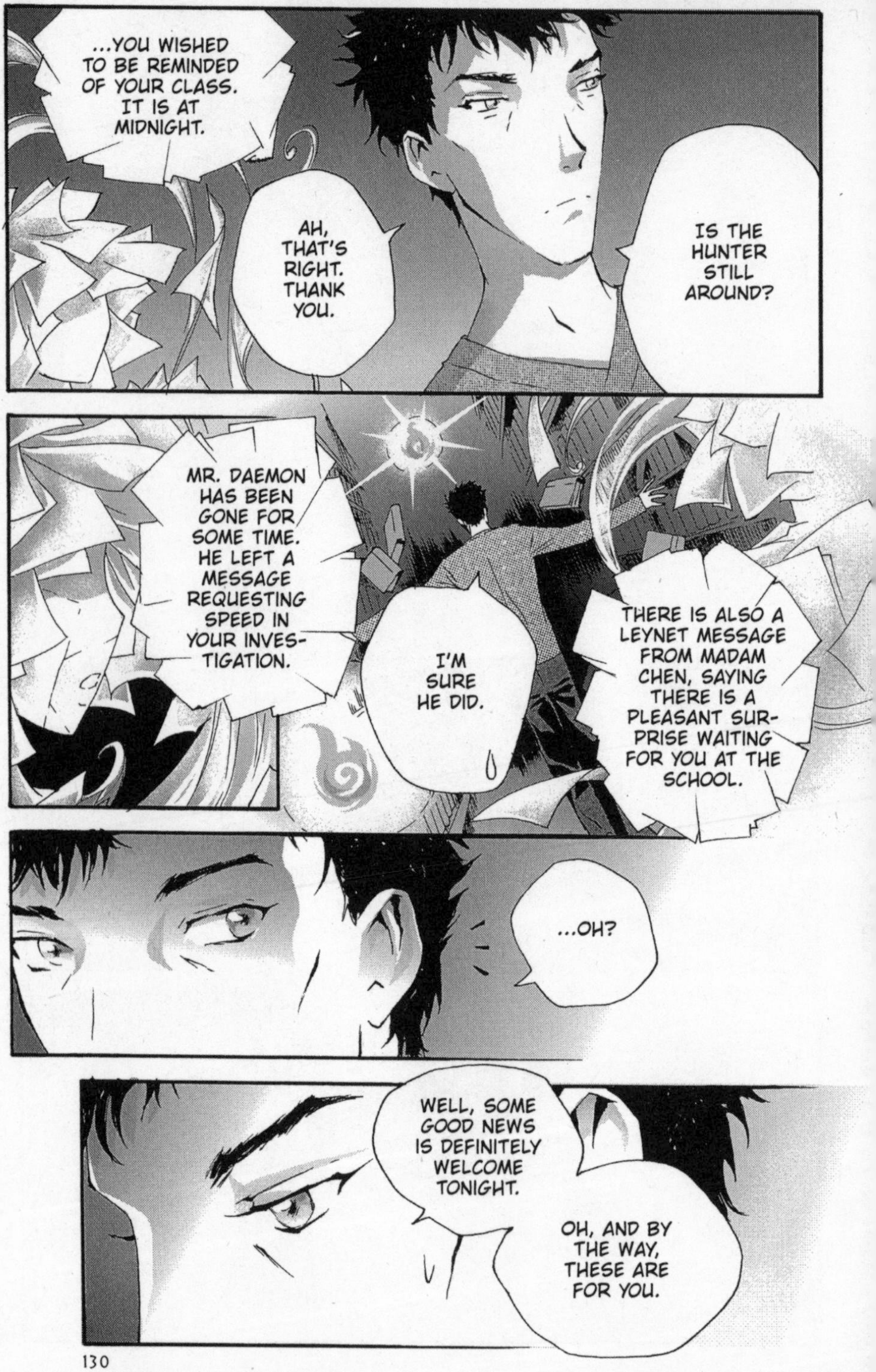
...YOU WISHED TO BE REMINDED OF YOUR CLASS. IT IS AT MIDNIGHT.
AH, THAT'S RIGHT. THANK YOU.
IS THE HUNTER STILL AROUND?
MR. DAEMON HAS BEEN GONE FOR SOME TIME. HE LEFT A MESSAGE REQUESTING SPEED IN YOUR INVES-TIGATION.
I'M SURE HE DID.
THERE IS ALSO A LEYNET MESSAGE FROM MADAM CHEN, SAYING THERE IS A PLEASANT SUR-PRISE WAITING FOR YOU AT THE SCHOOL.
...OH?
WELL, SOME GOOD NEWS IS DEFINITELY WELCOME TONIGHT.
OH, AND BY THE WAY, THESE ARE FOR YOU.

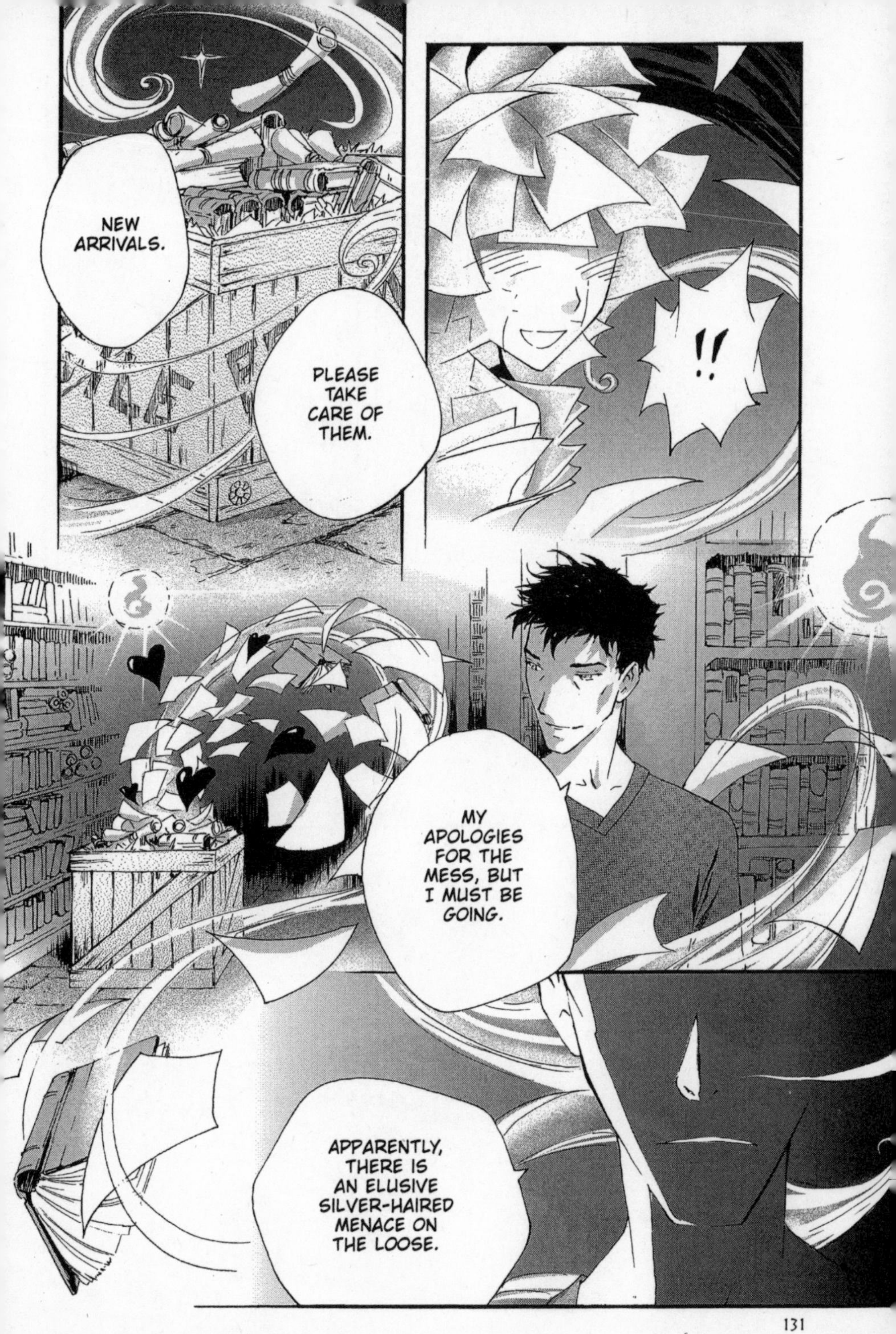
NEW ARRIVALS.
PLEASE TAKE CARE OF THEM.
!!
MY APOLOGIES FOR THE MESS, BUT I MUST BE GOING.
APPARENTLY, THERE IS AN ELUSIVE SILVER-HAIRED MENACE ON THE LOOSE.

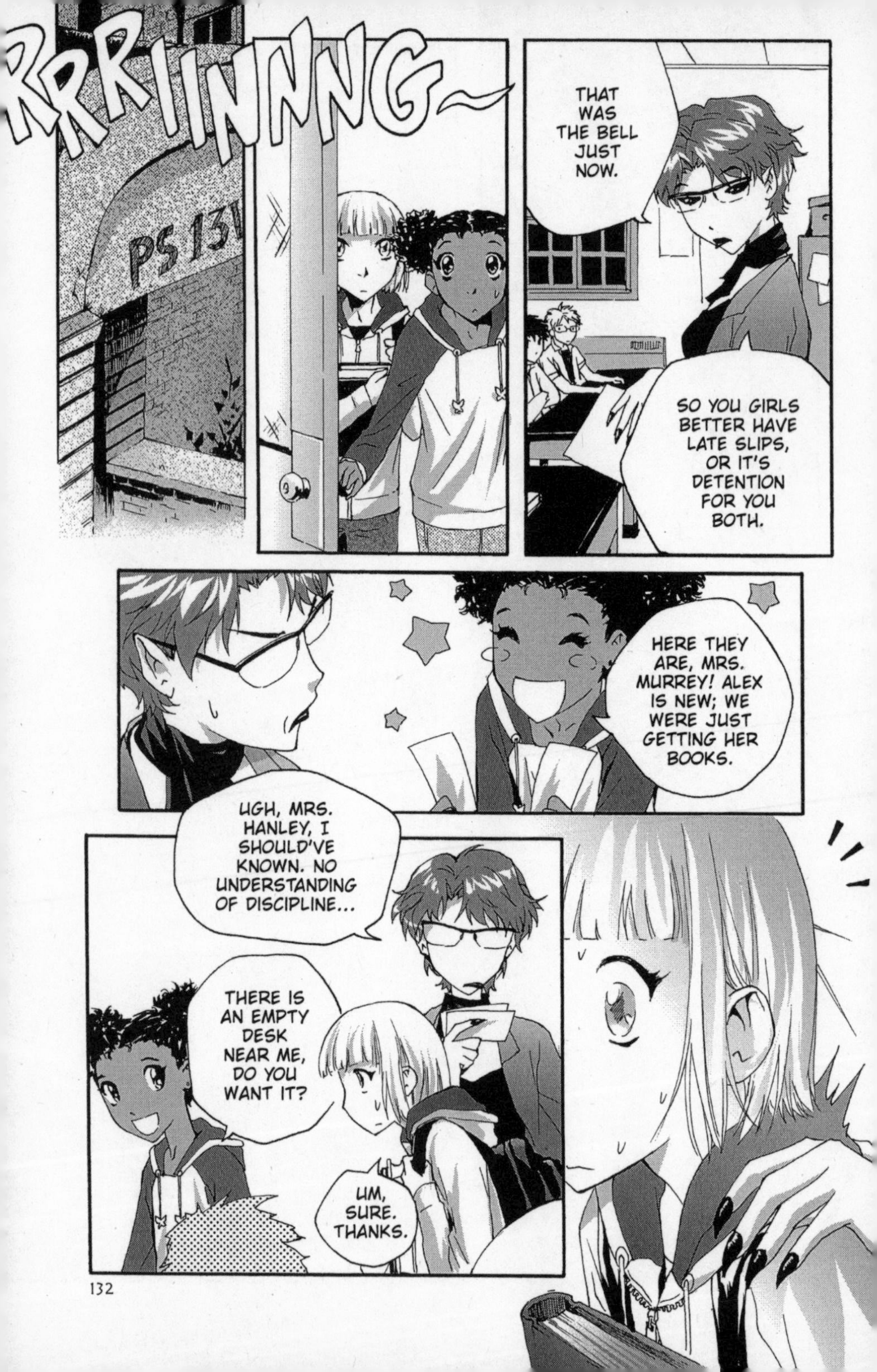
RRRIINNNG~
PS 13
THAT WAS THE BELL JUST NOW.
SO YOU GIRLS BETTER HAVE LATE SLIPS, OR IT'S DETENTION FOR YOU BOTH.
HERE THEY ARE, MRS. MURREY! ALEX IS NEW; WE WERE JUST GETTING HER BOOKS.
UGH, MRS. HANLEY, I SHOULD'VE KNOWN. NO UNDERSTANDING OF DISCIPLINE...
THERE IS AN EMPTY DESK NEAR ME, DO YOU WANT IT?
UM, SURE. THANKS.

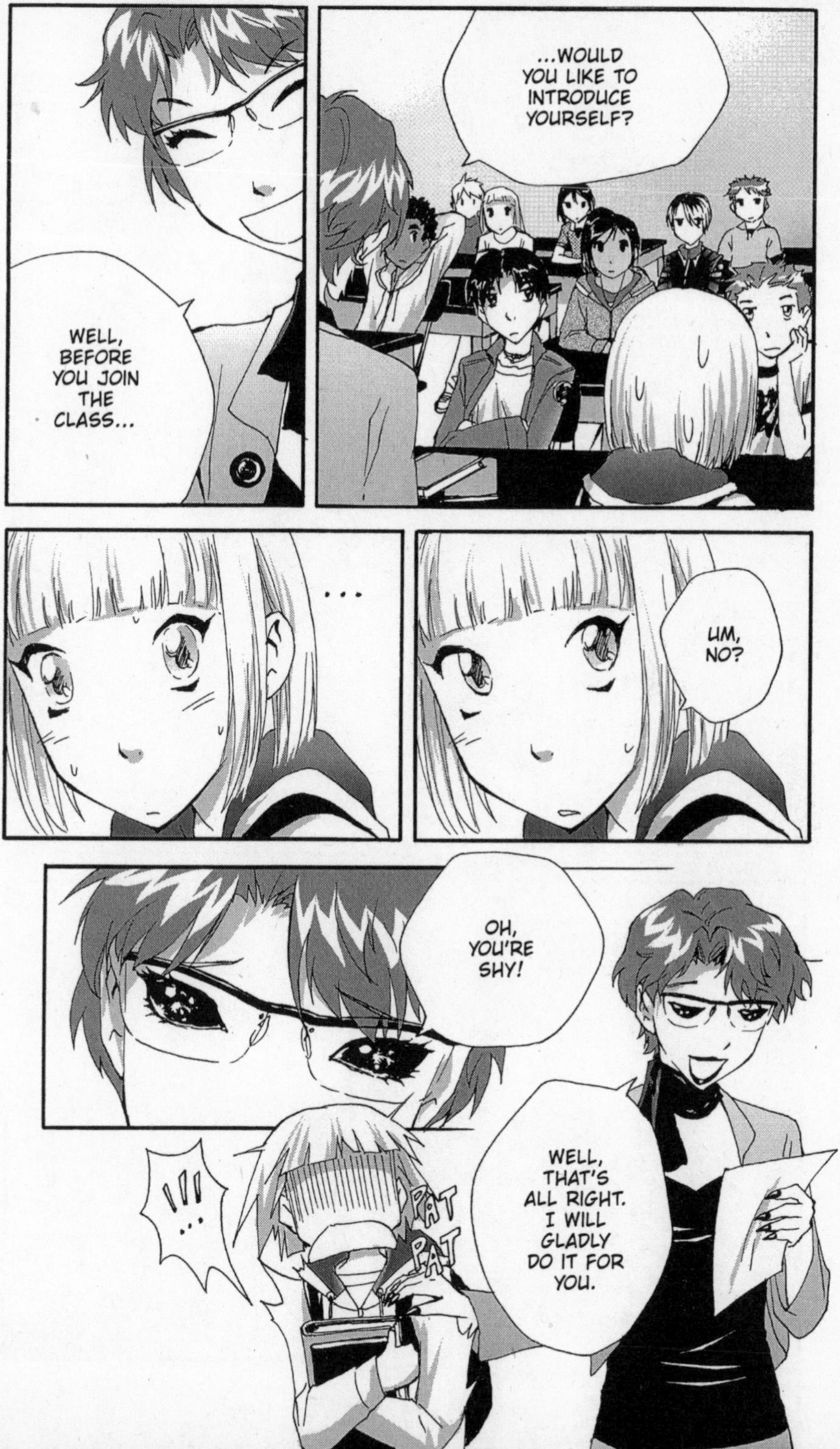
WELL, BEFORE YOU JOIN THE CLASS...
...WOULD YOU LIKE TO INTRODUCE YOURSELF?
...
UM, NO?
OH, YOU'RE SHY!
!!! ...
PAT PAT
WELL, THAT'S ALL RIGHT. I WILL GLADLY DO IT FOR YOU.

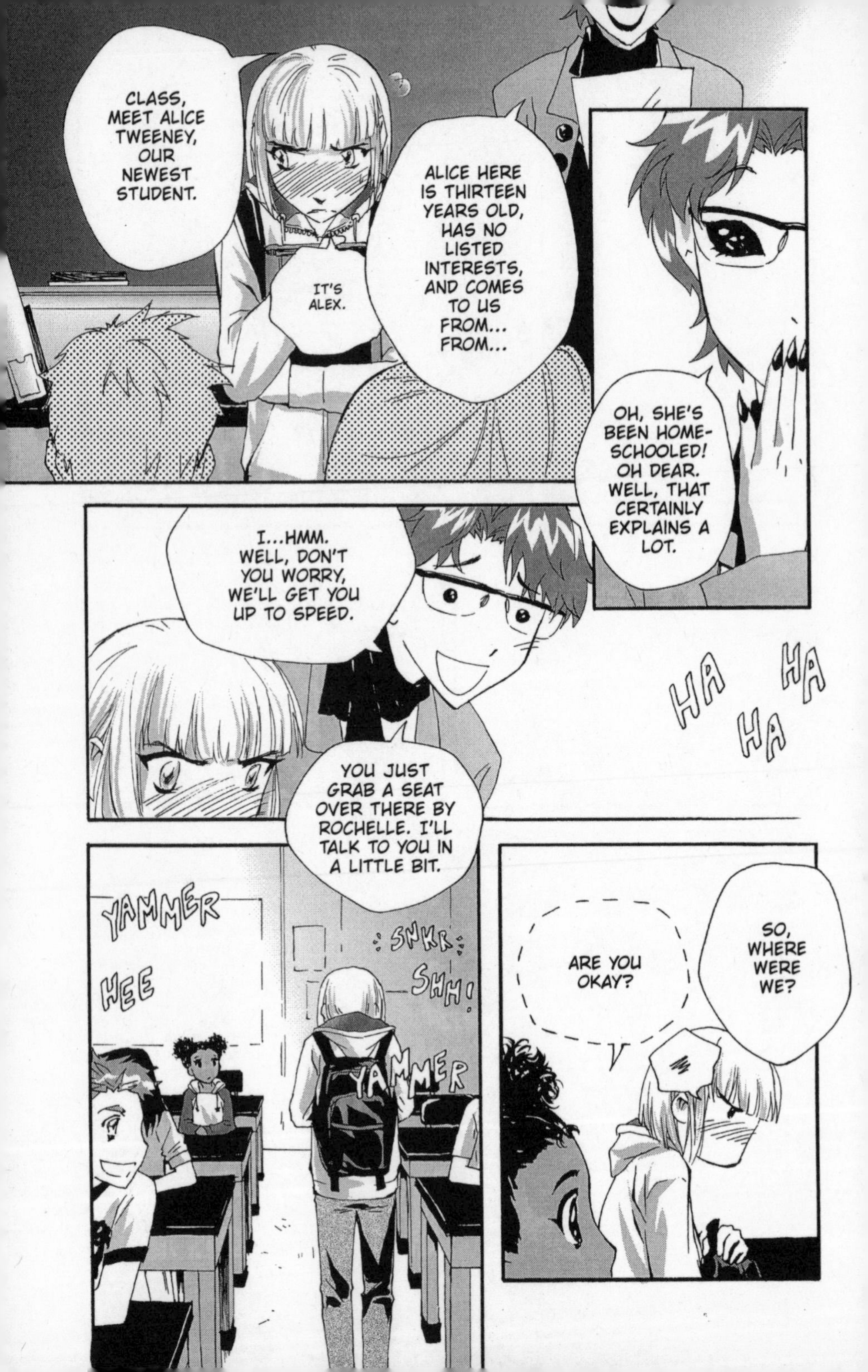
CLASS, MEET ALICE TWEENEY, OUR NEWEST STUDENT.
IT'S ALEX.
ALICE HERE IS THIRTEEN YEARS OLD, HAS NO LISTED INTERESTS, AND COMES TO US FROM... FROM...
OH, SHE'S BEEN HOME-SCHOOLED! OH DEAR. WELL, THAT CERTAINLY EXPLAINS A LOT.
I...HMM. WELL, DON'T YOU WORRY, WE'LL GET YOU UP TO SPEED.
YOU JUST GRAB A SEAT OVER THERE BY ROCHELLE. I'LL TALK TO YOU IN A LITTLE BIT.
HA HA HA
YAMMER
HEE
SNKR
SHH!
YAMMER
ARE YOU OKAY?
SO, WHERE WERE WE?

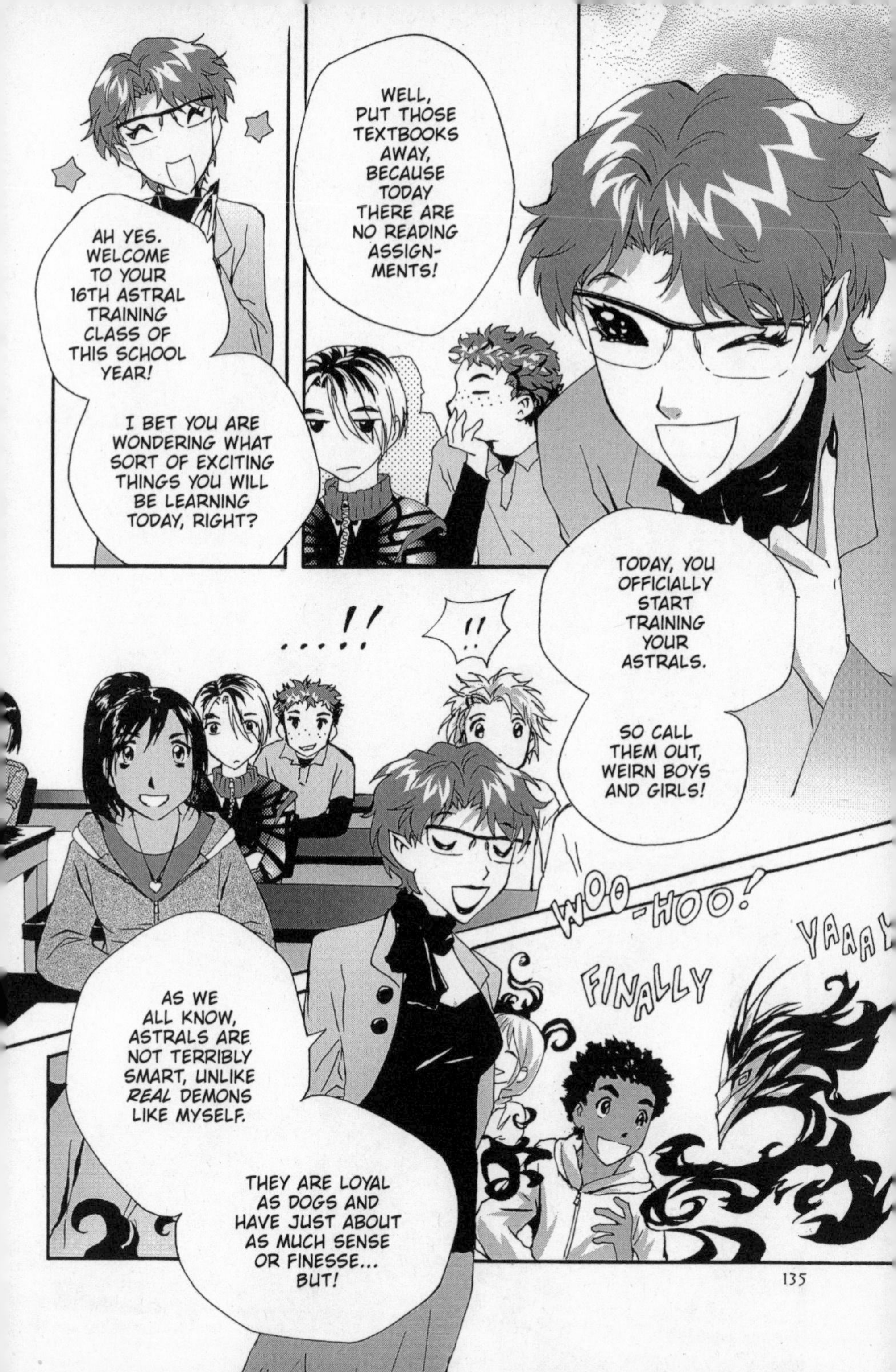

AH YES. WELCOME TO YOUR 16TH ASTRAL TRAINING CLASS OF THIS SCHOOL YEAR!
I BET YOU ARE WONDERING WHAT SORT OF EXCITING THINGS YOU WILL BE LEARNING TODAY, RIGHT?
WELL, PUT THOSE TEXTBOOKS AWAY, BECAUSE TODAY THERE ARE NO READING ASSIGN-MENTS!
TODAY, YOU OFFICIALLY START TRAINING YOUR ASTRALS.
SO CALL THEM OUT, WEIRN BOYS AND GIRLS!
...!!
!!
WOO-HOO!
FINALLY
YAAAY
AS WE ALL KNOW, ASTRALS ARE NOT TERRIBLY SMART, UNLIKE *REAL* DEMONS LIKE MYSELF.
THEY ARE LOYAL AS DOGS AND HAVE JUST ABOUT AS MUCH SENSE OR FINESSE... BUT!

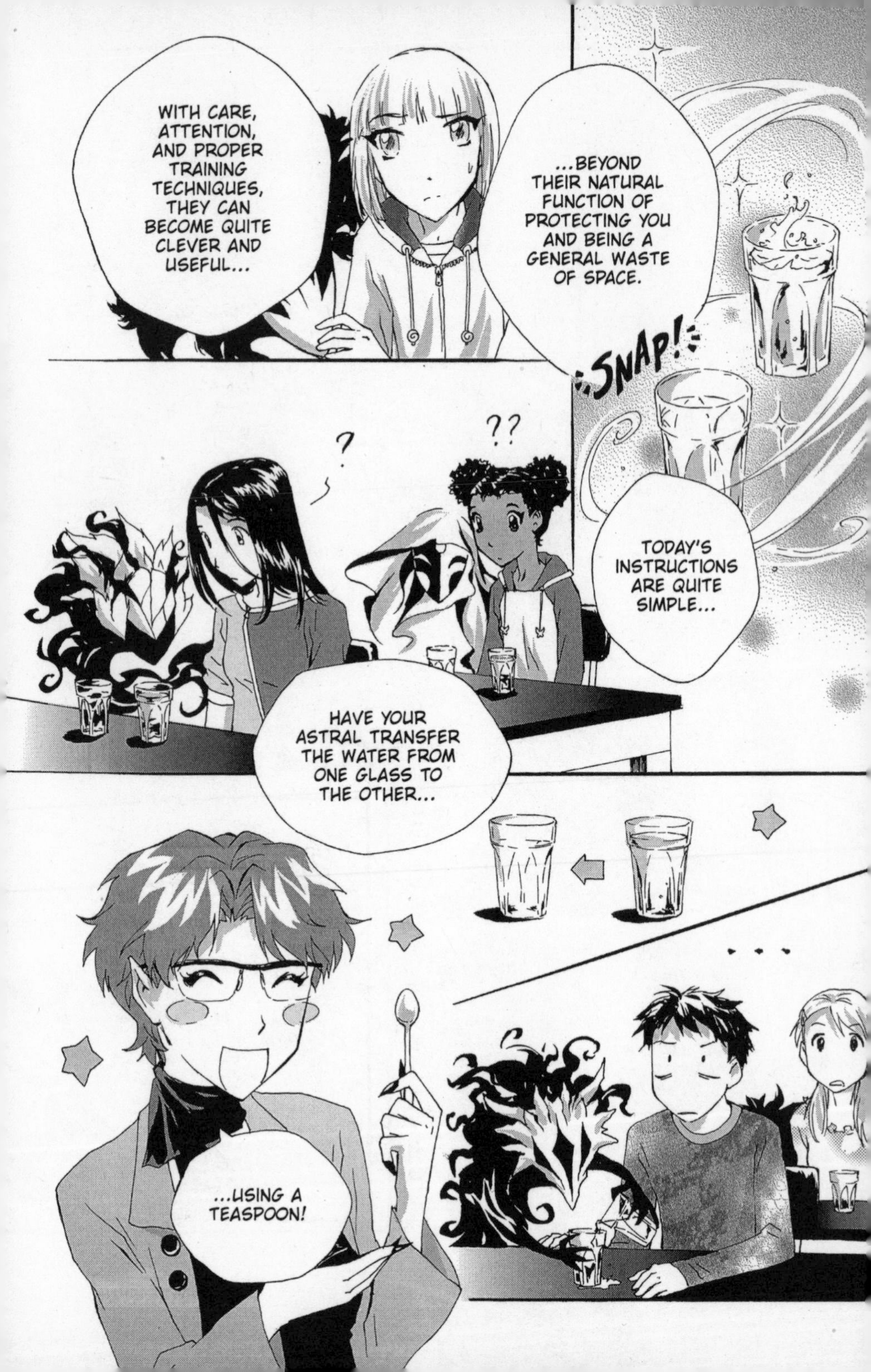
WITH CARE, ATTENTION, AND PROPER TRAINING TECHNIQUES, THEY CAN BECOME QUITE CLEVER AND USEFUL...
...BEYOND THEIR NATURAL FUNCTION OF PROTECTING YOU AND BEING A GENERAL WASTE OF SPACE.
SNAP!
?
??
TODAY'S INSTRUCTIONS ARE QUITE SIMPLE...
HAVE YOUR ASTRAL TRANSFER THE WATER FROM ONE GLASS TO THE OTHER...
...USING A TEASPOON!
. . .

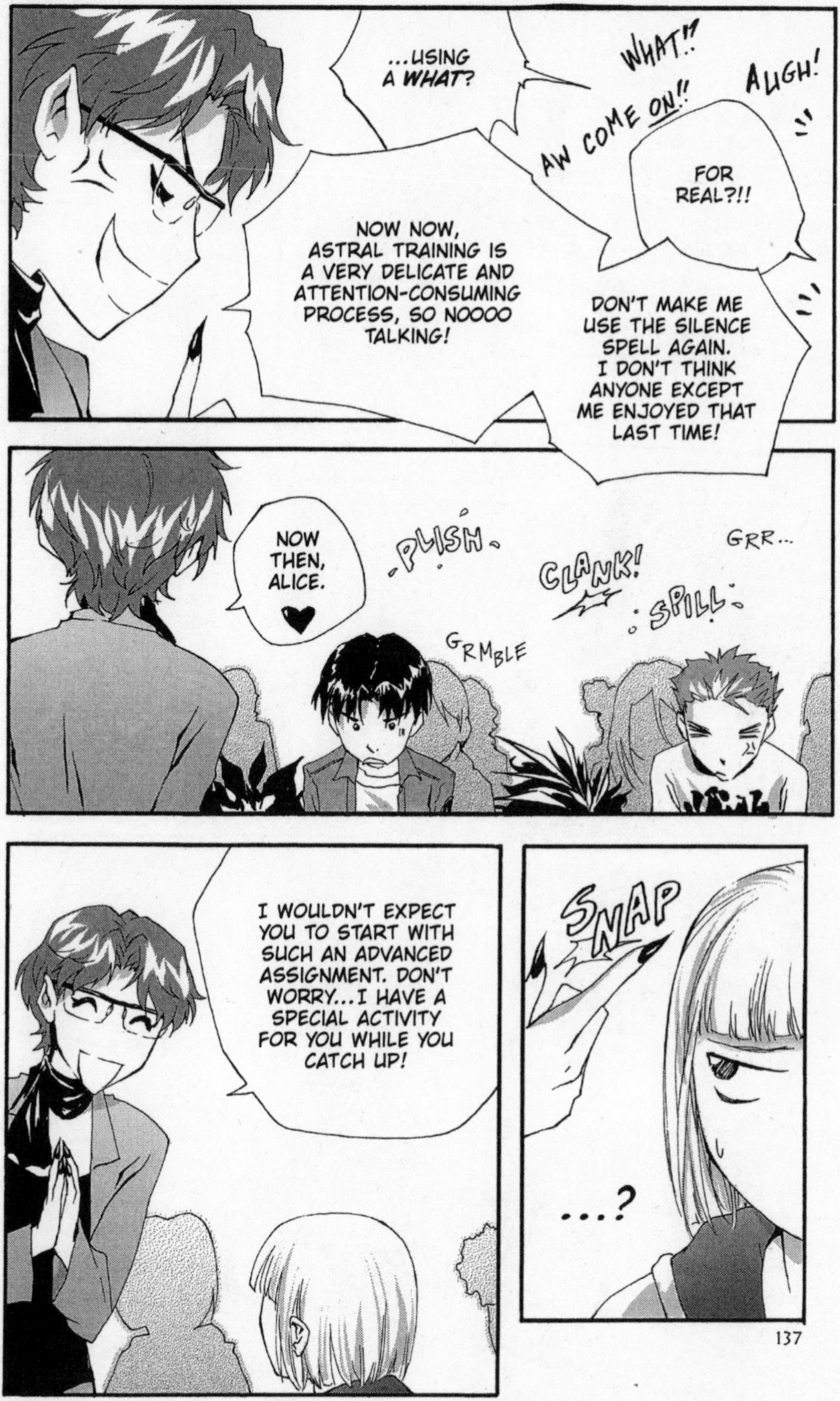
...USING A *WHAT*?
WHAT!!
AUGH!
AW COME ON!!
FOR REAL?!!
NOW NOW, ASTRAL TRAINING IS A VERY DELICATE AND ATTENTION-CONSUMING PROCESS, SO NOOOO TALKING!
DON'T MAKE ME USE THE SILENCE SPELL AGAIN. I DON'T THINK ANYONE EXCEPT ME ENJOYED THAT LAST TIME!
NOW THEN, ALICE.
PLISH
CLANK!
GRR...
SPILL
GRMBLE
I WOULDN'T EXPECT YOU TO START WITH SUCH AN ADVANCED ASSIGNMENT. DON'T WORRY...I HAVE A SPECIAL ACTIVITY FOR YOU WHILE YOU CATCH UP!
SNAP
...?

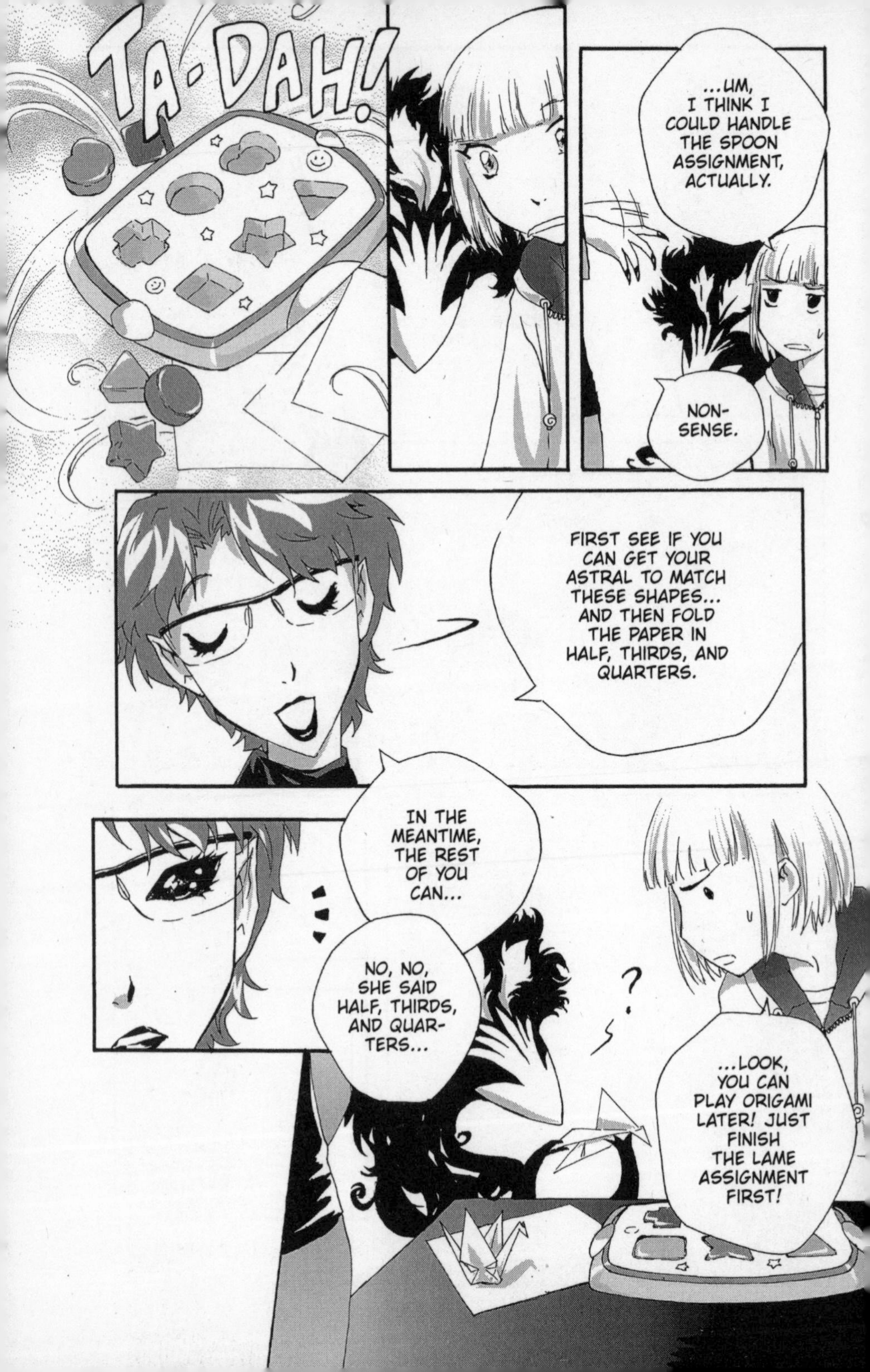
TA-DAH!
...UM, I THINK I COULD HANDLE THE SPOON ASSIGNMENT, ACTUALLY.
NON-SENSE.
FIRST SEE IF YOU CAN GET YOUR ASTRAL TO MATCH THESE SHAPES... AND THEN FOLD THE PAPER IN HALF, THIRDS, AND QUARTERS.
IN THE MEANTIME, THE REST OF YOU CAN...
NO, NO, SHE SAID HALF, THIRDS, AND QUAR-TERS...
...LOOK, YOU CAN PLAY ORIGAMI LATER! JUST FINISH THE LAME ASSIGNMENT FIRST!

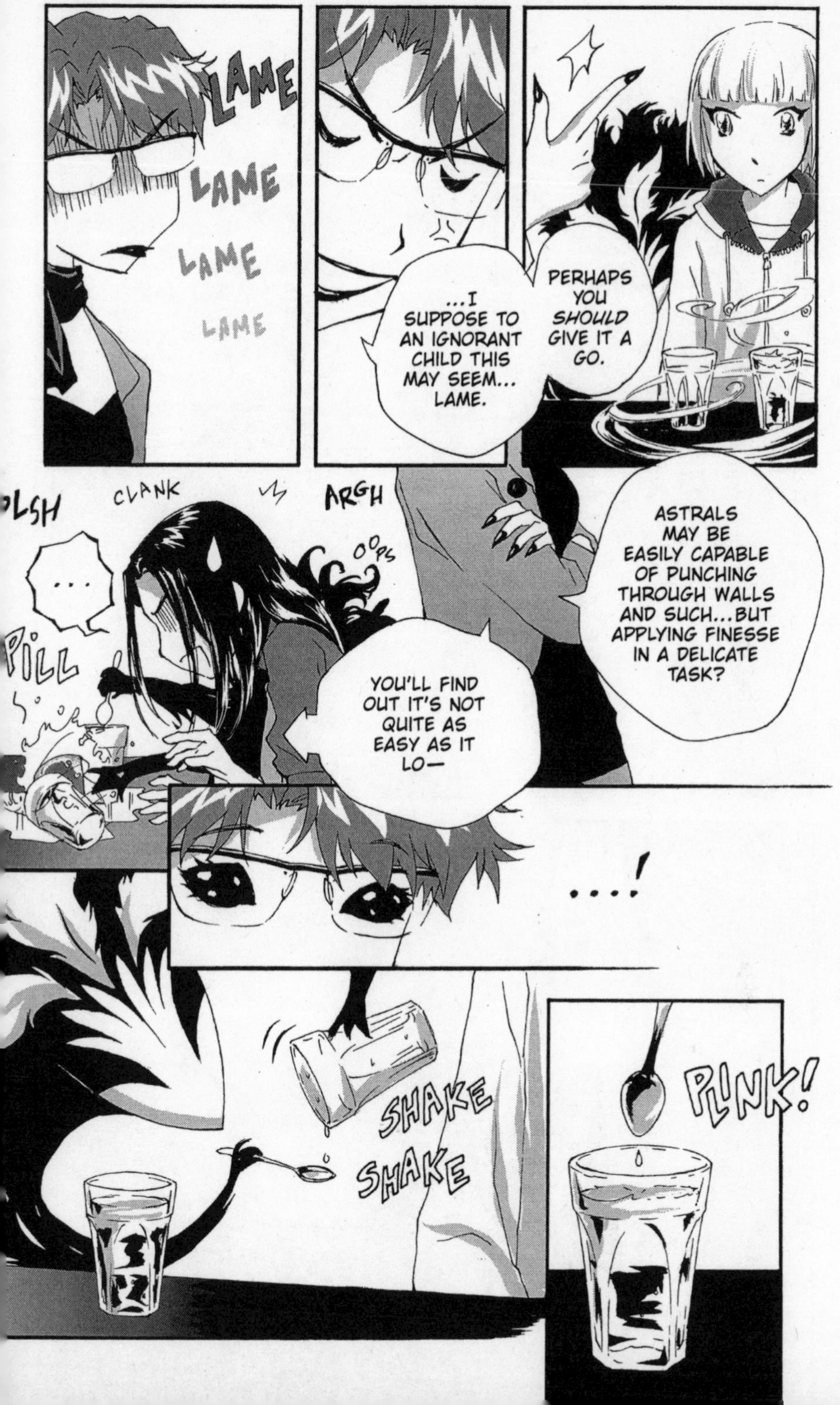
LAME
LAME
LAME
LAME
...I SUPPOSE TO AN IGNORANT CHILD THIS MAY SEEM... LAME.
PERHAPS YOU SHOULD GIVE IT A GO.
CLANK
ARGH
...
OOPS
ASTRALS MAY BE EASILY CAPABLE OF PUNCHING THROUGH WALLS AND SUCH...BUT APPLYING FINESSE IN A DELICATE TASK?
YOU'LL FIND OUT IT'S NOT QUITE AS EASY AS IT LO—
...!
SHAKE
SHAKE
PLINK!

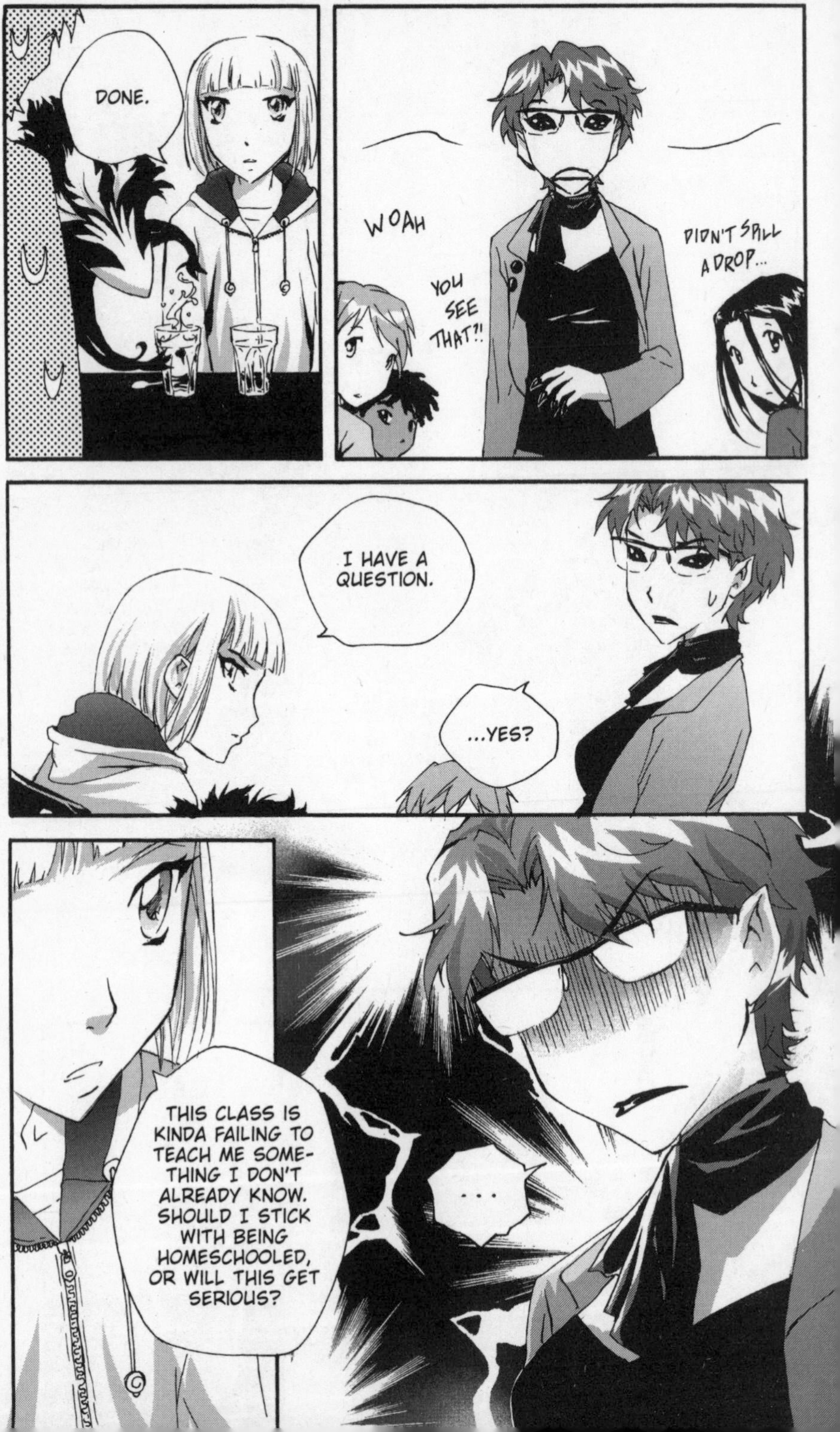
DONE.
WOAH
YOU SEE THAT?!
DIDN'T SPILL A DROP...
I HAVE A QUESTION.
...YES?
THIS CLASS IS KINDA FAILING TO TEACH ME SOME-THING I DON'T ALREADY KNOW. SHOULD I STICK WITH BEING HOMESCHOOLED, OR WILL THIS GET SERIOUS?
...

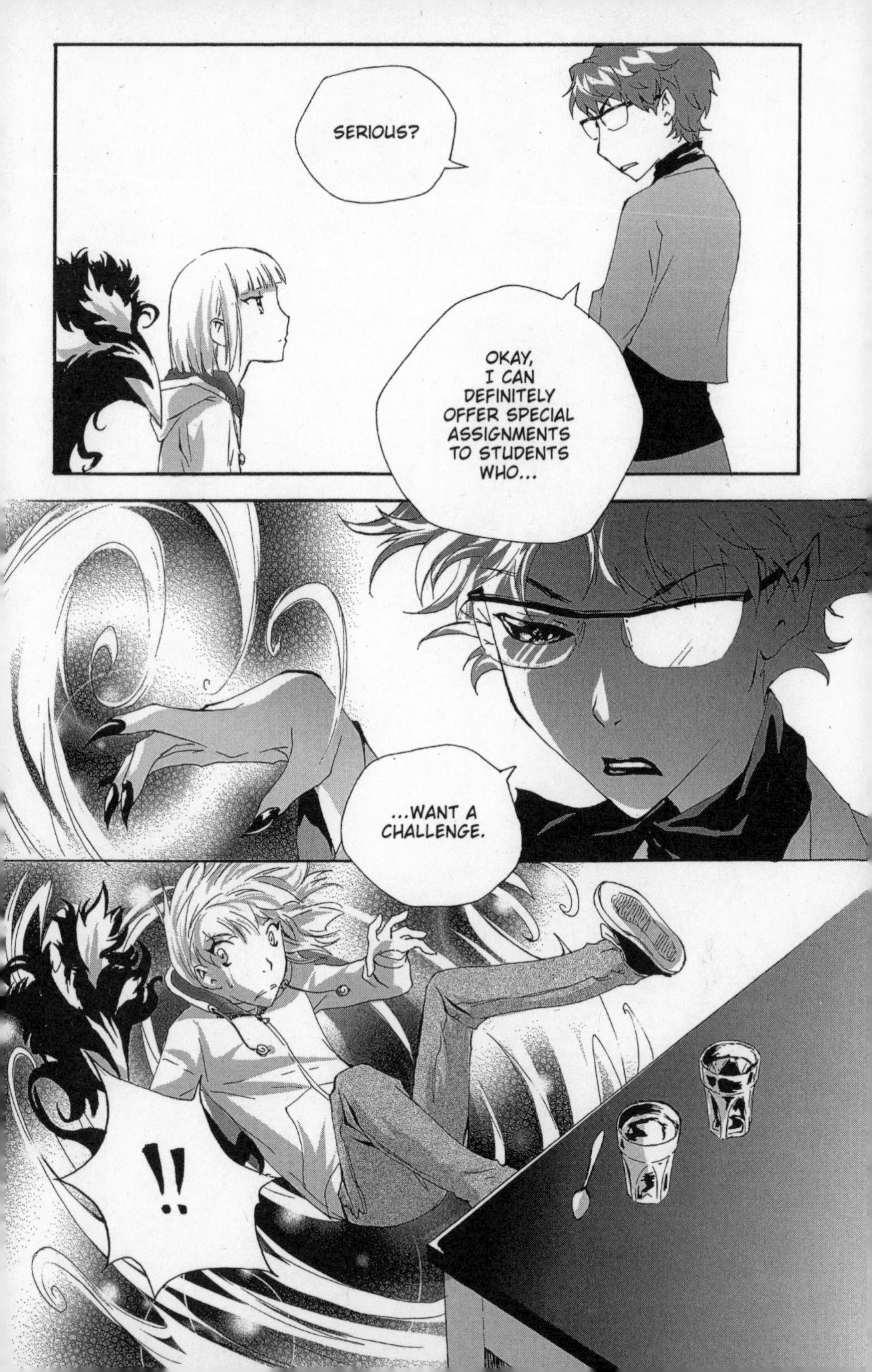
SERIOUS?
OKAY, I CAN DEFINITELY OFFER SPECIAL ASSIGNMENTS TO STUDENTS WHO...
...WANT A CHALLENGE.
!!

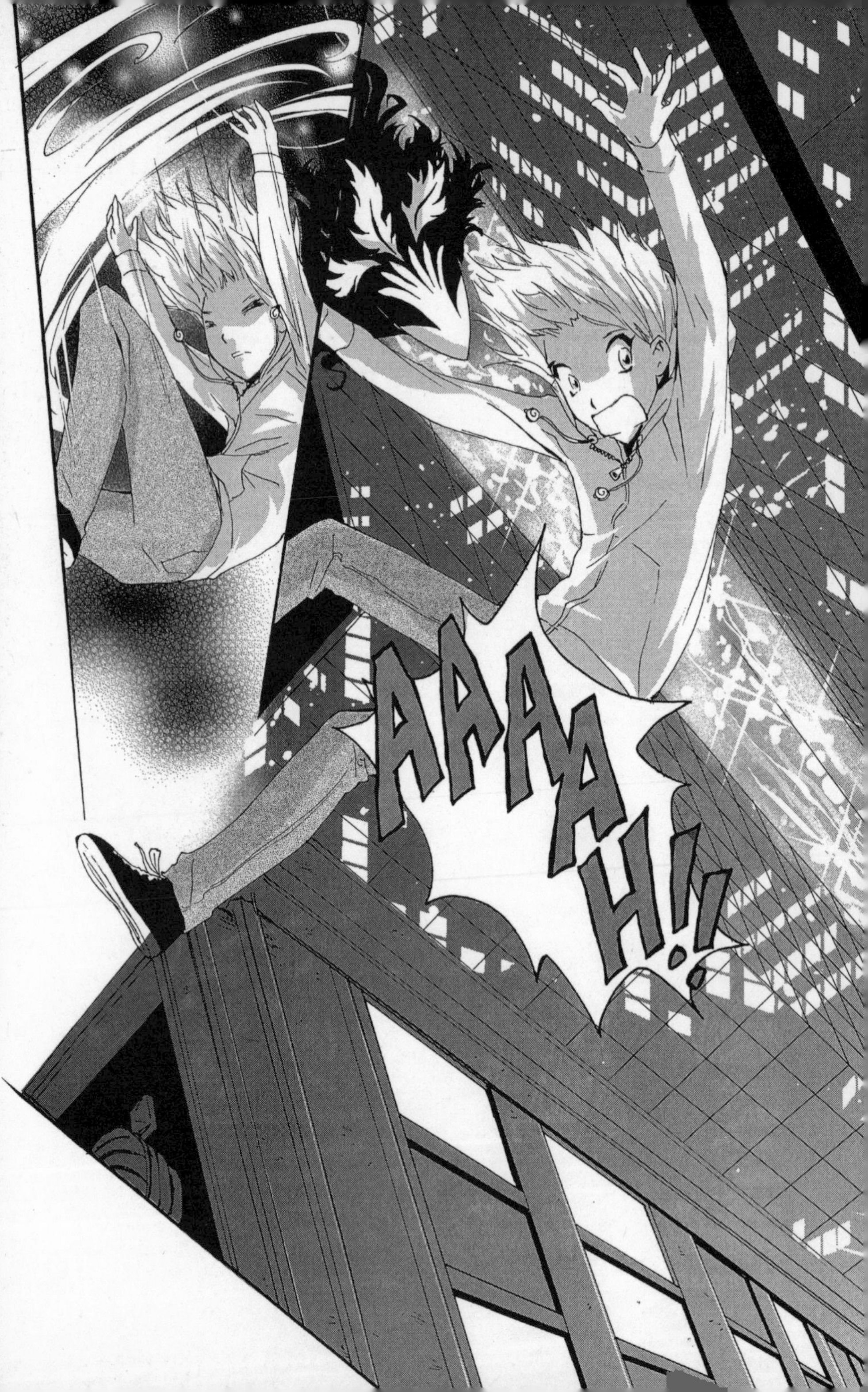
AAAAH!!

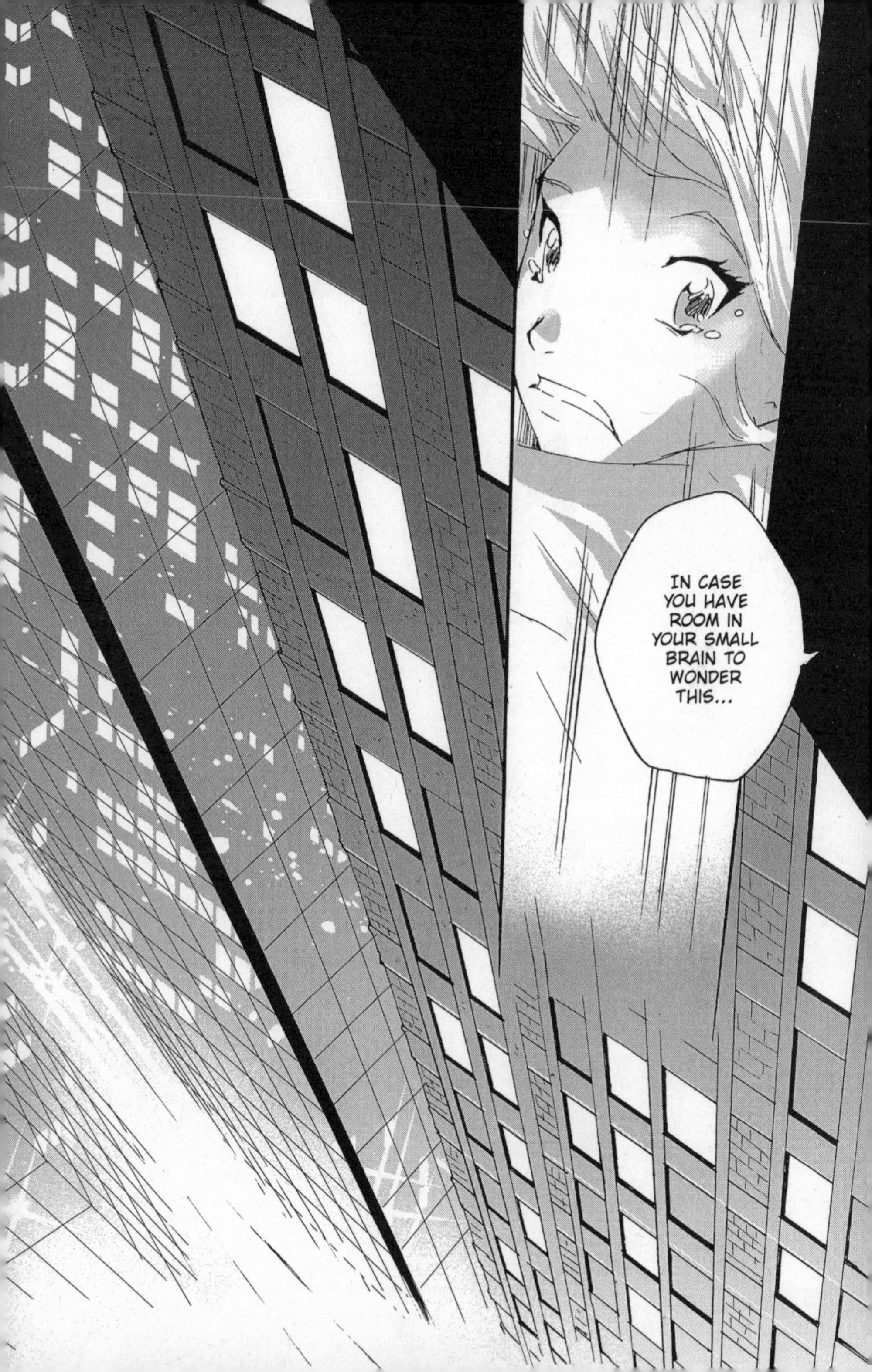
IN CASE YOU HAVE ROOM IN YOUR SMALL BRAIN TO WONDER THIS...

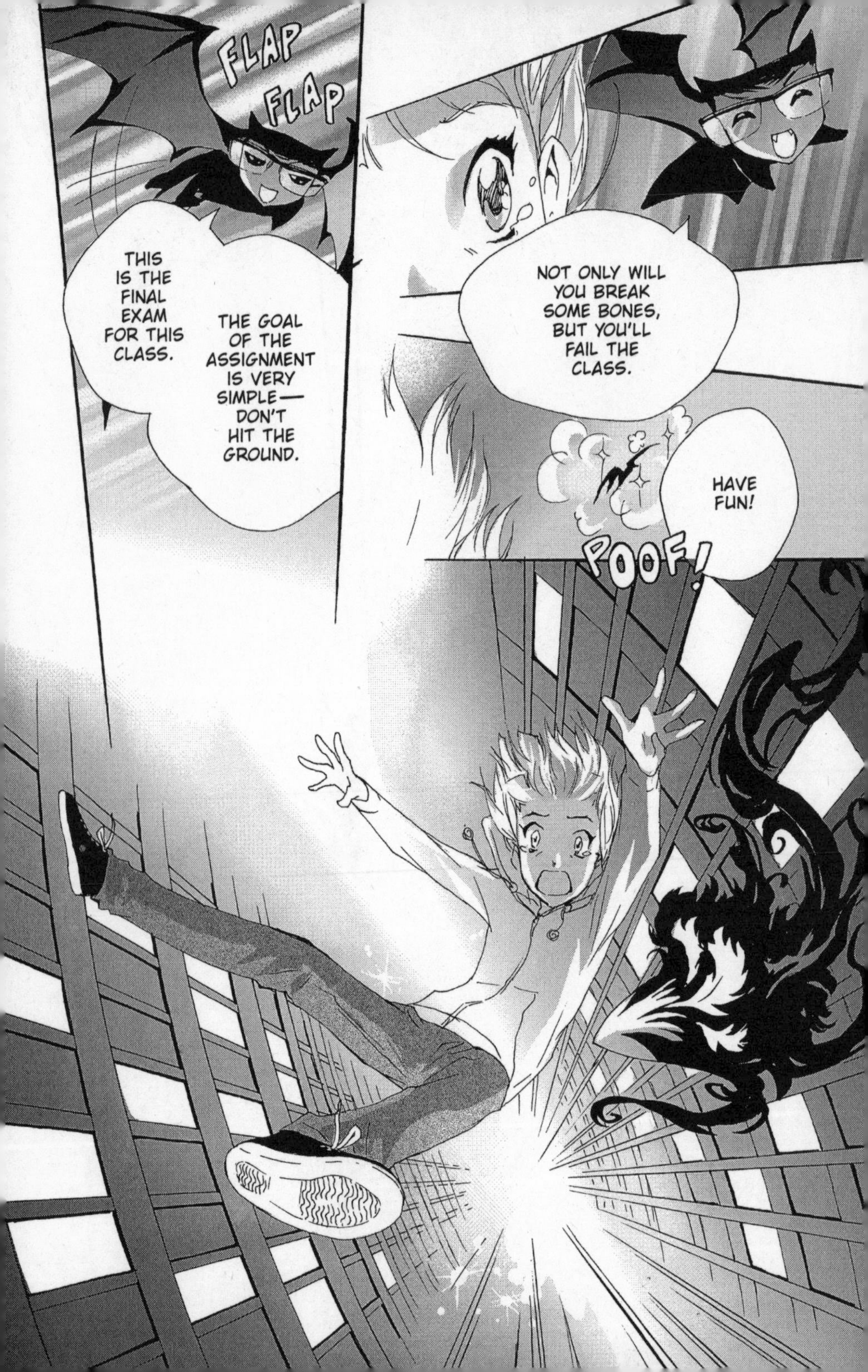
FLAP
FLAP
THIS IS THE FINAL EXAM FOR THIS CLASS.
THE GOAL OF THE ASSIGNMENT IS VERY SIMPLE— DON'T HIT THE GROUND.
NOT ONLY WILL YOU BREAK SOME BONES, BUT YOU'LL FAIL THE CLASS.
HAVE FUN!
POOF!

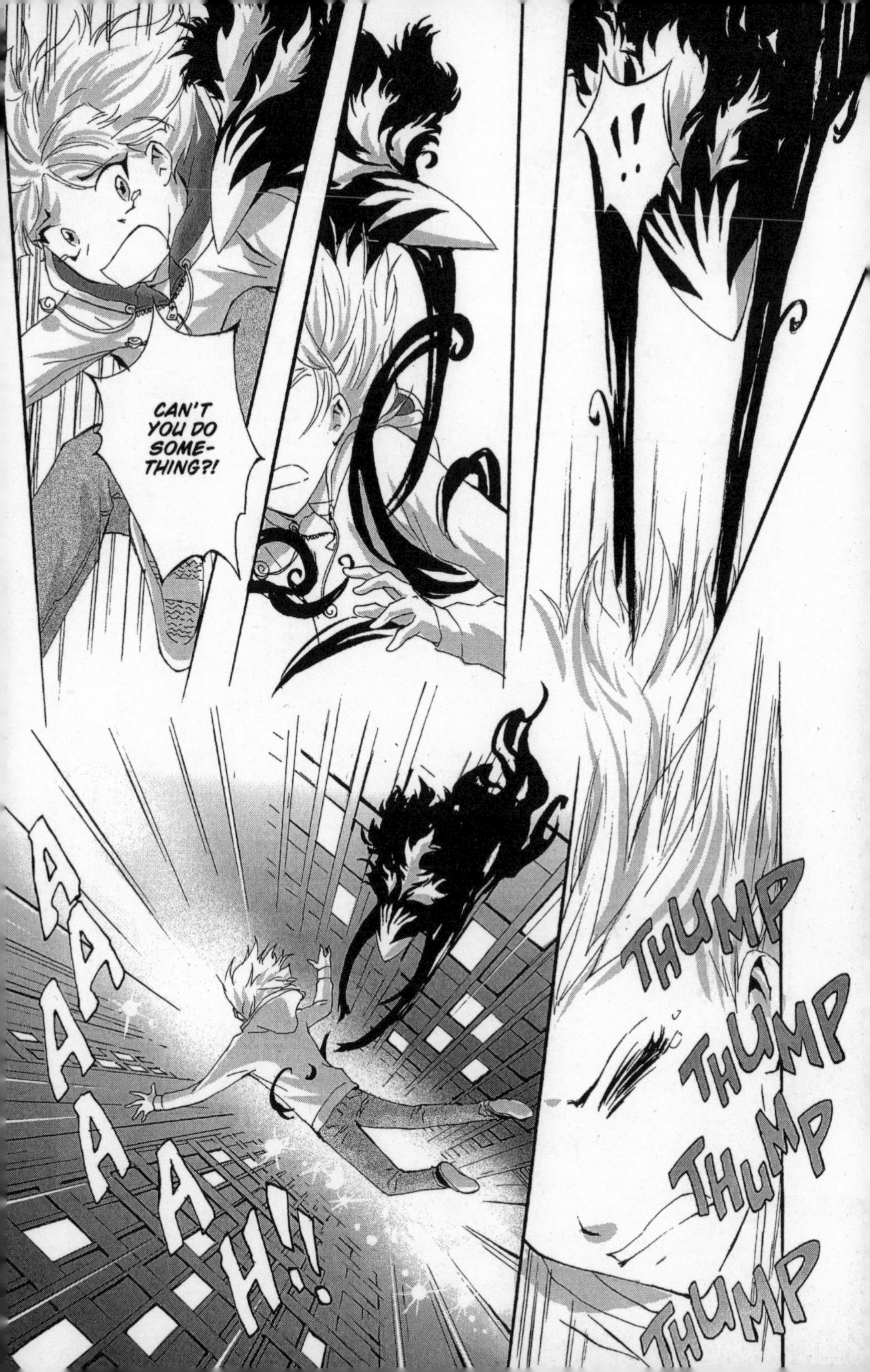

CAN'T YOU DO SOME-THING?!
!!
AAAAAH!!
THUMP THUMP THUMP THUMP

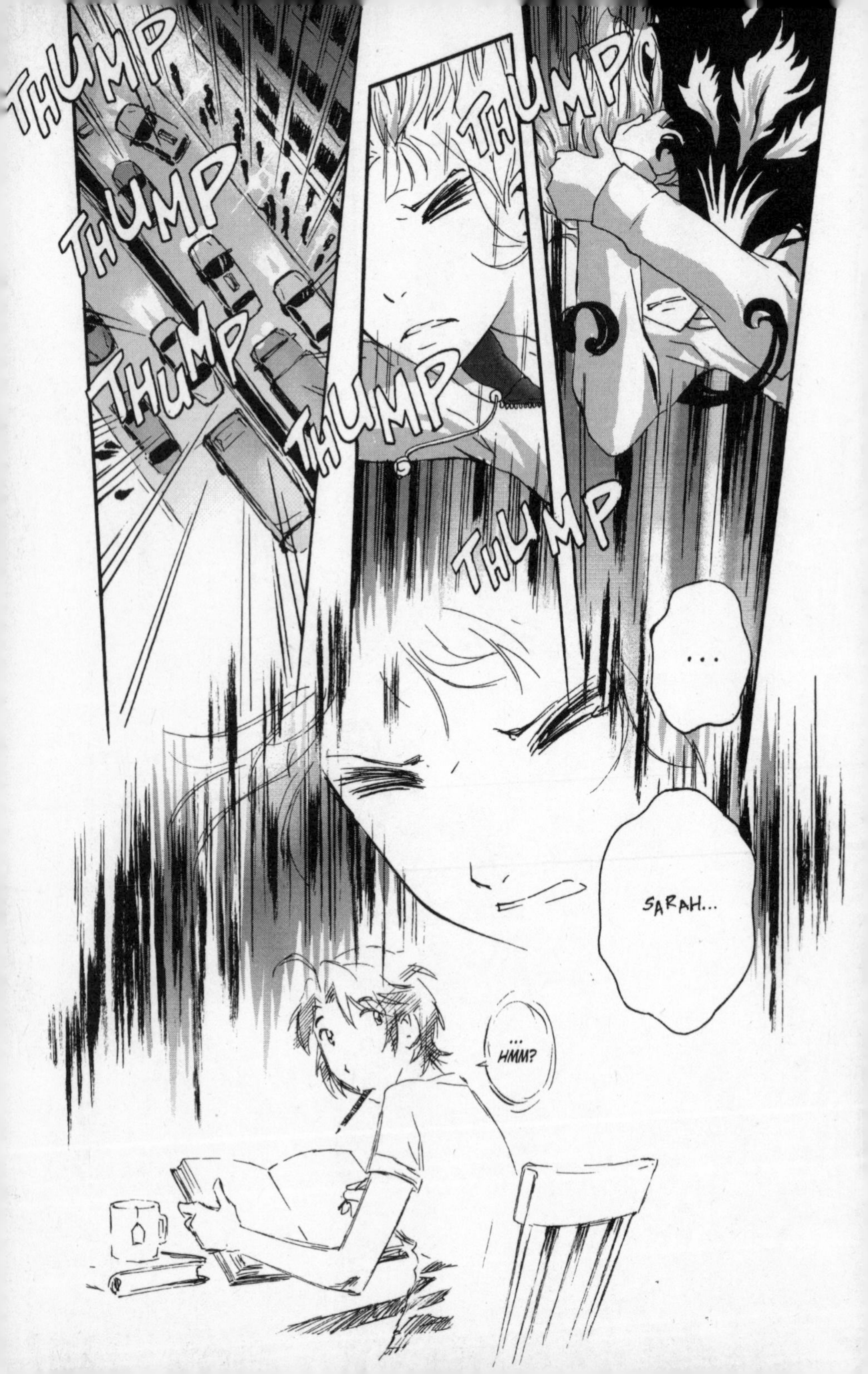
THUMP
THUMP
THUMP
THUMP
THUMP
THUMP
...
SARAH...
... HMM?

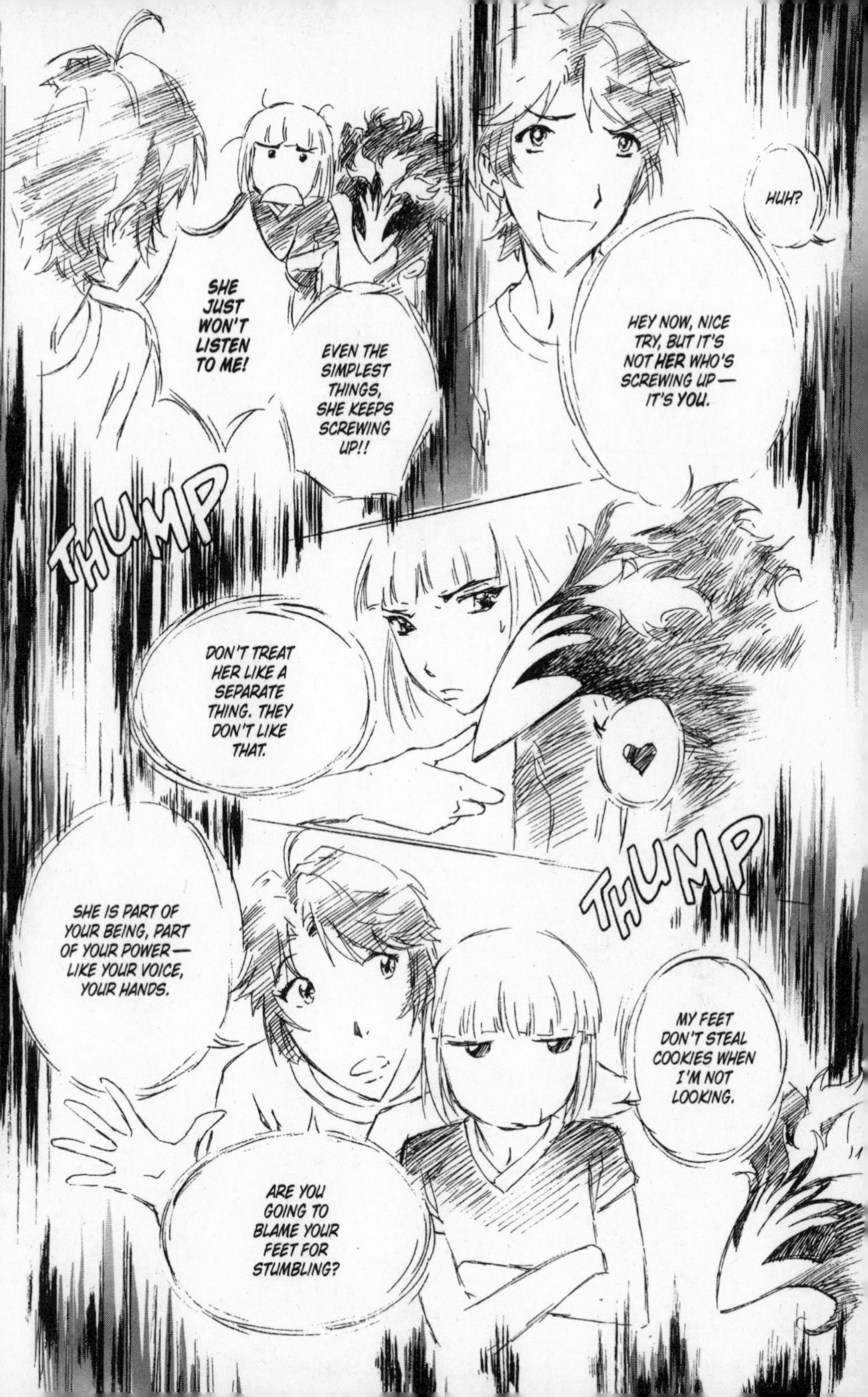
SHE JUST WON'T LISTEN TO ME!
EVEN THE SIMPLEST THINGS, SHE KEEPS SCREWING UP!!
HUH?
HEY NOW, NICE TRY, BUT IT'S NOT HER WHO'S SCREWING UP— IT'S YOU.
THUMP
DON'T TREAT HER LIKE A SEPARATE THING. THEY DON'T LIKE THAT.
THUMP
SHE IS PART OF YOUR BEING, PART OF YOUR POWER— LIKE YOUR VOICE, YOUR HANDS.
ARE YOU GOING TO BLAME YOUR FEET FOR STUMBLING?
MY FEET DON'T STEAL COOKIES WHEN I'M NOT LOOKING.

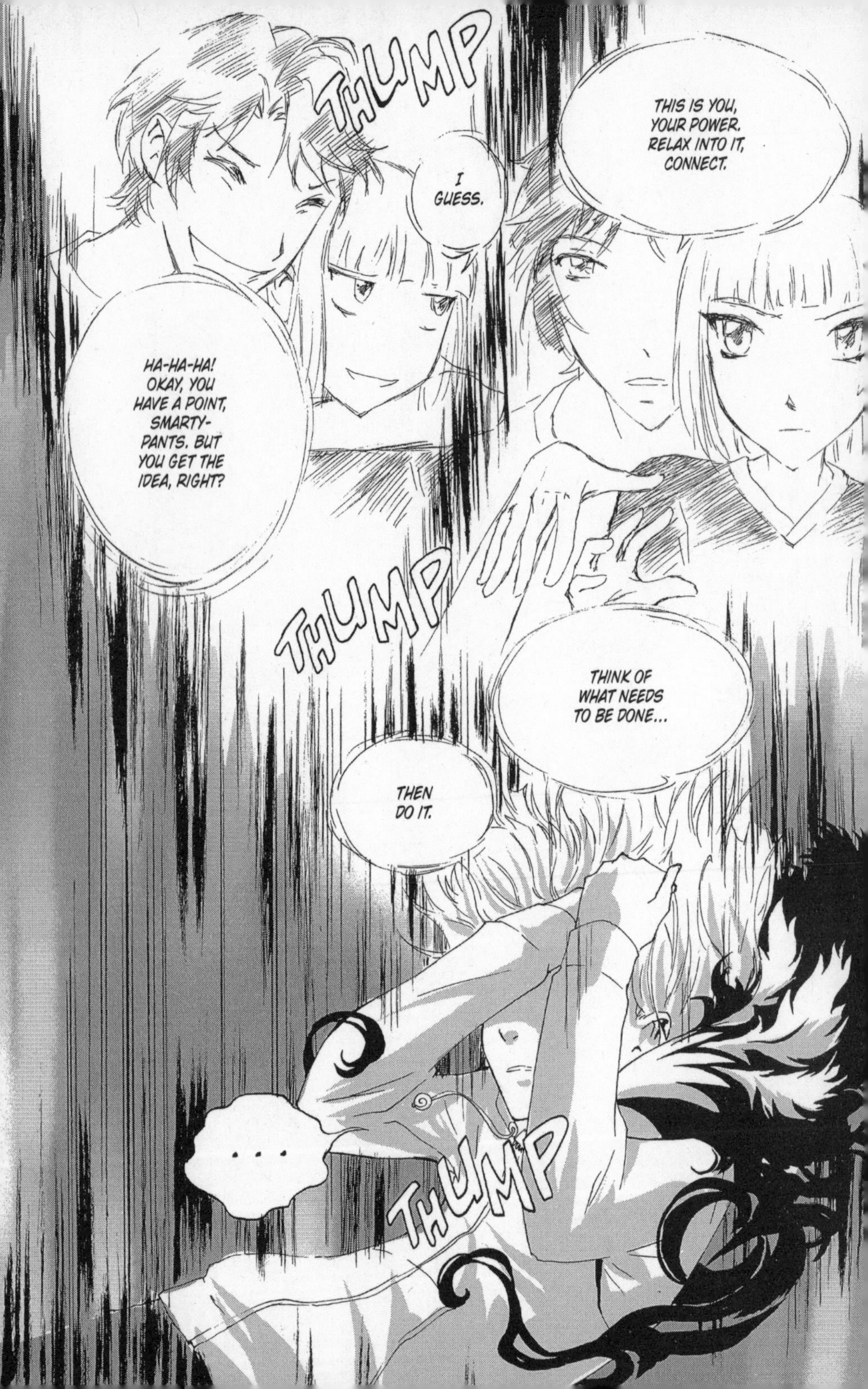
THUMP
I GUESS.
THIS IS YOU, YOUR POWER. RELAX INTO IT, CONNECT.
HA-HA-HA! OKAY, YOU HAVE A POINT, SMARTY-PANTS. BUT YOU GET THE IDEA, RIGHT?
THUMP
THINK OF WHAT NEEDS TO BE DONE...
THEN DO IT.
...
THUMP

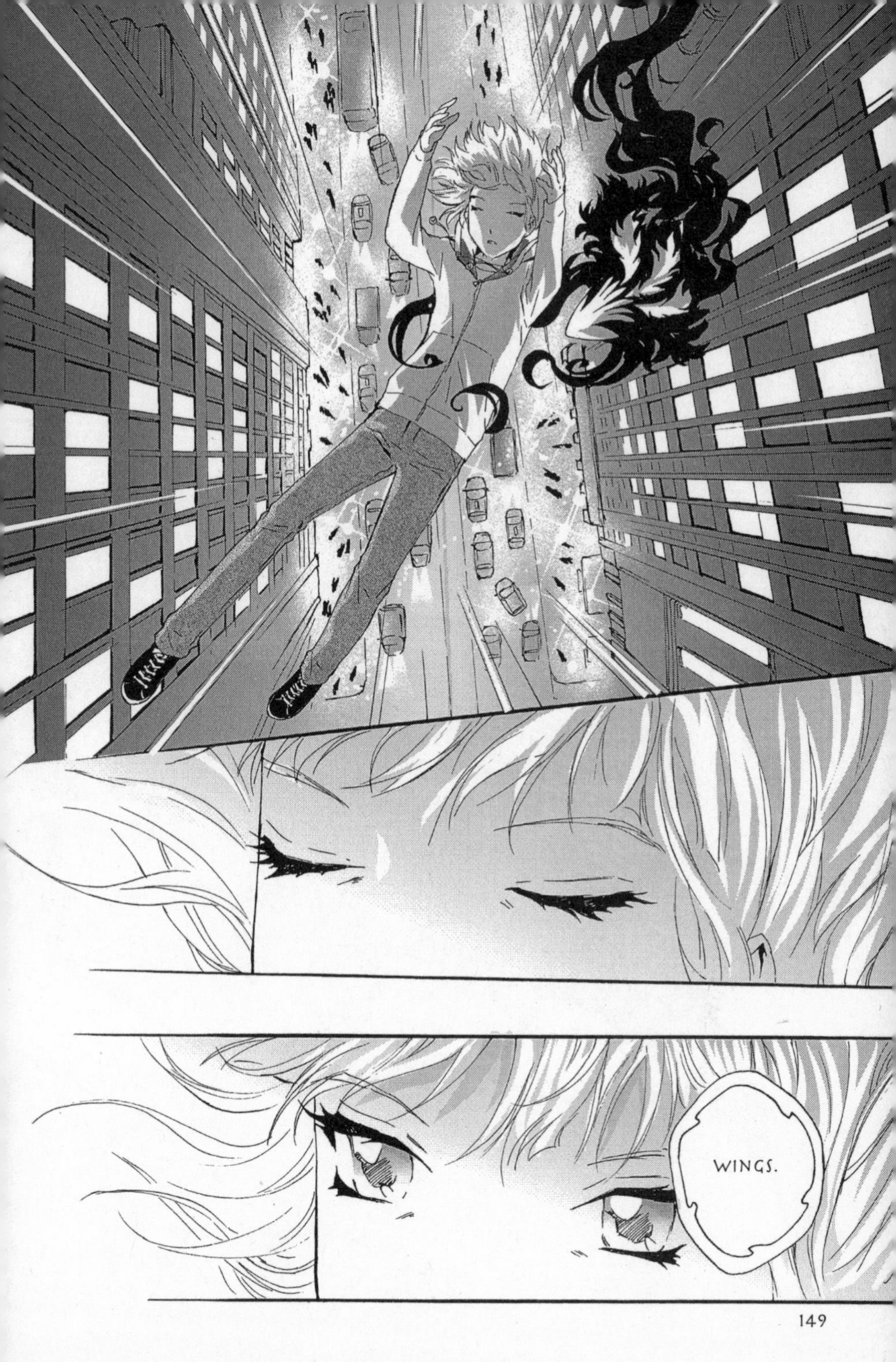
WINGS.

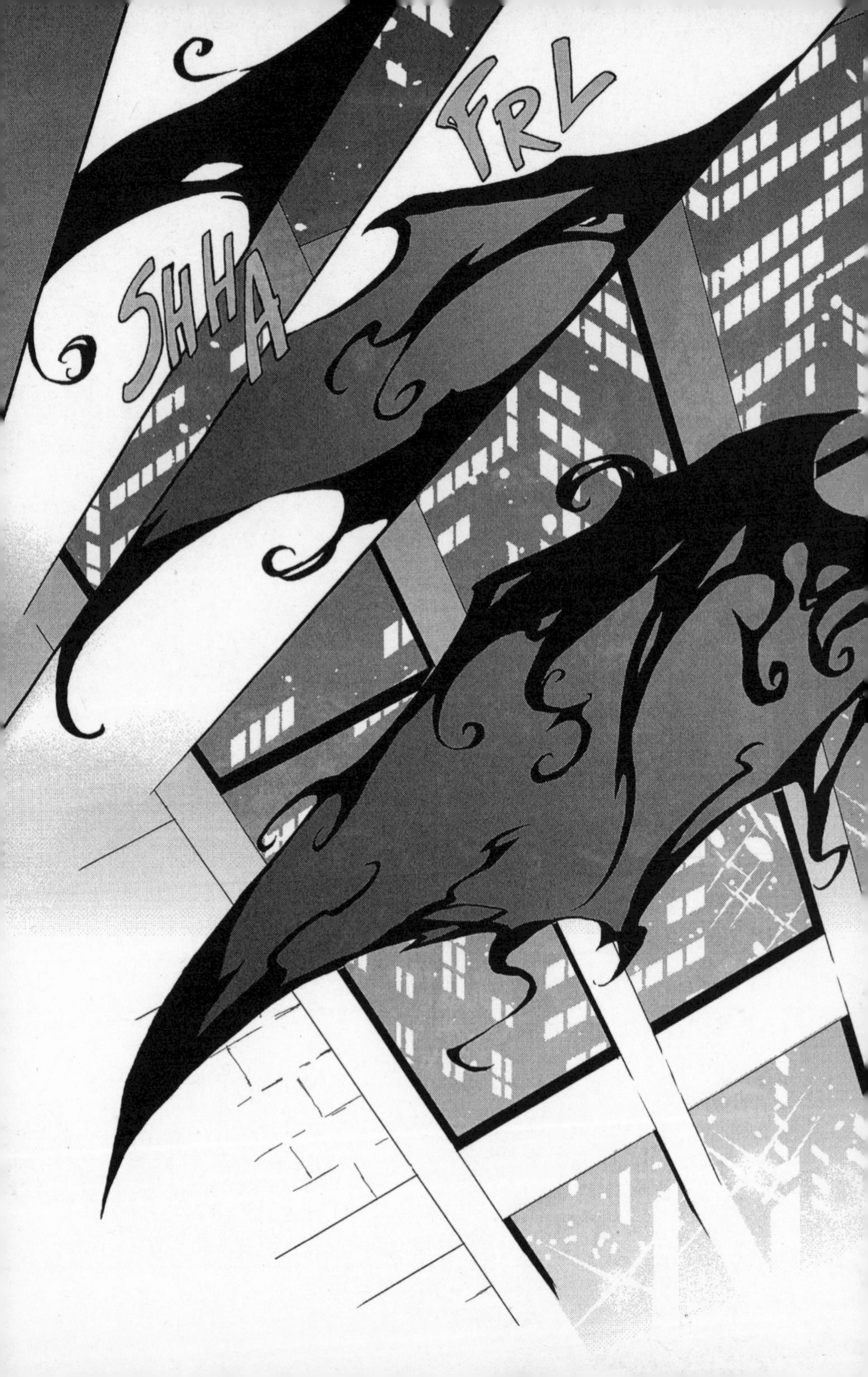
SHHA
FRL

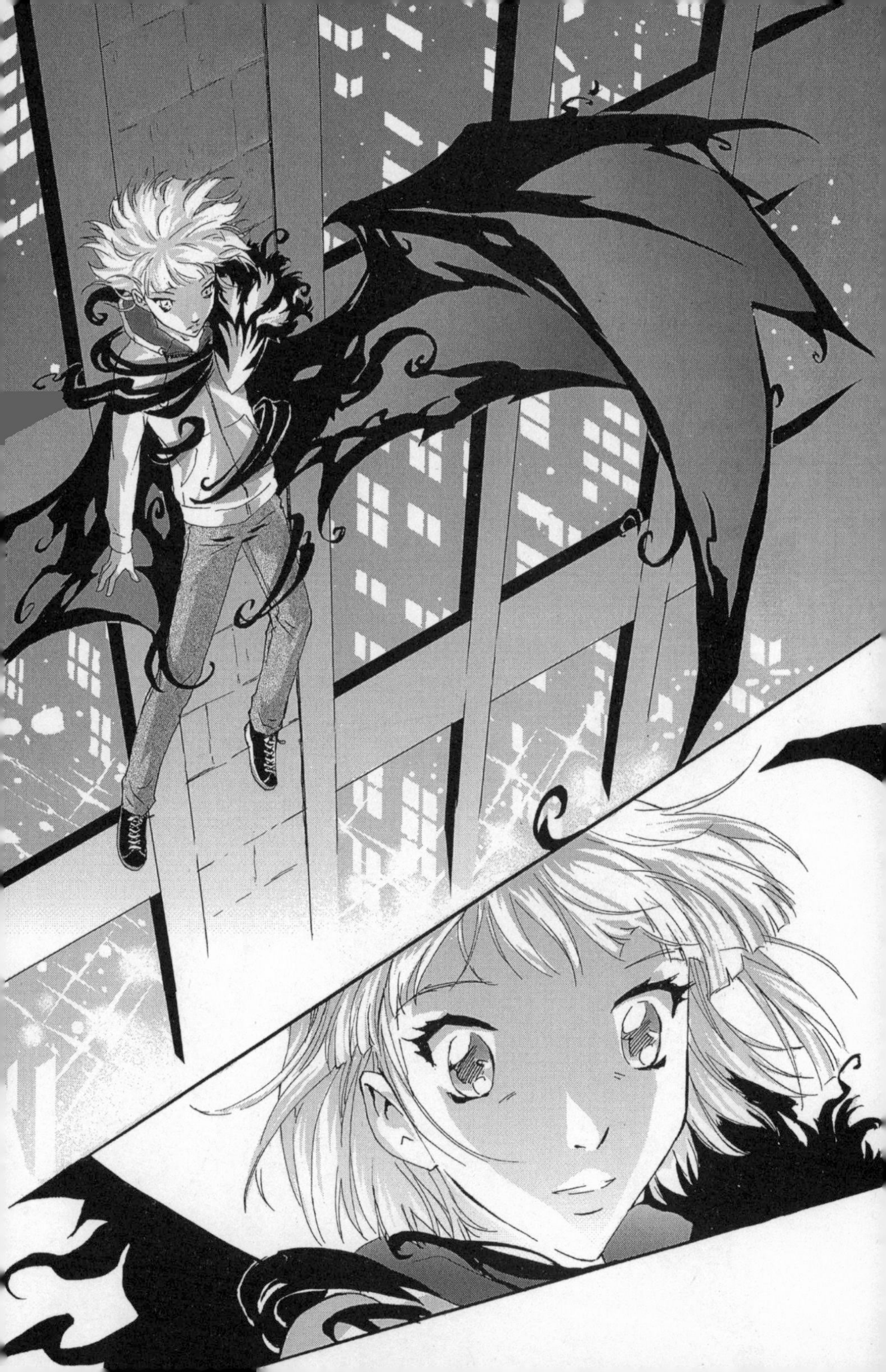

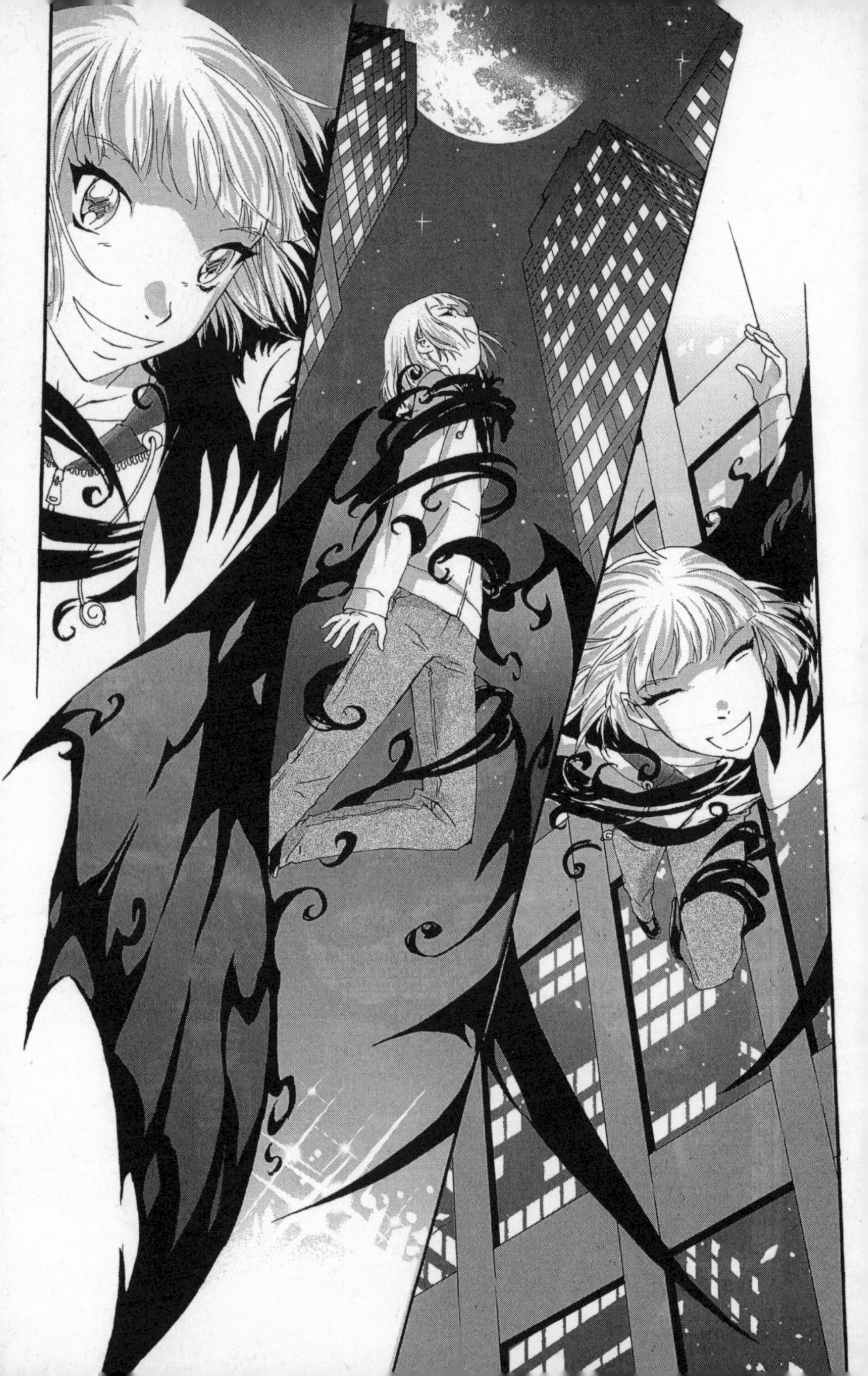

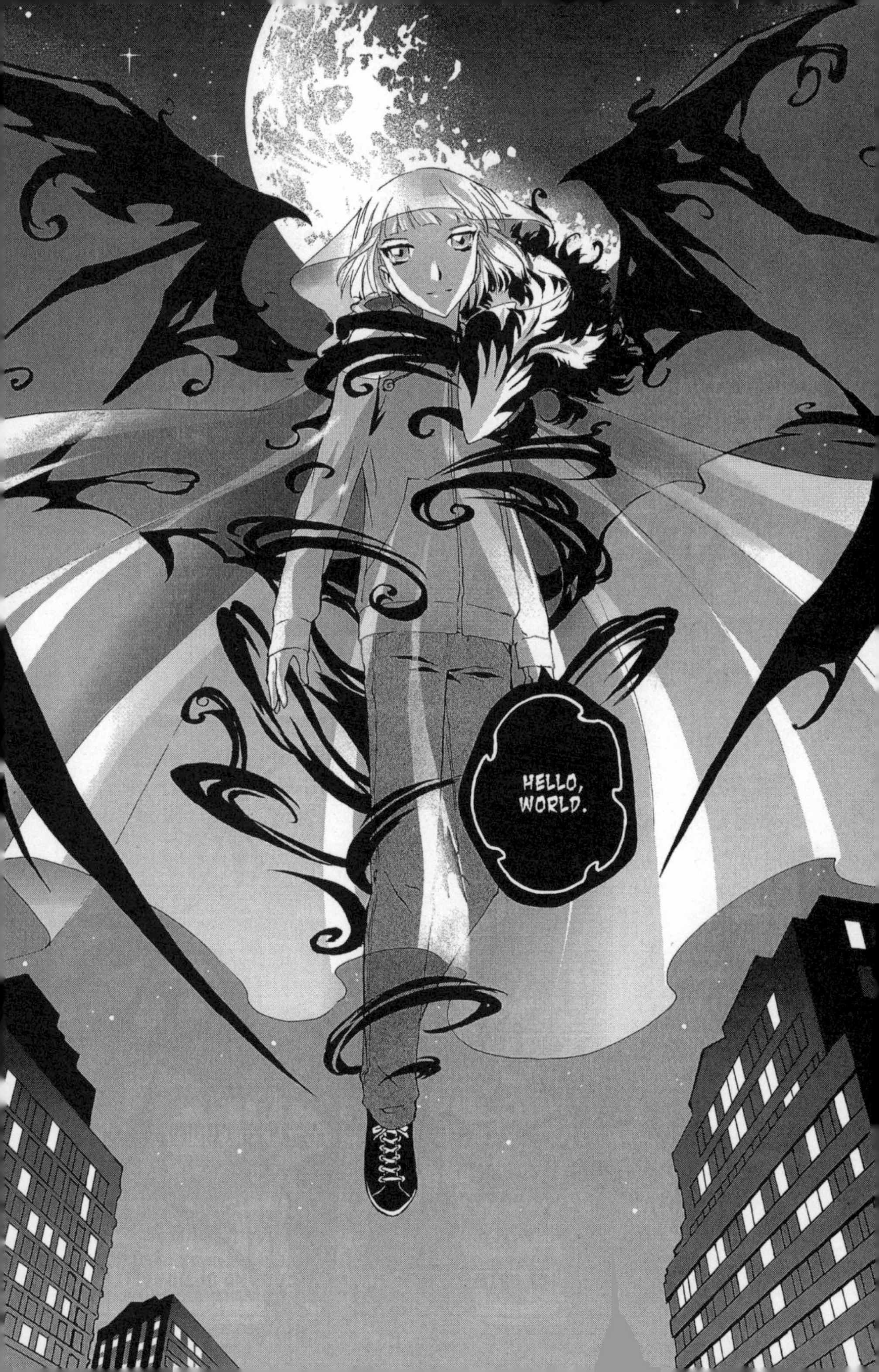
HELLO, WORLD.

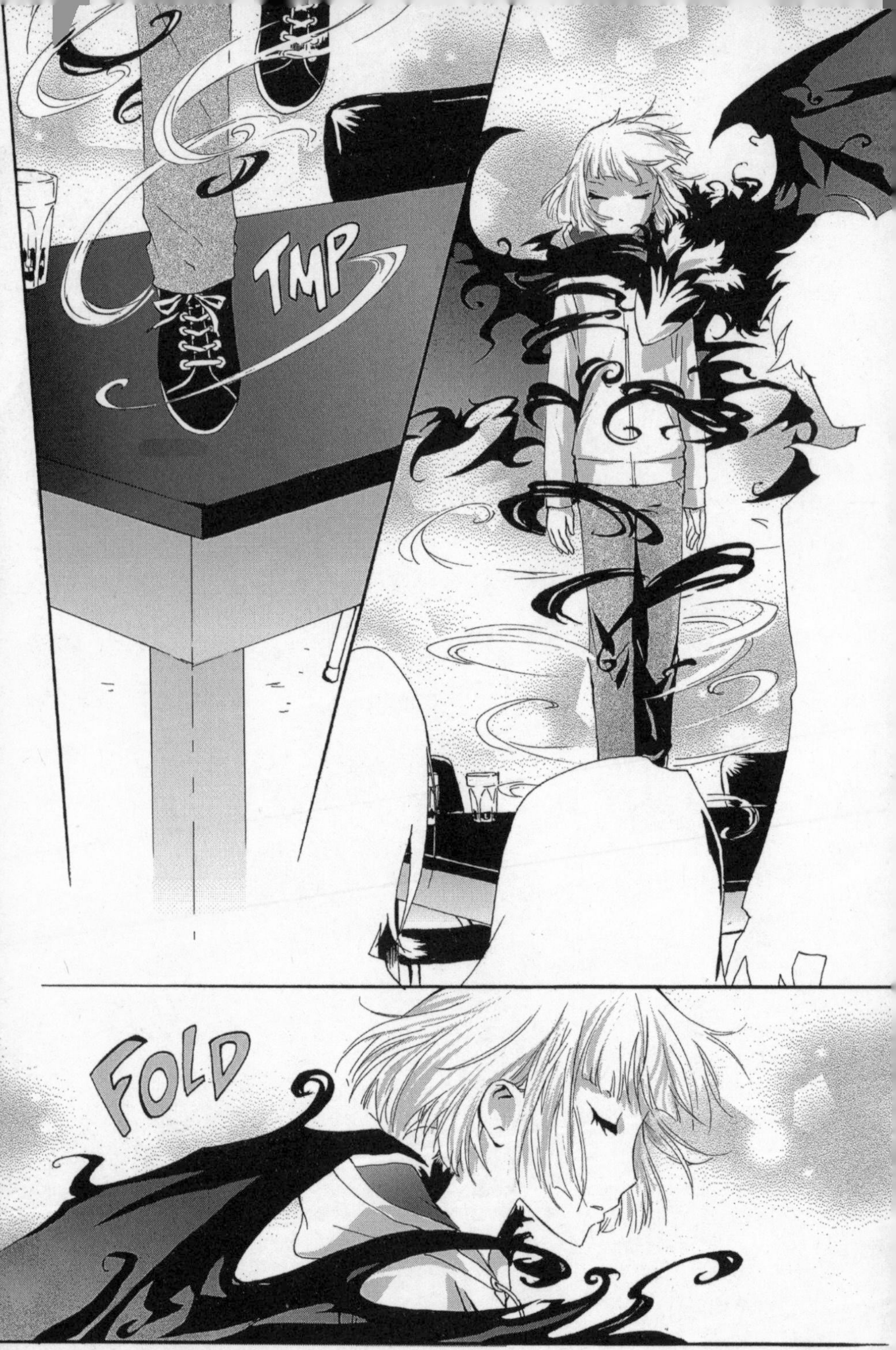
TMP
FOLD

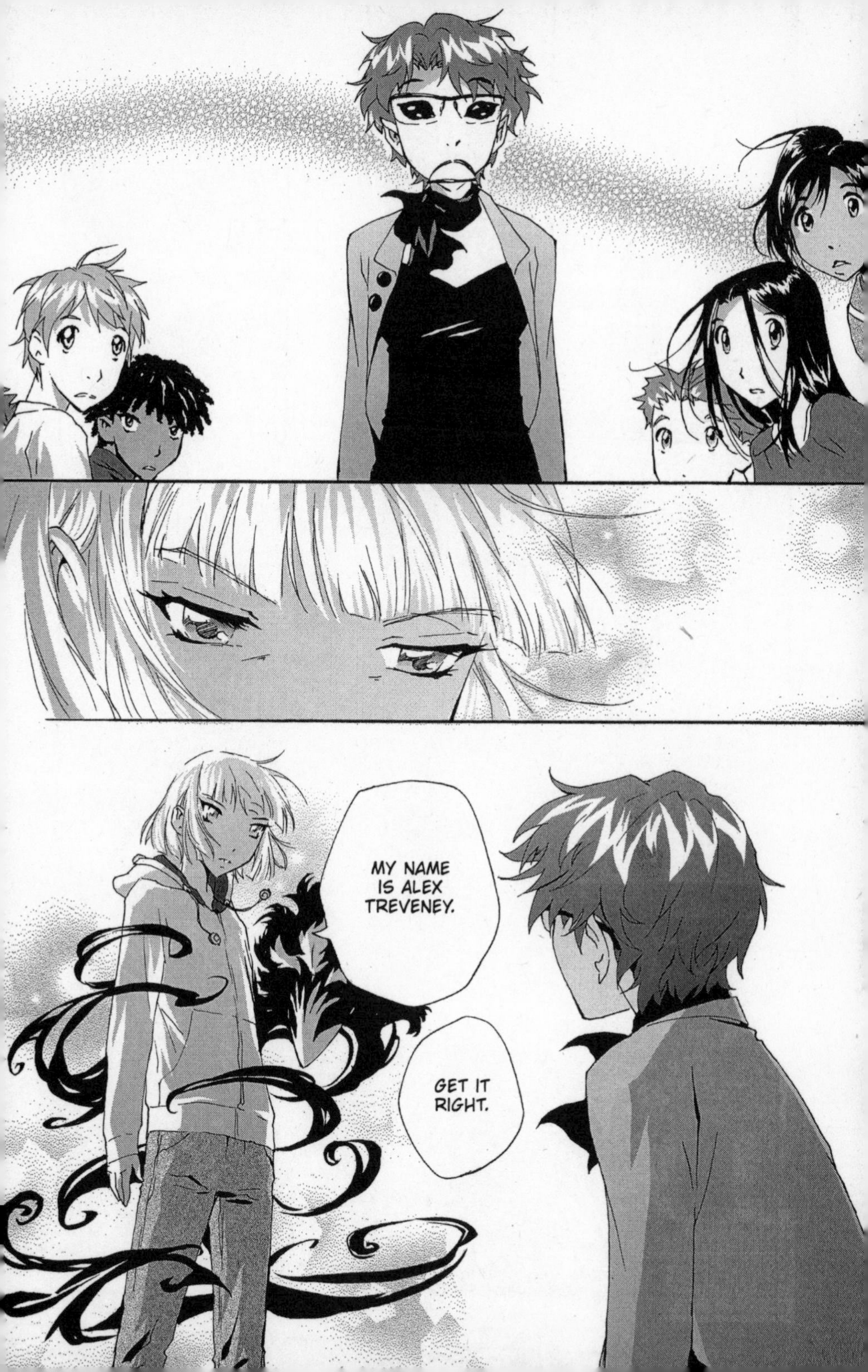
MY NAME IS ALEX TREVENEY.
GET IT RIGHT.

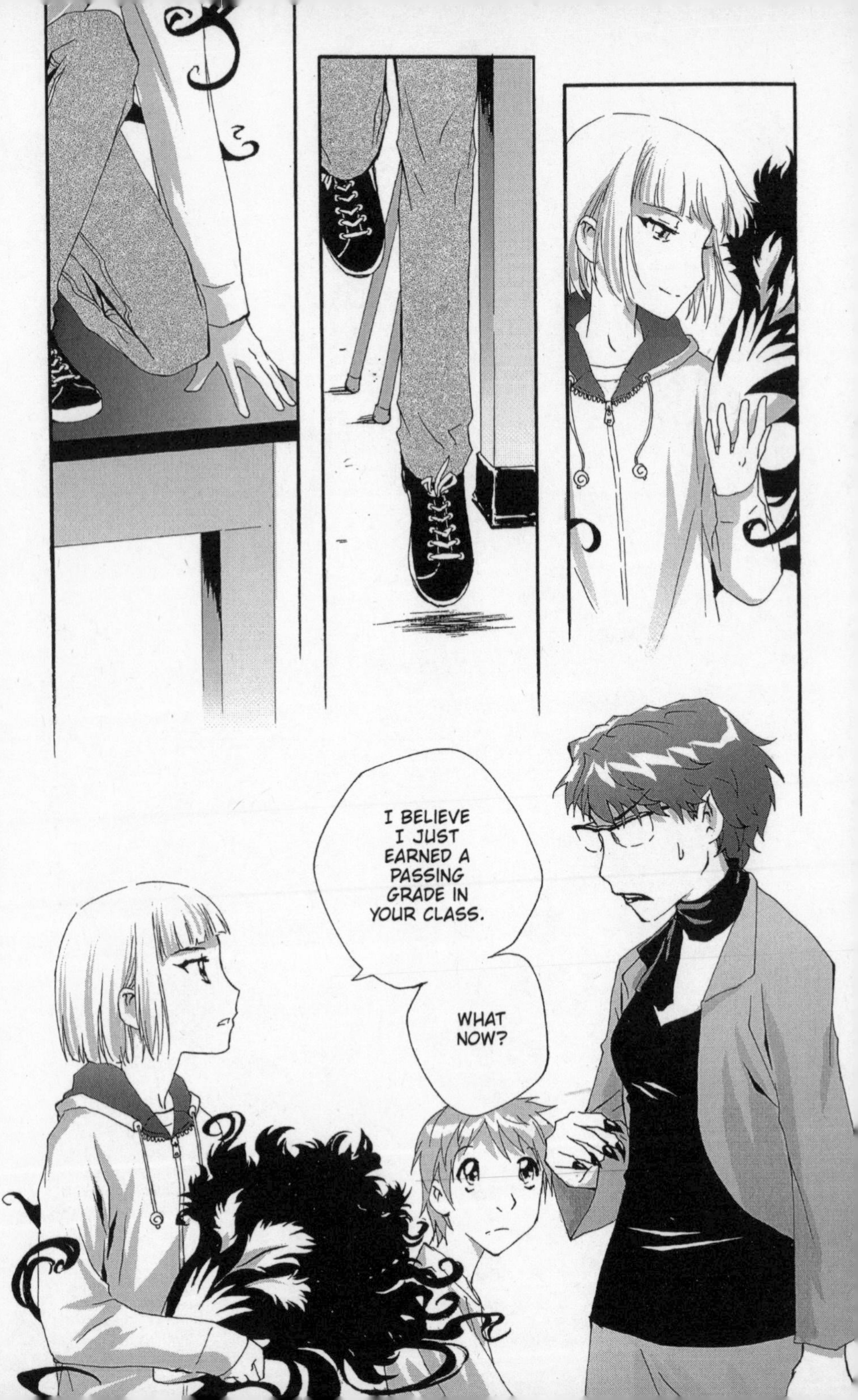
I BELIEVE I JUST EARNED A PASSING GRADE IN YOUR CLASS.
WHAT NOW?

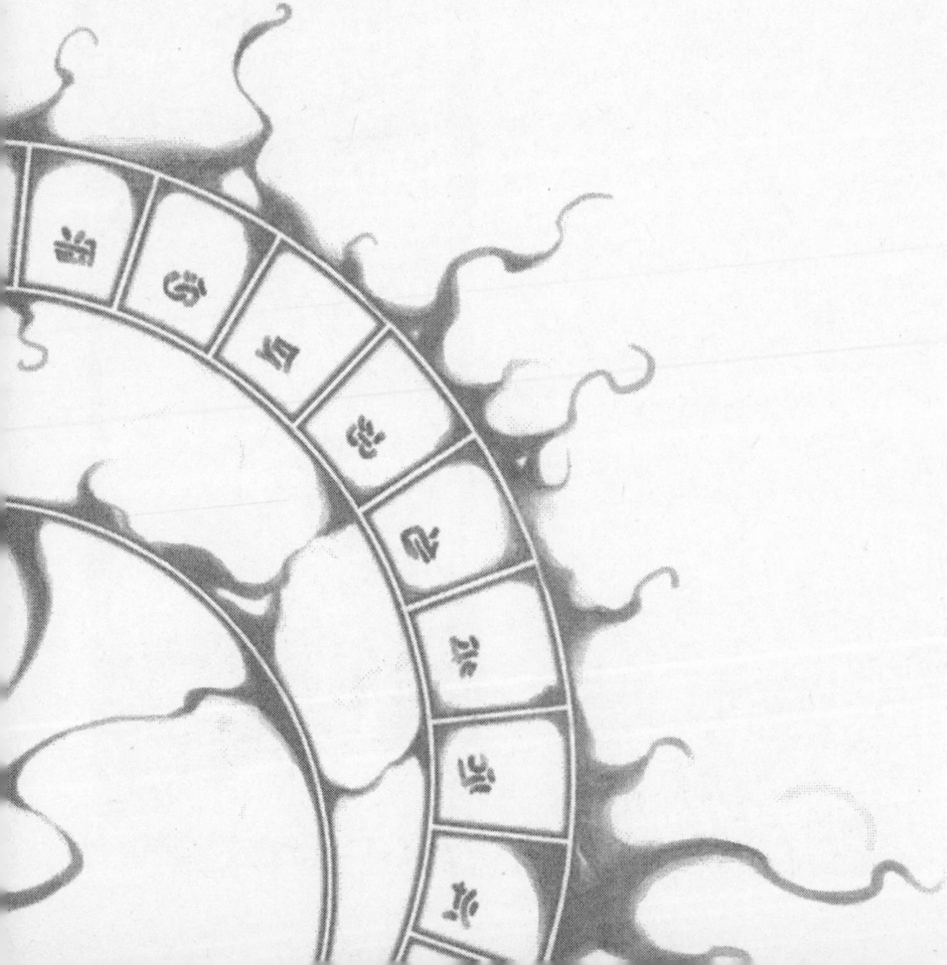

Chapter 12

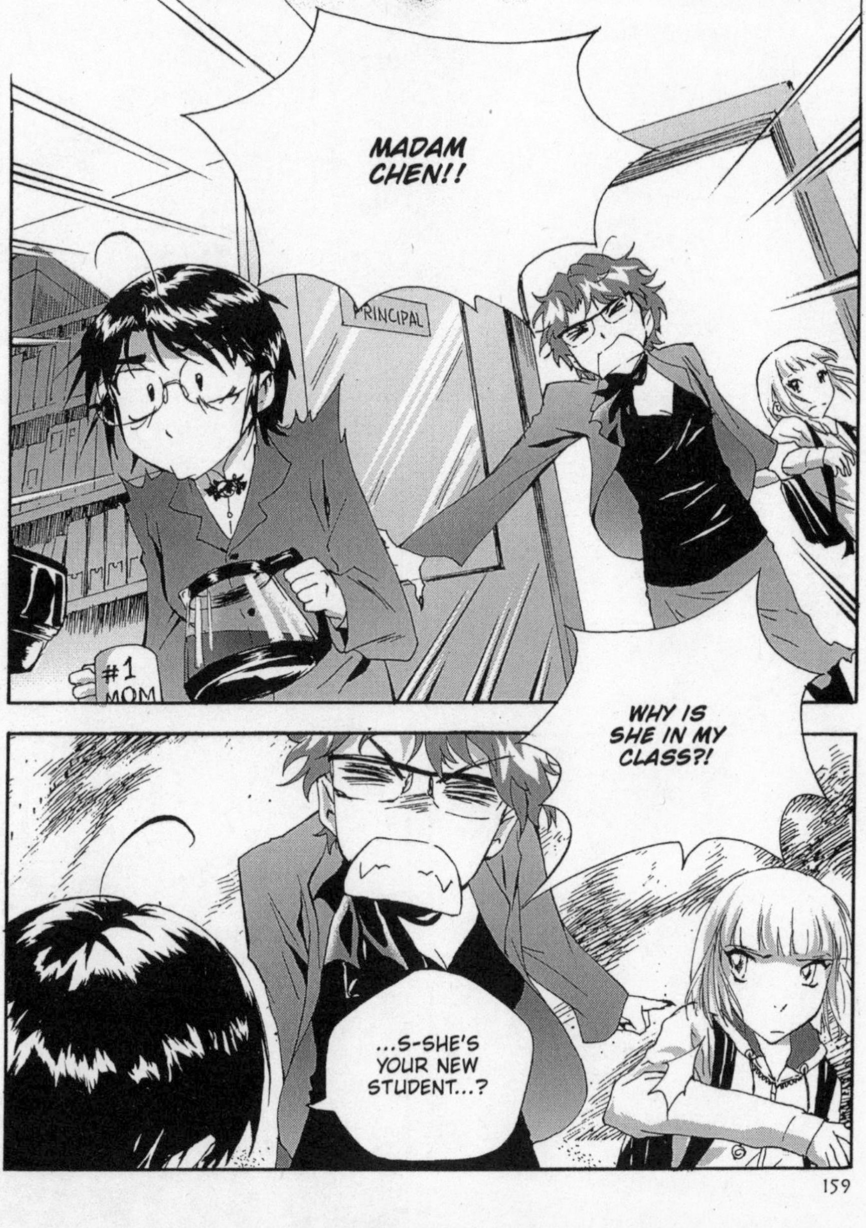

MADAM CHEN!!
WHY IS SHE IN MY CLASS?!
PRINCIPAL
#1 MOM
...S-SHE'S YOUR NEW STUDENT...?

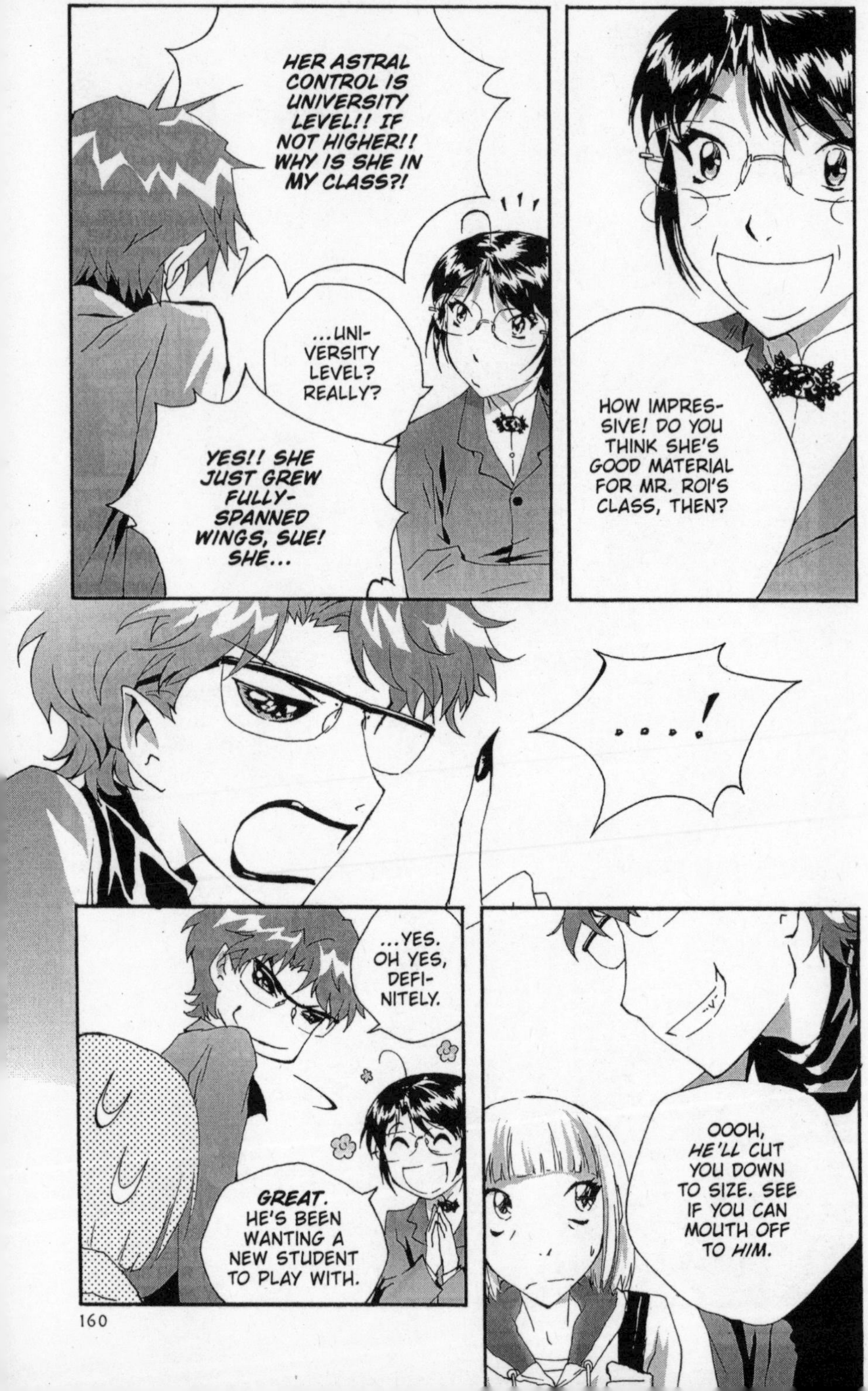
HER ASTRAL CONTROL IS UNIVERSITY LEVEL!! IF NOT HIGHER!! WHY IS SHE IN MY CLASS?!
...UNI-VERSITY LEVEL? REALLY?
YES!! SHE JUST GREW FULLY-SPANNED WINGS, SUE! SHE...
HOW IMPRES-SIVE! DO YOU THINK SHE'S GOOD MATERIAL FOR MR. ROI'S CLASS, THEN?
...!
...YES. OH YES, DEFI-NITELY.
GREAT. HE'S BEEN WANTING A NEW STUDENT TO PLAY WITH.
OOOH, *HE'LL* CUT YOU DOWN TO SIZE. SEE IF YOU CAN MOUTH OFF TO *HIM*.

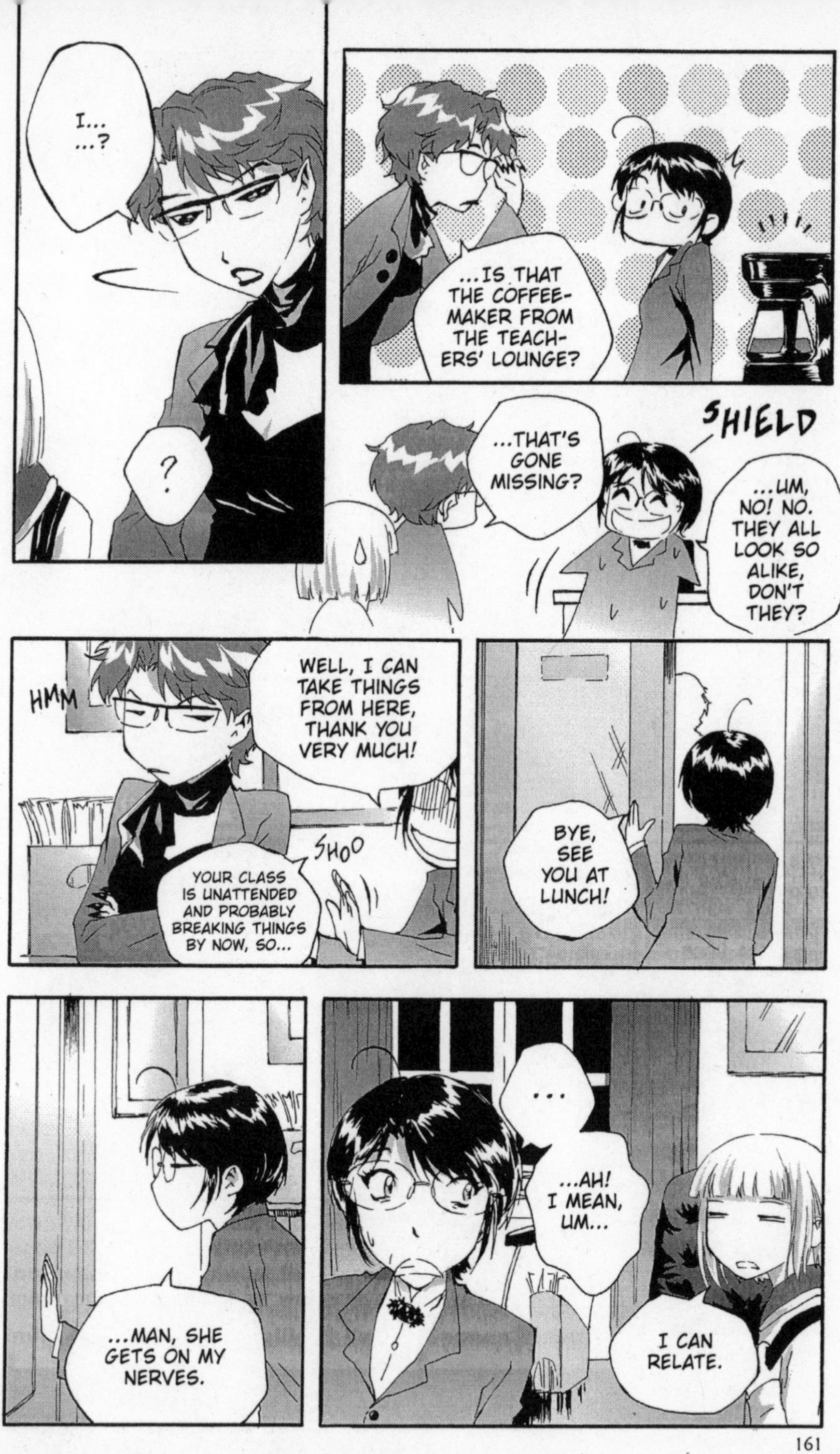
I...
...?
?
...IS THAT THE COFFEE-MAKER FROM THE TEACHERS' LOUNGE?
...THAT'S GONE MISSING?
SHIELD
...UM, NO! NO. THEY ALL LOOK SO ALIKE, DON'T THEY?
HMM
WELL, I CAN TAKE THINGS FROM HERE, THANK YOU VERY MUCH!
SHOO
YOUR CLASS IS UNATTENDED AND PROBABLY BREAKING THINGS BY NOW, SO...
BYE, SEE YOU AT LUNCH!
...MAN, SHE GETS ON MY NERVES.
...
...AH! I MEAN, UM...
I CAN RELATE.

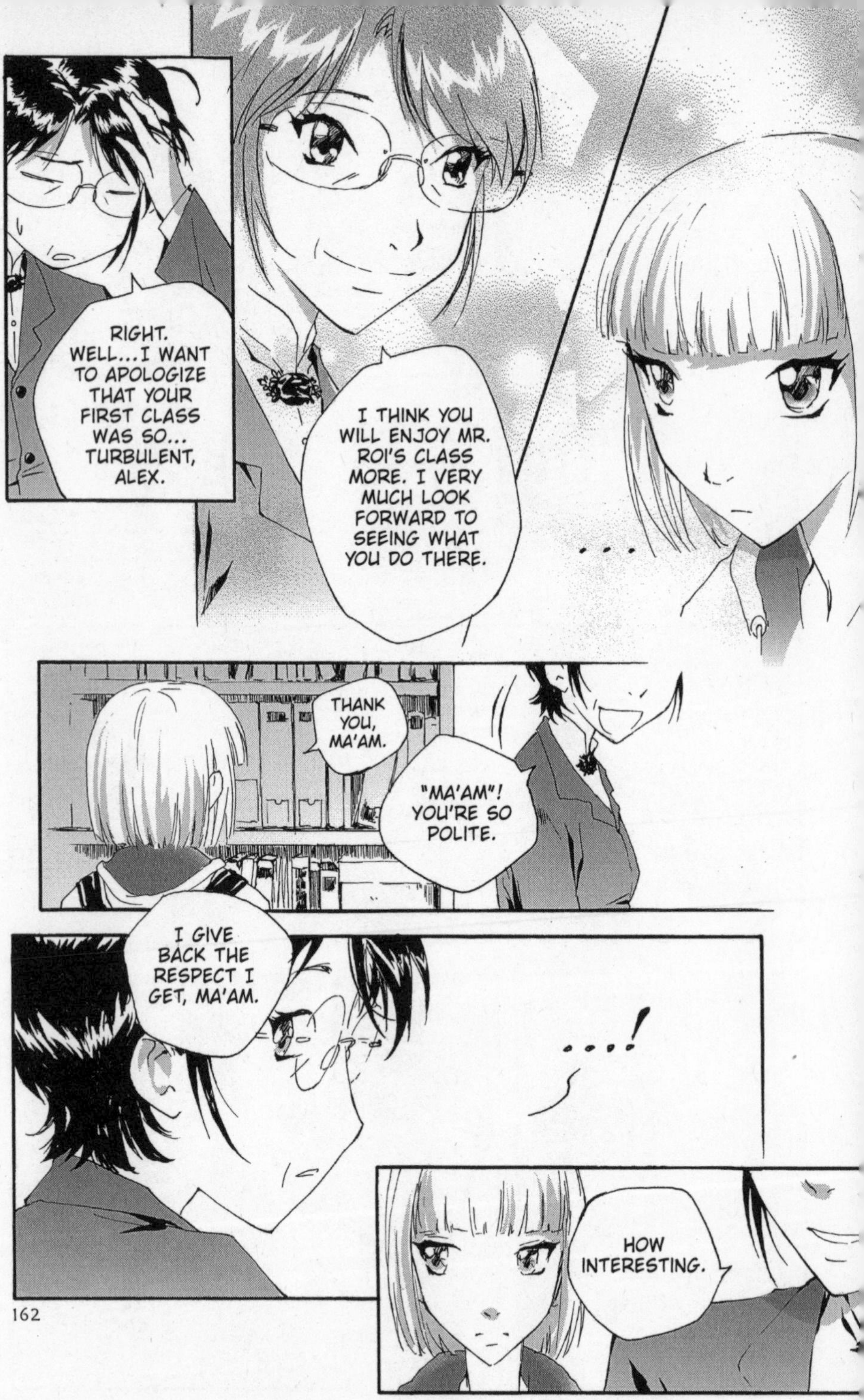
RIGHT. WELL...I WANT TO APOLOGIZE THAT YOUR FIRST CLASS WAS SO... TURBULENT, ALEX.
I THINK YOU WILL ENJOY MR. ROI'S CLASS MORE. I VERY MUCH LOOK FORWARD TO SEEING WHAT YOU DO THERE.
...
THANK YOU, MA'AM.
"MA'AM"! YOU'RE SO POLITE.
I GIVE BACK THE RESPECT I GET, MA'AM.
...!
HOW INTERESTING.

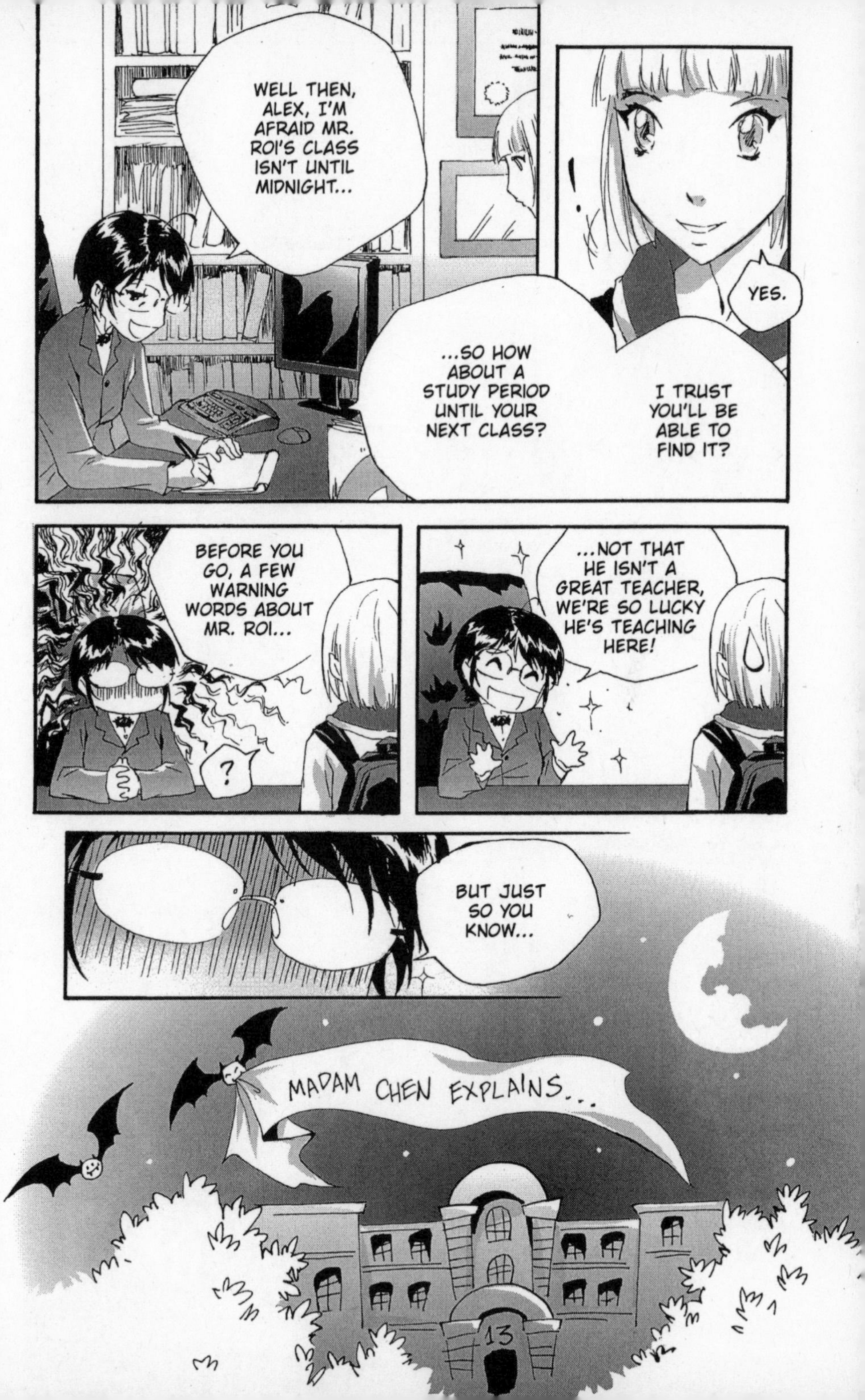
WELL THEN, ALEX, I'M AFRAID MR. ROI'S CLASS ISN'T UNTIL MIDNIGHT...
...SO HOW ABOUT A STUDY PERIOD UNTIL YOUR NEXT CLASS?
I TRUST YOU'LL BE ABLE TO FIND IT?
YES.
BEFORE YOU GO, A FEW WARNING WORDS ABOUT MR. ROI...
?
...NOT THAT HE ISN'T A GREAT TEACHER, WE'RE SO LUCKY HE'S TEACHING HERE!
BUT JUST SO YOU KNOW...
MADAM CHEN EXPLAINS...
13

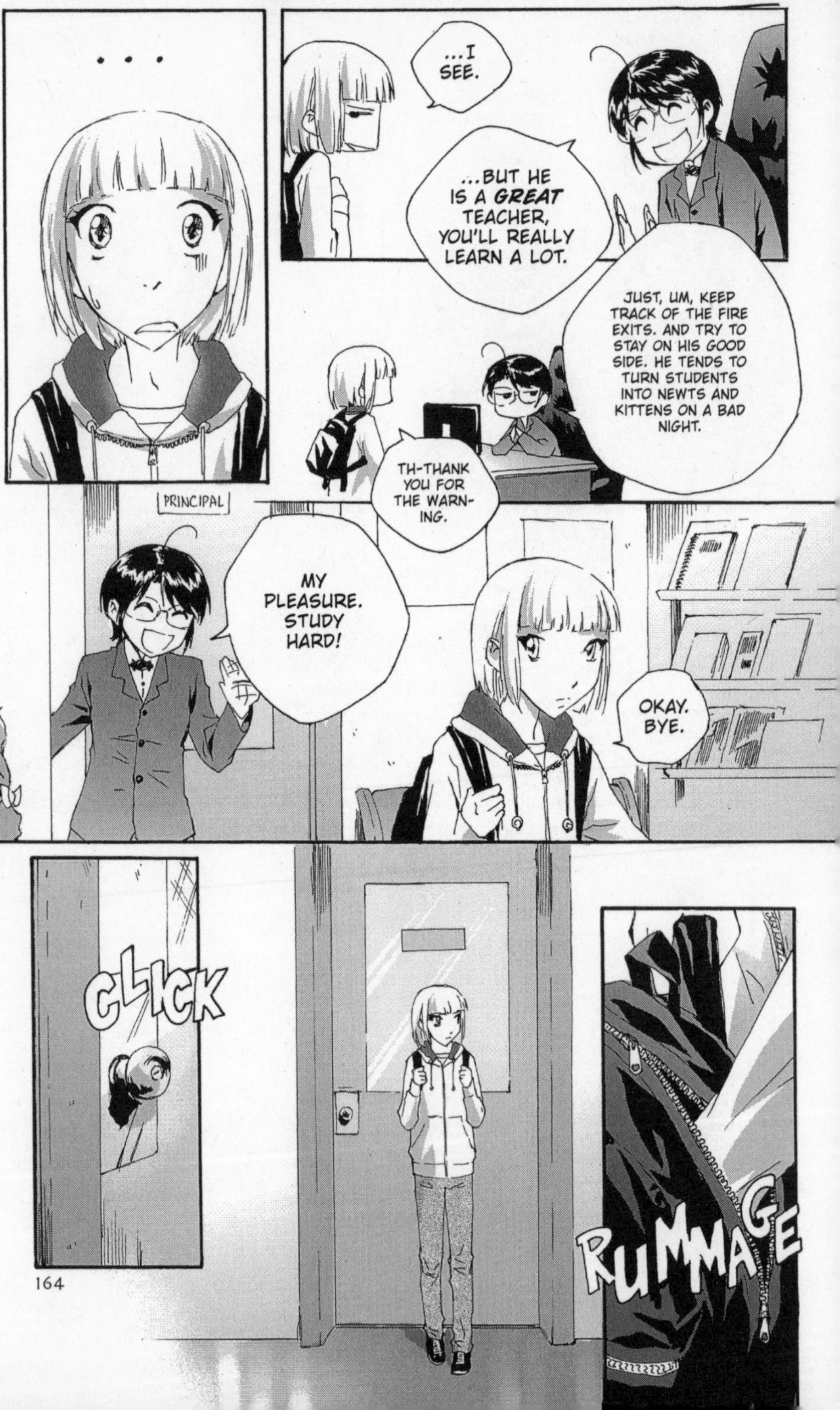
. . .
...I SEE.
...BUT HE IS A GREAT TEACHER, YOU'LL REALLY LEARN A LOT.
JUST, UM, KEEP TRACK OF THE FIRE EXITS. AND TRY TO STAY ON HIS GOOD SIDE. HE TENDS TO TURN STUDENTS INTO NEWTS AND KITTENS ON A BAD NIGHT.
TH-THANK YOU FOR THE WARN-ING.
PRINCIPAL
MY PLEASURE. STUDY HARD!
OKAY. BYE.
CLICK
RUMMAGE

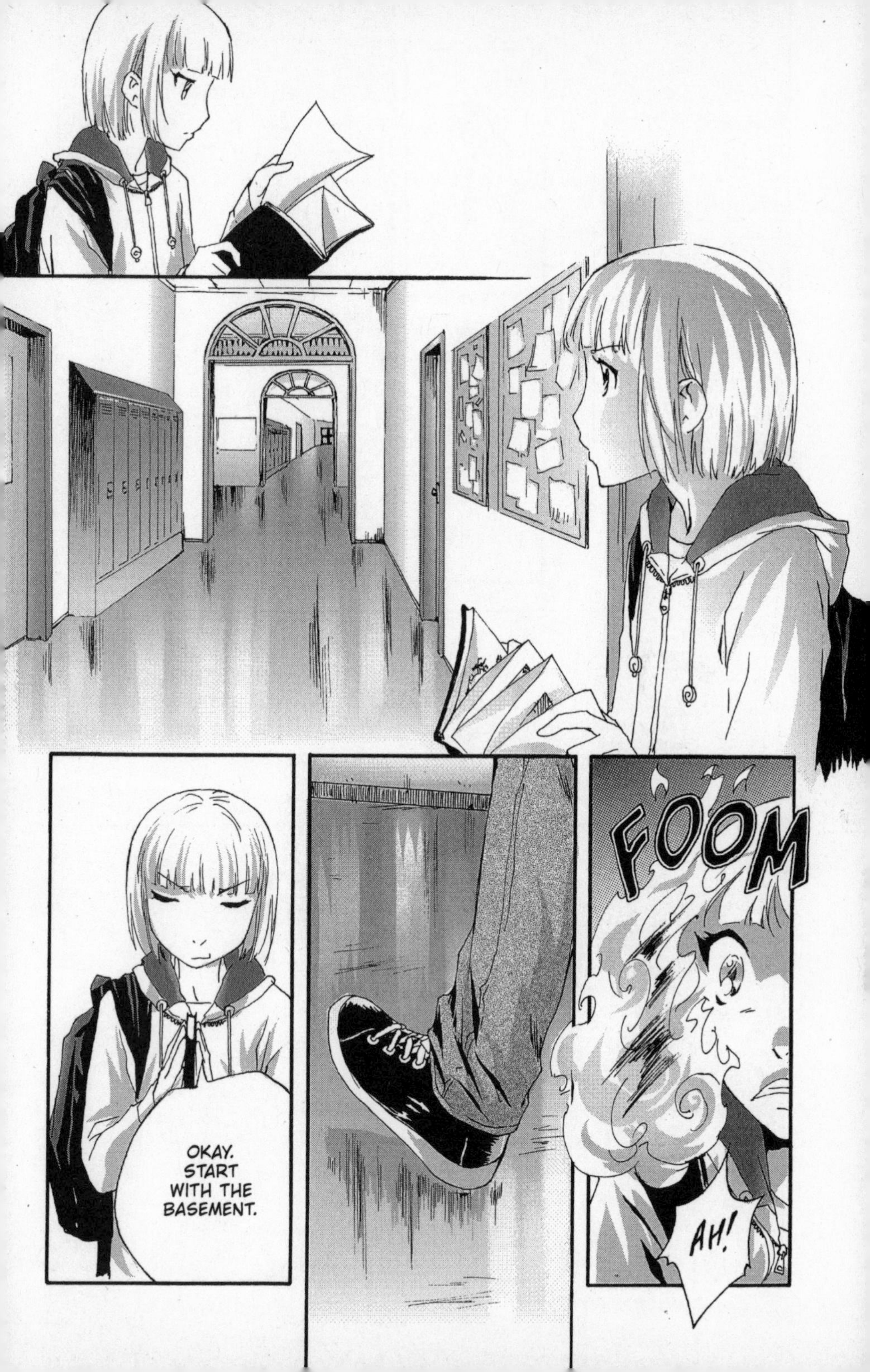
OKAY. START WITH THE BASEMENT.
FOOM
AH!

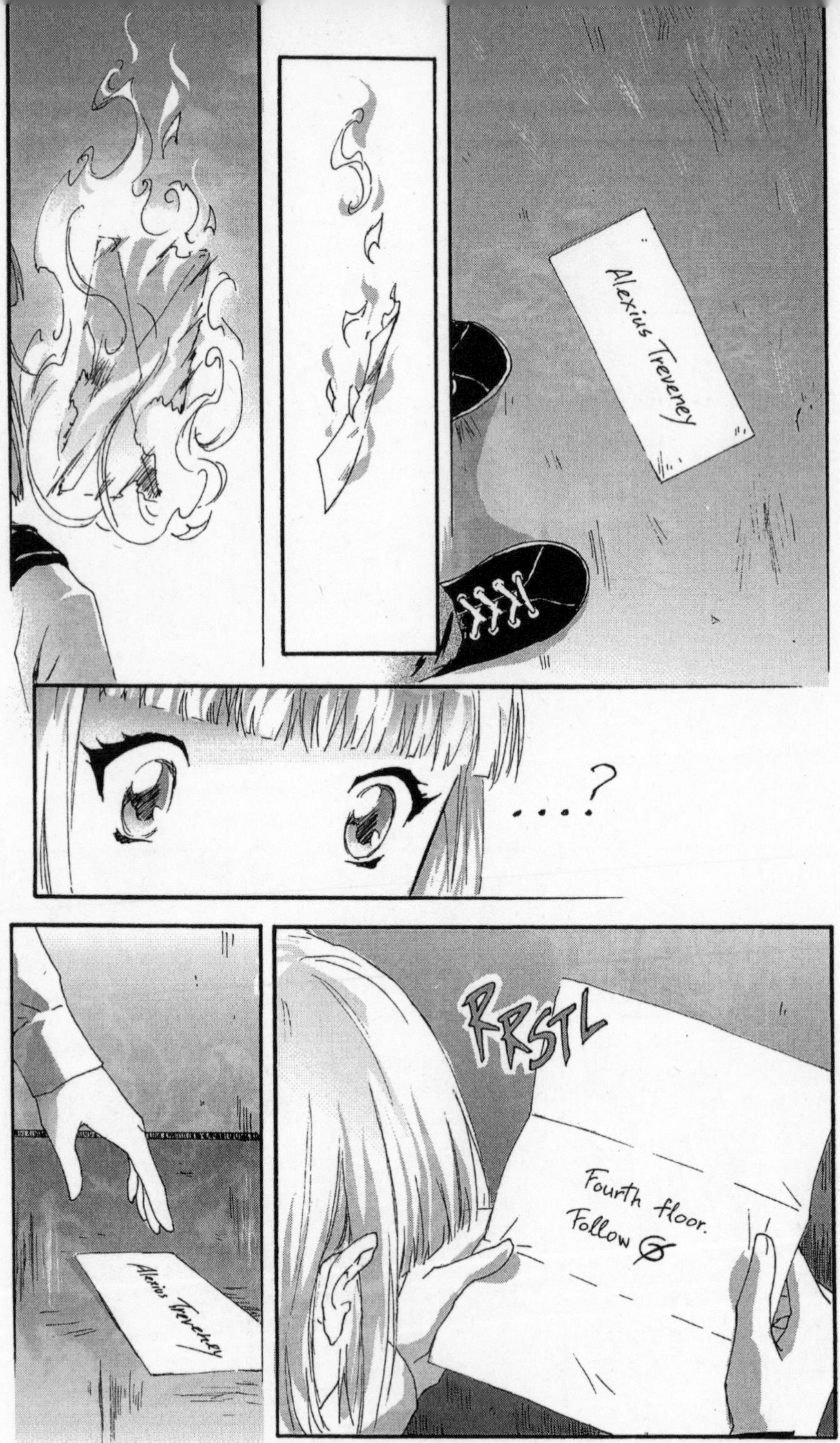
Alexius Treveney
...?
Alexius Treveney
RRSTL
Fourth floor.
Follow Ø

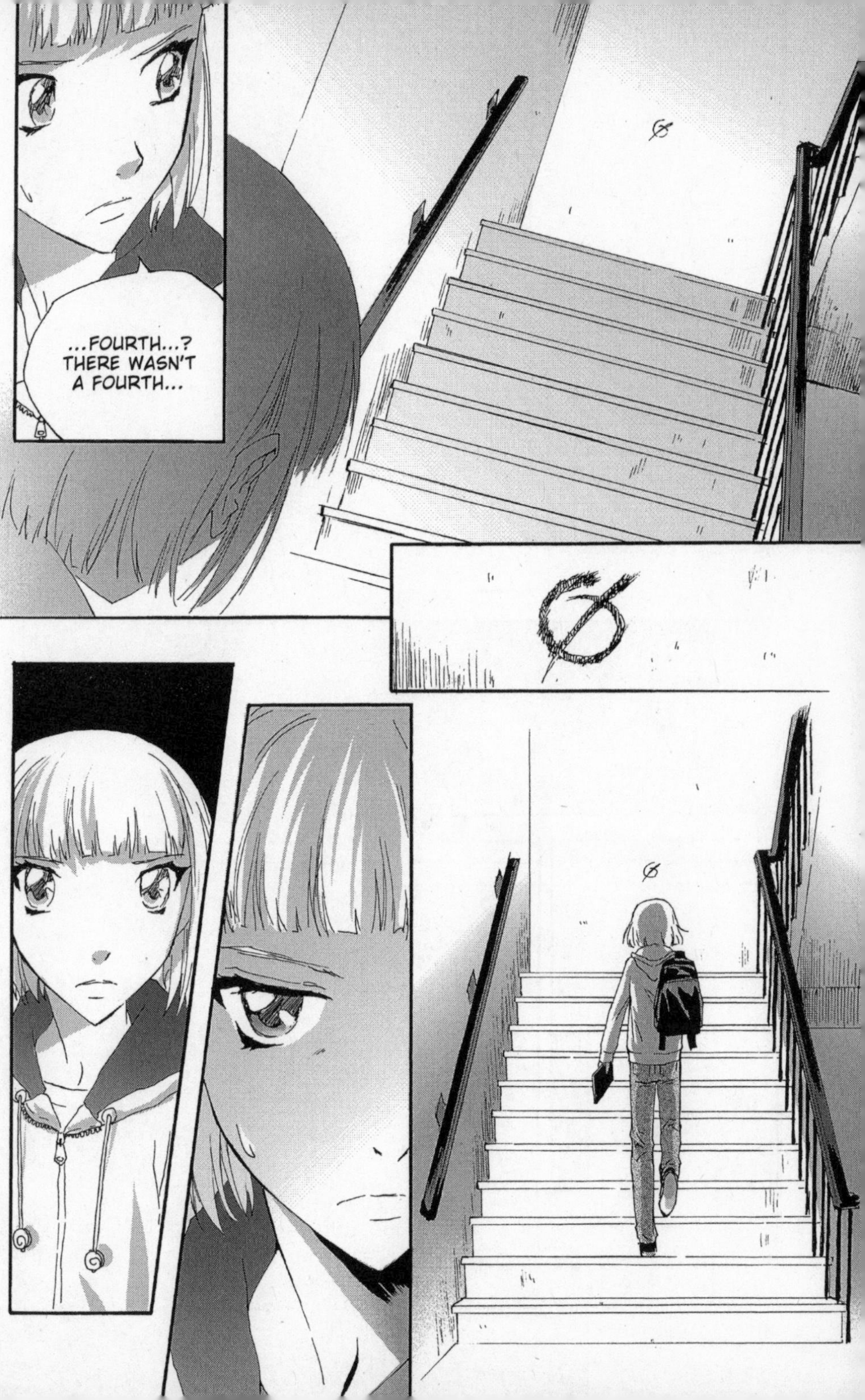
...FOURTH...? THERE WASN'T A FOURTH...

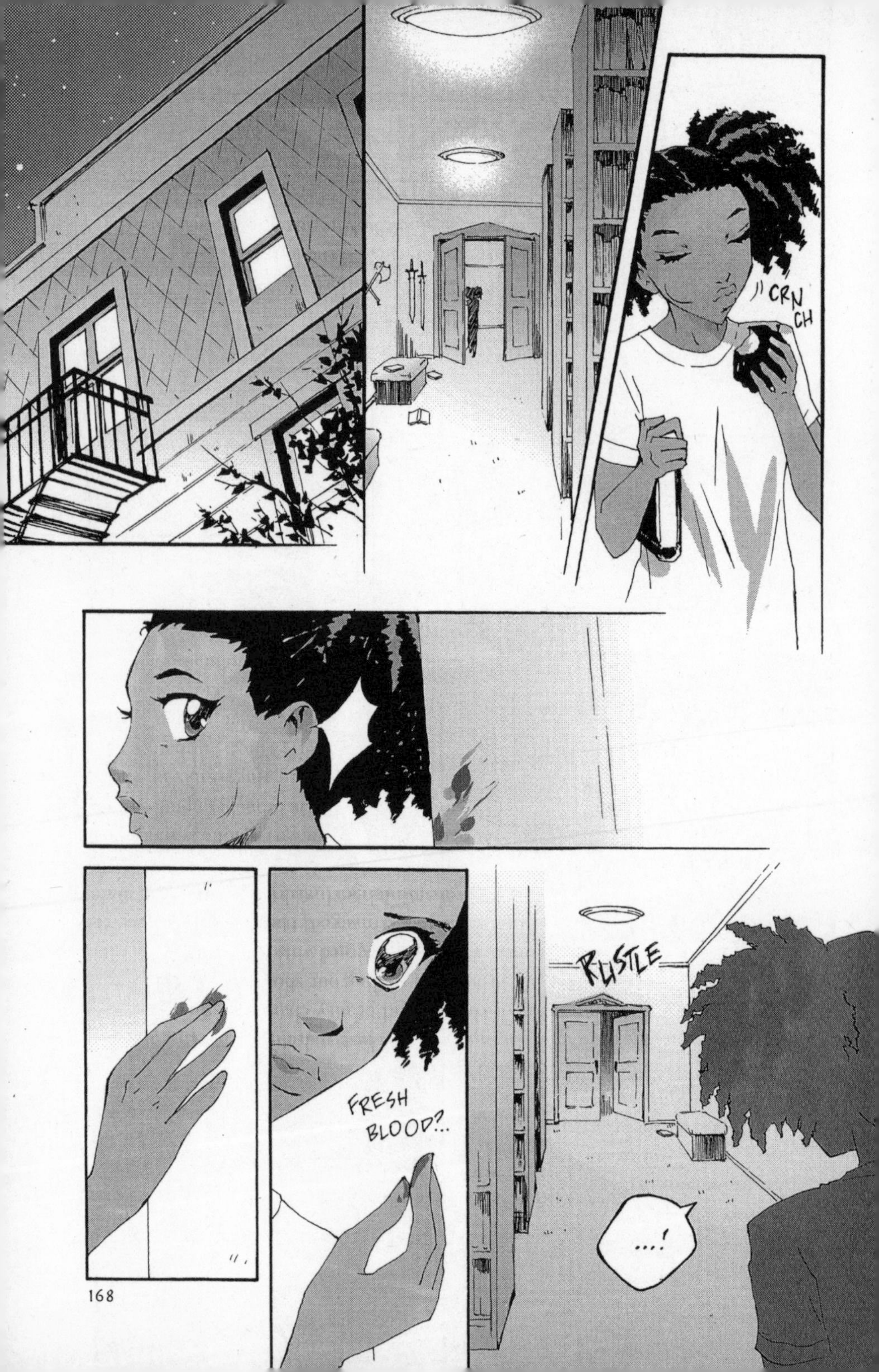
CRNCH
FRESH BLOOD?..
RUSTLE
...!

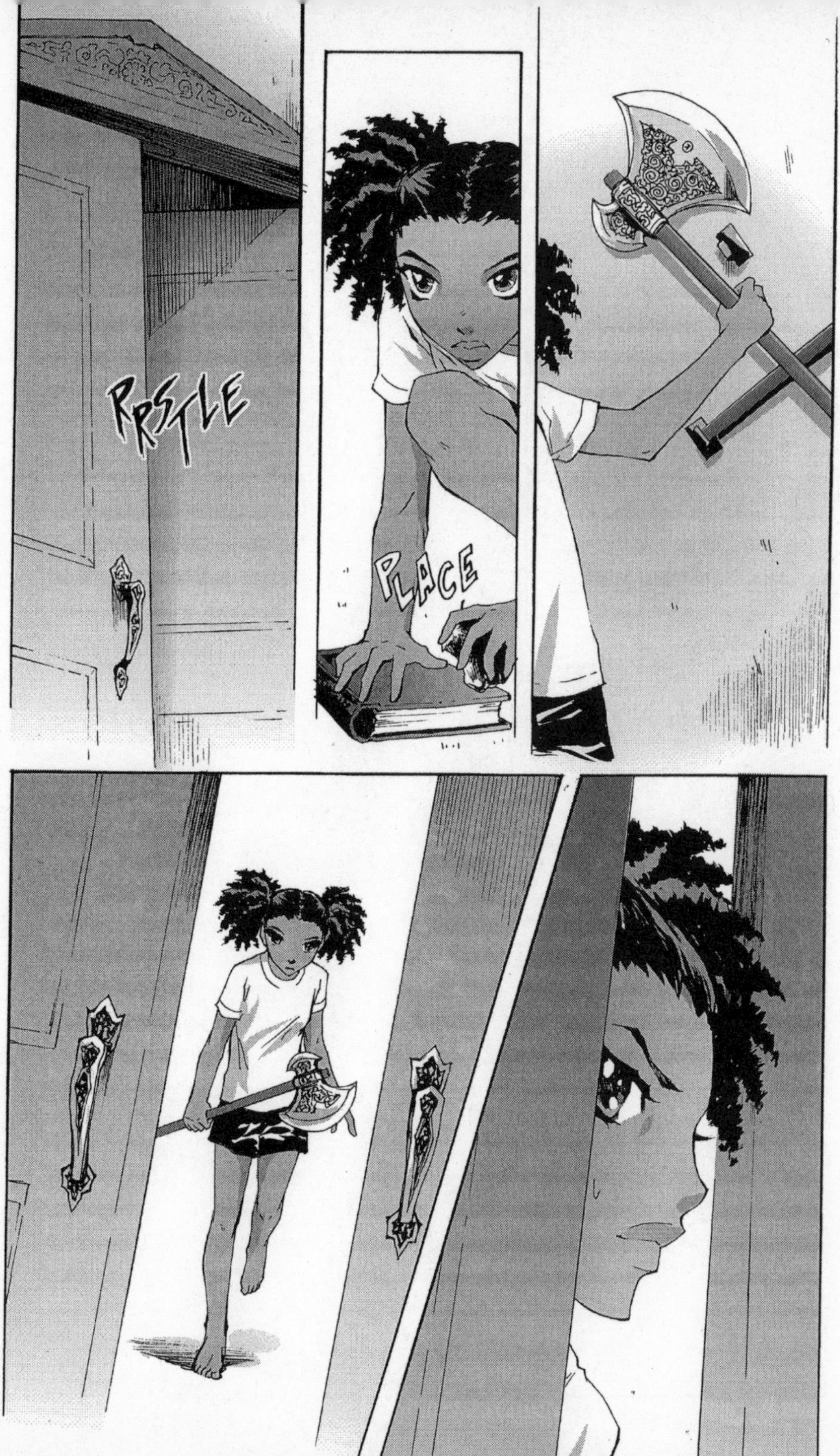
RRSTLE
PLACE

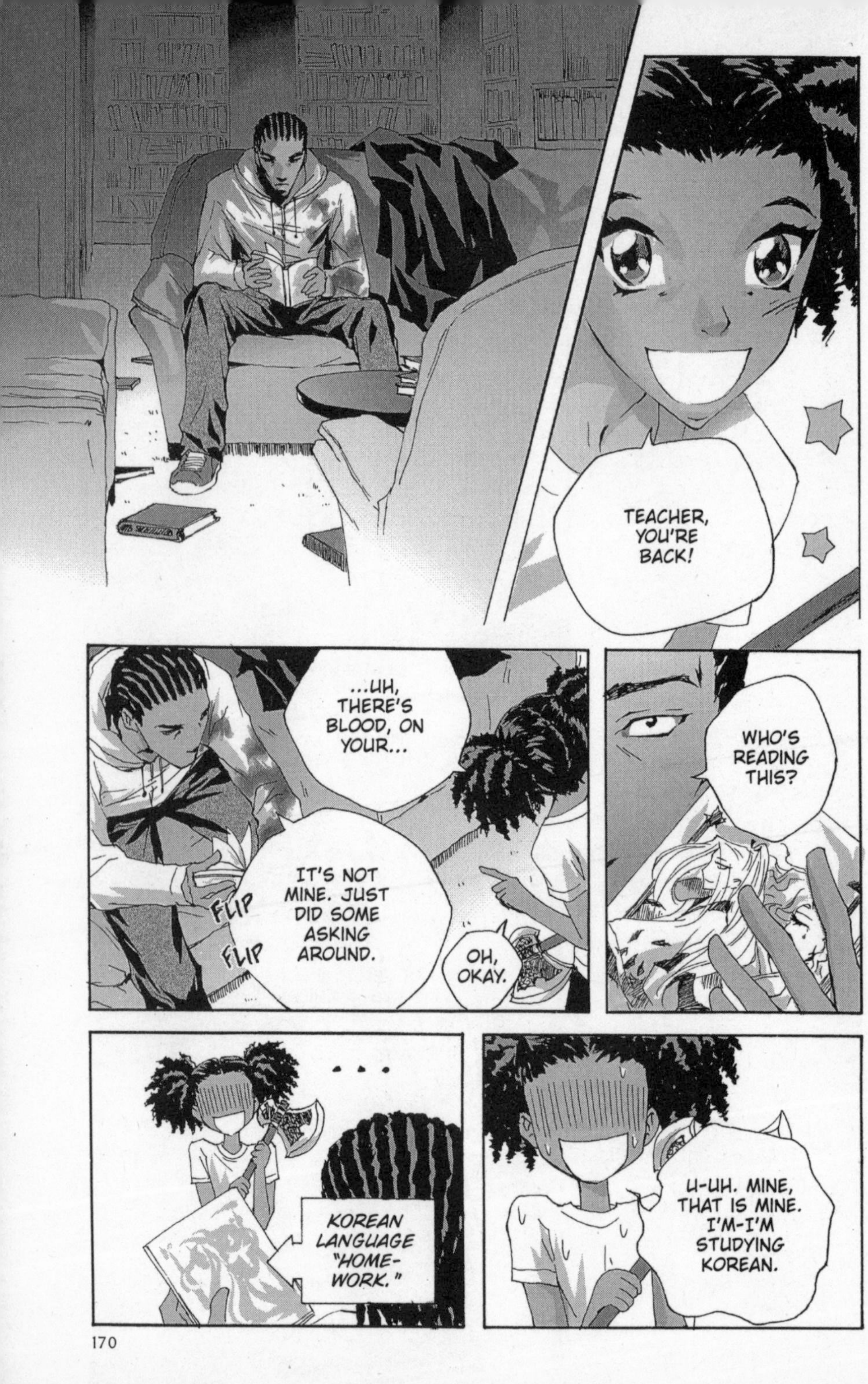
TEACHER, YOU'RE BACK!
...UH, THERE'S BLOOD, ON YOUR...
IT'S NOT MINE. JUST DID SOME ASKING AROUND.
FLIP
FLIP
OH, OKAY.
WHO'S READING THIS?
...
KOREAN LANGUAGE "HOME-WORK."
U-UH. MINE, THAT IS MINE. I'M-I'M STUDYING KOREAN.

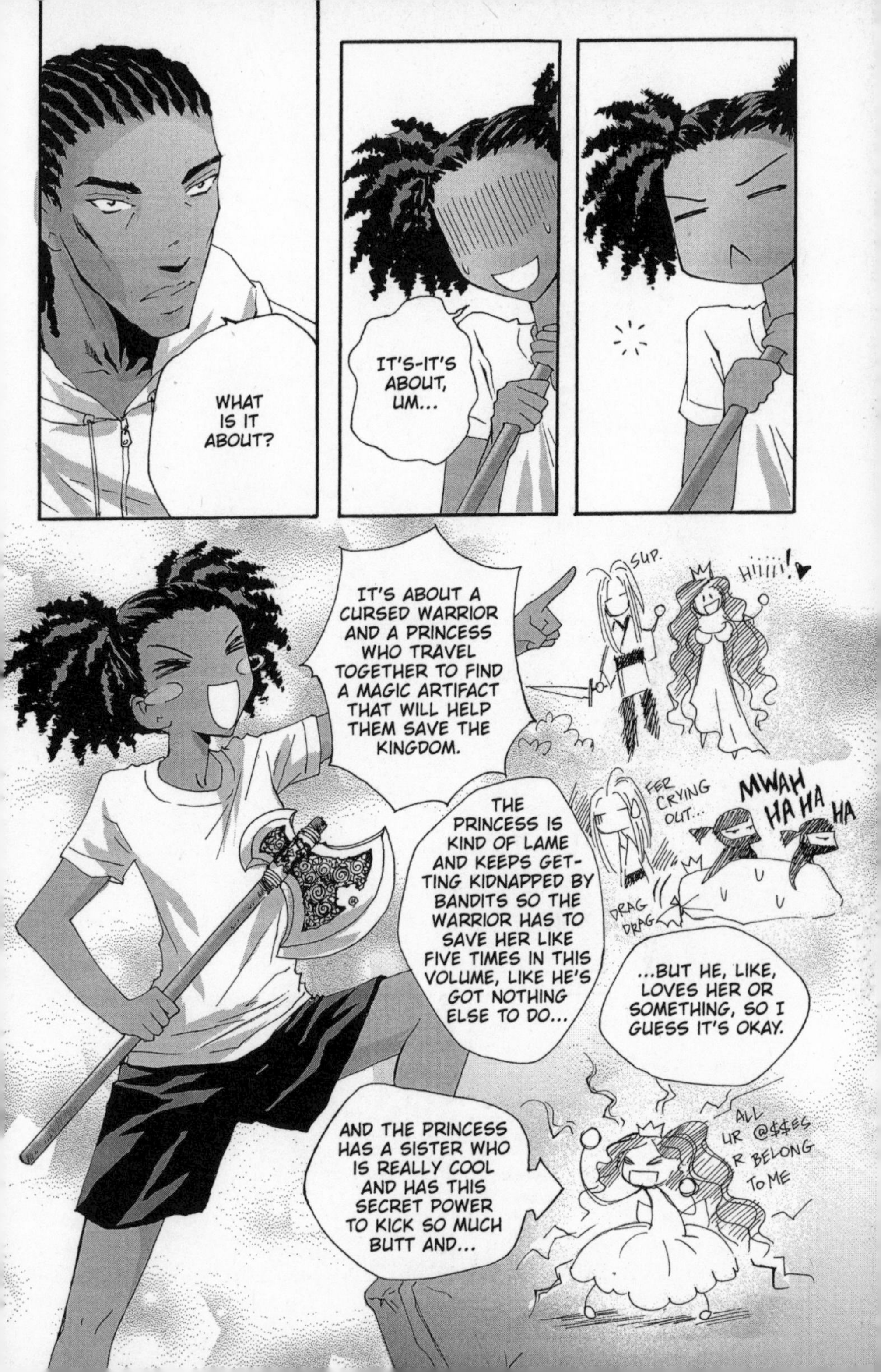
WHAT IS IT ABOUT?
IT'S-IT'S ABOUT, UM...
IT'S ABOUT A CURSED WARRIOR AND A PRINCESS WHO TRAVEL TOGETHER TO FIND A MAGIC ARTIFACT THAT WILL HELP THEM SAVE THE KINGDOM.
SUP.
HIIIIII!♥
THE PRINCESS IS KIND OF LAME AND KEEPS GET-TING KIDNAPPED BY BANDITS SO THE WARRIOR HAS TO SAVE HER LIKE FIVE TIMES IN THIS VOLUME, LIKE HE'S GOT NOTHING ELSE TO DO...
FER CRYING OUT...
MWAH HA HA HA
DRAG DRAG
...BUT HE, LIKE, LOVES HER OR SOMETHING, SO I GUESS IT'S OKAY.
AND THE PRINCESS HAS A SISTER WHO IS REALLY COOL AND HAS THIS SECRET POWER TO KICK SO MUCH BUTT AND...
ALL UR @$$ES R BELONG TO ME

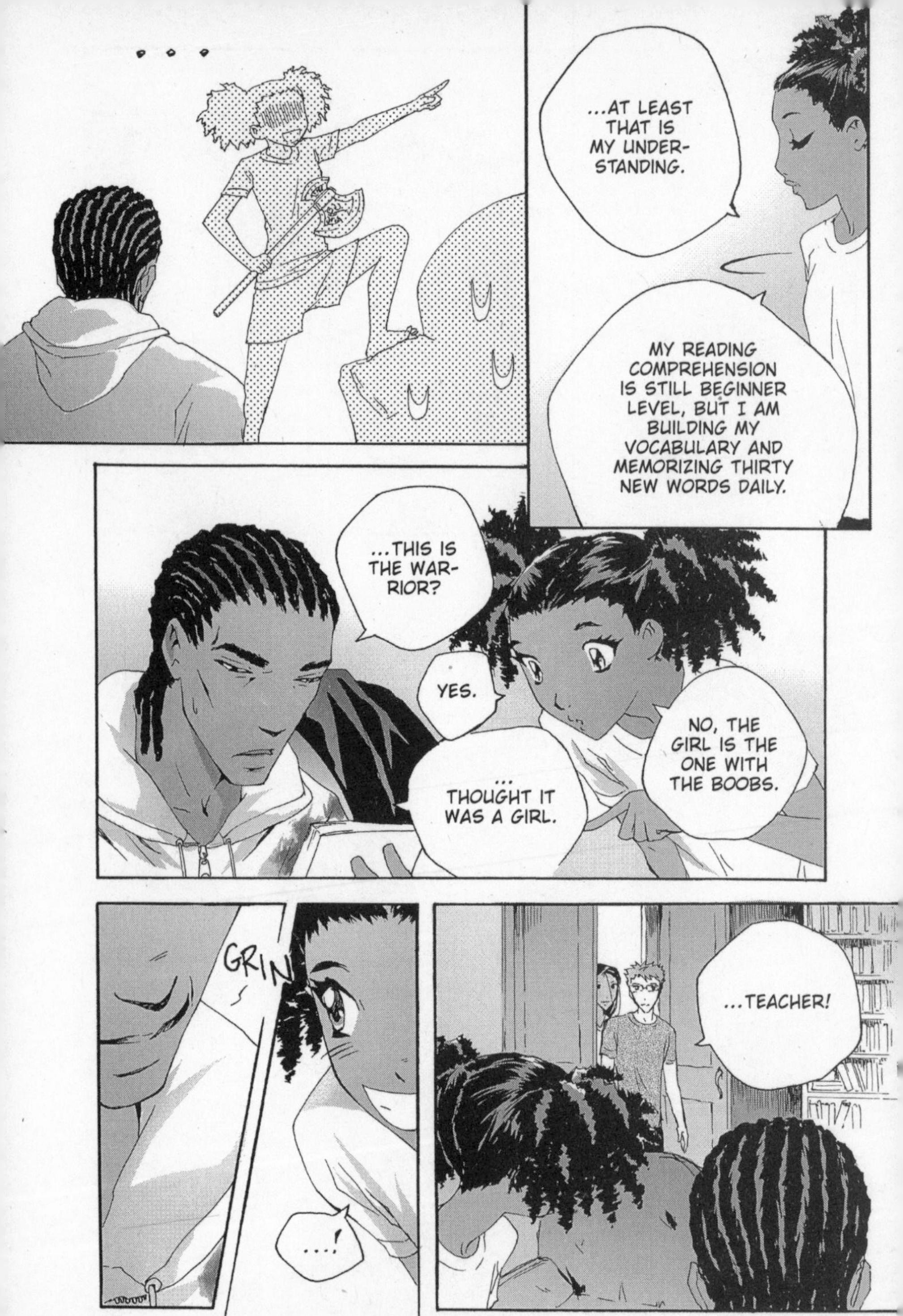
...AT LEAST THAT IS MY UNDER-STANDING.
MY READING COMPREHENSION IS STILL BEGINNER LEVEL, BUT I AM BUILDING MY VOCABULARY AND MEMORIZING THIRTY NEW WORDS DAILY.
...THIS IS THE WAR-RIOR?
YES.
... THOUGHT IT WAS A GIRL.
NO, THE GIRL IS THE ONE WITH THE BOOBS.
GRIN
...!
...TEACHER!

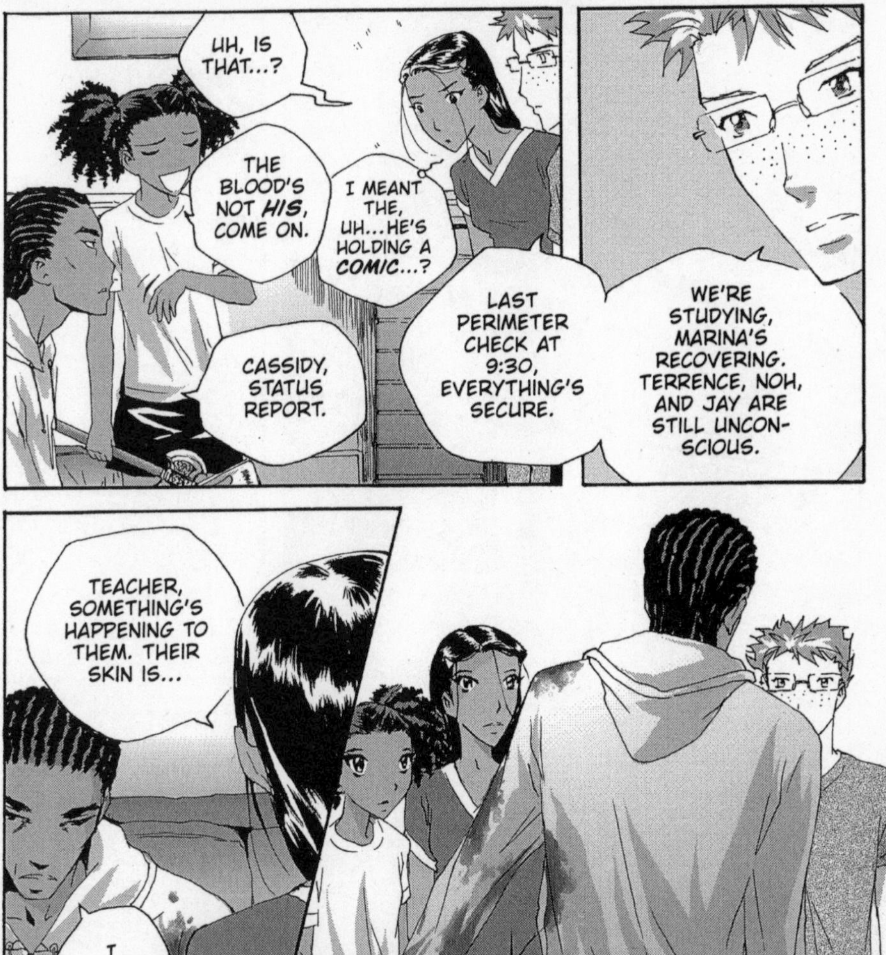
UH, IS THAT...?
THE BLOOD'S NOT *HIS*, COME ON.
I MEANT THE, UH...HE'S HOLDING A *COMIC*...?
CASSIDY, STATUS REPORT.
LAST PERIMETER CHECK AT 9:30, EVERYTHING'S SECURE.
WE'RE STUDYING, MARINA'S RECOVERING. TERRENCE, NOH, AND JAY ARE STILL UNCONSCIOUS.
TEACHER, SOMETHING'S HAPPENING TO THEM. THEIR SKIN IS...
I KNOW.
WHERE IS MARINA?

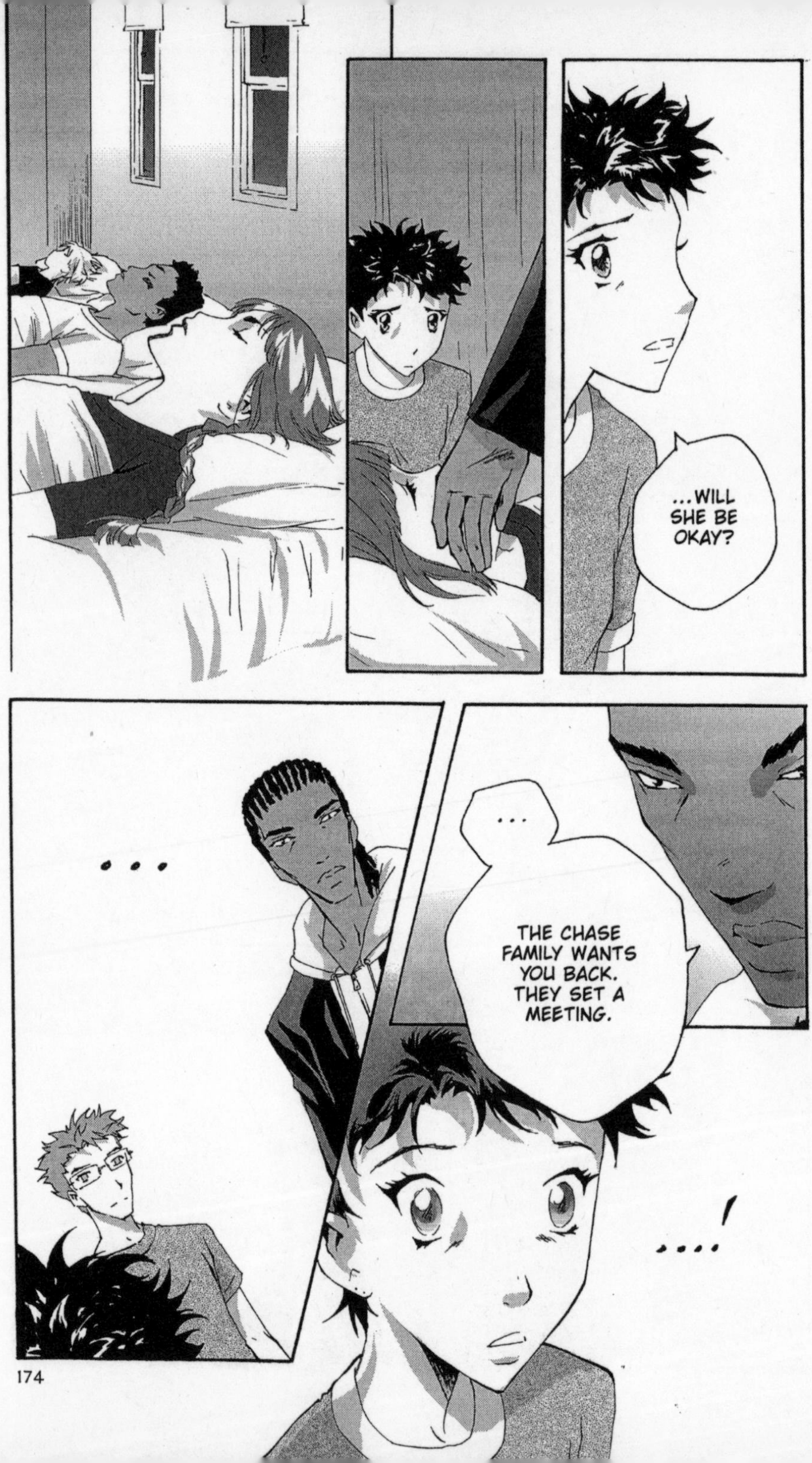
...WILL SHE BE OKAY?
...
...
THE CHASE FAMILY WANTS YOU BACK. THEY SET A MEETING.
...!

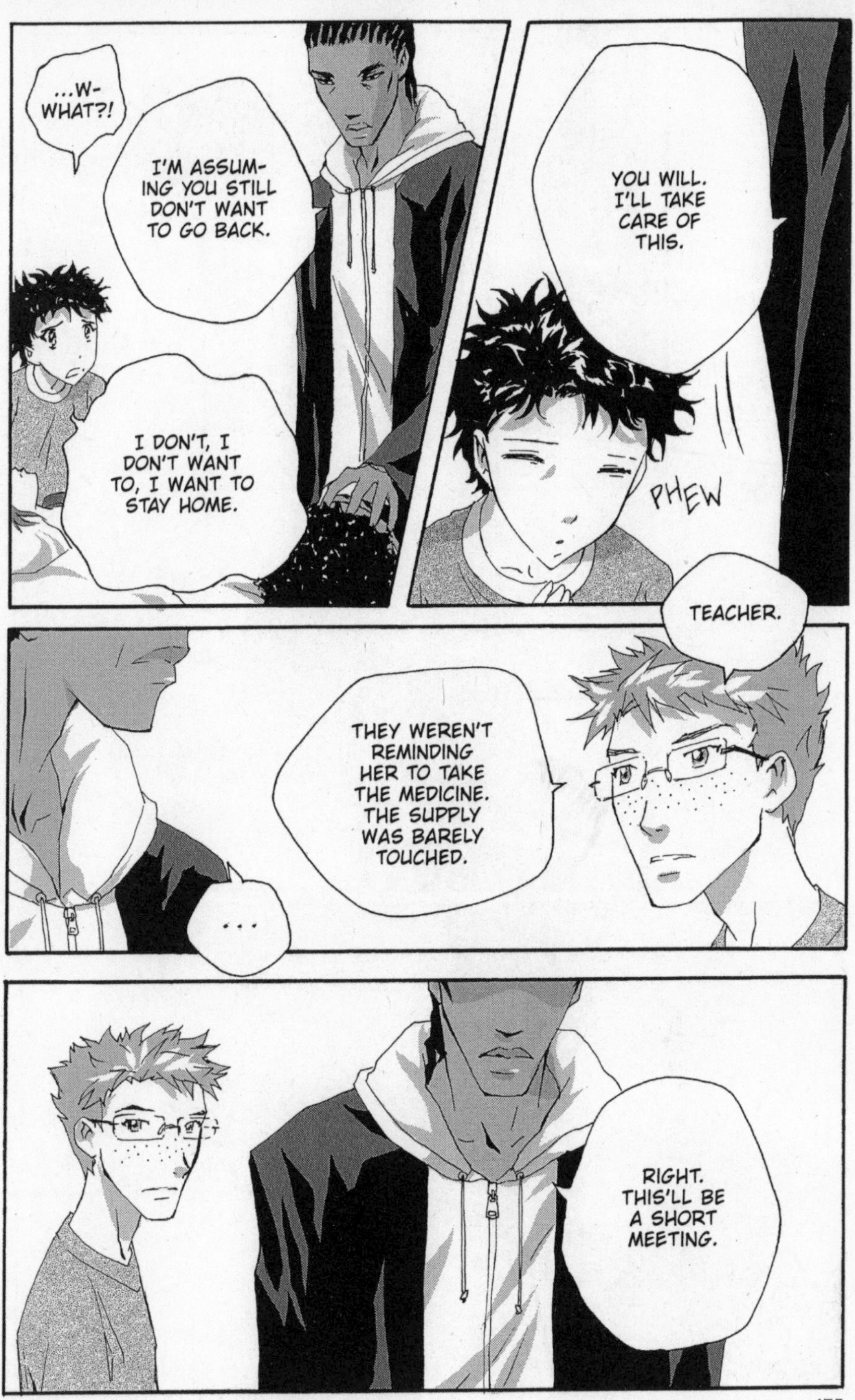
...W- WHAT?!
I'M ASSUMING YOU STILL DON'T WANT TO GO BACK.
I DON'T, I DON'T WANT TO, I WANT TO STAY HOME.
YOU WILL. I'LL TAKE CARE OF THIS.
PHEW
TEACHER.
THEY WEREN'T REMINDING HER TO TAKE THE MEDICINE. THE SUPPLY WAS BARELY TOUCHED.
...
RIGHT. THIS'LL BE A SHORT MEETING.

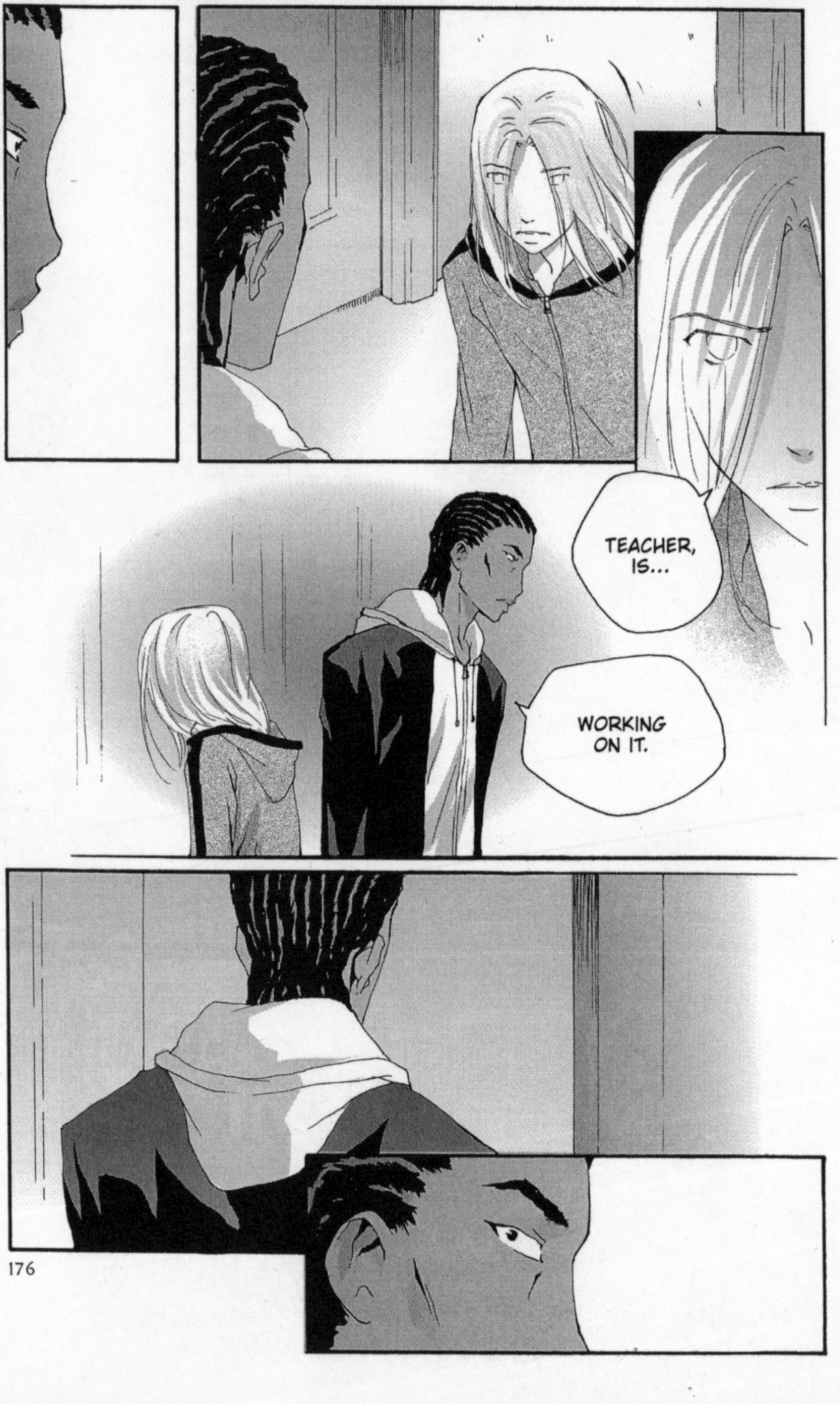
TEACHER, IS...
WORKING ON IT.

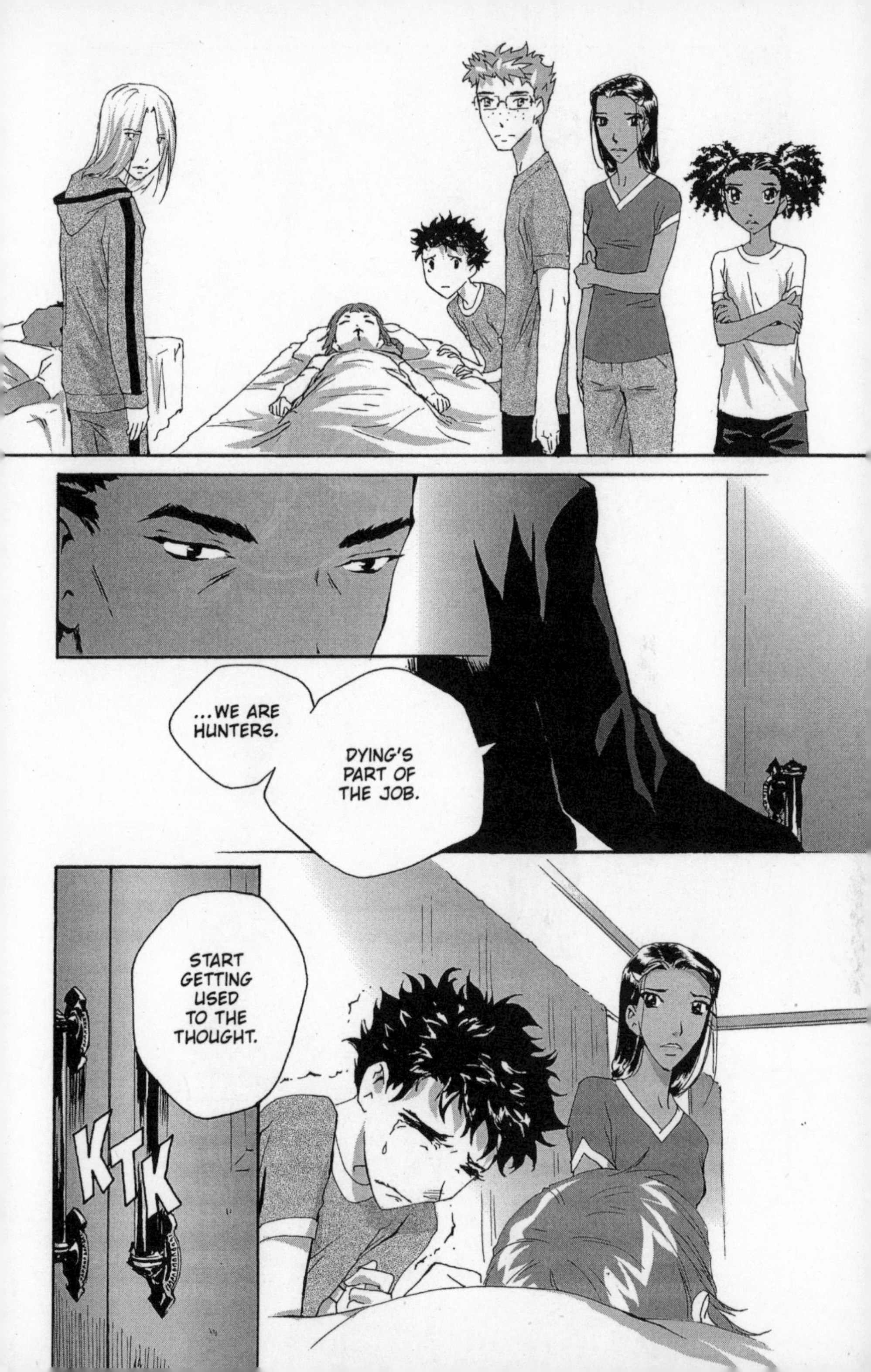
...WE ARE HUNTERS.
DYING'S PART OF THE JOB.
START GETTING USED TO THE THOUGHT.
KTK

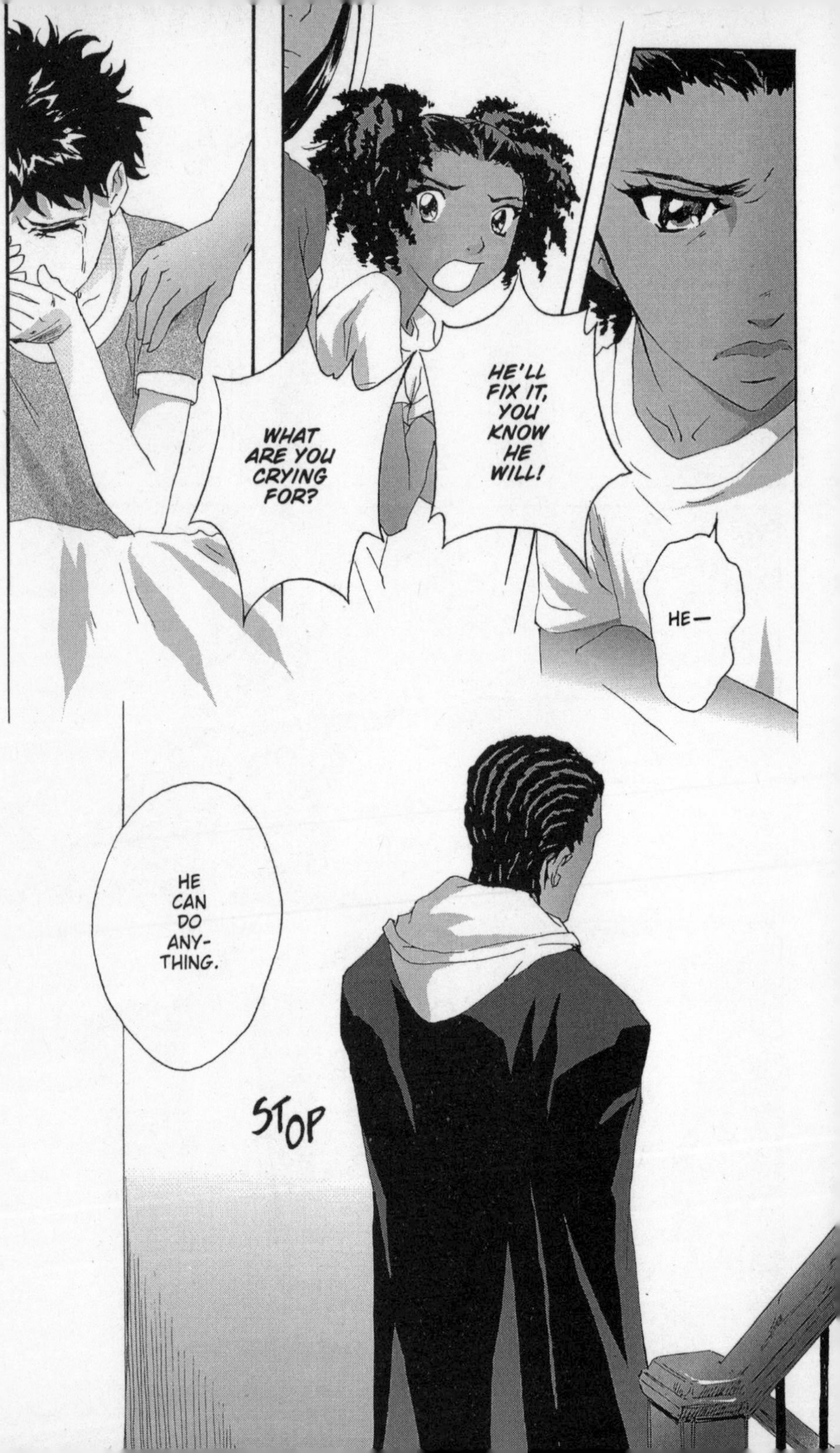
WHAT ARE YOU CRYING FOR?
HE'LL FIX IT, YOU KNOW HE WILL!
HE—
HE CAN DO ANY-THING.
STOP

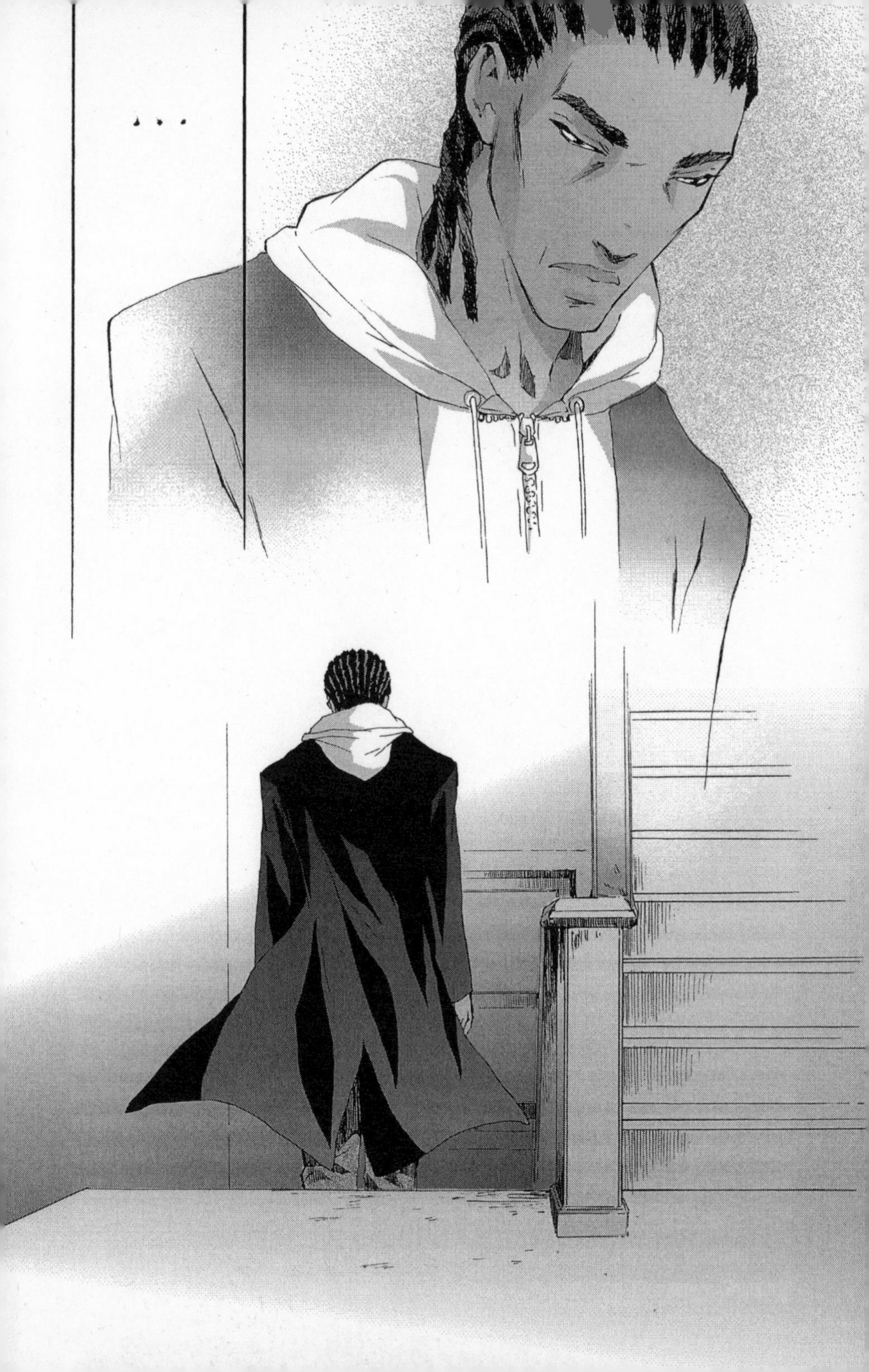
...

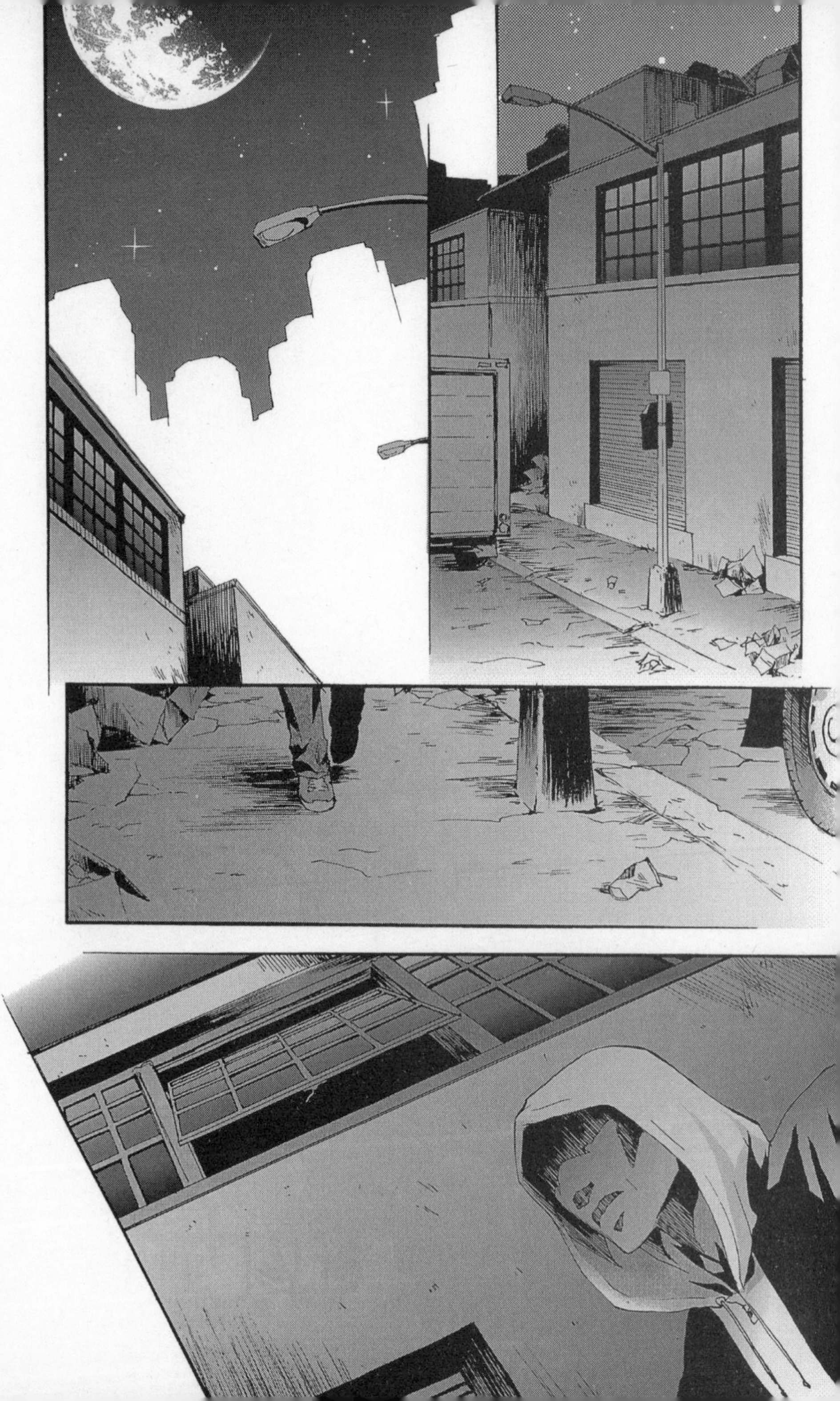

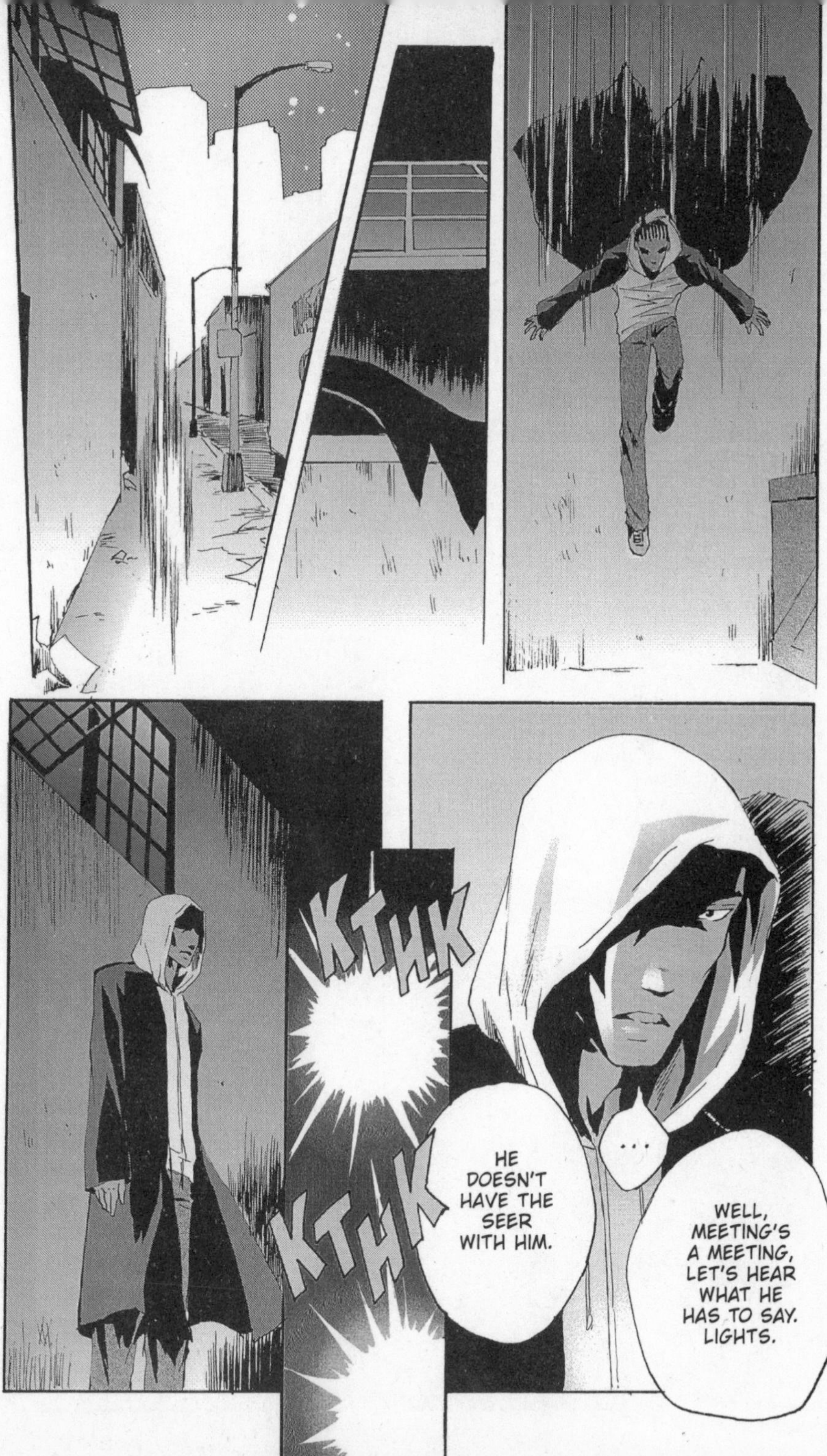
KTHK
KTHK
HE DOESN'T HAVE THE SEER WITH HIM.
...
WELL, MEETING'S A MEETING, LET'S HEAR WHAT HE HAS TO SAY. LIGHTS.

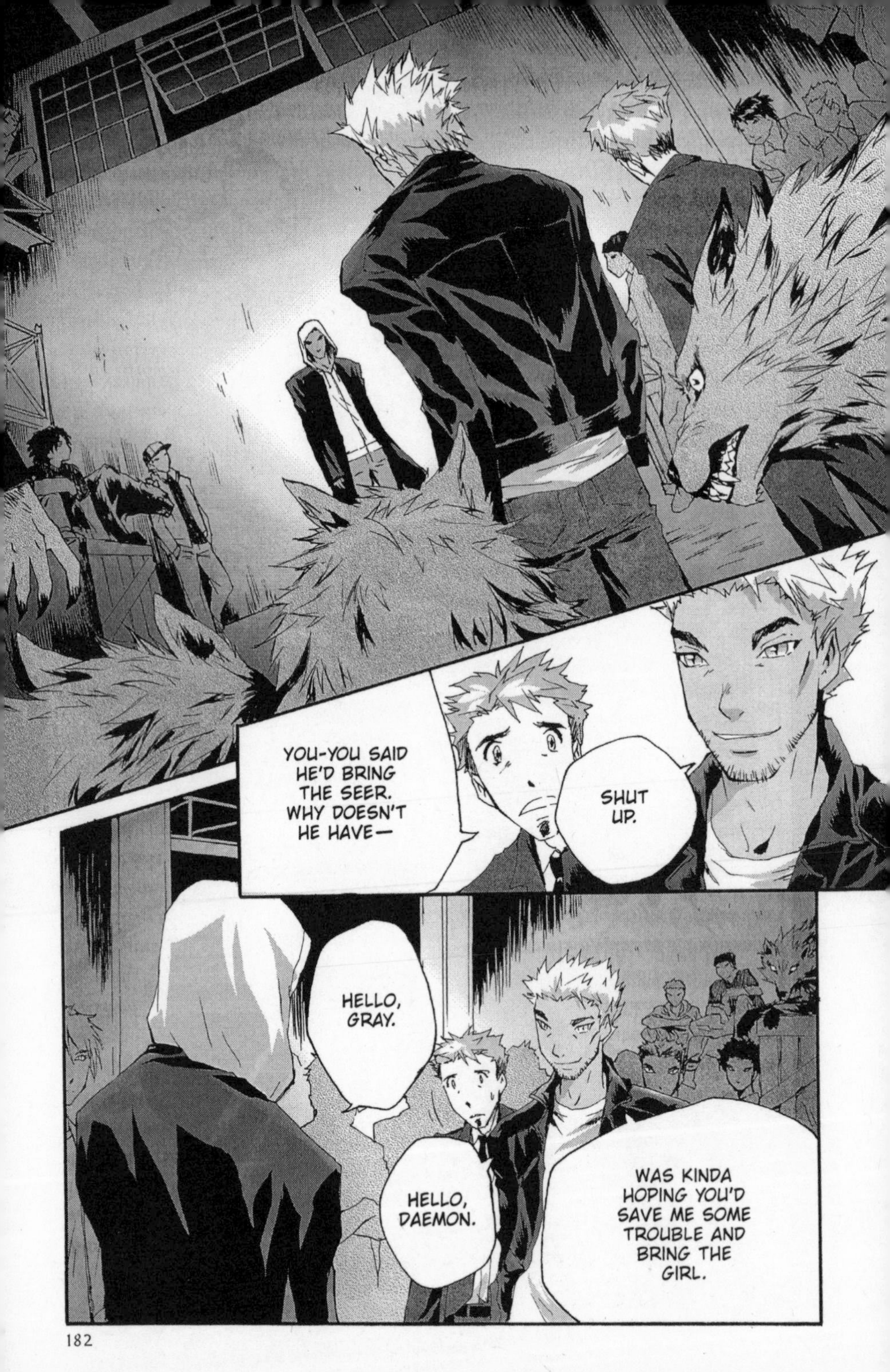
YOU-YOU SAID HE'D BRING THE SEER. WHY DOESN'T HE HAVE—
SHUT UP.
HELLO, GRAY.
HELLO, DAEMON.
WAS KINDA HOPING YOU'D SAVE ME SOME TROUBLE AND BRING THE GIRL.

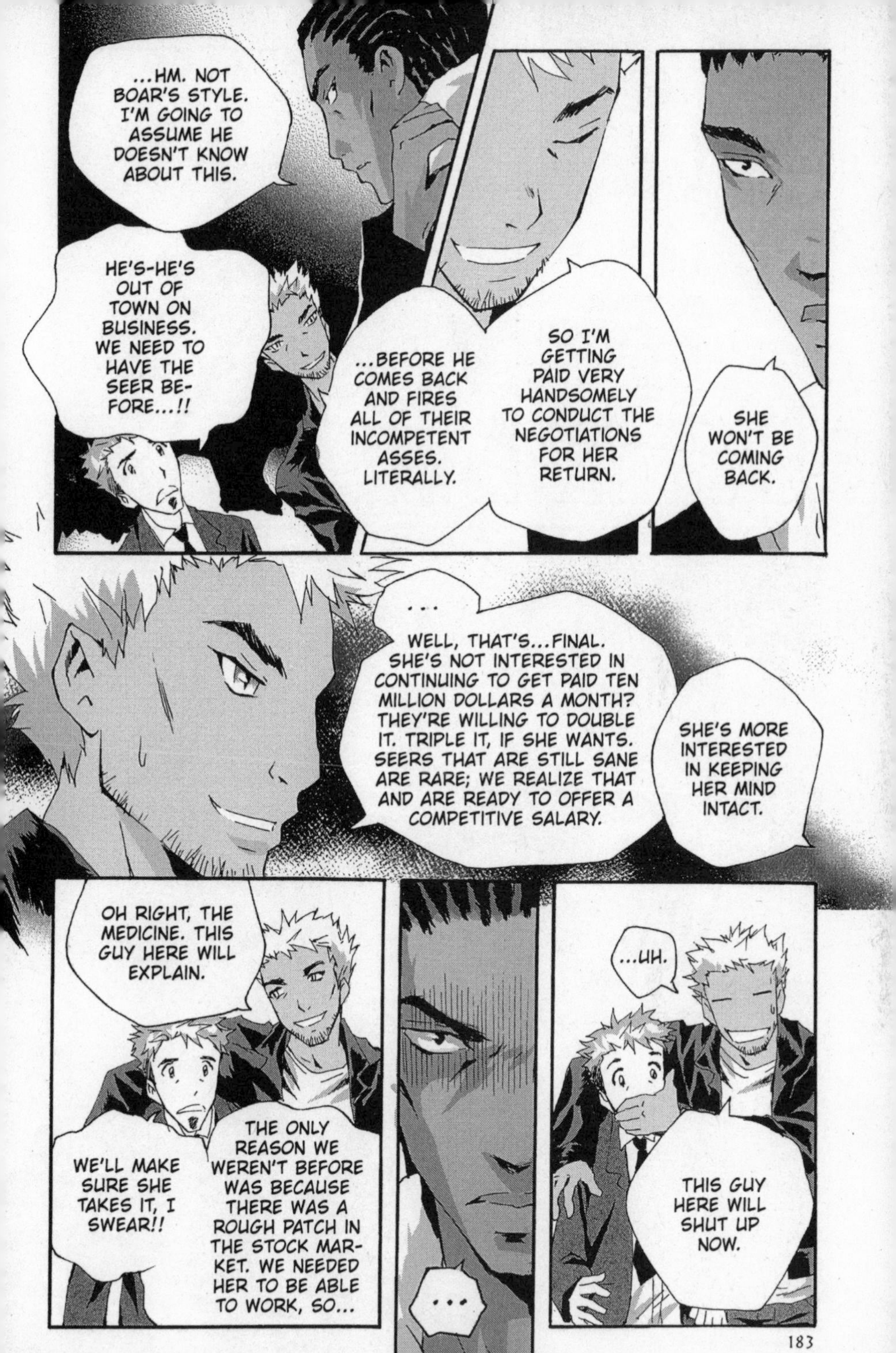
...HM. NOT BOAR'S STYLE. I'M GOING TO ASSUME HE DOESN'T KNOW ABOUT THIS.
HE'S-HE'S OUT OF TOWN ON BUSINESS. WE NEED TO HAVE THE SEER BE-FORE...!!
...BEFORE HE COMES BACK AND FIRES ALL OF THEIR INCOMPETENT ASSES. LITERALLY.
SO I'M GETTING PAID VERY HANDSOMELY TO CONDUCT THE NEGOTIATIONS FOR HER RETURN.
SHE WON'T BE COMING BACK.
...
WELL, THAT'S...FINAL. SHE'S NOT INTERESTED IN CONTINUING TO GET PAID TEN MILLION DOLLARS A MONTH? THEY'RE WILLING TO DOUBLE IT. TRIPLE IT, IF SHE WANTS. SEERS THAT ARE STILL SANE ARE RARE; WE REALIZE THAT AND ARE READY TO OFFER A COMPETITIVE SALARY.
SHE'S MORE INTERESTED IN KEEPING HER MIND INTACT.
OH RIGHT, THE MEDICINE. THIS GUY HERE WILL EXPLAIN.
WE'LL MAKE SURE SHE TAKES IT, I SWEAR!!
THE ONLY REASON WE WEREN'T BEFORE WAS BECAUSE THERE WAS A ROUGH PATCH IN THE STOCK MAR-KET. WE NEEDED HER TO BE ABLE TO WORK, SO...
...
...UH.
THIS GUY HERE WILL SHUT UP NOW.

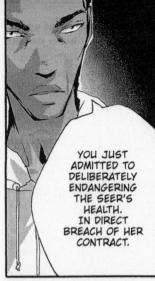

YOU JUST ADMITTED TO DELIBERATELY ENDANGERING THE SEER'S HEALTH. IN DIRECT BREACH OF HER CONTRACT.

THIS MEETING'S DONE.

WHOA, HEY! WAIT!

COME ON, MAN, HEAR ME OUT! I STILL GOT IMPORTANT THINGS...

...TO SAY.

KCHK

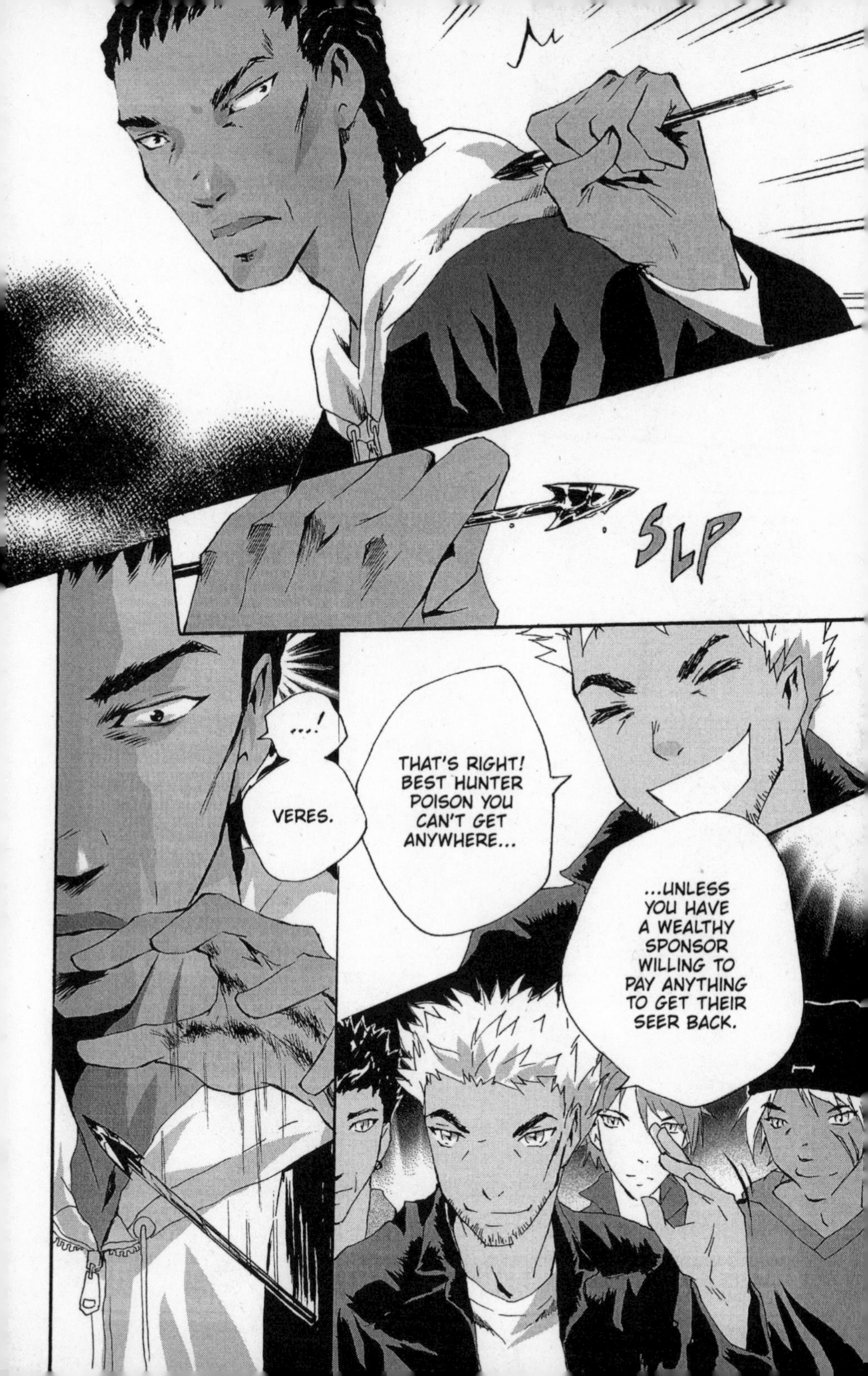
SLP
...!
VERES.
THAT'S RIGHT! BEST HUNTER POISON YOU CAN'T GET ANYWHERE...
...UNLESS YOU HAVE A WEALTHY SPONSOR WILLING TO PAY ANYTHING TO GET THEIR SEER BACK.

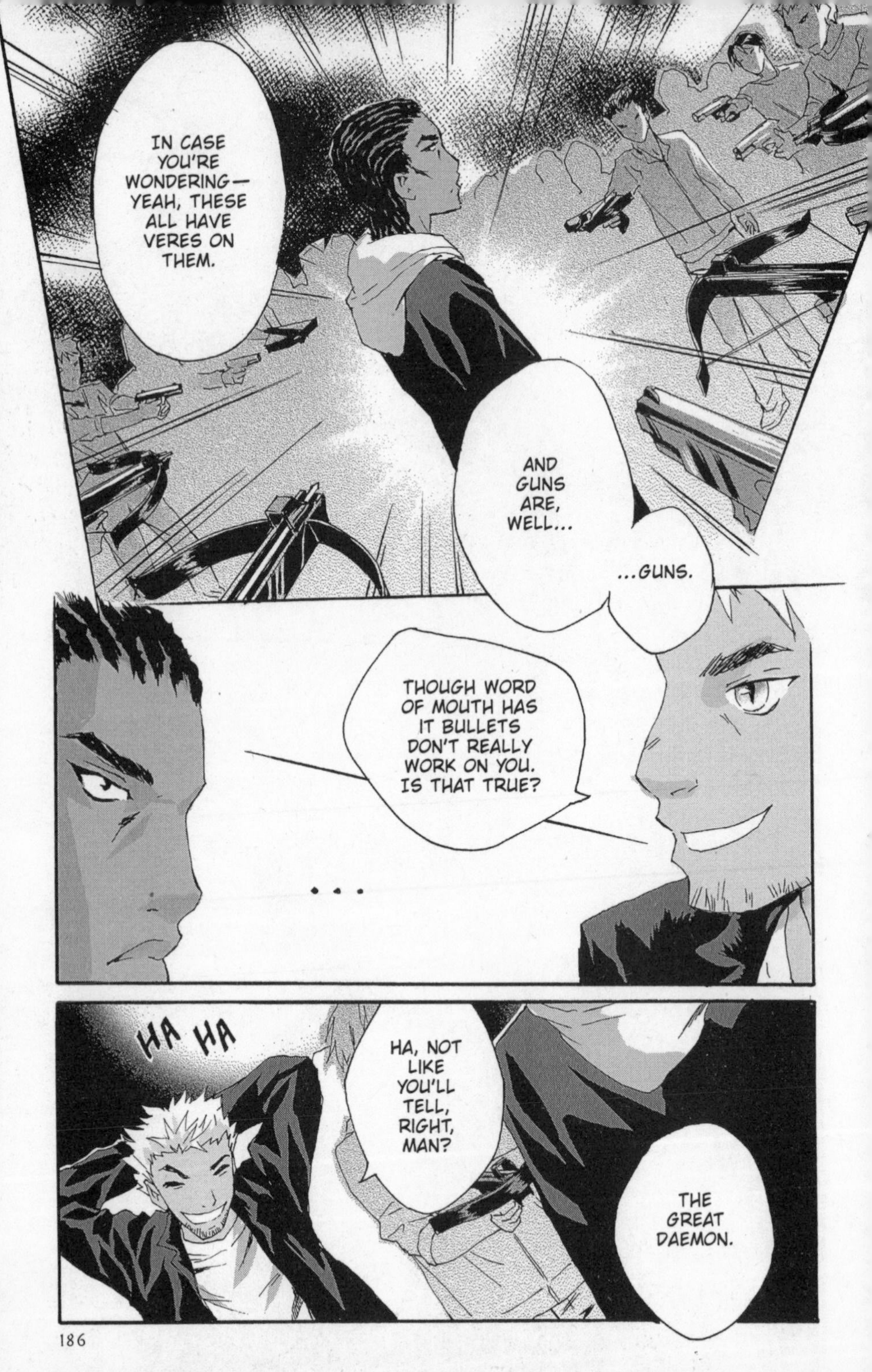
IN CASE YOU'RE WONDERING—YEAH, THESE ALL HAVE VERES ON THEM.
AND GUNS ARE, WELL...
...GUNS.
...
THOUGH WORD OF MOUTH HAS IT BULLETS DON'T REALLY WORK ON YOU. IS THAT TRUE?
HA HA
HA, NOT LIKE YOU'LL TELL, RIGHT, MAN?
THE GREAT DAEMON.

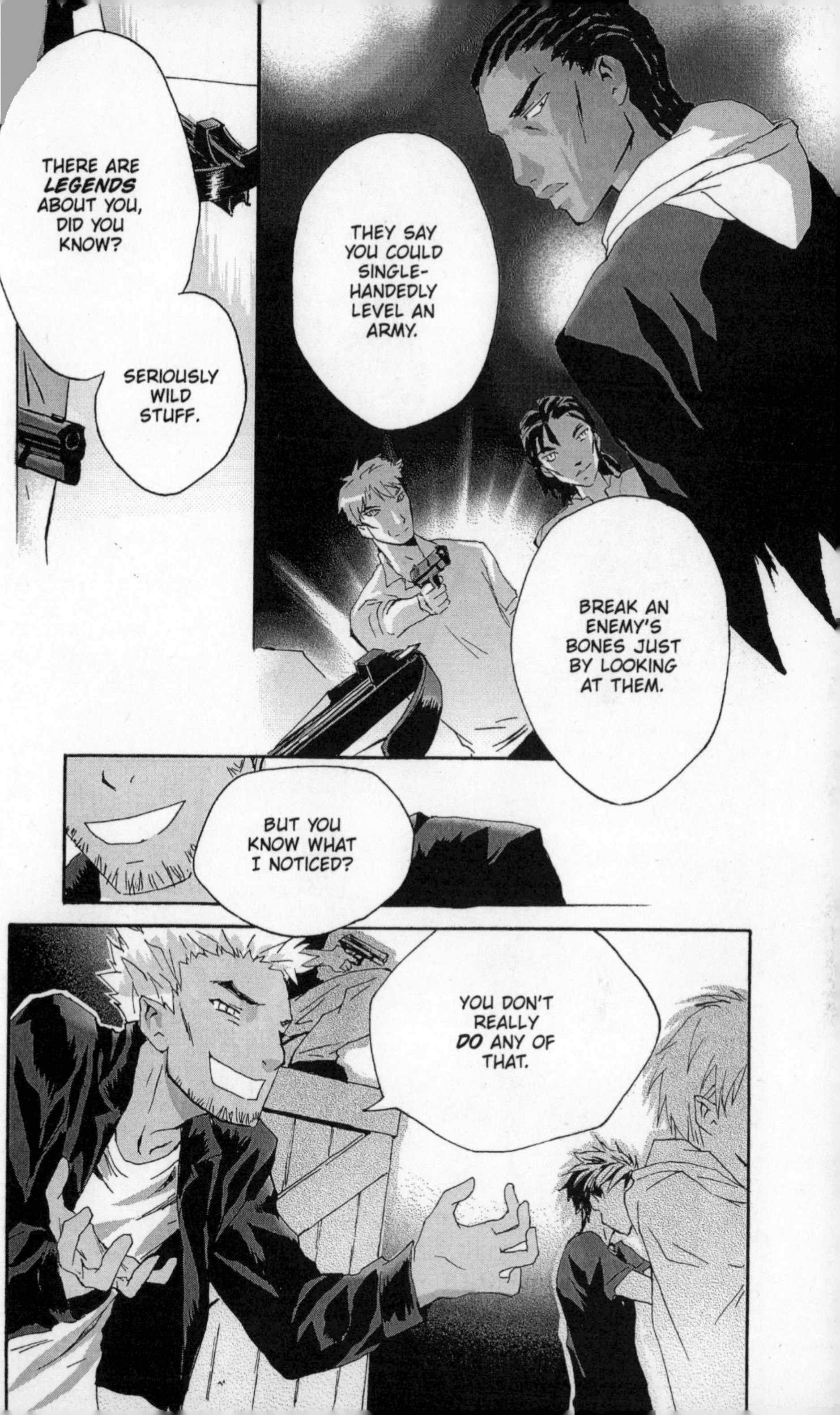
THERE ARE *LEGENDS* ABOUT YOU, DID YOU KNOW?
SERIOUSLY WILD STUFF.
THEY SAY YOU COULD SINGLE-HANDEDLY LEVEL AN ARMY.
BREAK AN ENEMY'S BONES JUST BY LOOKING AT THEM.
BUT YOU KNOW WHAT I NOTICED?
YOU DON'T REALLY *DO* ANY OF THAT.

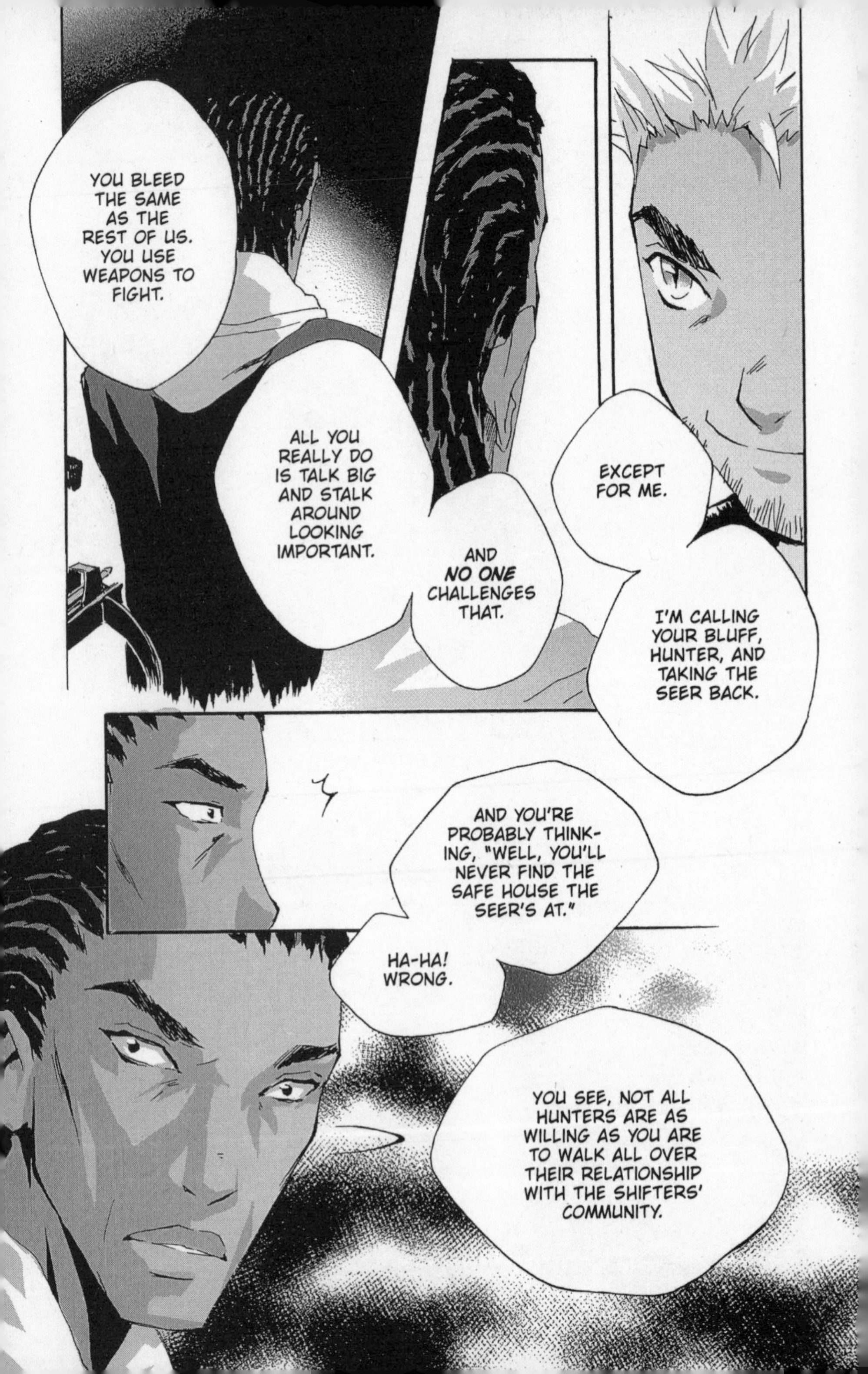
YOU BLEED THE SAME AS THE REST OF US. YOU USE WEAPONS TO FIGHT.
ALL YOU REALLY DO IS TALK BIG AND STALK AROUND LOOKING IMPORTANT.
AND *NO ONE* CHALLENGES THAT.
EXCEPT FOR ME.
I'M CALLING YOUR BLUFF, HUNTER, AND TAKING THE SEER BACK.
AND YOU'RE PROBABLY THINKING, "WELL, YOU'LL NEVER FIND THE SAFE HOUSE THE SEER'S AT."
HA-HA! WRONG.
YOU SEE, NOT ALL HUNTERS ARE AS WILLING AS YOU ARE TO WALK ALL OVER THEIR RELATIONSHIP WITH THE SHIFTERS' COMMUNITY.

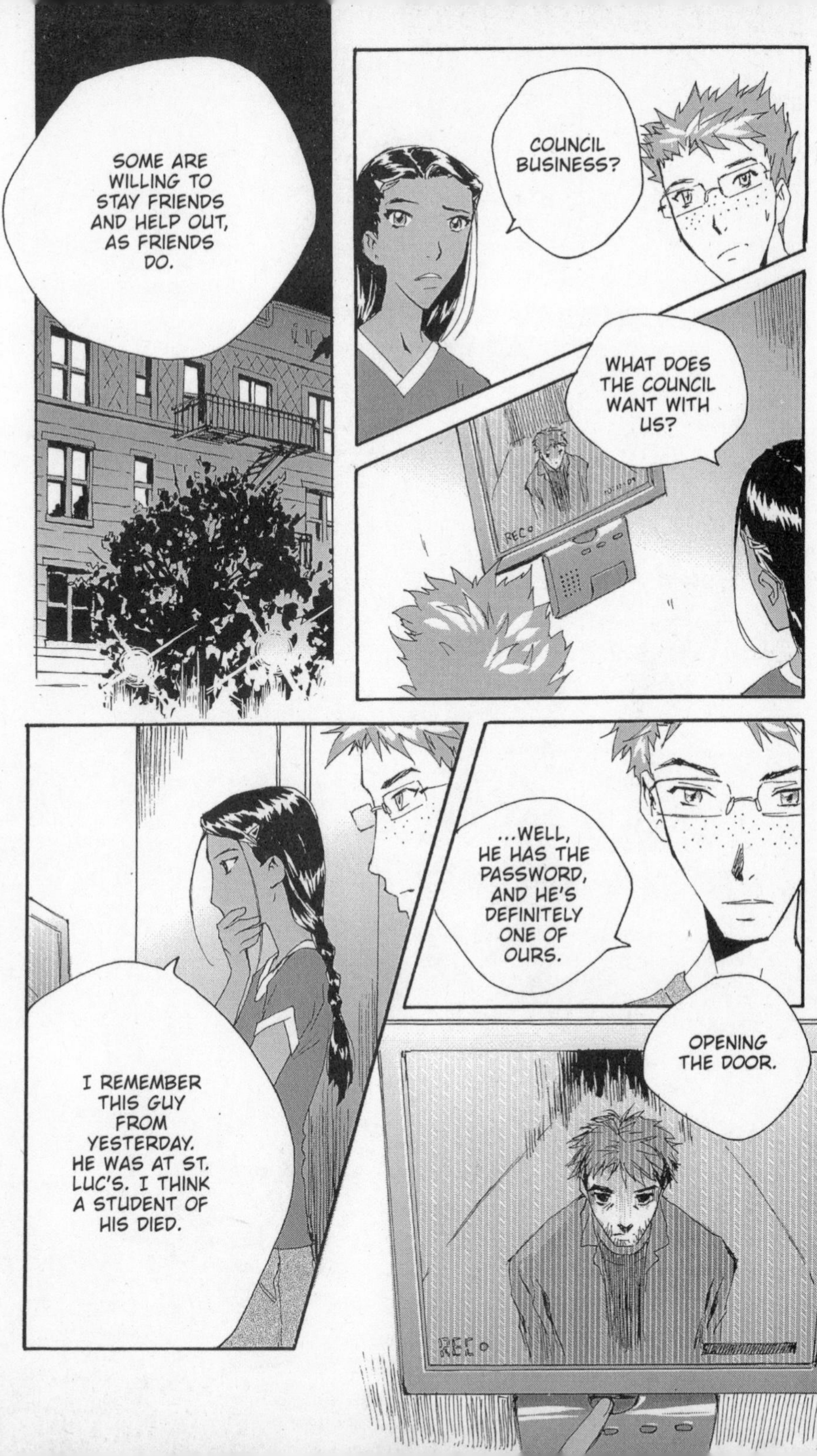
SOME ARE WILLING TO STAY FRIENDS AND HELP OUT, AS FRIENDS DO.
COUNCIL BUSINESS?
WHAT DOES THE COUNCIL WANT WITH US?
I REMEMBER THIS GUY FROM YESTERDAY. HE WAS AT ST. LUC'S. I THINK A STUDENT OF HIS DIED.
...WELL, HE HAS THE PASSWORD, AND HE'S DEFINITELY ONE OF OURS.
OPENING THE DOOR.

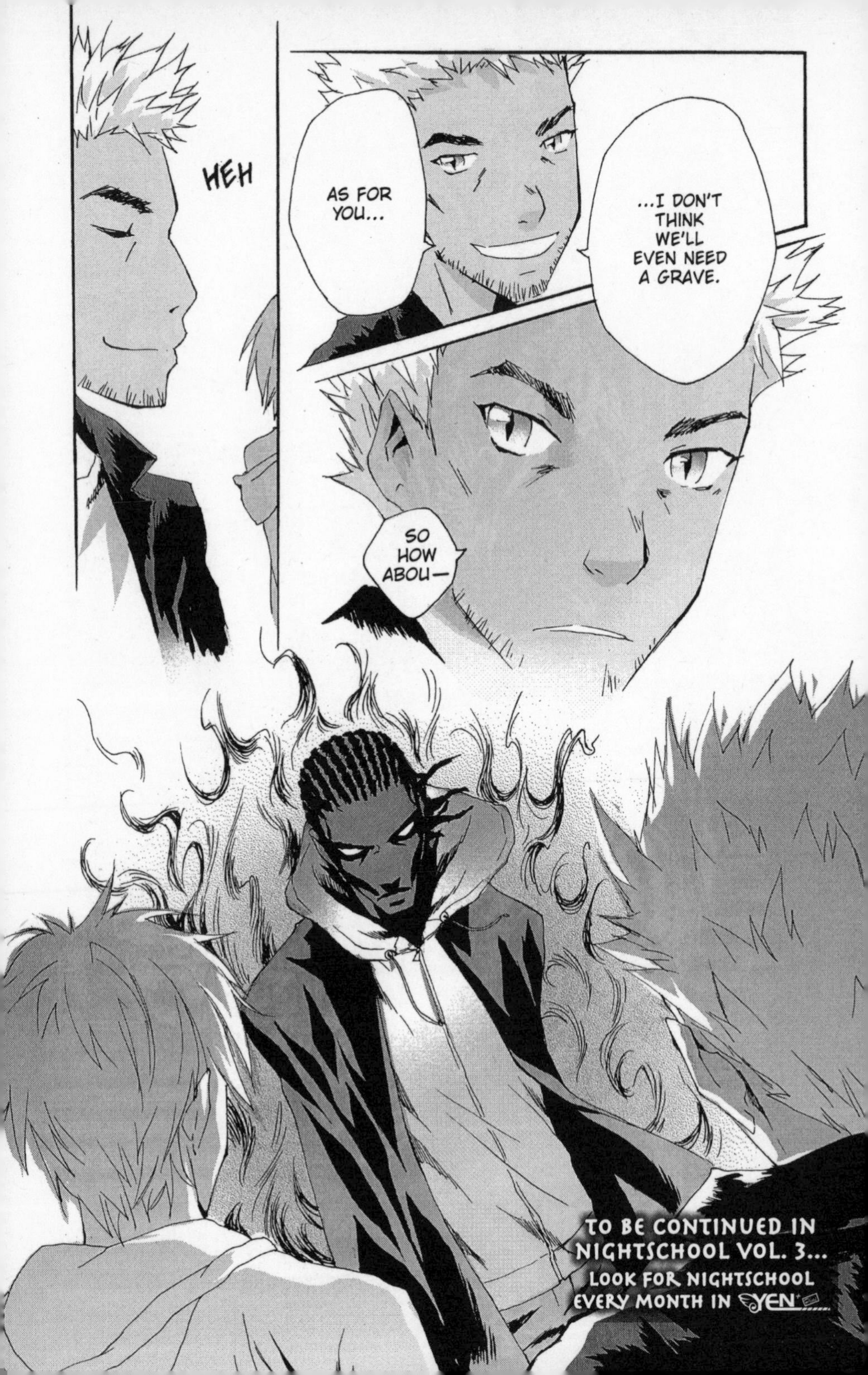
HEH
AS FOR YOU...
...I DON'T THINK WE'LL EVEN NEED A GRAVE.
SO HOW ABOU—
TO BE CONTINUED IN NIGHTSCHOOL VOL. 3...
LOOK FOR NIGHTSCHOOL EVERY MONTH IN YEN

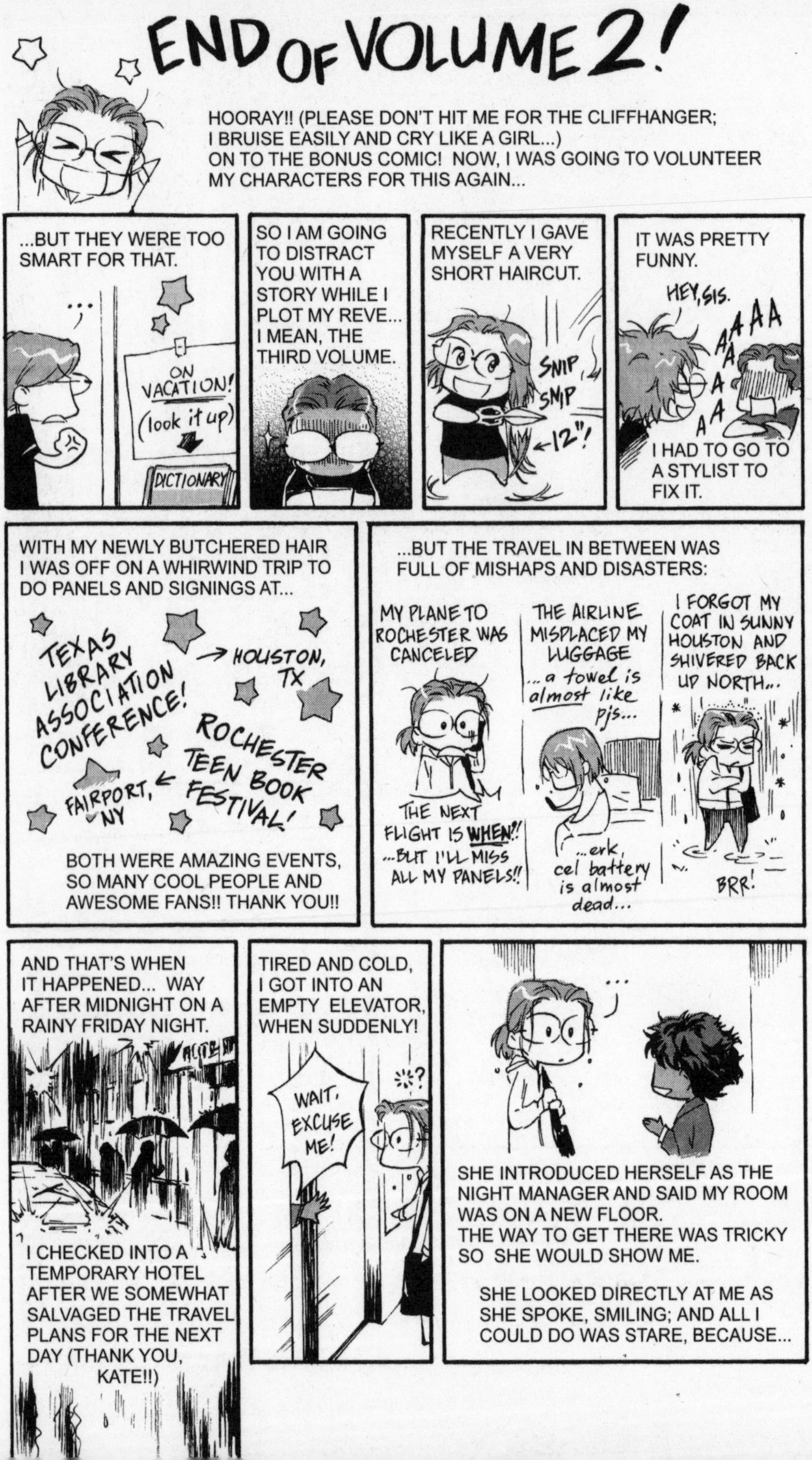
END OF VOLUME 2!
HOORAY!! (PLEASE DON'T HIT ME FOR THE CLIFFHANGER; I BRUISE EASILY AND CRY LIKE A GIRL...) ON TO THE BONUS COMIC! NOW, I WAS GOING TO VOLUNTEER MY CHARACTERS FOR THIS AGAIN...
...BUT THEY WERE TOO SMART FOR THAT.
...
ON VACATION! (look it up)
DICTIONARY
SO I AM GOING TO DISTRACT YOU WITH A STORY WHILE I PLOT MY REVE... I MEAN, THE THIRD VOLUME.
RECENTLY I GAVE MYSELF A VERY SHORT HAIRCUT.
SNIP SNIP
←12"!
IT WAS PRETTY FUNNY.
HEY, SIS.
AAAAAAAA
I HAD TO GO TO A STYLIST TO FIX IT.
WITH MY NEWLY BUTCHERED HAIR I WAS OFF ON A WHIRWIND TRIP TO DO PANELS AND SIGNINGS AT...
TEXAS LIBRARY ASSOCIATION CONFERENCE! → HOUSTON, TX
ROCHESTER TEEN BOOK FESTIVAL! → FAIRPORT, NY
BOTH WERE AMAZING EVENTS, SO MANY COOL PEOPLE AND AWESOME FANS!! THANK YOU!!
...BUT THE TRAVEL IN BETWEEN WAS FULL OF MISHAPS AND DISASTERS:
MY PLANE TO ROCHESTER WAS CANCELED
THE NEXT FLIGHT IS WHEN?! ...BUT I'LL MISS ALL MY PANELS!!
THE AIRLINE MISPLACED MY LUGGAGE
...a towel is almost like pjs...
...erk, cel battery is almost dead...
I FORGOT MY COAT IN SUNNY HOUSTON AND SHIVERED BACK UP NORTH...
BRR!
AND THAT'S WHEN IT HAPPENED... WAY AFTER MIDNIGHT ON A RAINY FRIDAY NIGHT.
I CHECKED INTO A TEMPORARY HOTEL AFTER WE SOMEWHAT SALVAGED THE TRAVEL PLANS FOR THE NEXT DAY (THANK YOU, KATE!!)
TIRED AND COLD, I GOT INTO AN EMPTY ELEVATOR, WHEN SUDDENLY!
WAIT, EXCUSE ME!
!?
...
SHE INTRODUCED HERSELF AS THE NIGHT MANAGER AND SAID MY ROOM WAS ON A NEW FLOOR. THE WAY TO GET THERE WAS TRICKY SO SHE WOULD SHOW ME.
SHE LOOKED DIRECTLY AT ME AS SHE SPOKE, SMILING; AND ALL I COULD DO WAS STARE, BECAUSE...

...HER EYES WERE BRIGHT YELLOW, WITH TINY HINTS OF ORANGE.
SHE TOOK ME UP TO THE TOP FLOOR... WHERE THERE WAS ANOTHER ELEVATOR, OFF TO THE SIDE.
VNNN
IT ONLY WENT UP ONE FLOOR (THOUGH IT FELT LIKE IT PASSED SEVERAL).
...IT OPENED ON THE WRONG SIDE.
FSSS
!
SHE UNLOCKED MY ROOM WITH HER MASTER KEY, AND I REALIZED THAT THE ROOM WAS...
...IN THE ATTIC.
DARKNESS AND RAIN WERE SCRAPING AT THE SLANTED WINDOWS.
THE NIGHT MANAGER LOOKED AT ME WITH HER YELLOW EYES, SMILING, FRIENDLY.
I'M JUST DOWNSTAIRS IF THERE ARE PROBLEMS.
ENJOY YOUR STAY.
CLICK
...
THERE WERE NO VAMPIRES HIDING IN THIS STRANGE ROOM (ALAS... I CHECKED), AND I DIDN'T SEE HER AGAIN THE NEXT MORNING.
WOW.
BUT THE SURREAL MAGIC OF THOSE FEW MINUTES STAYED WITH ME FOR MONTHS AFTER.
I WONDER IF THEY KNOW I'M MAKING A BOOK ABOUT THEM...
HEE.
I FELT LIKE I BRUSHED AGAINST THE VERY WORLD I WAS WRITING ABOUT.

Now, without further ado, I will introduce the awesomeness that is the next two pages!! Many *Nightschool* readers are also talented artists, so we ran a **Fan Art Contest** to show you what they can do. It was incredibly difficult to pick only eight from all the great art we received, so we ended up with several runners-up:

Emily Adams **Julien Faille** **Kaitlin Gagnon** **Sarah Miller** **Karen Yen**

Thank you!! We hope you enjoy your prizes :).

And finally... *drumroll* The contest winners are...!

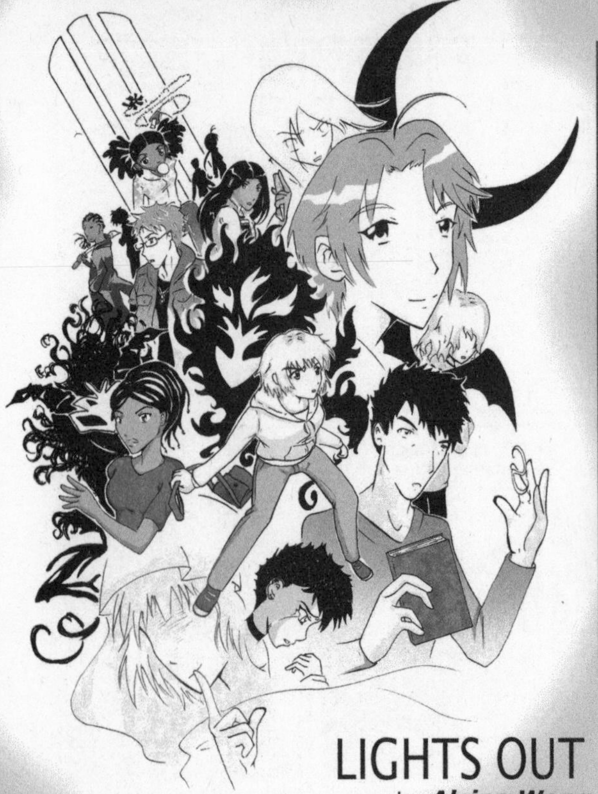

LIGHTS OUT

by ***Alcina Wong***

(I-I think half the characters are here... IMPRESSIVE)

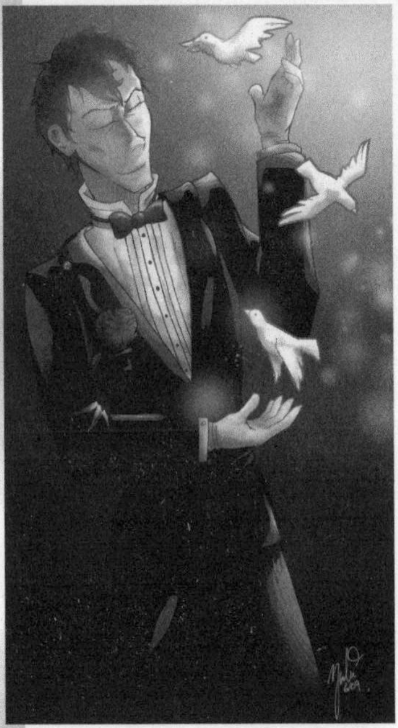

by ***Morgan Zamboni***

(Yay, Mr. Roi, looking sharp in a suit!!)

by ***Omnaya Omar***

(The rose in the original is a beautiful blue)

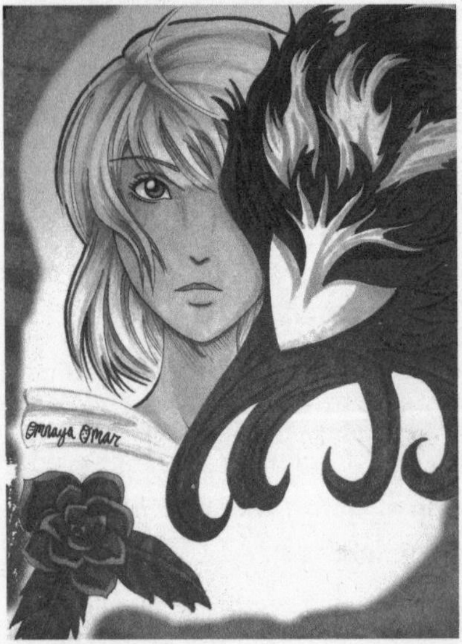

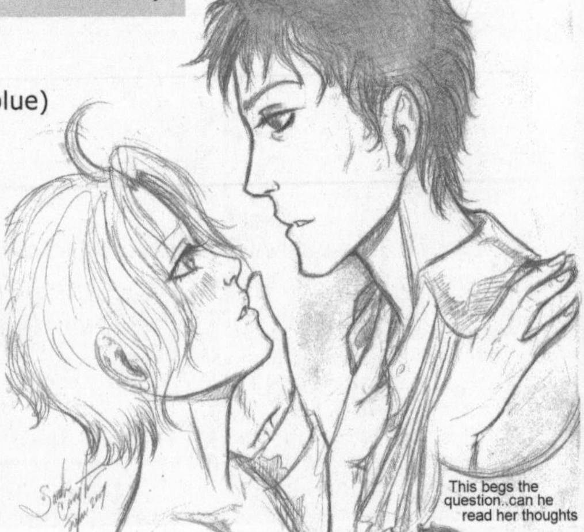
This begs the question..can he read her thoughts
Work place dating may = can of worms
Workplace Fanatasies are an entirely different matter.

by ***Sarah Covington***

(Wakey wakey, Sarah :D)

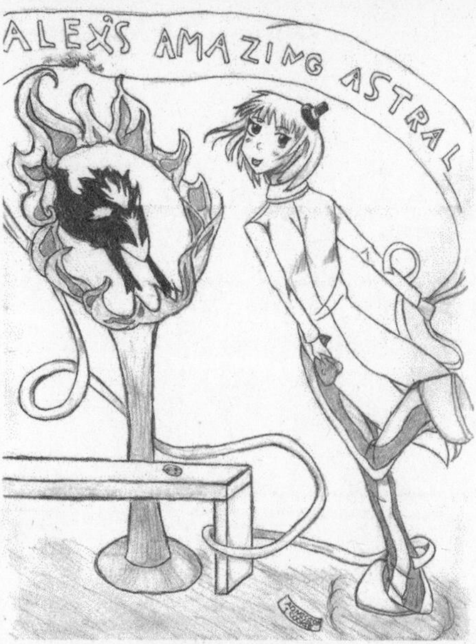
ALEX'S AMAZING ASTRAL

by ***Merritt Zamboni***
(Alex's Amazing Astral!! Too right! <3)

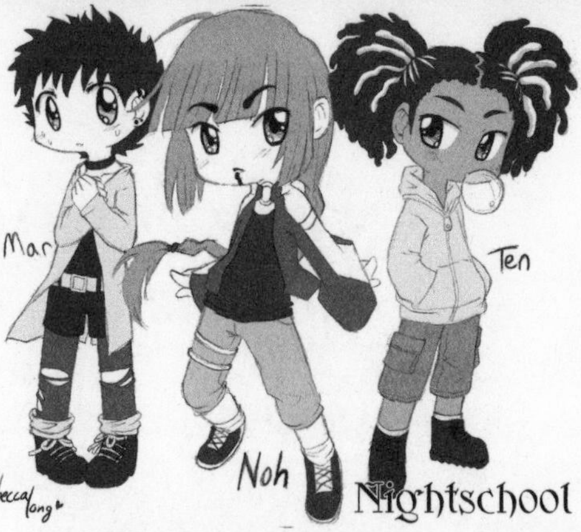
Mar
Noh
Ten
Rebecca Long
Nightschool

by ***Rebecca Long***
(SO. CUTE.)

by ***Starlia Prichard***
(The family! Personalities captured *perfectly.*)

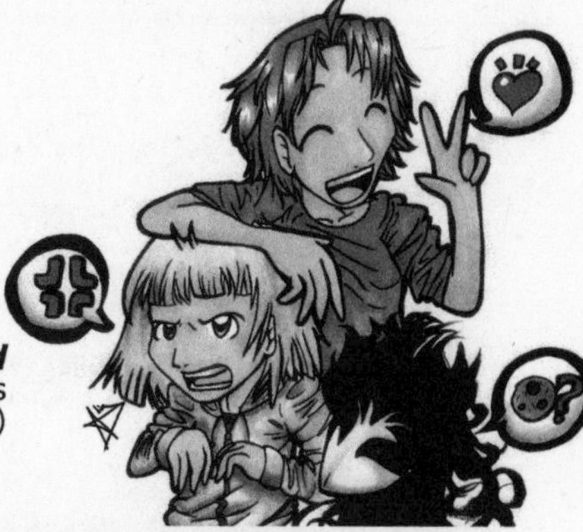

by ***Kaia Dumoulin***
(Originally in color, and SO beautiful...)

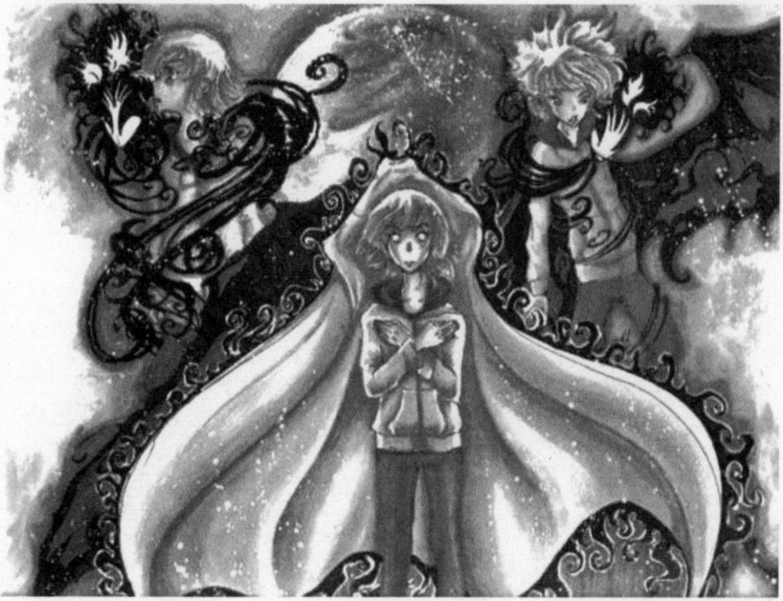

NIGHTSCHOOL
THE WEIRN BOOKS ②

SVETLANA CHMAKOVA

Toning Artist: Dee DuPuy

Lettering: JuYoun Lee

NIGHTSCHOOL: The Weirn Books, Vol. 2 © 2009 Svetlana Chmakova.

Yen Press
Hachette Book Group
1290 Avenue of the Americas, New York, NY 10104

Visit our Web sites at www.HachetteBookGroup.com
and www.YenPress.com.

Yen Press is an imprint of Hachette Book Group, Inc. The Yen Press name and logo are trademarks of Hachette Book Group, Inc.

First Yen Press Edition: October 2009

ISBN: 978-0-7595-2860-4

10 9 8 7 6 5 4

BVG

Printed in the United States of America